Essays in Jewish Theology

Essays in Jewish Theology

by
Samuel S. Cohon

Hebrew Union College Press
Cincinnati, Ohio
1987

Library of Congress Cataloging-in-Publication Data

Cohon, Samuel Solomon, 1888–1959.
  Essays in Jewish thought and theology.

  1. Judaism—Doctrines. I. Title.
BM601.C615   1987   296.3   86-25697
ISBN 0-87820-117-3

Manufactured in the United States of America

To the memory of
Prof. Samuel S. Cohon
from his grateful students

Contents

Preface

Samuel S. Cohon was a professor at the Hebrew Union College from 1923 until 1959. Through his years at the College, and his extensive writing, he influenced two generations of Reform rabbis. In this period, he was the theological spokesman for the American Reform movement. We, as editors, have prepared a selection of his essays; some have been previously printed and others have come from his literary legacy. These essays are intended to represent the broad scope of Samuel Cohon's work and thought. Some of them are timeless; others are associated with a particular era and its problems. The editors hope that this tribute will continue the influence of Samuel Cohon into succeeding generations.

We wish to acknowledge permission to reprint a number of essays which have previously appeared in the *Hebrew Union College Annual* and the *Yearbooks of the Central Conference of American Rabbis*. Our thanks are extended to Frances Stein for her help with the manuscript.

Walter Jacob
Stanley Dreyfus
Sidney Brooks

A Note from the Editors

The essays collected in this volume were published, or planned for publication, in various periodicals over a lengthy span of time. As a result, there is considerable variance with respect to the handling of footnotes, the transliteration of Hebrew words and terms, etc. No attempt has been made to create uniformity throughout this volume; the aim of the editors rather was consistency within each article.

Introduction

If, as someone in the Talmud (b. *Sotah* 47b) claims, "grape-cluster" (*eshkol*) means "a man in whom there is everything" (*ish shehakkol bo*), and if, with a view expressed in the Midrash (*Canticles Rabbah* I, 14, ii), "everything" is defined as "Scripture, Mishnah, Talmud, *Tosephta* and *Aggadoth*," then the Mishnah (*Sotah* 9:9) made a somewhat premature announcement when it claimed that the *eshkoloth* ceased with the demise of Jose ben Joezer of Zeredah and Jose ben Johanan of Jerusalem. Those who have had the privilege of studying with the late Professor Samuel S. Cohon, and those who now have the opportunity of reading some of his writings, know that he, too, was "a man in whom there was everything." Indeed, for Cohon, the "everything" included far more than merely "Scripture, Mishnah, Talmud, *Tosephta* and *Aggadoth*." It also embraced a knowledge of all branches of Hebrew and Jewish literature, of philosophy, of psychology, of comparative religion, of Jewish and general history, of Christian and of Jewish theology, and of the vast area of Jewish liturgy. The highways and the byways of *Wissenschaft des Judentums*, the modern scientific study of Judaism, were as familiar to him as were the streets of Neharde'a to his Babylonian namesake (b. *Berakhoth* 58b).

Born on March 22, 1888, in Lohi, Minsk, Russia, Cohon experienced his first exposure to intensive Jewish learning in his native country. Thus, when he came as a student to the Hebrew Union College in Cincinnati, where he was ordained in 1912, neither the Hebrew language nor the staples of rabbinic study were an unknown territory to him, while his mind was receptive to the modern emphases and methodologies which the Hebrew Union College, then under Kaufmann Kohler's direction, had to impart to its students. Upon ordination as a rabbi, Cohon first served the congregation in Springfield, Ohio, for a year, and then, from 1913 to 1918, he was the rabbi of Zion

Temple, Chicago, and from 1918 to 1923 he ministered to Temple Mizpah, Chicago, a congregation he himself had organized. It was from Chicago that President Julian Morgenstern called him to Cincinnati in 1923, offering him the chair of Jewish theology, which had been vacant since Kaufmann Kohler's retirement in 1921. Cohon occupied that position, teaching liturgy as well, until 1956, when he moved to California and took an active part in the development of the Los Angeles school of the Hebrew Union College until his death on August 22, 1959.

Samuel S. Cohon in his time was *the* Jewish theologian on the American scene. His mastery of the field was, and has remained, unequaled. His literary productivity was immense. By 1956, Cohon had some three hundred publications to his credit, as itemized by Theodore Wiener in "The Writings of Samuel S. Cohon" (in *Studies* in *Bibliography and Booklore*, vol. II, 1956, pp. 160–178). A few books have since been published posthumously.

Yet notwithstanding his impeccable academic credentials, Cohon continued to be the "rabbi" to whom students would turn with their personal problems, religious or otherwise, and to whom Reform Judaism as a movement would turn in matters ideological and liturgical. He was the architect of the Columbus Platform of 1937, which charted the Reform movement's changed perspectives in a new period of Jewish history. He it was who turned the *Union Haggadah,* in its 1923 revision, into a more recognizably *Jewish* liturgical text. He provided practical guidance to his "colleagues in the field" by means of the 1928 edition of the *Rabbi's Manual*; and he was responsible for introducing more Hebrew and a more traditional liturgical structure into the newly revised edition (1940/45) of the *Union Prayer Book.* He addressed himself to halakhic questions, balancing traditional claims with modern needs, even as he was one of the very first to engage, on a serious theological level, in the Christian-Jewish dialogue. (See the book he wrote with Harris Franklin Rall, *Christianity and Judaism Compare Notes,* 1928.) Far from being content to rest upon his academic laurels, he was ever responsive to the spiritual needs of the people, of *'ammekho,* even as, in his theological thinking, he was always alert to the concrete situation in which Jews found themselves.

That, however, did not mean that Cohon would let himself be swayed by all of the latest fads and fashions which had gained currency among both colleagues and students. Reform Judaism, for him, was a body of beliefs and practices which could not be made to mean all things to all people. And theological statements did not become "Jewish theology" simply because those who made them happened to be Jews. Something claiming to be "Jewish theology" had to show some organic relationship to what had been believed by Jews before — even though Cohon fully acknowledged the fact that, through the millennia, Judaism had undergone a constant process of development.

It was, moreover, this finely honed historical consciousness which, as it were, dictated Cohon's theological methodology. Without ever committing the "fallacy of primitivism," which sees the end-all or be-all of the meaning of a belief, a practice, or an institution in its origin alone, Cohon always paid very serious attention to origins — but also to developments — of whatever he discussed in class or committed to writing. If, for example, the subject was "Original Sin," as the reader can discover upon reading one of the studies included in this collection, Cohon chose a path quite different from that of many modern Jewish teachers, who simply dogmatize to the effect that "Judaism has no doctrine of Original Sin!" Instead, Cohon painstakingly examined all the relevant sources, finding that *some* Jews in *some* periods of history *did*, in fact, entertain a notion of this kind. Only then would he be led to the conclusion that what was to become a central Christian belief remained a peripheral notion in Judaism, never shared by all Jews.

Or take Cohon's approach to the problem of particularism in Judaism. Particularism had been frowned upon and as far as possible eliminated in Reform Judaism's so-called classical phase. Cohon had a different perception of particularism. He could appreciate the role which it had played throughout Jewish history. After all, without a Jewish people, there would not have been any Judaism. The Jewish religion is not some highly abstract religion-in-general; it is, rather, the religion of the Jews. And the Jews are a concrete, a particular people. The Hebrew language, too, is a vehicle of something uniquely Jewish; and so is the role played in Jewish religious devotion by the Holy City of Jerusalem. Cohon loved the Hebrew language. He encouraged its use by students; and he himself wrote essays and edited books in it. He also paid tribute, in one of the essays included hère, to Jerusalem. In that tribute as well as in his cultivation of the Hebrew language, Cohon represented a marked departure from the sentiments and the attitudes which had almost crystallized into an antiparticularist "orthodoxy" within Reform Jewish ranks. But it was his own profound knowledge of Judaism and the dynamics of its development, not the popularity of recent fads, which determined Cohon's position of independence. He would never accept a Jewish particularism which was unbalanced by the universalist view of God and the world. He could never get himself to espouse a secularist Jewish nationalism and a godless vision of Jewish peoplehood as an authentic modern manifestation of the millennial Jewish tradition. He was steeped too much in all facets of Jewish development to settle for any partial reading of the facts or any truncated version of Jewish commitments.

Cohon's aim in all of his theological efforts was to bridge two worlds: the world of rational inquiry and scientific methodology, to which he remained committed throughout his life, and the world of the holy, the nonrational basis of religion, toward which his personal piety inclined him, and for which the pioneering study undertaken by Rudolf Otto provided some of the conceptual framework and vocabulary. This "bridging" required a far more strenuous effort than many thinkers are willing to expend. It is always so much easier to reach an either/or decision than to follow the advice of Koheleth: "It is good that thou shouldest take hold of the one; yea, also from the other withdraw not thy hand; for he that feareth God shall discharge himself of them all" (Ecclesiastes 7:18). Cohon took the more strenuous approach, for he feared God. His vast knowledge of religion in general, and of Judaism in particular, made him beware of any simplistic solutions.

The essays in this collection, many of them garnered from earlier publications, others appearing in print here for the first time, are samples of Cohon's efforts to bridge the two worlds. Their erudition instills awe; their rationality, admiration; and their piety, the longing that we, too, may partake thereof. May they also inspire their readers with the desire to continue the work so lovingly and conscientiously begun by that great Master in Israel, that rabbi of rabbis, Samuel S. Cohon, whose memory is for blessing.

Jakob J. Petuchowski

Hebrew Union College–
Jewish Institute of Religion,
Cincinnati, Ohio

Essays in Jewish Theology

Faith and Reason

1. Biblical Ideas of the Holy and of the Covenant

With the psychological character of the holy, we dealt in an earlier study. Here we shall confine ourselves to the concrete expression of the experience of the holy in the life of the people. The root meaning of the Hebrew term *kadash* is "to be set apart from ordinary use or profane contact and be devoted to God, the sanctuary, or the priesthood." *Kodesh* approximates the idea of *taboo*. This idea of apartness or separateness marks the biblical usage of the term.

In its highest sense the term "holy" applies to God Himself, who is other than anything in existence, unlike any object known to man, removed from human frailties and weakness, whether physical or moral, exalted in might, wondrous in works, awe-inspiring in majesty. He is high and lofty, inhabiting eternity. The heavens declare His glory, and the earth, His creative power and wisdom. His thoughts are very deep, and His deeds baffling. Though He is transcendent, He is near to the lowly and the humble. He redeemed Israel from bondage and took it unto Himself. As the Holy One of Israel, He sanctifies Israel, i.e., He set Israel apart for His own care and for His worship. Thereby Israel is distinguished and honored. From among the people of Israel, He singled out certain men for His service: the firstborn, Nazarites, Levites,

Editor's note: This study assumes a previous one dealing with the psychological character of the holy, and a succeeding one on the creedal and dogmatic aspect of *emunah* (as mentioned on page x and xx). While these manuscripts have not been found, the subjects are treated in other parts of the collected works.

3

priests, and prophets. His presence in Israel bestows sanctity (i.e., religious distinction) upon certain places: the Tabernacle, the Sanctuary at Zion, the Temple mount, and the entire land. The objects associated with His worship, too, are sacred: the furniture of the Tabernacle, the altar, the menorah, the ark, the sacrificial offerings, the tithes, the heave-offerings, the first loaves of the new harvest, etc. Similarly, certain days are holy, such as the Sabbath and the special days of convocation. Everything which is in any way connected with God and with the cult is considered sacred, and is removed from ordinary contact.

The experience of the holy, which encompassed the entire religious life of ancient Israel, is woven into the conception of the covenant between God and the people. The idea is rooted in Semitic mythology. With the refinement of the religious consciousness, its primitive elements fell away and it came to express the sense of communion with God and obedience to His will. In its early forms, it betokens a mutual agreement between two parties, whether individuals or nations. At Sinai, Israel entered into an alliance with Yahveh. He was to be Israel's God, and Israel His people. A condition attached to this relationship. God would protect and help the people if they would fulfill their obligations to Him. It was confirmed by an oath. A curse threatened the violation of the covenant, and a blessing would crown its fulfillment. The priests emphasized the ritual side of the covenant. The whole institution of sacrifice may be viewed from the standpoint of the covenant. The sacrificial meal, which God was believed to share with the people, confirmed the covenant between them. The covenant was further sealed in the flesh of every male Israelite. Circumcision is still characterized as *berit,* a covenant (or *berit Avraham*). Similarly the Sabbath was to be observed as a sign of the everlasting covenant between God and Israel.

The prophets viewed the contractual relationship between Israel and God in ethical terms. It betokened for them the sense of Israel's belonging to God and of dedication to Him. From God's side, the covenant was based on the idea of a divine purpose or mission for Israel, and His desire that Israel give it effect in life. That purpose, as Amos and his successors interpreted it, is to act rightly, to do justly, to show compassion, etc. In the words of Isaiah, "the Holy One is sanctified [i.e., shows Himself holy] through righteousness."[1] The

---

[1] Isa. 5:16.

other ethical attributes of truth, justice, mercy, etc., similarly disclose the holiness of God and point the way in which man may fulfill His will. The command "be ye holy" may be carried out in two ways: (1) by abstaining from objects and ways that are offensive to God, viz. idolatry, immorality, violence, etc., and by honoring Him through proper ritual and moral acts. Some ritual forms, associated with magical practice or Baal cults, are offensive to Him. The worshiper, therefore, must be on his guard against things which defile and offend the honor of God.[2] (2) Above all, He must be honored through upright moral behavior, i.e., by conduct toward one's fellowmen in a manner worthy of children of God. The ceremonial and moral ways demanded by the covenant between God and the people form the content of the Torah, which covers all phases of the religious life and governs all human relations, whether private or public. The covenant at Sinai, which was symbolized by sacrifice, is also reported to have been embodied in a book.[3] Both the small collection of laws in Exodus[4] and Exodus's larger body of laws,[5] which is preceded by the Decalogue,[6] are introduced as the terms of the covenant between Israel and God.

The covenant relationship of men and God was based on the principle of mutual reciprocity, which served as the basis for regulating ceremonial purity, dietary and moral laws. It entails acts of worship, consisting of sacrifice and prayer, and was, therefore, designated *avodat elohim* or *avodat adonai.* This term covered both religion as a whole and also the religious worship in the Temple. By the side of *avodah,* which represents the ceremonial and formal part of religion, the psychological terms *yireah* and *emunah,* "fear" and "faith," are occasionally used for religion as a whole. We meet also with *daat elohim* and *Torah,* "knowledge of God" and "instruction" or "law," as approximations of religion in its pragmatic intellectualistic aspect.

The fulfillment of the obligations of the covenant was to be rewarded not only with worldly goods but also with God's favor and salvation. Even when the people shall be punished because of faithlessness to the obligations of the

---

[2] Cf. תועבה.

[3] Exod. 24.

[4] Exod. 34:12–26.

[5] Exod. 21–23.

[6] Cf. Deut. 5:6–18.

covenant, God, in His boundless mercy, will remember the covenant and save them. Instead of remaining external, Jeremiah declares, the words of the covenant will be inscribed upon the hearts of the people, so that Israel and God will truly belong to each other.[7] Israel thus is a "covenant people" and a "people who know righteousness, in whose heart is the Law."[8]

2. Biblical Conception of Faith

On the subjective side, the covenant relationship constituted fidelity and loyalty to God, designated in the Bible as *emunah,* a term which came to express both the psychological and the cognitive aspects of religion, covering both faith and belief. Derived from the root *aman* ("confirm, support, establish"), it denotes firmness, steadfastness, confidence.[9] It is closely related to the word for "truth," *emet,* which, as a contraction of *emenet,* is derived from the same root, and likewise expresses the idea of firmness, faithfulness, and reliability.[10] While *emet* applies primarily to objective knowledge, *emunah* refers to the subjective, to the personal relation to truth, and is employed with respect to human conduct.[11] It is personal confidence in God's benevolence toward us, in the steadfastness of His purpose, and in the ultimate wisdom and rightness of His ways.

Emunah, esteemed as the key to the spiritual life, was regarded by the prophet as the means whereby the righteous live.[12] The psalmists accounted it a divine attribute and a revelation of God's nature and works.[13] The prophet Hosea combined faith with mercy and righteousness in his conception of the bond which unites man with God. *Emunah,* expressing the sense of reliability, confidence, and loyalty to God, recommended itself as an indispensable

[7] Jer. 31:33.

[8] Isa. 51:7.

[9] Exod. 17:12, Isa. 33:6.

[10] Gen. 24:48, Jer. 2:21, Pss. 25:10, 31:6.

[11] Ps. 119:30. Accordingly, it is sometimes associated with *zedek* and *zedakah,* "righteousness." See Prov. 12:17. Cf. 1 Sam. 26:23, Isa. 59:4, Jer. 5:1.

[12] Hab. 2:4.

[13] Pss. 36:6, 119:90, 33:4. Also Deut. 32:4.

prerequisite of piety. Abraham's righteousness consisted in his confidence in, or reliance on, God.[14] Isaiah warned his contemporaries that if they did not have *emunah*, i.e., trust in God's saving power, they would not endure.[15] To the psalmists, faith meant unquestioned reliance upon God's goodness. It is the prophylactic of the soul against fear and danger. Filled with faith, one may walk through the valley of the shadow of death, without fear of harm. Though a host rise up against him, he remains confident. Out of the deepest darkness and in the stormiest seas, he retains the assurance of God's salvation.[16] The subjective side of faith combines with the objective, with reliance upon God's saving power. Faith is directed not only toward God, but also toward His messengers.[17] The chronicler quotes King Jehoshaphat as declaring to the people: "Believe in the Lord your God, so shall ye be established; believe His prophets, so shall ye prosper."[18]

The element of trust which enters into the conception of faith is represented by the Hebrew word *bittahon*, which is often interchangeable with *emunah*.[19] Hezekiah is praised for trusting in the Lord.[20] Jeremiah sang of the blessedness of the man who trusts in God. He flourishes as a tree planted by the waters, untroubled by the drought of adversity.[21] For the psalmists, too, the attitude of trust stands for the highest piety. He who trusts in the Lord is surrounded with loving-kindness.[22]

The religious consciousness, as reflected in the Bible, represents the sense of personal confidence in God's fidelity to His covenant, in His boundless might, righteousness, and goodness, and in His readiness to help. He who turns away from God and trusts in his own might is like a shrub in a parched desert.[23] Even Moses and Aaron are rebuked for having failed, on one occa-

[14] Gen. 15:6.
[15] Isa. 7:9.
[16] Ps. 27.
[17] Exod. 14:31.
[18] 2 Chron. 20:20.
[19] 2 Kings 18:19–22.
[20] 2 Kings 18:5, 19:10.
[21] Jer. 17:7 ff.; Ps. 1.
[22] Ps. 9:11, 21:8, 22:5–6 (25:2, 26:1), 28:7, 32:6–7, 84:13, 62:9, 37:2, 115:11, 112:6–7; also 125:1.
[23] Jer. 17:5–6.

sion, in their belief in God's help, and consequently impatiently striking the rock for water.[24] The children of Israel are denounced for their perverseness in lacking faith.[25] Their faithlessness came to light in their setting up of the golden calf in place of the living God; in their tendency to idolatry, the arch sin of Israel, in disregard of the covenant with God; and in their moral looseness.[26]

While the predominant aspect of the biblical conception of faith is psychological or volitional, i.e., showing itself in complete dependence upon and surrender to God, in loyalty and in trust in His purposes, and in obedience to His will, the cognitive side steadily came to the fore. This, too, was inherent in the covenant idea. The prophets continually called upon Israel to *believe* in Yahveh's superiority over the deities of the surrounding nations. Elijah challenged the people to choose between Yahveh and Baal. His successors not only thundered against the idolatrous cults, but endeavored to demonstrate the superiority of the national religion, the lofty character of their God, and the high standards of His ethical demands. "For Yahveh your God," the Deuteronomist declares, "He is the God of gods, and the Lord of lords, the great, the mighty, and the awful, who regardeth not persons nor taketh reward. He doth execute justice for the fatherless and widow, and loveth the stranger, in giving him food and raiment."[27] The dawn of monotheism with its challenge to all polytheistic cults evoked reflection. The prophetic ideas regarding God's unfailing justice and love, His government of the affairs of individuals and of nations, called for proofs from history and experience. Reason, accordingly, was summoned to bolster belief. This tendency is prominent in Jeremiah's soliloquy on the question of theodicy and his parable of the potter (concerning world judgment), in Ezekiel's argumentation with the elders for justifying the ways of God, in Deutero-Isaiah's rhapsodic expression of the grounds of faith in the universal God, and in the searching debates of Job and his friends, on the same themes.[28]

---

[24] Num. 20:12.

[25] Deut. 32:20.

[26] Exod. 32, Hos. 4:11-12, Ps. 10:3, etc.

[27] Deut. 10:17-18.

[28] Jer. 12:1 ff., 18; Ezek. 14, 18; Isa. 40 ff.; etc.

The emphasis on the rational side of the beliefs of Judaism was accentuated by its contact with Zoroastrian dualism and to a still greater degree by its clash with the protean forms of Hellenistic worship and thoughts. The prevalence of evil in a world governed by the one God, the mediacy of angels in His government of the affairs of men and of nature, the revelation of His will, Israel's destiny, the beliefs in the Messiah, the resurrection of the body, and the immortality of the soul, agitated the hearts of thinking believers. Amid these challenging conditions to faith, Ben Sira's stress on the importance of faith as an anchor of the soul, takes on new meaning: "Woe unto the faint heart, for it believeth not; therefore shall it not be sheltered."[29] But the questioning mind could be satisfied only with rational answers to the riddles that confronted it. When Judaism entered upon its career of propaganda for universal acceptance, the content of Jewish belief steadily grew in clarity. Greek philosophy was utilized to demonstrate the excellence of the teachings of Judaism: Plato "Mosaized." The intellectualization of the Jewish faith, as evidenced in Hellenistic Jewish writings, led to new developments in the spheres of dogma and philosophy.[30]

3. Rabbinic Views of Faith

The Jewish conception of faith was subjected to a thorough testing by the appearance of Christianity. With the Paulinian theology, faith entered upon a new career, as a dogmatic message, viz. that Jesus is Lord and Christ. Under the influence of current mystery religions, salvation became dependent not upon conduct or works but upon a mystic faith in Jesus.

> Confess *with your mouth* that "Jesus is Lord," believe *in your heart* that God raised him from the dead, and you will be saved, for
> > With his heart man believes and is justified,
> > With his mouth he confesses and is saved.[31]

---

[29] Sira 2:13.

[30] Philo, *On the Creation of the World*, chap. 61, *De Abrahamo*; Josephus, *Against Apion*.

[31] Rom. 10:9–10 (Moffat's trans.); also Rom. 3:23–31, 4, 9:30 ff.

And more explicitly:

> Before this faith came, we were confined by the Law and kept in custody, with
> the prospect of the faith that was to be revealed; the Law thus held us as wards
> in discipline, till such time as Christ came, that we might be justified by faith.
> But faith has come, and we are wards no longer; you are all sons of God by
> your faith in Christ Jesus (for all of you who had yourselves baptised into
> Christ have taken on the character of Christ). Christ ransomed us from the
> curse of the Law by becoming accursed for us (for it is written, *cursed is every-
> one who hangs on a gibbet)*, that the blessing of Abraham might reach the
> gentiles in Christ Jesus, so that by faith we might receive the promised Spirit.[32]

The Epistle to the Hebrews replaces the old covenant between Israel and God
as embodied in the Torah with the new covenant made by God through the
sacrifice of His Son, the mediator between Himself and sinful humanity.[33]

In the name of the new dispensation, the Jews were urged to abandon
their ceremonial Law. The Christian argument declared that the destruction
of the Temple, and the consequent cessation of its ceremonial laws, evidenced
God's indicating the abrogation of the Law.[34] In reply, the rabbis emphasized
the intrinsic validity of the ceremonial law in all its parts and for all times.
The laws connected with the Temple stood suspended, and would be reinstituted promptly with the rebuilding of the Temple. Whereas Abraham had
earlier been regarded as vindicated by his faith alone,[35] the rabbis now
asserted that he observed not only the seven Noachian laws and circumcision,
but also all the commandments of the Torah.[36] Trained to express their faith

---

[32] Gal. 3:23–27, 13–14. See art. "Faith," Hastings, *Encycl. Rel. and Ethics*, V, p. 689.

[33] Heb. 8–9. In Heb. 11–12:2, the mystical vein of faith is linked with the Judaic. It forms a
midrashic development of the text of Isa. 40:31: "They that wait for the Lord shall renew their
strength; they shall mount up with wings as eagles; they shall run and not be weary; they shall
walk and not be faint." It is illustrated by the record of the fathers from Adam to David, of the
prophets and saints. It utilizes the Psalms (e.g., Ps. 107). The passage seems also to refer
specifically to 4 Macc. (See 11:25–26), and presents a tinge of Philo's teaching. For the intellectualistic aspect of faith in Jesus, see John 20:31; also 4:53, 14:11, 15:5, 17:23, etc.

[34] Justin Martyr, *Dial. cum Trypho* XI, 132.

[35] *Mechilta* (ed. Weiss), *Beshalaḥ* 6, p. 40b. Cf. Rom. 4:1 ff.

[36] *Yoma* 28b: אמר רב קיים אברהם אבינו כל התורה כולה שנ' עקב אשר שמע אברהם בקלי וגו' (Gen.
26:5) א"ל רב שימי בר חייא לרב ואימא שבע מצות הא איכא נמי מילה, אימא שבע מצות ומילה א"ל א"כ

in deeds rather than in verbal confessions, and assured of the divine origin of
the Torah, they answered with renewed attachment to the word of God. As
when tried by the Syrian Greeks, so now — though crushed by the Roman
heel and threatened by the vigorous rival faith — they again demonstrated,
through their martyrdom, that their love for God was stronger than death.
The Torah now appeared as the manifestation of God's love for them.
"Exceedingly great love was shown to them [the people of Israel]," Akiba
declared, "in that the precious instrument [the Torah] whereby God created
the world, was entrusted to them."[37] He demonstrated this spirit by defying
the Roman prohibition of the study of the Torah, and by indefatigably
preaching in many communities and firing the hearts of the people with faith
in God and with loyalty to Israel. When a certain Papus warned him of the
danger to which he exposed himself, he replied with this parable:

> It is like a fox that ran to the river bank and beheld fishes hurrying in all direc-
> tions. "Why this excitement?" he asked. "Because nets are spread for us,"
> replied the harassed creatures. "Then would you not come ashore," the crafty
> fox suggested, "where we should live together in safety even as did our fathers
> in the past?" To which the fishes answered: "Art thou he who is famed as the
> wisest of animals? Thou speakest as a fool. If, within our element, we are beset
> with fear, how much greater will be our danger outside thereof!" Even so are
> we. If, while engaged in the Torah, of which it is written: "It is thy life and the

מצותי ותורותי למה לי. אמר (רב) ואיתימא רב אשי קיים אברהם אבינו אפי' עירובי תבשילין שנא' תורותי
פ"שבע תורה ואחת שבכתב תורה אחת. See also *Kid.* IV, 14; Tos. *Kid.* 5. See J. Z. Lauterbach, art.
"Nomism," *Jew. Encyc.* IX, 328. See Kasher, *Encyc. Bib. Interpretation* IV, 24–26, on Gen.
26.5. וימלא אותו רוח אלהים (Exod. 35:31) ולא זה בלבד אלא כל מי שנתעסק במלאכת המשכן נתן בו
וכל הבינה שהיתה (Job 32:8) הקב"ה חכמה ובינה ודעת וכו' . . . א"ר חנינא הה"ד אכן רוח היא באנוש.
בבצלאל משל שדי היא. הוי ואמלא אותו רוח אלהים. בחכמה שהיה חכם בתורה. ובתבונה שהיה מבין בהלכה,
ובדעת שהיה מלא דעת בתלמוד. אמר הקב"ה לישראל בעולם הזה היתה רוחי נותנת בכם חכמה אבל לעתיד
לבא רוחי מחיה אתכם שנאמר (Exod. R. XLVIII. 3–4) ונתתי רוחי בכם וחייתם. (Ezek. 37:14)
מים רבים לא יוכלו לכבות את האהבה, מים רבים אלו (Song 8:7) הה"ד. (Exod. 36:8) ויעשו כל חכם לב
כהמות ימים יהמיון. ואם מתכנסין כל האומות לבטל את האהבה שבין (Isa. 17:12) אומות העולם, שנאמר
ואוהב את יעקב1 (Mal. 1:2) הקב"ה לישראל אינם יכולין. הוי מים רבים לא יוכלו לכבות את האהבה, שנאמר
את מי הנהר העצומים והרבים את מלך אשור וכו' ד"א כל (Isa. 8:7) ונהרות לא ישטפוה. אלו המלכיות שנא'
שחורה אני ונאוה. אם שחורה למה נאוה. וכי יש שחורה נאוה? אלא אמרה כנסת (Song 1:5) חכם לב. הה"ד
ישראל שחורה אני במעשי ונאוה אבותי וכו' (Exod. R. XLIX, 1–2).

[37] *Abot* 3:18.

length of thy days," we are in danger, how much greater will be our peril if we should abandon the study of the words of the Torah![38]

When this noble soul, together with a number of like-minded associates, was exposed to martyrdom for his patriotism and his religion, he died with the word *eḥad* ("one") of the *Shema Yisrael*, on his lips. According to a Midrash, "The people of Israel said: 'We know the power of the Torah; hence shall we not move from the Holy One, blessed be He, and from His Torah,' as it is said: 'I sat down under his shadow with great delight, and his fruit was sweet to my taste.'"[39] The words "many waters cannot quench love" were interpreted to mean that, should all the nations unite to annul the love between the Holy One, blessed be He, and Israel, they would not succeed.[40] As counterclaim to Christian negation of the authority of the Torah, and Christian emphasis on salvation through faith, the rabbis taught that while "heaven and earth rest on faith,"[41] that very faith is buttressed by works and grounded in the Torah. R. Levi asserts that the Jewish people are preserved through the merit of faith and of Torah. Without either one of them, there can be no life.[42] Instead of Paul's thesis of freedom *from* the Law, the rabbis taught that true freedom is achieved *through* the Law. Discussing the verse in Exodus "And the tables were the work of God and the writing was the writing of God, *graven upon the tables*,"[43] the Midrash suggests that the word *ḥarut*, "graven," be read *ḥerut*, "freedom," and asks "What kind of freedom?" Rabbi Judah replies: "freedom from political oppression." Rabbi Nehemiah says: "freedom from the angel of death [i.e., saving the soul for eternal life]; for when Israel accepted the Torah at Sinai, God said unto the angel of death: 'Over all nations thou art free to exercise thy might, but not over this nation, for it is My own portion.'"[44]

Commenting on the verse of the pastoral psalm, "Thy rod and Thy staff,

---

[38] *Berachot* 61b.

[39] *Exod. R.* XVII, 2. The biblical quotation is from Song 2:3.

[40] *Exod. R.* XLIX, 1 on Song 8:7.

[41] *Mid. Ps.* 119:37 ff.

[42] *Gen. R.* LXXIV, 12; *Mid. Ps.* 27:7, 94:5.

[43] Exod. 32:16.

[44] *Exod. R.* XXXII, 1 on Exod. 32:16.

they comfort me," the rabbis said that "'Thy rod' refers to suffering and 'Thy staff' to the Torah."[45] Both betoken God's care and love for His people. The words of the Song of Songs "stay me with flagons [ashishot]"[46] expressed for them the belief that they were being upheld by the two fiery (esh) laws: the Written Torah and the Oral Torah. Hosea's prophecy, "I shall be as dew unto Israel; he shall blossom as the lily,"[47] suggested the thought that even as the lily is preserved for its fragrance, so Israel will not cease to be, because of the Torah and the practice of good deeds. The same spirit is voiced in the old prayer, which may date from Temple times:

> With everlasting love, Thou hast loved the house of Israel, Thy people; a Law and commandments, statutes and judgments hast Thou taught us. Therefore, O Lord our God, when we lie down and when we rise up we will meditate on Thy statutes; yea, we will rejoice in the words of Thy Law and in Thy commandments forever, for they are our life and the length of our days; and we will meditate on them day and night. And mayest Thou never take away Thy love from us. Blessed art Thou, O Lord, who lovest Thy people Israel.[48]

And in the private morning devotions, the Jews were taught to pray:

> Make pleasant therefore, we beseech Thee, O Lord our God, the words of Thy Law, in our mouth and in the mouth of Thy people, the house of Israel, so that we, with our offspring and the offspring of Thy people, the house of Israel, may all know Thy name and learn Thy law. Blessed art Thou, O Lord, who teachest the Law to Thy people Israel.[49]

Faith in the covenant made for the assurance of salvation not alone in the present but also in the future.[50] As the reward of their faith, the people were promised their ultimate messianic redemption. An early Midrash extols faith

---

[45] *Song. R.* II.1 (end), commenting on Ps. 23:4d.

[46] Song 2:5.

[47] Hosea 14:6.

[48] See *Authorized Daily Prayer Book*, trans. by S. Singer, p. 113a; also pp. 39–40.

[49] Ibid., p. 4.

[50] Lev. 26:42–45, Isa. 59:21.

as causing the Holy Spirit to rest upon the people, making them sing for joy in God's salvation, and adds:

> Thou findest that Abraham inherited both this world and that of the hereafter, only through the merit of his faith, as it is stated: "And he believed in the Lord."[51] Similarly thou findest that our fathers were delivered out of Egypt only through the merit of their faith, as it is pointed out: "And the people believed."[52] ... Thus too thou findest that the dispersed exiles will be gathered [into the Holy Land] only as the reward of faithfulness, as [God says unto Israel]:[53] "Come with me from Lebanon, my bride.... Look from the top of Amana [= faith]."[54]

Faith, accordingly, came to mean for the Jew, steadfastness in his religious life as prescribed in the Torah, and loyalty to his people and to his God. "It is known," writes R. Bahia ben Asher (d. 1340), "that the holy seed of Israel, though being in *Galut* [Exile] in the lands of their enemies, scattered over all the ends of the earth, do not forget the principles of their Torah and the commandments, but guard them steadfastly and are firm in their faith, resisting the endeavors of the nations to convert them to another religion. And because of this firmness in their faith, the Holy One, blessed be He, will cause His Shechinah to rest upon them, and restore them to Jerusalem as of yore."[55]

Faith thus embraces the whole of religion and presents a complete program of Jewish life. In his famous sermon, R. Simlai (3d cent.) reduces the 613 commandments of the Torah to the fifteen ethical qualities indicated in the Psalm,[56] then to the six named in Isaiah,[57] the three of Micah,[58] the two of Deutero-Isaiah,[59] and finally to the one of Amos, "Seek ye Me, and live,"[60]

---

[51] Gen. 15:6.

[52] Exod. 4:31.

[53] Song 4:8.

[54] *Mechilta, Beshalah* VI; and in *Yalkut Shimeoni, Beshalah* XIV, 240.

[55] *Kad Hakkemah,* art. "Emunah."

[56] Ps. 15.

[57] Isa. 33:15.

[58] Micah 6:8.

[59] Isa. 56:1.

[60] Amos 5:4.

and of Habakkuk,[61] "The righteous shall live by his faith."[62] The entire body of ethical and ceremonial law ultimately rests upon the foundation of faith. The complete *Halachah* the rabbis found in faith, as expressed in Isaiah: "And the *faith* [or stability] of thy *times* shall be a *hoard* of *salvation* — *wisdom* and *knowledge* and the fear of the Lord, which is His treasure."[63] Each noun in the text suggested to the rabbis one of the six bodies of religious practice codified in the Mishnah, which are crowned by the fear of God.[64]

In the view of the rabbis, faith is a practical relation of confidence in God and in His revealed Law. A mystic Haggadah speaks of it as the first of the seven attributes that minister before the throne of glory, the others being righteousness and justice, loving-kindness and mercy, truth and peace.[65] Like the other virtues, it figures as the means whereby man draws near to his Maker. "He who puts trust in the Holy One, blessed be He, has a protection in this world and in the world-to-come."[66] This confidence is not a mere matter of belief; it translates itself into right conduct. "When man is brought to judgment, he is asked: 'Didst thou *deal faithfully*, didst thou set aside time for Torah; didst thou hope in God's salvation?'"[67]

By the side of the psychological and moral nature of *emunah*, its creedal or dogmatic aspect grew into ever greater prominence. We deal with this subject in another study. Here we shall refer only to R. Ḥananel (990–1050), who writes in his commentary on Exodus that *emunah* is divided into four parts: (1) belief in God, (2) belief in the prophets, (3) belief in the hereafter, and (4) belief in the Messiah. *Emunah* of this nature secures for man future bliss. In his commentary on Genesis, he stresses the binding character of tradition. He considers it part of prophetic revelation, the whole of which must be accepted on trust. Tradition must be recognized as the supreme guide in religious life.[68] For Baḥia ibn Pakudah, faith in the principles of Judaism,

---

[61] Hab. 2:4.
[62] *Maccot* 23b–24b. Cf. Ps. 119:26.
[63] Isa. 33:6.
[64] *Sabbath* 31a.
[65] *Abot de-R. Nathan.* 37.7.
[66] *Men.* 29b.
[67] *Sab.* 31a.
[68] Cited in Baḥya b. Asher's commentary to Exod. 14:31 and to Gen. 18:19. See S. J. Rappaport, "Toledot R. Ḥananel, Likkutim," in *Bikkure Ha'ittim*, XII. 34–55.

which form the basis for its practices, is the foremost of "the duties of the heart."

For Baḥia b. Asher, as for R. Ḥananel, *emunah* ceased to be a mere psychological element of childlike trust and confidence in God, and assumed the character of *reasoned belief* — steeled into *conviction* — in the existence of God and in His providential care of the world and of man — a belief embodying a well-defined program of ethical relationships. The element of *trust, bittaḥon,* in Baḥia's opinion, ranks above *emunah.*

> *Bittaḥon* resembles the fruit of the tree, and *emunah* the tree itself. While the presence of the fruit proves the existence of a tree or plant upon which it grew, the presence of a tree by no means signifies that there is fruit upon it, for certain trees are not fruit-bearing. Even so, *trust* shows the presence of belief, but belief does not necessarily testify that its possessor is trustful.[69]

4. *The Sovereignty of Reason*

The transfer of *emunah* from the realm of psychology to that of dogmatics, on the one hand, and of philosophy, on the other, occurred as a gradual process, influenced by the conflict of Judaism with Zoroastrianism, Hellenism, Christianity, and Islam, and also by the sectarian divisions within Judaism.[70] The Karaites played a significant role in this development. Their denial of rabbinic tradition called forth a revaluation of the inherited faith. In direct opposition to them, Saadia Gaon (882 or 892–942) wrote his classic work *Emunot Vedeot.*[71] His use of the term *emunot* in this title already carries a speculative

---

[69] *Kad Hakkemaḥ,* art. "Bittaḥon."

[70] In the development of ideas regarding the relation of faith and reason, we note the influence of Arabic philosophy, of the Kalam, which placed faith by the side of reason as a source of religious knowledge, of Neoplatonism, which ranked revelation above reason, and of Aristotelianism, which ranked reason above revelation. *Jew. Encyc.* II, 56–58.

[71] Saadia Gaon's high regard for tradition as the foundation of human culture can be appreciated in the light of his anti-Karaism. He writes: "The All-Wise, blessed be He, knowing that His laws would, in course of time, require transmitters in order to be accepted by the later generations as by the former ones, implanted in human reason the faculty of receiving

connotation.[72] Judah ibn Tibbon, in imitation of the Arabic *amanat*, employed it "in the sense of a philosophic doctrine," and occasionally applied it also in its nonphilosophical sense of religious beliefs (*i'tikâd*).[73] "*Emunah,*" Saadia says,

> appears in two ways: one true and one false. True belief consists of knowing the thing as it is, the great thing as great and the small as small, the white as white and the black as black, the existing as existing and the nonexisting as nonexisting. False belief consists of knowing the opposite of the real, such as holding the great small and the small great, the white black and the black white, the existing nonexisting and the nonexisting existing. The wise man that is deserving of praise is he who makes reality the root, adjusts his mind to it, and in his wisdom trusts that which should be trusted and takes heed of that which should be heeded. The contemptible fool, on the other hand, is he who makes his own opinion the root, and imagines that reality adjusts itself to his opinion. In his folly, he relies upon that which he should guard against, and he guards against that in which he should trust.[74]

Since *belief* derives its value from its reasonableness, Saadia devotes himself to the presentation of Judaism from the standpoint of reason or philosophy.

> All knowledge is commonly derived from three sources: (1) sense perception, (2) direct cognition or apprehension of the mind [intuitive or immediate knowledge], (3) syllogistic reasoning [inferential or mediate knowledge]. In addition to these three general sources of knowledge, "we, the followers of monotheism," recognize also a fourth one, i.e., the Bible. If, as often happens, the word of Scripture appears to contradict what we had assumed as true on the basis of one of the other three general sources of truth, or even of all of them, it becomes our duty first to submit the assumed truth to a careful examination. For it may be found that it is based either on an imaginary

prophetic truth and in the soul room for its welcome, that thereby His stories and traditions may be verified." *Emunot* III, 3-5.

[72] Its Arabic title is *Kitab al' Amanat wa'l I'tikadat*, i.e., "Book of Philosophic and Religious Beliefs." Dr. Neumark renders the title "Dogmas and Beliefs." See his *Principles of Judaism*, p. 39.

[73] See Malter, *Saadia Gaon*, p. 193, n. 455.

[74] *Emunot*, Introduction, IV.

experience or on false reasoning. If, upon conscientious revision, we still feel
convinced that the biblical word is in conflict with experience or reason, then
we are not only entitled, but in duty bound, to interpret the scriptural passage
in question allegorically,[75] so as to bring it into harmony with the accepted
truth.[76]

It is evident that in Saadia's view, reason ranks as primary, and Scripture
and revelation as secondary sources of truth. For him, "both reason and
religion sprang from the same divine Source"; and human reason is needed to
discover what divine reason declares as truth.[77] Hence "any interpretation [of
Scripture] agreeing to what is in reason, is the truth, but any [interpretation]
that leads to something that is at variance with reason is fallacious."[78]
However, his intellectualism, though apparently enjoying complete autonomy,
in reality seeks to serve the cause of religion. The purpose of all speculation is
to appropriate through reason what was first acquired through tradition and
to secure the means of "refuting anyone who will argue against us in any of
the matters of our religion."[79]

Abraham ibn Daud (1110–1180) — the first strict Aristotelian and
forerunner of Maimonides — devoted his *Emunah Ramah*, "Sublime Faith,"
to the interpretation of Judaism from the standpoint of reason. "In our time,"
he complains,

> it often happens that a person who has studied a little science has no strength to
> hold in his hands the two lights, the light of religion in his right hand and that

[75] or figuratively.

[76] H. Malter, *Saadia Gaon*, pp. 195–96. See also note 459.

[77] D. Neumark, *HUCA* I, pp. 525 ff. A Geniza fragment of Saadia's lost "Testimonies and
Agreements" (אלותאיק = Hebrew השטרות 'ס) contains the following definition of truth: "In the
beginning, I say: Praised be God, the God of Israel, who is Truth manifest, who makes Truth
the noblest object of knowledge, Now Truth is that which finds its place in intellects which are
immune to all damage, and clear in the souls which think by their means." This definition of
truth resembles that of Saadia's contemporary Isaac Israeli, viz., that truth is that [conception]
which is identical with the thing [conceived]. Hartwig Hirshfield, *JQR*, XVI (1904), 294–95.

[78] *Emunot* III, 1 and Neumark, op. cit., 526 and 563.

[79] *Emunot*, Introduction VI, 2.

of his science in his left; but as the light of science is kindled, that of religion is extinguished. And not only in our generation, but also in former generations it happened thus, as our rabbis tell us concerning Elisha Aḥer. They state that four entered the Pardes [= garden, i.e., of philosophic speculation]: R. Akiba, Ben Azzai, Ben Zoma, and Elisha Aḥer. Ben Azzai gazed [into the heavenly chambers] and died; Ben Zoma gazed and was injured; Elisha Aḥer cut down its plants [i.e., became an apostate]; only Akiba entered in peace and went out in peace.[80] On this account, many of our contemporaries consider the study of these high sciences as injurious, and do not turn to them for anything. For this reason, too, they know nothing of either the foundations of religion and its principles, although these should command their constant attention, or even of its branches which require but a little investigation.

True philosophy, far from leading us away from religion, only confirms us in it, for that which is in reason is also in Scripture.[81]

With Maimonides (1135–1204), reason attained its apotheosis. What distinguishes man from brute-creation is his rationality. While at birth this element forms but a part of his psychic powers, it may develop in the course of time into its full and unique being. From a state of potentiality it may reach that of actuality. As the "acquired intellect," it ceases to be a "power in the body; it is rather distinct from the body" and does not decay with the decay of the body.[82] Thus reason endows man with immortality. The whole aim of man is to cultivate his intellect through the study of philosphy and theology. To facilitate the cultivation of men of high intellectual attainment constitutes the chief aim of society. Religion itself serves this end, for it represents a popular philosophy, and, on its practical side, a body of morality and social pedagogy. Religion is, accordingly, subordinated to reason. Hence Maimonides, discussing the doctrine of the eternity of matter, states that he would accept it in preference to that of the creation of matter if he had convincing proofs for it.[83]

The Torah itself, in his view, figures as the revelation of the divine Mind

---

[80] *Haggiga* 14b.
[81] See Introd. to *Emunah Ramah*.
[82] *More Neb.* I, 70, 72, and Preface to *Com. on Zeraim*.
[83] *Kovetz Teshuboth* (Leipzig, pt. II, p. 23, Letter to R. Hisdai Halevi.

and, on this account, must be in agreement with the highest truths known to man. In this spirit, he set himself to interpret away all the anthropomorphic and anthropopathic expressions from the Bible, and to make it voice ideas that stand in conformity with reason or philosophy. In the fifty-first chapter of the third part of his *Guide of the Perplexed,* he pictures six groups of people who set out to visit the king in his palace. One group is wholly out of the king's province, i.e., is devoid of all religion and morals, like animals. Another group of men is headed in the opposite direction from the palace. The farther it goes, the farther it is from its goal. The third group consists of people who had never seen the palace, i.e., the common folk who observe the practical religious duties without being aware of the speculative principles. The fourth group is composed of men who circle around the palace but do not enter, i.e., they have acquired by tradition certain true beliefs, but do not enter to examine the roots of the Torah. To the fifth group belong all those who have gained entrance into the vestibule, i.e., those who have already investigated the principles of faith or who have mastered the physical sciences. Only those enter into the king's chamber and behold his presence who have mastered the science of metaphysics. *Reason* thus becomes the bond of union between man and God. Through its acquisition, man comes under the care of divine Providence, and secures his immortality.

5. *The Opposition*

While Maimonides' view reappears in Gersonides and in numerous other thinkers of the synagogue, it *also* called forth sharp protests from men of influence. R. Shem Tob comments on the fifty-first chapter of the third part of the *Guide* to this effect:

> Many rabbinical scholars declare that the Master did not write this chapter, and, if he did, it must be hidden, or, more fittingly, burned; for how could he have placed those who know natural things in a higher rank than those who occupy themselves with religion, and especially, how dared he place them in the inner court of the king? If so, then the philosophers who concern themselves with science and with metaphysics rank above those who devote themselves to the Torah.

Quite naturally, some leaders of Judaism apprehended the danger of rationalizing religion. Reliance upon syllogistic reasoning inevitably leads to the depreciation of truth derived in other ways.[84] Religion, by becoming subservient to philosophy, is shorn of its distinction and power. Some philosophers, both before and after Maimonides, were, therefore, content to use reason as the handmaid of revelation. Thus Bahia ibn Pakudah (first half of 11th cent.) recognized reason together with Scripture and tradition as a source of religious truth. Its exercise constitutes, in his view, one of the "duties of the heart," which man owes his Maker. However, its office consists primarily in confirming the data obtained through the other two channels.[85]

For Bahia's contemporary, the Neoplatonic poet-philosopher Solomon ibn Gabirol (b. 1022), *reason* loomed as the native element of man. Yet it is faith that leads him to salvation. In his rapturous poetic version of his religious philosophy, "The Royal Crown," he views the soul as drawn "from the fount of light" and its radiance as wrought "from the sphere of intelligence," imbued with the spirit of wisdom and endowed with the faculty of knowledge, so that "science is the very fount of her glory."

> My soul was precious in Thy sight,
> Nor didst Thou send me empty away.
> But all this didst Thou yet exceed and add to
> When Thou gavest me a perfect faith
> To believe that Thou art the God of Truth
> And that Thy Law is true and Thy prophets are true.
> For Thou hast not set my portion with the rebels and those
> who rise up against Thee,
> And the foolish multitude that blaspheme Thy name.[86]

The other outstanding poet-philosopher of the synagogue, Jehuda Halevi (1085–1142), similarly glories in man's intellectual endowments. Dealing with the order of the middle prayers in the *Amidah,* the central portion of all three daily services, he writes:

---

[84] See Jehiel of Pisa, *Minhath Kenaoth,* p. 9.

[85] See Introd. to *Hobot Halebabot.*

[86] Zangwill and Davidson, *Selected Religious Poems of Solomon Ibn Gabirol,* pp. 104–5, 112.

It is proper that the first of the specific petitions be for reason and knowledge,[87] for it is through them that man endeavors to draw near unto his God. Therefore, the prayer for understanding is placed directly before the one for repentance, that wisdom, knowledge, and understanding be applied to Torah and to the service of God, as stated: "Cause us to return, O our Father, unto Thy Law."[88]

However, the chief source of religious knowledge for Halevi is not reason but prophecy. The goal of wisdom is the mastery of the Torah. Unquestioning acceptance of the Torah is superior to philosophizing about it. The Torah represents the supreme manifestation of wisdom with which only the Jews were graced and to which the Greeks failed to attain. Aristotle "belabored his reason and thought because he lacked a well-authenticated tradition."[89]

The distinguished exegete Abraham ibn Ezra (1092–1167) considered reason as "the mediating angel between man and his God."[90] "Wisdom of every kind," he writes, "gives life to its owner. There are many kinds of wisdom, and each kind is useful; they are like the steps of a ladder, leading upward to true wisdom. Happy they whose mental eyes are open, that they may in the future approach the Lord and His goodness."[91] However, in addition to his reason and to his intuitive distinction between right and wrong, man needs the guidance that came through God's direct communication to man in the form of the Torah. Commenting on the words "the Law of the Lord is perfect,"[92] he writes: "David — after having described in the preceding verses how the wise man can find a proof for the existence of God, and how he can learn to understand God's works — adds that there is yet another proof which is much better and more trustworthy, viz., the divine Law. . . . It is called 'perfect' because in its presence no other evidence is needed."[93]

[87] Cf. S. Singer, *Authorized Daily Prayer Book*, p. 46.

[88] *Cuzari* III, 19.

[89] *Cuzari* I, 63.

[90] Introd. to *Commentary on the Pentateuch*: השכל שליח השם.

[91] *Yesod Mora*, Introd., cited by M. Friedlander, *Essays on the Writings of Ibn Ezra*, p. 33, n. 1.

[92] Ps. 19:8.

[93] M. Friedlander, op. cit., p. 49, n. 1. Commentary to Exod. 20:1. כל המצות היו על ב' דרכים. והדרך הא' מצות שהם נטועות מהשם בלב כל אנשי דעת וכו'.

Substantially the same position is taken by Joseph Albo (1380–1444). Defending the validity of human knowledge, he also recognizes its limitations. It is obtained not only through sense perception and syllogistic reasoning, but also through faith. By faith, Albo understands "the mental representation of a thing in such manner as not to permit of its contradiction under any circumstance, even though the way in which to prove it is not known." He equates faith with axiomatic truth. It applies to that which the believer himself has not perceived through is own senses, but which some worthy person or persons perceived some time in the past, and has come down to him by direct tradition from father to son.[94] Such knowledge is indispensable for mankind. Inasmuch as human perfection depends upon the performance of deeds that are pleasing to God, and as the human mind cannot, through investigation, discover what they are, the Higher Wisdom had to find another way by which to assist men in knowing what is acceptable to God. This way consists in endowing a chosen individual with the gift of prophecy. The knowledge which he miraculously obains offers guidance to the rest of mankind. Man's happiness thus becomes dependent upon the study of the Torah.[95]

Even this moderate position regarding the office of reason failed to satisfy the ultra-Orthodox. They refused to compromise with any attempt at dragging the supernatural into the realm of the natural. The Kabbalist Moses de Leon (1250–1305), the probable author of the Zohar, protests that if the Torah contained nothing more than that which Aristotle attained without storm and noise, it was not necessary for God to reveal Himself at Sinai amid thunder, to give His people the Torah and commandments. Natural religion renders revelation superfluous.[96] Rabbi Solomon ben Abraham ibn Adret of Montpellier (13th cent.), the chief opponent of the philosophical tendency in Judaism, was not content with the elimination of the fifty-first chapter of the third book of the *Guide of the Perplexed*. He would have all the books written by the philosophers "burned in the public place, in their presence." In his interdict of the study of the sciences by persons under twenty-five years of age, i.e., until they have so filled themselves with traditional lore that "they

---

[94] *Ikkarim* I. 16, 19.
[95] Ibid., III. 8 ff.
[96] *Nefesh Haḥachama.*

will not remove it from being queen," he inveighs against those who study philosophy as enemies of religion. "Truth," he cries,

> has stumbled in the street, for some of them say that all that is written from the section of *Bereshit*, Genesis, as far as the giving of the Law is nothing more than an allegory. . . . Indeed they show that they have no faith in the plain meaning of the commandments; they inscribe on their hearts and on the walls of their altars that they have no portion in the God of Israel, nor in the Torah which their fathers had received on Sinai. They are more estranged than the gentiles; for the latter fulfill some of the commandments in the proper form, while they (may they have no remnant in the land!) strongly desire to uproot all. The chief reason of all this is because they are infatuated with alien sciences, Zidonian and Moabitish,[97] and pay homage to the Greek books. . . . Now a boy born upon the knees of natural science, who sees Aristotle's seven-fold proofs concerning it, really believes in it, and denies the Chief Cause; if we refute him, he becomes all the more impious. They only read the Law, but their heart is not right inwardly, and they pervert it in seven ways. For thus says one of their sages, who is esteemed as the chief of the heads of their sects: "It is good that the study of the Law should be combined with secular sciences; it is a good thing, but without the wisdom of the Greeks a man is called *a wild ass used to the wilderness*. They that study the Law, what manner of wisdom is in them? for they themselves are but as beasts."[98]

With the aid of the Dominicans, Rabbi Solomon succeeded in putting the torch to Maimonides' philosophical writings.[99] The issue was clear. Rabbi

---

[97] The allusion is to 1 Kings 11:1.

[98] B. Halper, *Post-Bib. Heb. Lit.* (Eng. trans.), pp. 176 ff. For the serious controversy concerning the relation of philosophy and Judaism, see *Kobetz Teshuboth HaRaMBaM*, (Leipzig, 1859), part III, and H. Graetz, *History of the Jews*, vol. III, chap. XVI. "Philosophy," R. Joel Sirkis (1561-1640) wrote, "is heresy incarnate and the 'strange woman' of whom Solomon warned [in Proverbs]." Responsa שו״ת הב״ח (ed. 1697), n. 4, pp. 3-4, cited by S. Dubnow, *Toledot Hahasidut*, p. 20, n. 2.

[99] In 1236. In 1210 and 1215 the University of Paris prohibited the reading of Aristotle's physical and metaphysical writings. *Environmental Factors in Christian History*, ed. McNiel, p. 220. In 1231 Pope Gregory IX appointed a commission to edit Aristotle so as to make him safe for Christianity. Ibid., p. 245.

Solomon's "fundamentalism" is still expressive of the ultra-Orthodox view-point, which finds in Scripture, as interpreted by talmudic tradition, the only authoritative source of religious knowledge. Not reason but unquestioned faith in God and in His revelation at Sinai leads man to salvation. This tendency is still not without adherents in Judaism.[100] However, the stars in their courses are fighting against it. Modern Orthodoxy itself has joined the side of reason,[101] while the ever-growing wing of Liberal Judaism may be considered an outgrowth of the philosophical tendencies in Judaism.

6. Conclusion

Faith is the life-breath of religion. Frequently it is regarded as a form of knowledge that is not derived from the usual sources of observation and deduction, through rational analysis and demonstration, but comes to us through inward perception in the absence of all proof. While this view still has its defenders in Judaism, there is the strong tendency to regard faith not as opposed to reason but supplementary to it. Faith and reason are the two eyes of the soul through which we look upon reality. When either of them fails to function, our vision is distorted. Only when they are properly focused do they afford us a balanced view of reality.

The continued emphasis on reason in religion has secured a firm place for science — whether in the form of Aristotelian or Darwinian thought — in Jewish life. Taught to regard all truth as the signet of God, the foremost representatives of Judaism welcomed the new revelations of truth. Elijah del Medigo voiced the conviction of many of our religious thinkers that "our revealed Law does not at all obligate us to believe contradictory things nor to deny axiomatic truths, those that resemble them, or perceptible verities. And if our religion had contained such a requirement, we would set it aside."[102]

---

[100] With the pious glossator of Eccles. 12:13, Orthodoxy holds: סוף דבר הכל נשמע את האלהים ירא וכו'. Cf. the modern trend to existentialism on the part of some Jewish teachers.

[101]Samson Raphael Hirsch, *Nineteen Letters of Ben Uziel*, Friedlander's *Jewish Religion*, and Schechter's *Studies in Judaism* and *Aspects of Rabbinic Theology*, may serve as examples.

[102] "תורתנו צו האלהית לא תחייבנו כלל להאמין הדברים הסותרים ולא לכפור המושכלות הראשונות או אשר המה כראשונות והמוחשות, ולו היה בזה בדתנו היינו מחליטים המאמר בדיחיית הדת, כי גם אם הונח שהאמת כן לא יגיענו עונש אלהי. על הותנו בלתי מאמינים בם אחר ששכלנו בטבעו אשר חקק לו האל לא יוכל

The human reason, which is the stamp of divinity upon man, must not be offended by credulity masquerading as faith. Montefiore wrote: "Faith concerns the reason as well as the feelings and the will. . . . The present conception of God has been won by reason as well as by love. Ignorance can never be a good, whether in religion or in anything else."[103]

Faith is not salutary if it cannot stand the test of truth. *Emunah* must not be divorced from *emet*. Only when it can justify itself before the bar of reason can faith create the state of personal reliance on and fidelity to God, to truth, and to right, which form the basis of the religious life, and serve as the spring of ethical conduct.

But faith has its contribution to add to that of reason. Reason is critical and analytical; faith is appreciative and practical. The eye of faith often beholds what the eye of reason may overlook. Thus it affords a deeper insight into the heart of things, strengthens the will for action, and, in so doing, transforms character. As the unguarded use of the X-ray may render the operator sterile, so, frequently, the employment of reason in the service of religion may exert a disastrous spiritual effect. Judaism claims the right of the mind to test and to purify its doctrines and practices; but it claims more than that. It also demands reverence, humility, and self-effacement. Its great command is not only "hear" or "know," but also "love" with all your heart and soul, "keep the covenant," and "do" the commands of God, in order to be holy. Faith and knowledge must be crowned by works that sanctify and bind the individual to the religious community.

Faith means steadfastness, hope, and courage. Its absence spells vacillation and anxiety. Faith is an anchor in the sea of uncertainty and trouble, delivering from the paralysis of fear, and liberating man's creative powers. In the religious sense, faith represents personal avowal of the values of religion: the purposefulness of life, the reality of God, and the rightness of His will; and speaks commitment to these truths, whether they be disclosed by reason, grasped by intuition, or delivered by tradition. Faith constitutes an affirmation of life.

Elijah Delmedigo, *Beḥinat* לקבל ולא להאמין באלה אבל יצייר תמיד וידע חלופם כאשר יונח כפי טבעו." *Hadat* (Basel, 1629), p. 3a (Vienna, 1833), p. 14.

[103] C. G. Montefiore, *Outlines of Liberal Judaism*, p. 351.

The Precepts of Judaism

By the side of the principles of Judaism, its *mitzvot* or precepts hold the place of greatest prominence. Philosophers like Maimonides valued the precepts as the rind that preserves the fruit.[1] Others, like Abravanel and R. David b. Zimra, refused to draw a line between the two. In their opinion, all the commandments of the Torah rank as principles and are equally binding. Thus Mendelssohn, while regarding the principles of Judaism — that is, the existence of God, revelation, immortality of the soul, etc. — as self-evident truths which underlie all religion, found the distinctiveness of Judaism in its being a divinely revealed legislation, a body of laws based on reason.

Thus from whatever angle Judaism is examined, it manifests itself as a religion of *mitzvot*, precepts or duties. The duties invest Judaism with a practical character. Josephus, in the second part of his polemic against Apion, gloried in the coextensiveness of the Torah with the life of the Jewish people. Indeed the distinguishing characteristic of Judaism has been that it did not remain in the realm of emotion or of abstract thought, and ever strove to embody itself in the life pattern of the individual and of the community. Its faith and its convictions were transmuted into *halacha,* rules for everyday conduct.

The claim has been made that the unity of Judaism was based not "upon orthodoxy in theology but upon uniformity of observance."[2] It is easy to

---

[1] *H. Yesode Hatorah* 4:13; Hones, *Toledot Haposekim*, p. 619, cites the following passage which does not appear in the printed edition: הלכות דעות הם עיקרי האמונה וכל איש אשר הולך בדרך זה הוא האיש הנאמן לאלהיו. המצות המעשיות הם רק כקליפה ושומר לפרי אשר בלתי הַקליפה לא ישתמר הפרי מכל רוח ובערה, מכל נגע וגע והוא כמו מליצת התלמוד ר' מאיר רמן מצא תוכו אכל לקיפתו זרק, הכוונה כי כיון שלבו תמיד בו עזה בשכל הישר. המצות המעשיות הן לו כמו רשות אם יעשה או לא יעשה אחת היא כי כל כוונת המעשיות היא רק אשר בהם ישתמר הפרי, הדעת הישרה באלהות והוא הוא האיש התם והישר בדרך ה'.

27

overestimate the uniformity of observance as well as to underestimate the uniformity of belief. In reality, vital differences of opinion prevailed with regard to practice as well as in the matter of doctrine, as, for example, the requirements of dietary laws, laws of marriage and divorce, civil legislation, calendation, and observance of the Sabbath and the holy days. These differences found expression in sectarian divisions, and continued within Rabbinic Judaism. Furthermore, while practice was considered all-important, and the formulated *halachah* was regarded as binding even upon those who argued against it, wide differences of opinion existed regarding the interpretation of the *halachah*, even as about the principles of the faith.

Basic to understanding the nature of historical Judaism[3] is the awareness that it recognizes its observances as divine commands. The taboos and prohibitions with which the sense of the holy invests itself have, as their extension, certain definite requirements. They figure in Judaism as *mitzvot aseh* and *mitzvot lo taaseh,* positive and negative precepts, which form the warp and woof of the entire *halachah.* The emphasis on commands marks the advance of Judaism over heathenism. In the pagan cults, conduct was regulated by taboos and the magic art. Judaism viewed all tribal mores and ritual observances as commands of God, the supreme Source of authority.

If the emphasis on belief is linked with the prophetic idea of the inwardness of faith, the stress on practice follows the priestly tradition. While the two often clash, there is also a measure of common agreement between them. The preaching of the prophets would have fallen on deaf ears but for the guidance of the priests. As the conservative guardians of the Law, they embodied some of the prophetic teachings in their legislative enactments. Prophecy thus found its way into the Torah, into the legal codes of the Pentateuch. The ideas of righteousness proclaimed by an Elijah and an Amos are re-echoed in the code of the covenant.[4] The Deuteronomic code, in both its

---

[2] Moore, *History of Judaism* I, p. 111.

[3] Some rabbis do not approve of the name "Orthodox," considering it a misnomer. They are critical also of the terms "historical Judaism" and "traditional Judaism," which, as Dr. Leo Jung maintains, "have been found to cover a multitude of sins." The Neo-Orthodox have adopted the clumsy name "Torah-true Judaism."

[4] Principally in Exodus 23.

legal and hortative sections, and the Code of Holiness[5] voice the doctrines of Isaiah, Jeremiah, and Ezekiel. While in the process of translation into Law, something of prophecy's compulsiveness was softened, prophecy would, without this compromise, have vanished from the consciousness of the people. Spirit must be tenanted in body. Ethical monotheism shaped itself into definite forms and rules, and the Law became the controlling factor of Jewish life. It holds the center of the Pentateuch and forms the main interest of the Talmud and the rabbinic codes. It combined the advancing ethical, philosophic, and mystical ideas into a legislative system that endowed Jewish life with organized structural forms.

Thus, on the practical side, Judaism may be regarded as a system of *mitzvot* or divine commands or rules of conduct. It includes not only ceremonial laws but also all moral requirements, which the prophets, by uniting religion with morality, represented as the requirements of God. The fulfillment of a precept, a *mitzvah*, constituted an act of merit; its violation or neglect, an *avera*, a transgression or sin. The fulfillment of certain commands must be accompanied by the intention of doing God's will, while others are considered valid even if observed without such intention. However, before assuming the yoke of the commandments, the Jew must accept the yoke of the divine Kingship.[6] The whole moral and spiritual life of man depends upon obedience to the will of God, as expressed in the Torah. In the closing words of Ecclesiastes, "The end of the matter, all being heard: fear God and keep His commandments, for this is the whole of man," or as the Authorized Version reads, "for this is the whole duty of man."

Positive and Negative Commands

God's will being the source and authority of every moral and ceremonial duty, His commands began with the birth of the human race. Thus the rabbis trace

---

[5] Lev. 19.

[6] *Ber.* 13a–b, 14b; *Naz.* 23a–b; art. "Kavvanah," *Universal Jewish Encyclopedia* VI, 346–48; *Jew. Encyc.* IV, 180; Schechter, *Aspects of Rabbinic Theology,* p. 116.

the revelation of God's will to Adam, to Enoch, to Noah, to Abraham, and principally to Moses at Mount Sinai, purposing to show that certain basic rules of life came into existence with the very appearance of man on earth. A Midrash comments that unto the ancients, God gave only the savor of the commandments: to Adam one, to Noah and his sons six; but to Israel at Sinai He poured out all of them as one pours out a whole barrel of wine.[7] Other rabbinic sources speak of six commands to Adam and seven to Noah. The Noachian commandments include the establishment of courts of justice and the prohibition of idolatry, incest, bloodshed, blasphemy, robbery, and eating the flesh of a living animal.[8] The Book of Jubilees adds to the Noachian laws, commands regarding honoring parents, loving the neighbor, "sinning against the beasts and birds," etc.[9] Rabbinic literature, too, made many additions to these laws, so that Hullin enlarges their number to thirty-two.[10] Generally, however, the number seven prevails. Some laws inferred from the traditions in Genesis and Exodus prior to the Sinaitic revelation were eliminated on the principle: "Every law that was enjoined upon the Noachides and was repeated at Sinai was intended to apply to both Israelites and non-Israelites, but laws that were not repeated at Sinai were meant only for Israel."[11] These commandments have been regarded as the foundation of the entire Torah, aiming to remove idolatry and to advance love for one's fellowmen.[12] Weber regards them as essentially similar to the Decalogue, accounting them "not unjustly named a compendium of natural pedagogy and morality."[13] They were effectively employed in the propaganda for the extension of Judaism among the nations, and were utilized by the early church, which succeeded the missionary propaganda of Hellenistic Judaism.[14]

[7] Tanhuma, Yitro.

[8] Gen. R. 16:9; Yalkut, Gen, 22; Deut. R. 2:11; Cant. R. 1:16 (Adam); Noah — Gen. R. 34:7; Sanh. 56b–57; Tos. Ab. Zara 9:4.

[9] Jub. 7:20–37. The translators misinterpreted birkat hashem as "blessing the Creator" and giluy arayot as "cover the shame of their flesh."

[10] Hullin 32a.

[11] Sanh. 59a; Bacher, Aggada d. Palestin. Amoraer I, 430 and note; Jew. Encyc. VI, 648–50, art. "Laws, Noachian," by Julius Greenstone.

[12] I. B. Levinsohn, Zerubabel I, 24, also 15, and II, 74–88.

[13] Juedische Theologie, no. 56.

[14] Acts 15:20, 29. See Kohler, Jew. Theol., p. 51.

It was at Sinai that the Law in all its fullness was revealed to Israel. At Sinai, according to Exodus 19–20 and Deuteronomy 5, the covenant of God and Israel was embodied in the Decalogue, whereas the sequel in both books suggests that the codes that follow similarly formed part of the covenant. Philo as well as the rabbis harmonized the two claims by regarding the Decalogue as the epitome of the entire Law. Philo writes: "The ten covenants are summaries of the special laws which are recorded in the Sacred Books and run through the whole legislation." The first set of five expresses man's relation to God, the second group of five "contains the actions prohibited by our duty to fellowmen." The Decalogue was given by God Himself, but the special laws were spoken by the mouth of Moses, "the most perfect of the prophets, whom He selected for his merits, and having filled him with the divine spirit, chose him to be the interpreter of His sacred utterances."[15]

Palestinian Judaism similarly accorded the Decalogue a place of pre-eminence and made it part of the daily liturgy in the Temple, by the side of the *Shema*. It was dropped out of the reconstructed liturgy of the synagogue because of the heretical contention of the type expressed by Philo, that only the Decalogue was given by God.[16] Nevertheless the Decalogue continued to be regarded as the core of the Torah. R. Ishmael seems to have held to Philo's distinction between the Decalogue and the rest of the Torah, considering the first as general principles and the other as special laws.[17] A Midrash attempts to read all the precepts of the Torah into the Decalogue by assuming that its 620 letters correspond to the 613 commands and the seven days of creation,[18] indicating that the world was called into being for the sake of the Torah.

---

[15] *The Decalogue*, XII, 50ff.; XXIV, 121; XXIX, 154 ff.; XXXIII, 175.

[16] *Tam.* 5:1; Jeru. *Ber.* 12a. An attempt was made to revive the custom at Sura and Nehardea, but without success. See Responsum of Hai Gaon in *Haeshkol* II, 1, cited by J. Mann, *Jews in Egypt*, I, 223. The *Seder R. Amram*, ed. Frumkin, I, 322 ff., shows that a compromise was effected and the recitation of the Decalogue was prescribed for individuals. On the other hand, in Palestine the custom was revived seven generations before Saadia. It was followed also in Fustat. After the reading of the psalm of the day (*Al-shir — shir shel yom*), a scroll was carried to the almemar; the Decalogue was recited; and the scroll, unopened, was carried back to the ark. J. Mann, op. cit.

[17] *Hag.* 6a ר׳ ישמעאל אומר כללות נאמרו בסיני ופרטות באהל מועד, ור׳ עקיבא אומר כללות ופרטות נאמרו בסיני ונשנו באהל מועד. Cf. *Hor.* 6a–b.

[18] *Num. R.* 13:16.

St. Jerome (4th cent. C.E.), in his commentary on Ezekiel, writes: "The Jews say that the pious scholars of Babylonia to this day bind their head with the Ten Commandments written on parchment. These they were commanded to append before their eyes on their forehead, in order that they might perpetually see the things they were commended." A. M. Hoberman thinks that this statement, far from being erroneous, as some have supposed, is corroborated by *Sifre*,[19] which controverts the view that the Decalogue should be included in the phylacteries.[20] The accuracy of the fact that this view had actual adherents in both theory and practice is established by the unearthing at Qumran of phylacteries which contain the Decalogue. Consequently it appears likely that originally the Decalogue was included in the phylacteries, and was removed on the same grounds on which it was eliminated from the liturgy, that is, to overcome the belief of the sectarians that only the Decalogue was given to Moses.

The number of the precepts of the Torah appears to have been familiar to the rabbis in the second century.[21] In the sermon of R. Simlai (3d cent.), we read that "613 precepts were given to Moses at Sinai: 365 prohibitions corresponding to the days of the solar year, and 248 affirmative commands corresponding to the number of bones in the human body."[22] He meant to impress the idea that the Torah applies to every day of the year and to every part of the body. Rabbinic literature treats this number as an accepted fact.[23]

Systematic Works on the Taryag (613)

The number of the commands appears to have been derived on purely homiletical grounds. The Talmud and the Midrashim offer no suggestion as to

---

[19] *Sifre, Devarim,* par. 35.

[20] Hoberman, "The Dead Sea Scrolls," *Judaism,* vol. 5, no. 4, (1956), p. 315.

[21] *Mekilta, Bahodesh,* Weiss (74a), is of the opinion that this number is a later addition since the *Yalkut* does not give it. See Halper, JQR, n.s. IV, p. 521. However, the number of the negative commands is given by R. Simeon b. Azzai in *Sifre,* Deut. 76, ed. Friedman, p. 90b.

[22] *Makkot* 23b.

[23] *Shabuot* 29a, *Ned.* 25a, *Exod. R.* 33:1, *Num. R.* 13:16, *Tanḥ.,* Buber, *Tetze* 1.

the method by which it was obtained. The first attempt at an actual enumeration of the commandments of the Torah is contained in the Halachot Gedolot, variously ascribed to R. Jehudai Gaon and, with greater reason, to R. Simeon Kayyara, both of the eighth or possibly the beginning of the ninth century. Maimonides remarks about this work that "all who occupied themselves with enumerating them [the precepts] or with composing a book on the subject, followed the author of the *Halachot Gedolot,* and they deviated only slightly from his opinions, as if the intellects of men stopped still at the decisions of this man."[24]

It has been suggested that not by accident were the first efforts to codify the *halachah* made in the time of the Geonim, shortly after the appearance of Karaism. The frequent controversies with the sectarians convinced the rabbis of the need of drawing up a concise compendium of the law, free from the controversies of the Talmud. Thus Jehudai Gaon, a contemporary of Anan, who composed a *Sefer Hamitzvot,* summarized the final results of the discussions in the Talmud in his *Halachot Pesukot* or *Halachot Ketuot.* R. Simeon Kayyara went beyond that effort in summarizing the whole *halachah* under the 613 commandments, thus overcoming the attack of the Karaites on the nonscriptural nature of rabbinic tradition.[25]

Of more scientific character is the *Sefer Ḥefetz* by Rab Ḥefetz b. Yatzliaḥ, a Resh Kallah of Babylonia.[26] Instead of arranging the precepts into one group of negative and another of positive commands, as was done by R. Simeon of Kayyara and most other codifiers, he arranged all precepts belonging to one category into one book, and then divided it into two or more sections according to subject matter. These in turn he subdivided into positive and negative commands. He also indicated which commands are obligatory for all times and all countries, and which were binding only during the existence of the Temple or only in Palestine. As a theologian he also assigned reasons to the commandments; and, in the treatment of the two precepts dealing with the existence and unity of God, he set forth *philosophical*

---

[24] *Sefer Hamitzvot.*
[25] Louis Ginzberg, art. "Kayyara," *Jew. Encyc.* VII, 640b–41.
[26] Ginzberg thinks him to have been a North African scholar.

reasons, which B. Halper, the editor of the Genizah fragments of this work, observes, contained "the kernel of medieval Jewish philosophy."[27]

Maimonides undertook to remove the difficulties in the way of numbering the Pentateuchal precepts by formulating a set of rules. As he reduced the principles of belief to thirteen, so he condensed the principles of the *halachah* to fourteen. These are treated in his *Sefer Hamitzvot,* which serves as an introduction to his *Mishneh Torah,* the towering monument of rabbinic literature, which, in fourteen books, restates the whole body of Jewish law. His work in the field of *halachah* as well as in that of philosophy called forth heated attacks and defenses, as well as numerous imitations.[28]

Like the thirteen articles of faith, so the 613 commandments furnished a theme for the poets of the synagogue. These productions are known as *Azharot,* a name derived from the first composition of this character, the opening word of which carries the numerical value of 613. It begins with the words *Azharat reshit leamecha natata* ("Of old Thou didst give exhortations unto Thy people"), and is known as "Exhortations of the Rabbis," also as "Exhortations of the Holy Academy of the Rabbis of Pumbedita." Poems of this nature appear to be of great antiquity, perhaps older than the *Halachot Gedolot.* Prior to the composition of this code, the *Azharot* dealt with the *Taryag* in general, but subsequently they contained the actual enumeration of the precepts. The poem *Atta hinhalta Torah leamecha* faithfully reproduces the code. A host of imitators followed. Their poems were recited in the ritual for Shabuot.

Of special interest are the versifications of the commandments by Saadia Gaon. In an introductory note, he criticizes the *Atta hinhalta* for its inexactness, repetitiousness, and verbosity, and adds: "I see fit to present a substitute for it, not because it is absolutely essential [to recite them], but because I find that the people are attracted to them." His poem begins with the words *Et adonai elohecha tira,* and is arranged in six parts of twenty-two double lines, following the Hebrew alphabet. One section gives the alphabetic acrostic in direct order and the next in its reverse order. Even more ambitious is his

[27] JQR, IV, 558–5.
[28] For literature on *Taryag,* see Yellinek, *Kuntres Taryag* and *Jew. Encyc.* IV, 181 ff.

earlier attempt to versify the *Taryag* in 128 four-membered stanzas. The introductory and concluding parts are worked into the seven benedictions of the *Musaf Amidah*, and the main body of the poem, in the form of straight and inverted alphabetic acrostics, presents the 613 commands in ten parts, following the order of the law in the Decalogue. The whole is cast in a framework of verses from Psalms 68: 8–20 and 19:8–10 and key words of the Song of Songs.[29]

One of the most successful compositions of this type is Solomon ibn Gabirol's *Elohecha esh ochla*. Jehudah Halevi and numerous other poets tried their hands at composing *Azharot*.

The reduction of the precepts of the Torah to 613, and their versification, did not fail to meet with opposition on the grounds of arbitrariness and of lack of value. We noted Saadia's criticism of previous attempts at versifying the *Taryag*. Abraham ibn Ezra compares the efforts of these versifiers to the counting of the number of herbs named in a book of medicine, without the counter's recognition of the use of any of them. Naḥmanides voices his doubt of the Talmud's intention to have the number 613 taken seriously.[30]

However arbitrary these efforts were, they demonstrate the determination of the masters of Judaism to link the entire body of the *halachah* with the revelation of the Torah at Sinai. This intention marks the classification of even some laws of uncertain origin as *halachot* given unto Moses at Sinai.[31] The same purpose of establishing the unity of Judaism was served by the efforts of the philosophers to interlink the rational and ethical precepts with the ceremonial. Whereas Saadia, Baḥia, and Abraham ibn Daud regard the rational commands as forming the essence of Judaism, and the revealed laws (*mitzvot shem'iyot*) as subsidiary to them, Halevi took the opposite view, placing the revealed above the rational, for the first are explicable only through the will of God, and the second are derived from the human intellect. Maimonides rejected the division of the ceremonial law into rational and

---

[29] *Siddur R. Saadia*, ed. by Davidson, Assaf, and Joel, pp. 156–216; Malter, *Saadia Gaon*, pp. 150, 330 ff.

[30] *Halper*, op. cit., pp. 525–26; art. "Azharot," *Jew. Encyc.* II, 370–71.

[31] See. W. Bacher, *Tradition und Tradenten*, pp.. 33–46; I.H. Weiss, *Dor Dor V'dorshav* II, 175 ff.

revealed as foreign to Jewish thought, borrowed from the Mutazilites. He was confident that the seemingly nonrational commands rest on rational grounds.[32]

Whatever the valuation of the ceremonies of Judaism, there is unanimity regarding their importance. While some view them as media for the expression of the spiritual content of religion, others consider them as ends in themselves, that is, as religion in action. Through them the soul is brought into union with God.

---

[32] *Shemoneh Perakim* VI, ed. Gorfinkle, pp. 36, 77. Ibn Ezra, *Yesod Moreh.*

Authority in Judaism

Religious authority represents the right which a religion exercises upon its followers as individuals and as a community. Conformity to its standards renders them religious in their own eyes and in the eyes of others. Authority inheres in the very nature of religion. Whether religion springs from the upward direction of the soul in solitariness or from the experience of groups in their struggle for self-preservation, it ever functions as both a personal and a social force. As the consciousness of the sacred, as a faith, and as a discipline, it affects and governs the feelings, thoughts, and actions of men and communities. It pervades their habits and customs, which are rooted in their common needs, reinforces the claims of the group upon the individual, supplies incentives and sanctions, and makes for social cohesion. The social imperative often underlies the religious command.

It is of the very essence of religion as a social phenomenon to gravitate toward the lives of men. A philosophy, no matter how profound, conceivably may exist as a purely speculative abstraction, detached from actuality. A body of science, too, may be concentrated in mathematical formulae. A religion lives and gives life only when wedded to human life. It is vital to the extent to which it incarnates itself in personal experience and in the social fabric and institutions. When true to itself, religion seeks to create a Kingdom of God on earth and to render man a willing citizen of the Kingdom. And citizenship, whether in a temporal or a spritual state, ever imposes obligations. Hence religion urges man "to receive the yoke of the Kingdom of God" and "the yoke of the commandments." The very freedom which religion holds out to

Editor's note: This essay is the author's revision of a monograph published in the *Hebrew Union College Annual*, 1936.

man as his greatest boon is through obedience to its authority. Only he is free upon whose heart the laws of God are inscribed.[1]

Thus conceived, religious authority assumes a twofold aspect. Seeking to set up a social order in accordance with its highest visions of righteousness, religion provides man with an objective and external standard of right. He is expected to conform to the laws of the ideal community. At the same time religion strives to find its way into the heart of man, to become part of his inward life, and to function from within as a spiritual light, as his moral inspiration and conscience. In this light, the sharp contrast which Sabatier draws between what he calls "religions of authority" and "religions of the spirit" loses its force. No religion is divested of the element of authority, nor is there a religion wholly without spirit. Authority may be both external and internal at one and the same time. Incorporated into social custom and into written law, religious authority appears heteronomous. Inscribed upon the tables of the heart, it is autonomous. While the inner law and the external command become disjointed in the lives of vast numbers of people, they blend into a perfect harmony in the lives of truly religious spirits.

Whether controlling human lives as an external discipline or as an inner compulsion, religion ever exhibits its trait of obligatoriness. It speaks with the stern voice of duty and lays burdens upon man. Science and philosophy appeal to man's mind and to his sense of utility. Art justifies itself by the sense of beauty and by personal taste. Religion, on the other hand, while not disregarding man's self-interest and social well-being, and not underestimating human reason, appeals primarily to man's will and conscience, to his higher self, and to his consciousness of the holy. Merging with morality, religion, in its advanced forms, commands man's conduct, sets up standards of right and wrong, holds out goals of personal and social striving, and prescribes ritual deeds and ceremonies. The obligatoriness of religion represents, on the one hand, the pressure of society upon the will of the individual, and, on the other, a power not ourselves that makes for righteousness, a power superior to the whim or pleasure of the individual and the group. Religion appeals to the deepest in man, in the name of the All-highest. "Thus saith the Eternal!" constitutes its characteristic claim upon men.

[1] Cf. *Abot* VI, 42.

It is this obligatoriness that invests religion with its greatest value. Most people live not so much by their own reason and personal taste as by the standards set up for them by others in the name of some clause or ideal. They do not arrive at their preferences, convictions, and beliefs through careful deliberation and reflection but rather by way of imitation, social contagion, convention — in a word, authority. Morality itself is binding for them because it is the popularly approved way of behavior. While usage does not always establish the objective validity of an idea or the rightness of an act, it tends to become the norm of conduct. Helping to unite individuals into a community, it recommends itself to reason as socially valuable. Even when the higher interests of the group or of humanity urgently require the breaking of certain mores and taboos, social and religious reformers immediately replace them with more ideal standards of conduct. Progress lies not in the abolition of all authority, which spells the disruption of society, but in replacing the lower forms of authority with higher ones. From this standpoint the history of each religion is the history of the changing forms which its authority has assumed.

The diverse forms of authority in Judaism are clearly reflected in the development of the conception of Torah in its twofold aspect of Scripture and Oral Law, or of revelation and tradition. It is the indelible stamp of authority that distinguishes Torah from other propducts of the mind, from *hochmah,* "wisdom," and *mada,* "knowledge" or "science." The historical analysis of the authoritative phases of revelation and tradition will show the role which authority plays in Orthodoxy, and prepare us for the consideration of the problem of authority in Reform Judaism.

Revelation

The whole structure of biblical religion rests upon a threefold view of revelation: (1) the manifestation of the Divine Presence, which the rabbis described as *gilluy shechinah,* whether in nature or in history; (2) the disclosure of the divine will and purpose to Israel by means of chosen instruments, i.e., *mattan torah* or *nebuah*; (3) the embodiment of the objective content of revelation in the Written Torah (*torah shebichtab*) and — according to the rabbis — in the

Oral Law, or tradition (*torah shebeal peh*). Whether as law or as prophecy, revelation figures as the creative force of religion. Unlike a Plato or an Aristotle, the Jewish lawgiver and prophet did not establish their truths by reasoning. Here and there, Jeremiah Deutero-Isaiah, Job, some of the psalmists, and the priestly author of the opening chapter of Genesis, turn to the wonders of creation and to the harmony of nature's operations for the vision of the glory of God. In the main, however, the spring of their knowledge is neither empirical observation nor speculative reflection but the spontaneous illumination of their spirits with a light from on high.

The idea of revelation is by no means confined to Judaism. We meet it in the religions of primitive as well as of the most advanced races. Wherever deities dawn in the human consciousness, revelation serves as the medium of communication between them and their worshipers. By signs and wonders, by omens and dreams, as well as by theophanies and oracles, they express their desires and commands. In the great ethical religions, one supreme revelation of the divine will to a prophetic ambassador holds the commanding position. The will of the deity manifested itself once and for all to a Zoroaster or a Mohammed, and, reduced to writing, became the foundation of the entire religion. The canonized scripture came to enjoy the authority which originally belonged to the personal revelation. Its very form acquired sanctity in the eyes of the believers. By the side of the revealed book, there developed a venerable and sacred tradition, which both preserves and advances the light of the original revelation, and may on this account be regarded as the continuation of revelation.

To understand the meaning which revelation has had for Israel, it may be helpful to note the terms denoting the process. The Hebrew verb *galah*, from which the technical terms for revelation, *hitgalut* and *gilluy shechinah*, are derived, means "to bare" or to remove the veil which obscures the vision of naked reality, "to uncover" the true nature of an object or event to human perception.[2] The form of the revelation is represented by derivations from the verbs *raah* and *hazah*, "to see." *Mareh*, *hazon*, and *hizayon* possibly convey the idea of internal sight imparted to the *hozeh*. Both terms for "seer," *hozeh*

---

[2] For example, 1 Sam. 9:15, Ps. 98:2.

and *roeh*, were replaced by *nabi*, "prophet," who expresses in words the message of God flashed upon his conscious or unconscious mind.

Revelation implies an interaction between God and man. Man seeks the presence of God, straining to fathom His designs and to secure His approbation. God, in turn, aids man's search by coming to meet him halfway. By the side of the general revelation of God in the physical order and in the history of humanity, the Bible speaks of special revelations to the people of Israel on significant occasions and to chosen individuals who merited His grace. Whether the revelation is general or special, its two factors are God and man, and its object is spiritual and ethical guidance, both communal and personal.

The Divine Factor

The cause of religion is not served by the mere manifestation of God's power and intelligence. To become a sanctifying force in the lives of men, God must be felt as the Holy One, as the awe-inspiring and indwelling Presence. The feeling that above the seething chaos both within and without us, the order-producing principle, God, is sovereign, heartens us and brings us peace. We are assured that the world, with its warring forces of light and darkness, of good and evil, and of life and death, is not a scene of the mere interplay of blind and aimless forces. Behind the pageantry of phenomena, "the Lord on high is mighty." The voice of faith sings: "Thy throne is established of old, Thou art from everlasting."[3] His creative energy, which has fashioned the world, is at work also in the lives of men. Here it manifests itself particularly in the moral order, in the values of righteousness and truth, of love and goodness.

The revelation of deities to their worshipers is almost as universal as religion. What is unique about the religion of Israel is the character of God as revealed to man. Unlike the deities of the neighboring nations, which but reflected the moral character of their worshipers, the God of Israel possessed a mind and a will of His own, embodying the highest ethical attributes.[4] Instead

[3] Ps. 93:2.
[4] Exod. 34:6–7.

of being pleased, as were the gods of Egypt, Babylonia, and Canaan, with a service of attractive ceremonial appealing to the people, He demanded worship expressed in righteousness, hard and exacting. He was conceived as a God who not only rewards His people with felicity but also punishes them for their evildoing. His judgments fall in no arbitrary or fickle fashion. He applies the plumb line of justice to His own as well as to strange nations. In the words of W. R. Smith, His is

> a fixed and consistent holy purpose, which has Israel for its object and seeks the true felicity of the nation, but at the same time is absolutely sovereign over Israel, and will not give way to Israel's desires or adapt itself to Israel's convenience. No other religion can show anything parallel to this. The gods of the nations are always conceived as arbitrary and changeful, or as themselves subordinate to blind fate, or as essentially capable of being bent into sympathy with whatever is for the time being the chief desire of their worshipers, or, in some more speculative forms of faith, introduced when these simpler conceptions broke down, as escaping the limitations only by being raised to entire unconcern in the petty affairs of men. In Israel alone does Jehovah appear as God to man, and yet maintaining an absolute sovereignty of will, a consistent independence of character.[5]

His very love and grace, which are boundless, strictly accord with His moral nature and purpose.

God is the giver of law. Justice and righteousness are the foundations of His throne. While among other peoples, too, deities are conceived as guardians of the mores and laws, nowhere else does this conception obtain the precision which it did in Israel, because nowhere else do deities display so sharply defined an ethical character as does the Holy One of Israel.

> The heathen gods are guardians of law, but they are something else at the same time; they are not wholly intent on righteousness, and righteousness is not the only path to their favor, which sometimes depends on accidental partialities, or may be conciliated by acts of worship that have nothing to do with morality. And here be it observed that the fundamental superiority of the Hebrew reli-

[5] W. R. Smith, *The Prophets of Israel*, pp. 70-71.

gion does not lie in the particular system of social morality that it enforces, but in the more absolute and self-consistent righteousness of the Divine Judge.[6]

The Human Factor

The human factor in the biblical conception of revelation is no less instructive. The Bible assumes the universality of the process. God speaks to all who would hear. Not alone to the fathers of the human race, to the patriarchs of Israel and to Israel's prophets, but also to non-Israelites like Abimelek, Laban, Balaam, Job, and Eliphaz, God communicated His purpose. However, the central aim of the revelation is to Israel. The underlying idea of the Bible is that God has chosen Israel from among all the nations and revealed Himself and His commandments to it as part of His plan of universal salvation. Though He spoke to individual prophets, it is to them as representatives of Israel that He spoke.[7] He disclosed His counsels to His servants the prophets that they might warn and guide Israel in the path of rectitude. His concern is first of all with the house of Israel. He would have Israel serve as a kingdom of priests and a holy nation, consecrated to His service for the welfare of all humanity. It is the conviction of Amos that of all the families of the earth, Israel was cared for in a special degree.[8] Hosea speaks of Israel now as the spouse of God and now as His son.[9] While pinning his hope in the faithful remnant, Isaiah refers to the people of Israel as the sons of God, to Zion as the mountain-house of God, and to Jerusalem as the hearth of God.[10] For Jeremiah, too, Israel is the community of God's revelation.[11] Deutero-Isaiah carries the ideas of his prophetic predecessors to an exalted height in his presentation of Israel as the servant of the Lord, charged with the task of bringing light and salvation to all the nations of the earth.[12] Religion, for the

---

[6] Ibid., pp. 72–73.

[7] Amos 2:10 f.

[8] Amos 3:2.

[9] Hos. 1–3, 11:1.

[10] Isa. 1:2, 2:2f., 29:1.

[11] Jer. 2:2 ff., 5:20 ff., etc.

[12] Isa. 42:1–7; 49:1 ff., 53, etc.

masters of the Bible, is the affair of the people of Israel rather than of the individual Israelite. "This is your wisdom and your understanding," the Deuteronomist announces," "in the sight of the peoples, that, when they hear all these statutes, shall say: 'Surely this is a wise and understanding people.' For what great nation is there, that hath God so nigh unto them, as the Lord our God is whensoever we call upon Him? And what great nation is there, that hath statutes and ordinances as all this law which I set before you this day?"[13] Though God is near to all who call upon Him in truth, He is specially close to Israel, the people of His covenant, in whose heart is His law.

> He declareth His word unto Jacob,
> His statutes and ordinances unto Israel.
> He hath not dealt so with any nation;
> And as for His ordinances, they have not known them.[14]

Even with the emergence of the individual as directly responsible to God, and the rise of universalism and of absolute ethical monotheism, Israel continued to figure as the religious unit, as the *Adat Adonai*, the congregation of the Lord. Though the Deuteronomist declares: "sons are ye of the Lord your God,"[15] he deals not only "with the faith and obedience of individual persons but with the faith and obedience of a nation as expressed in the functions of a national life."[16] No matter how universalistic a religion may be in its outlook, it cannot exist without a community or church. In Israel the religious circle was not limited to a special body of believers or to an organized association; it coincided with the entire people. The conception of the *Keneset Yisrael*, which emerged after the fall of the state, represented a continuation of the classical tradition.

The authoritativeness of biblical religion is thus derived from its constituting the revelation of the will of God, on the one side, and, on the other, from its social character as the governing principle of the nation. To foster

---

[13] Deut. 4:6–8.
[14] Ps. 147:19–20.
[15] Deut. 14:1.
[16] W. R. Smith, op. cit., p. 20.

and to advance this double phase of religious authority represented the burden of both prophet and priest.

Prophet

The prophet holds the place of preeminence in the religious history of Israel. In every crisis, his leadership pointed the path of duty and of honor. His place was in the vanguard of Israel's progress. In his personality, the religious ideas of Israel germinated and grew. The prophet figured as the herald and mouthpiece of God. Amos affirms:

> For the Lord God will do nothing,
> But He revealeth His counsel unto His servants the prophets.
> The lion hath roared.
> Who will not fear?
> The Lord God hath spoken.
> Who can but prophesy?[17]

The prophet proclaims God's message under an irresistible compulsion. A power not himself, making for righteousness, seizes him and employs him as its instrument. He is possessed by the divine spirit, or overpowered by "the hand of the Lord" or "the power of the hand." The divine message is a burning fire in his heart; it sears his flesh and consumes his stength. Having caught the overtones of the divine voice and beheld the vision of His triumphant righteousness, he cannot but speak out that all may hear.[18] He but reechoes the voice of God. Hence he introduces his words with the formula "Thus saith the Lord," "The word of the Lord," "The oracle of the Lord," etc. The true prophet, unlike the false one, does not speak out of his own heart or in accordance with the wishes of the hearers, but in agreement with what he considers to be the will of God. His very intelligence, though often active during the reception, is the mere interpreter of the revelation. It but places a rational

[17] Amos 3:7 f.
[18] Jer. 20:9, 23:22.

construction upon that which was apprehended intuitively. As the trumpet of God, the prophet wished to be judged not for his personal gifts and mental powers but for his faithfulness to the heaven-inspired message.

Popular judgment considered prophecy true when its predictions were fulfilled. In the opinion of the great prophets themselves, their credentials consisted in the correspondence of their claims with the purest and noblest conception of the character and purpose of God. Their words, issuing from the depths of sincerity, carried the stamp of authenticity for those whose hearts were alive to divine truth. They were marked by simplicity and obviousness. "Thy judgment," says one of their foremost representatives, "goeth forth as the light."[19]

In Israel, as among other nations, revelation assumed the form of (a) theophanies, (b) prophecy, and (c) inspiration. God is conceived as making Himself known through extraordinary physical phenomena, like the burning bush, the thunder and lightning at Sinai, and the cloud-pillar. Outward presentations of God's revelation figure also in the prophecies of Isaiah, Ezekiel, and Zechariah.[20] And we encounter frenzied utterances of mantic prophets, possessed of the divine spirit. However, in the higher ranges of prophecy, the notion of revelation grew ever more inward and ethical. Micah announces that he is

> full of power by the spirit of the Lord,
> And of justice and of might,
> To declare unto Jacob, his transgression,
> And to Israel, his sin.[21]

Trito-Isaiah, voicing the loftiest ideal of prophecy, states:

> The spirit of the Lord God is upon me,
> Because the Lord hath anointed me
> To bring good tidings unto the humble;

[19] Hos. 6:5.
[20] Isa. 6, Ezek. 1–2, Zech. 1–6.
[21] Mic. 3:8.

He hath sent me to bind up the broken-hearted,
To proclaim liberty to the captives,
And the opening of the eyes to them that are bound.[22]

With the growing inwardness of the religion of Israel, the channel of revelation was shifted from external phenomena to the human spirit, and God came to be conceived as revealing Himself principally through the conscience and mind of the prophet, i.e., by means of inward inspiration. The spirit of God impressed itself upon the sensitive consciousness of men of religious genius and laid bare to their souls the reality and imperativeness of the divine commands. The divine element penetrated and transformed the human. In turn, the human factor in revelation came to ever greater prominence. The consciousness of the divine disclosed new levels of value to man. The holy spirit dwelling in man, manifests to him the reality of the ideal, and inspires him to follow its light.

Inspiration figures in other spheres of human experience besides religion. It is the source of the poet's insight, of the artist's vision, and of the sage's understanding. It is a sort of awakening of dormant energies and powers within a person, enabling him to sense and to see truth, beauty, and goodness. The eyes of the soul are suddenly opened to the inner core of things. A flash of light, coming as from another world, illuminates the heart of things and bares the mind and the purpose of God.

The prophecies of the Bible, deriving their glow from the consciousness of the divine, are molded by the individual character and genius, diverse tastes, and idiosyncrasies of the prophecies, and are determined by the conditions of the age in which they lived and by the position of the people to whom they addressed themselves. They deal with specific circumstances in the national experience, with the concrete policies pursued by the state, and with definite moral infractions. They were bound up with their times and generations. Driver appropriately spoke of the "relativity of inspiration" and stressed the progressive nature of biblical revelation. Though their words have resounded through the ages and speak with authority to the hearts and consciences of

[22] Isa. 61:1.

men today, the prophets addressed themselves in the first place to the special circumstances of their own day.

As the prophet's search after God was not along the path of speculation, so too was his discovery neither philosophical nor scientific. Instead of looking for an abstract notion of the divine essence, the prophet sought God and His strength, His presence and His will, in holiness, righteousness, justice, truth, mercy, compassion, etc. His truths were not metaphysical but spiritual and moral, constituting the values by which men live. "Seek ye Me and live" is the prophet's version of the divine behest. "Seek ye the Lord while He may be found, call upon Him while He is near. Let the wicked forsake his way and the man of iniquity his thoughts, and let him return unto the Lord, and He will have compassion upon him, and to our God, for He will abundantly pardon."[23] "Let the heart of them rejoice that seek the Lord."[24] The manifestation of the divine purpose to the human mind and conscience brings to light a knowledge which is bound up with the deepest issues of life, affecting the well-being of the individual, the community, and humanity. Amid the moral chaos of their day and amid the selfishness and greed of society and its leaders, the prophets envisaged the clear white light of the spiritual and ethical ideal, transcending popular mores and expediency. This ideal recommended itself as grounded in the mind and will of God, the foundation of all life and of all order, and, therefore, constituted an absolute standard by which to judge the customs and conduct of the people. It consequently imposed duties, to ignore which constituted disloyalty to the Holy One; and to follow which, reverently and humbly, secured divine approval and inner contentment. The motive of authority, in the prophets' view, is not merely fear of the consequences of disobedience of the commands of God and the expectation of reward for obedience. A higher motive asserted itself in their teaching. It is the motive of the love of God, of unconditioned loyalty and devotion to Him as the All-Holy and All-Perfect. Man's action should spring from joyous self-surrender and filial relationship to God. Because the words of the prophets touched the deepest springs of human life they have gone forth "to meet the centuries." Though spoken in particular crises, they have lighted up the paths of the generations that followed.

[23] Isa. 55:6 f.
[24] Ps. 105:3.

Priest

The prophet was not the only vehicle of revelation. The people went "to inquire of the Lord,"[25] i.e., to consult the oracle at the sanctuary through the attendant priest. The Arabic *kahin*, which corresponds to the Hebrew *kohen*, signifies a "soothsayer," or one who has a familiar spirit to reveal secret things to him. The Hebrew *kohen* may have arisen from the seer's function. Thus Judaism possibly inherited from ancient Semitic religion the common bond between seer or prophet and priest. This bond is evident in the characters of Moses, who figures as priest as well as prophet, of Aaron, the father of priesthood, who is referred to also as prophet, and of Samuel, who combines the offices of priest and prophet.[26]

Before becoming the exclusive officiant at the altar, the *kohen* served as the interpreter of the will of God. By means of the *ephod* and the *urim vetummim*, he sought to obtain divine guidance for the people in war and in peace. The sanctuary where the oracle was consulted served as a seat of judgment. The *kohen*'s instruction, direction, or decision was technically known as *torah* (from the root *yarah*, "to cast" the lot, "to direct," "to teach"). With the growing complexity of the religious life and the increase of ritual observances, the *kohen* became indispensable as sacrificer as well. He best knew "the manner of the God of the land,"[27] and was, therefore, best qualified to represent his people before God. However, his function as revealer of the will of God was not obscured by his newer task of minister at the altar. The levitical priests, according to the Blessing of Moses, were to

> . . . teach Jacob Thine ordinances,
> And Israel Thy law;
> They shall put incense before Thee,
> And whole burnt-offerings upon Thine altar.[28]

The priest stands as the embodiment of the social side of religion, as

---

[25] Gen. 25:22 ff.
[26] Exod. 33:7, Num. 12:2, I Sam. 9, Ps. 99:6 f.
[27] 2 Kings 17:27.
[28] Deut. 33:10.

guardian of tribal traditions, customs, taboos, and religious rites. While the prophet represented — to use Bergson's terminology — "dynamic religion," the priest represented "static religion." In giving response to questions addressed to him, the priest assumed the office of judge. The Deuteronomic Code refers all litigations too difficult for settlements by local courts, whether criminal or civil, to the arbitrament of "the priests the Levites [of the central sanctuary] and unto the judge that shall be in those days," i.e., to the secular head of the state. Refusal to abide by their decisions was punishable with death.[29] In Ezekiel's plan of the restored sanctuary, the tasks of the priests were to teach the people "the difference between the holy and the common, and cause them to discern between the unclean and the clean. And in the controversy they shall stand to judge; according to Mine ordinances shall they judge it."[30] Jeremiah characterizes the priests as "they that handle the law" (*tofse hatorah*).[31] The prophets themselves looked up to the priests as the custodians of the Law, and castigated them for their violation of their trust.[32] Malachi declares:

> The priest's lips shall keep knowledge,
> And they [the people] should seek the law at his mouth;
> For he is the messenger of the Lord of Hosts.[33]

The Torah

The priests derived their authority from being the organs of the law or Torah. The beginnings of the law generally go back to tribal custom. By reason of the close relationship between ancient tribes and their deities, tribal custom displays a religious complexion. Its observance expressed loyalty to the deity.

---

[29] Deut. 17:8–13; see also 2 Chron. 19:8–10.
[30] Ezek. 44:23 f.
[31] Jer. 2:8.
[32] Hos. 4:1–12, 6:9; Mic. 3:11; Zeph. 3:4; Isa. 28:7; Jer. 2:8; 6:13; 8:10; Ezek. 22:26.
[33] Mal. 2:7.

Accordingly, the laws of ancient Israel, even when closely parallel to those of other Semitic peoples, are presented as of divine origin.[34] Many of these laws antedate the consecration of Israel to the worship of Yahveh, and have their roots in the Semitic heritage. By them the tribes, newly emancipated from Egyptian slavery, were governed. When difficulties arose for which the older tribal law made no provision, God was consulted directly. The complicated cases arising from the conditions of Israel's intertribal union, from the exigencies of the wearying journey, and from the perils of the desert, were brought to Moses, who was believed to stand in close communion with God.[35] At Sinai, he formulated the Decalogue (i.e., the brief commands, minus the explanatory glosses which reflect later conditions) as the terms of the covenant between Israel and God, which became the Magna Charta of Judaism. Special authority was claimed for this document as having been proclaimed by God Himself to the people of Israel, and inscribed by the finger of God upon the tables of stone.[36] At Kadesh, Moses continued to administer the affairs of the people, teaching them "the statutes and the laws." The decisions which he made served as precedents for later legislation. He thus laid the foundation for the whole development of the law in Israel. However, the new statutes and ordinances which he established did not set aside the customary laws which Israel shared as part of its Semitic heritage. The ordinary judges were still the elders, who ruled the people in most cases.[37]

The administration of the sacred oracle constituted the prerogative of the kinsmen and the successors of Moses, who were the priests not only of the portable sanctuary but also of the local shrines of Canaan, at Shiloh, Dan, Nob, Gibeah, etc. In these seats of justice, the law was dispensed by the priests in the name of God, in the form of "decisions," "directions," or "instructions" (*torot*) in ritual, civil, and moral matters. These rulings, which grew

[34] Similarly the Code of Hammurabi is presented as coming "by the command of Shamash, the judge supreme of heaven and earth, that justice might shine in the land." Though the whole code is ascribed to Hammurabi, it rests upon older foundations.

[35] Exod. 33:7-11.

[36] Exod. 19-20, 31:18, 32:16; Deut. 9:10; cf. Exod. 34:27 ff. and 24:4.

[37] Exod. 18:25 f.

out of consuetudinary law, in turn furthered the growth of "the community of custom and of feeling in matters of law."[38]

In the course of transition from a nomadic to an agricultural economy, the force which tribal custom exercised through the family was weakened; and this weakness contributed to the lawlessness of the age of the Judges.[39] Custom required the reinforcement of externl authority, which was supplied by the establishment of the monarchy. The king as "God's anointed" combined in himself all authority, civil and religious. David's priests seem to have acted as his substitutes and appointees.[40] The "anointed" was the fountain of law and order in the land. As in Tyre and elsewhere, the king in Israel presided as supreme judge.[41] The ideal ruler was expected to be animated with the spirit of God, so that he might rule the people with unerring justice.[42] The king, even as the tribal elders, who continued to act as judges by the side of the priests, seems to have been guided by customary law, and issued new laws only when unprecedented situations presented themselves.

The oldest collection of precepts, contained in the Book of the Covenant,[43] bears the impression of being a compendium of current procedure, based on tribal custom and established precedents, some of which may have grown out of priestly decisions. Its reduction to writing was probably due to the practical need of providing the priests and the elders with detailed guidance in their tasks as judges. The Deuteronomic Code, which is an expansion of the older legislation, displays a distinctly religious motive. The norm of right conduct is no longer determined by the antiquity of the law or custom, but by the unique relation of Israel to God. "Ye are children of the Lord your God" forms the ground for the prohibition of practices current among the worshipers of other gods. "For thou art a holy people unto the Lord thy God, and the Lord hath chosen thee to be His own treasure out of all peoples that are upon the face of

[38] Examples may be found in Gen. 34:15–16, Josh. 7:15–24, Judg. 19:23 ff., 20:10; 1 Sam. 30:25; 2 Sam. 12:1–12, 13:12; 1 Kings 21.

[39] Judg. 17:6 ff., 18.

[40] 2 Sam. 8:17–18, 20:25–26.

[41] 2 Sam. 15:2–6; 1 Kings 3:16–28.

[42] Isa. 11; Pss. 45, 73.

[43] Exod. 21–23.

the earth."[44] The demand for holiness in matters ceremonial and ethical is carried further in the Priestly Code and in the Code of Holiness.[45]

The promulgation of the Deuteronomic Code marked a thorough reform in Jewish life. Much of the old customary law is here modified by the spirit of humanitarianism. Proper measures are provided to guard the religion of Israel from sinking to the level of Semitic paganism. Furthermore, the respective limits on the authority of the prophets, the priests, the civil magistrates, and the king are carefully defined.[46] Despite these innovations, the Deuteronomic Code purports to go back to Moses. It carried the additional authority of having been adopted by the people in solemn covenant,[47] rendered binding upon both the covenanters and their descendants by a sacred oath, the violation of which was to call forth the wrath of God and carry the direst consequences.[48] The Priestly Code, or possibly the entire Pentateuchal Torah, was promulgated under similar circumstances. The representatives of the people, princes, Levites, and priests, set their seal to a written covenant and "entered into a curse, and into an oath, to walk in God's law, which was given by Moses the servant of God, and to observe and do all the commandments of the Lord our Lord, and His ordinances and His statutes."[49]

The term *Torah*, once expressing a moral or spiritual precept of a prophet,[50] or designating an oral decision or teaching of a priest, was transformed to signify the written body of law contained in the Pentateuch. The entire collection of narrative, poetry, admonition, and legislation embodied in this five-volume work was now presented as the revelation of God's will to Israel through Moses. Different sections of the law are introduced with the statements: "And the Lord said unto Moses: Thus shalt thou say unto the children of Israel"; "And the Lord spoke unto Moses, saying"; "And thou shalt command the children of Israel"; "And the Lord called unto Moses, and

---

[44] Deut. 14:1 f.
[45] Lev. 17–26.
[46] Deut. 13:1–6, 16:18–chap. 18.
[47] 2 Kings 23:1–3.
[48] Deut. 29:9–chap. 30.
[49] Neh. 10:29–30.
[50] Amos 2:4; Hos. 4:6, 6:6, 8:1, 12; Isa. 1:10, etc.; Jer. 6:19.

spoke unto him out of the tent of meeting, saying: Speak unto the children of Israel and say unto them:" The introductory part of Deuteronomy makes the still larger claim: "And this is the law which Moses set before the children of Israel; these are the testimonies which Moses spoke unto the children of Israel, when they came forth out of Egypt."[51]

The Torah, like prophecy, is progressive in character. It grew out of the conditions of the people of different ages, in response to varying circumstances. The extent to which its laws reflect the developing religious and moral ideas of the Jewish people may be judged by a comparison of the *lex talionis* in Exodus 21:24 with the law of *humanity* in Leviticus 19:17–18. The teachings of the prophets found their way into the codes of law and were translated into detailed rules of conduct. In the Decalogue and in sections of the Code of the Covenant, of Deuteronomy, and of the Priestly and Holiness Codes, the dynamic religion of the prophets was crystallized into definite patterns of behavior, into practical legislation adapted to varying situations. From flaming ideals of righteousness, there developed righteous laws, designed to protect the poor and the needy, the servant and the stranger, the weak and the helpless, to curb avidity and malpractice, and to safeguard life and property. The occasional conflicts between prophet and priest, i.e., between the representatives of dynamic and static religion, disappear from the Torah. Here the priest legislates with the voice of the prophet. Thus the accumulation of customary laws, social mores, and taboos, and priestly rites and directions, modified and irradiated by prophetic idealism, and embodied in the Pentateuch, came to be the supreme source of authority for the Jewish people.

From the time of the Reformation of Ezra, the Torah constituted the pivot around all Jewish life revolved. Its absoluteness was questioned neither by the Samaritans (except regarding certain variations in the text) nor by the Sadducees. Pharisaic teaching on this subject is free from all ambiguity. *Torah min hashamayim*, i.e., the divine origin of the Law, was fixed as a ruling dogma. From the first verse of Genesis to the last verse of Deuteronomy, the Pentateuch is equally perfect and binding, inasmuch as it comes

---

[51] Exod. 20:19, 25:1–2, 27:20; Lev. 1:1–2; Deut. 4:44 f.

from God. Jewish life was no longer directed, as of old, chiefly by ancient custom, nor by special decisions of the priests, nor even by the occasional revelations of the divine will to prophets, but rather by the fixed word of the Torah. Actions were recognized as right when they conformed to that which is "written in the Law of Moses, the man of God." The use of the word *kakatub*, "as it is written," came to be the customary manner of supporting the rightness of an act or an idea.[52]

The words of the prophets, though coming as divine revelations, and the teachings of the sages, while recognized as inspired, were subordinated to the Torah. The prophetic canon closes with the admonition: "Remember ye the Law of Moses My servant, which I commanded unto him in Horeb for all Israel, even statutes and ordinances."[53] And the pious psalmist finds his supreme happiness in the study and observance of the torah.[54] The second and third parts of the Bible canon, the *Nebiim* and *Ketubim*,[55] i.e., the Prophets and the Hagiographa, were considered *dibre kabbalah*, tradition, without the power vested in the Law. The belief that the Torah in its entirety was given by God to Moses produced the unhistorical view that the Pentateuch came first and that the prophets came to reinforce its teachings, a view which was reversed only in recent times, in consequence of the critical study of the Bible.

With the establishment of the Torah as the supreme source of authority in Jewish life, certain difficulties presented themselves. As a compilation of several older codes, the Pentateuch exhibited some discrepancies between its parts. In addition, as the product of past legislation, it did not cover all new

---

[52] Ezra 3:2, 6:18; Neh. 8:14–15, 13:1–3; 2 Chron. 23:18, 25:4, 30:5, 31:3, 35:12, etc.

[53] Mal. 3:22. See also 2 Kings 17:37.

[54] Ps. 119.

[55] *Taan.* 9a: אין לך דבר כתוב. *Num. R.* X. 6: מי איכא מידי דכתיבי בכתובי דלא רמיזי באורייתא. *Tanh. Yitro* XI: בנביאים וכתובים שלא רמזו משה בתורה אמר רבי יצחק אף מה שהנביאים עתידין. . . . ולא הנביאים בלבד אלא אף כל החכמים שהיו ושעתידין להיות שנ' להתנבאות כלם קבלו מהר סיני וגו'. Also *Exod. R.* XXVIII. 6 את כל הדברים דבר ה' אל כל קהלכם. קול גדול ולא יסף (Deut. 5:19) (ibid.). ר' יוחנן אמר קול אחד נחלק לז' קולות והם נחלקים לע' לשון. רשב"ל אמר שממנו נתנבאו כל הנביאים *Meg.* 2b: אלה המצות (Lev. 27.34) שאין נביא רשאי לחדש דבר מעתה. *Meg.* 14a: ת"ר ארבעים שעמדו ושמונה נביאים ושבע נביאות נתנבאו להם לישראל ולא פחתו ולא הותירו על מה שכתוב בתורה חוץ ממקרא מגילה.

conditions facing late postexilic Jewry. Accordingly, a twofold activity resulted. On the one hand, room was left by the side of the Written Torah for the play of ancient customary law which had continued in the life of the people; and, on the other hand, efforts had to be made to expound the meaning of the "Written" Torah so as to reconcile its inner difficulties and to apply its precepts to the new situations. To this twofold tendency the "Oral" Law owes its existence.

Tradition

The transformation of Judaism into a religion based on a canonized Scripture contributed to the silencing of prophecy and to curbing the power of the priest as the revealer of the will of God. In consequence it led to the replacement of the authority of revelation with that of tradition. The priest's decision now had to be based upon the text of the Torah. Nonetheless, he continued to function as the guardian of the law. With the disappearance of prophecy, the priest emerged as the only authentic representative of the established religion. Jewish unity was changed from a political to an ecclesiastical character. The Jewish nation turned into a "kingdom of priests," or a "theocracy," as Josephus called it. In place of a king, the high priest headed the state. The people continued to seek guidance and instruction from the priests and regarded them as the messengers of the Lord of Hosts.[56] The priests were, indeed, the logical interpreters of the Torah, inasmuch as they possessed a living tradition of ritual ministration in the Temple and of administration of civil law. Their tradition, as we have seen, went back to most ancient times. Since life did not remain at a standstill, and ever new exigencies continued to arise, for which neither the Torah nor tribal custom presented precedents, special enactments or decrees, *gezerot*, were passed. A complete book of such ordinances is referred to in *Megillat Taanit*.[57] However, the priests drew a fine line between the Written Torah and the oral tradition as well as the special enactments, deeming only the first authoritative, to which, in accordance with

[56] Mal. 2.7.
[57] *Meg. Taan.* IV.

Deuteronomy 4:2, nothing was to be added, and from which nothing was to be subtracted. As has often happened in the history of religions, this hyperconservatism of the priests defeated its own purpose. The Torah was steadily pushed into the background and was in danger of being divorced from life.

The difficulty was corrected from another direction. The Reformation of 444, while inspired by Ezra, a descendant of the leading priestly family of Zadok, aimed at raising all Israel to the rank of priestly holiness. By making the study of the Torah obligatory for all Jews, Ezra's Reformation liberated forces hitherto chained in the fetters of ignorance. Among the scribes that followed Ezra, lay scholars (*hachme yisrael*) appeared by the side of the priests. For the new party of Pharisees, which emerged out of the activity of the scribes, the Torah appeared as the unerring guide of all life. They refused to recognize the gap between Torah and life or to reconcile themselves to the dualism of Torah and tradition. In their belief, the Torah was all-embracing. They therefore devoted themselves to the task of refashioning tradition in such manner as to make it the protective armor of the Torah, and the means of applying the Torah's precepts to the life of the people. Their task may be considered fivefold. They set out (1) to establish their right as trustees of the Torah; (2) to demonstrate that tradition is not extraneous to the Torah; (3) to set up a hedge around the Torah; (4) to define the content of the Oral Torah; and (5) to endow it with means for self-preservation.

The Rabbis

The lay scholars gained their right to interpret the Torah not without a struggle. Earlier precedents favored their claim. Eldad and Medad had not been restrained from prophesying.[58] The prophets and sages were not necessarily of priestly origin. Lay elders had shared in the administration of civil law from the very beginnings of the nation. 2 Chronicles 19:8–10 reflects the state of affairs in the period following the Reformation of Ezra. By the side of the priests, the "lay heads of families" are named as being in charge of all judgments, laws, commandments, statutes, and ordinances. The only condition was that they adminster the law "in the fear of the Lord, faithfully, and

---

[58] Num. 11:24–29.

with a whole heart." Shemaiah and Abtalion voiced the sentiment of the entire Pharisaic party when they told the high priest that what matters is not so much descent from the house of Aaron as following in the ways of Aaron.[59] "In matters of the Torah, defer not to the sons of the elders, the sons of the great, or the sons of the prophets, for all are equal, as Scripture says: 'Moses commanded us a Law; it is the heritage of the congregation of Jacob.' It does not say the heritage of priests, Levites, or lay Israelites, but of the whole congregation of Israel."[60] While emphasizing the democratic nature of Judaism, the Pharisees would not deprive the priests of the special prerogatives given by the Torah. The *Sifre* interprets the statement in Deuteronomy 33:10, "They [the priests] shall teach Jacob Thine ordinances and Israel Thy Law," to mean that all decisions in ritual matters must be pronounced by priests only. The *Sifra* states similarly that while a lay scholar may inspect leprosy, only a priest may declare it "clean" or "unclean." If the priest is ignorant, a lay scholar prompts him.[61] The Pharisees, having gained the upper hand in the Sanhedrin,[62] and considering themselves the true interpreters of the Torah, ventured to dictate to the Sadducean priests in matters of ceremonial.[63] The high priest himself was obliged to receive instruction from "two scholars of the disciples of Moses," i.e., Pharisaic representatives, in preparation for his ministrations at the Temple on Yom Kippur.[64] Jesus is reported to have said correctly: "The Scribes and Pharisees sit on Moses' seat; all things therefore whatsoever they bid you, these do and observe."[65] Josephus reports likewise that the Pharisees "were the real administrators of the public affairs; they removed and readmitted whom they pleased; they bound and loosed at their pleasure."[66] While the Deuteronomic law refers all difficult cases to the supreme court consisting of Levitical priests as well as of

[59] *Yoma* 71b.
[60] *Sifre* to Deut. 11:22 and 31:4.
[61] *Negaim* 1.
[62] *Meg. Taan.* X.
[63] *Parah* III.8.
[64] *Yoma* I. 1–5.
[65] Matt. 23:2 ff.
[66] *Wars* I.5.2.

a lay judge or head of state, the Pharisees did not consider the presence of either priests or Levites indispensable. The court could act without them.

As for themselves, so for their supreme court or Sanhedrin, the Pharisaic masters claimed direct succession to Moses, the first "Sanhedrin" having been formed by him to assist him in caring for the people.[67] The great Sanhedrin claimed jurisdiction over the high priest but not over the king. (Its consent was necessary for the king to declare war.)[68] Even when its political powers were clipped, the Sanhedrin remained the supreme authority and court of highest appeal in all matters pertaining to ritual, whether in the Temple or Synagogue, arrangement of calendar, and civil justice. While the Sanhedrin was originally stationed in the Chamber of Hewn Stones at the Temple, its power of legislation was not wholly contingent upon that place.[69] When transferred to Yabneh, it continued as the highest court, in all but criminal cases.[70] The later academies, too, were regarded as continuations of the Sanhedrin.

The supreme court was presided over by the high priest and the chief civil ruler.[71] Combining the two functions, the Maccabean high priestly rulers, owing to their frequent engagements in wars, seem to have appointed a *nasi* to preside over the Sanhedrin in their stead. We are told that John Hyrcanus appointed the *zugot*, or "pairs," i.e., a *nasi* and an *ab bet din*, "head of the court," one acting as president and the other as vice-president of the Sanhedrin.[72] The authority of the two occasionally clashed.[73] Whereas in the smaller courts the *ab bet din* acted as head, in the great Sanhedrin he was subordinated to the *nasi*. Furthermore, while any competent scholar could serve as *ab bet din*, only one of aristocrat lineage, generally a descendant of the house of Hillel, was eligible for the office of *nasi*. In the years following

---

[67] Num. 11:16–17; *Sanh.* I.6.

[68] *Sanh.* 19a, I.5–II.

[69] *Sanh.* 14b, *A.Z.* 8b.

[70] *Sifre* to Deut. 16:8 ff. Maimonides, *Sefer Hamitzvot, Mitzvot Aseh*, no. 153, and the discussion by Naḥmanides ad loc.

[71] 2 Chron. 19:11.

[72] Jeru. *Maaser Sheni* V.5; *Hag.* II.2, 16b.

[73] *Ber.* 28a, *Hor.* 13b, Jeru. *Sanh.* I.2.

the destruction of Jerusalem, the *nasi* acted not only as the religious head of the Jewish people but also as their representative before the Roman government.[74]

As all religious and civil authority was vested in the Sanhedrin participation in its deliberations could be granted only to duly authorized scholars, so that the *amme haaretz* (i.e., non-Pharisees, which included the Sadducees) would be eliminated. This qualification led to the institution of *semichah,* or "ordination," as a prerequisite for admission not only to the great Sanhedrin but also to the lower Sanhedrins and to any college of judges empowered to issue decisions. In course of time, the right to make decisions relating to matters of law was limited to those who were properly authorized by scholars who themselves had been ordained. The institution of ordination was modeled after the example of Moses, who ordained the seventy elders and Joshua by laying his hands upon them, thus imparting his spirit to them.[75] Originally every master could ordain his disciples. In the interest of harmony, the right to ordain was vested in the *nasi.* Finally, the consent of the Sanhedrin (according to Maimonides: of the *ab bet din*) was made necessary for ordination.[76] With the suppression of the *semichah* after the Bar Kochba rebellion, the practice arose of announcing in public the names of the authorized scholars, *minuy zekenim.* As part of their ordination, the disciples of Hillel and Shammai began to be invested with the title *rabbi.* The *nasi* was distinguished by the higher title *rabban.* To maintain the hegemony of Palestine and of the *patriarchate,* the right of ordination was made their exclusive prerogative. As full ordination could not be conferred in the diaspora, Babylonian scholars received a partial ordination, marked by the title *rab.*[77] Such a scholar, after obtaining permission (*reshut*) from the exilarch or from the head of a Babylonian academy, could act, within the limited jurisdiction allowed the Jews by the government, in civil and religious matters. However, unlike an appointee of the *nasi* in Palestine, he did not enjoy the full powers of

[74] M. Guttman, *Maphteah Hatalmud,* vol. I, art. "Ab Bet Din," pp. 81–91.

[75] Num. 11:16–17, 24–25; 27:18–23; Deut. 34:9.

[76] *Sanh.* 5a, b; 13b–14a; Jeru. *Sanh.* I.2; Maimonides, *H. Sanh.* IV.5.

[77] *Ber.* 63a, b; *Sanh.* 13b–14a; Jeru. *Hag.* I.8, II.2.

a justice, which included issuing decisions regarding firstlings (i.e., whether any blemish rendered them ritually unfit for sacrifice), exacting fines (*kenas*), inflicting stripes (*malkot*), and still less imposing capital punishment.[78] He could imprison and inflict light bodily punishment.

Thus the lay scholars established their right as authoritative expounders of the Torah. They regarded themselves as in the direct line of succession to Moses. The opening Mishnah of *Abot* teaches: "Moses received the Torah at Sinai and handed it down to Joshua, and Joshua to the elders, and the elders to the prophets, and the prophets to the men of the Great Synagogue." From the men of the Great Synagogue, according to the rest of the first chapter of *Abot,* the Torah came down through the "pairs" to the rabbis of the schools of Hillel and Shammai. No reference whatever is made in this Pharisaic statement to the priests as depositories of the Law. The sages, whether of lay or priestly origin, are its sole custodians.

The next concern of the Pharisees or rabbis was to demonstrate the authoritative nature of their traditions. Josephus writes: "The Pharisees have delivered to the people a great many observances by succession from the fathers, which are not written in the laws of Moses; and for that reason it is that the Sadducees reject them, and say that we are to esteem those observances to be obligatory which are in the written word, but are not to observe what are derived from the tradition of our forefathers."[79] It must not be inferred from this statement that the Sadducees rejected all tradition. As a matter of fact, the priests, as we have shown above, were guided in both their ritual and judicial duties by ancient usage and custom. It was the contention of the Sadducees, however, that whatever is not plainly in the written Torah cannot be on a par with it. Whereas the Torah, being of divine origin, is binding for all times, traditional laws, being man-made, may be altered when

---

[78] *Sanh.* 31b. On the entire question, see Serira Gaon's Second Letter in B. Lewin's *Iggeret Rab Serira,* pp. 125–27; Maimonides, *H. Sanh.* IV.6–15; Estori Haparhi, *Kaftor Waferah,* chap. X, ed. A. M. Luncz, pp. 149–50; Frankel, *Darke Hamishnah,* p. 71, n. 7; Bacher, "Zur Geschichte der Ordination," *MGWJ,* XXXVIII, pp. 122–27; J. D. Eisenstein, art. "Hattarat Horaah," *Jew. Encyc.* VI, 261–64; J. Z. Lauterbach, art. "Ordination," *Jew. Encyc.* X, 428–30.

[79] *Antiq.* XIII.10.6.

occasion demands.[80] The Pharisees, on the other hand, refused to consider tradition as something extraneous to the Torah. In the words of G. F. Moore, "Since religion with all its duties and observances was revealed by God, the revelation necessarily included the unwritten as well as the written law."[81] From the doctrine of the Torah as the totality of revealed religion, the Pharisees drew the conclusion that, alongside of the written Torah, God had entrusted Moses with an unwritten Torah.[82]

To justify this novel conception of the Oral Law, it became necessary to find a scriptural basis both for the ancient customs and practices that were current among the people and for the required innovations of doctrine and observance. A method of exegesis (*midrash*) had to be evolved that would permit the interpretation of the Torah beyond its literal meaning (*peshat*).[83] The rules of Hillel, R. Ishmael, R. Akiba, and R. Eliezer b. Jose the Galilean represent the subtle devices whereby tradition established itself as the complement of revelation. R. Ishmael claimed for his rules of interpretation,

---

[80] On this phase of the problem, see J. Z. Lauterbach, "The Sadducees and Pharisees," in *Studies in Jewish Literature Issued in Honor of Prof. K. Kohler* (1913), pp. 176–98.

The Judeo-Christians appealed to the gentiles to observe the moral laws of the Torah, known as the Noachian commandments (Acts 15). The ceremonial laws were understood to belong only to Israel. Paul's total rejection of the Torah meant a rejection of the ceremonial law, which he claimed was given to Israel because of the hardness of their hearts. This belief became basic in Christian teaching. Thus Justin Martyr (*Dialogue* 11) states: "The law given in Horeb is now antiquated, and concerned only you [Jews]." He continues (ibid., 23): "Observe that the material universe, στοιχεῖα, is neither idle nor observes any Sabbath. Remain as you were born. For if before Abraham there was no need of circumcision, nor before Moses of Sabbath-keeping and feasts and offerings, neither is there now." Further (ibid., 43): "It has been shown that these things were commanded you because of your people's hardness of heart." (Cited by Huidekopper, *Judaism at Rome*, p. 343, n. 34.)

In Paul's teaching, the literal interpretation of the Law gave way to the allegorical. Christ was made the center of the new faith, and Moses and the prophets became nothing more than his forerunners. The Scripture became Old Testament, to be read and interpreted in the light of the New Testament, as mere background for the new religion.

[81] G. F. Moore, *Judaism*, I, 254.

[82] The earliest expressions of the doctrine of two Torahs are represented in the *Sifre* on Deut. 33:10, *Sab.* 31a, *Yoma* 28b.

[83] *Mas. Soferim* XVI.5–7.

Sinaitic origin.[84] The *Sifra* asserts likewise that along with the Torah, its principles of interpretation came from Sinai.[85]

Despite their skill in stretching Scripture, the rabbis were unable to find any ground in the written word for certain important traditions. Of these, some were assumed to date back to the fathers, to the prophets, to Moses, etc. Others were considered "laws given to Moses on Mount Sinai" (*halachah lemosheh misinai*). These, according to Bacher, hail partly from the school of Gamaliel I and partly from that of Jabneh.[86] In other instances the biblical text but faintly supported the weighty beliefs and practices. This was the case with the doctrine of the resurrection and of the Messiah and with so important an institution as the ritual mode of slaughter (*sheḥitah*). The latter institution probably grew out of the general tendency of the Pharisees to extend the laws of priestly holiness to the common people. Accordingly, the *Sifre* derives the regulations for the slaughter of animals for food from those governing the preparation of the sacrifices at the Temple. But all that R. Judah Hanasi could adduce in proof of this practice are the three words of Deuteronomy 12:21: *vezabaḥta ... kaasher tziviticha*, "and thou shalt slaughter ... as I commanded thee."[87] The Mishnah frankly states that for some laws (*halachot*) there are but slender scriptural proofs.

> The dissolution of vows floats in the air, and has no foundation in the Torah. The *halachot* concerning the Sabbath, private festival offerings, and the misappropriation of consecrated property are like mountains suspended by a hair; their scriptural basis is scant and the *halachot* are abundant. On the other hand, the regulations of civil and criminal law, Temple worship, purity, and incestuous relations have strong support in the Torah. Indeed they constitute the essential parts of the Torah.[88]

The skillful use of the midrashic method in setting up a hedge around the

---

[84] *Mechilta of R. Simeon b. Joḥai*, ed. Hoffmann, p. 117.

[85] *Sifra, Behar*, Introduction; *Beḥukotai* VIII, end.

[86] Bacher, *Tradition und Tradenten*, p. 33.

[87] *Sifre* on this verse; *Ḥul.* 28a.

[88] *Ḥag.* I.8; cf. *Abot* III.23. In some instances, the rabbis state: דבר זה מתורת משה רבינו לא למדנו מדברי קבלה למדנו *R.H.* 7a.

Torah justifies the statement of Josephus that the Pharisees followed "the government of reason; and what that prescribes to them as good for them, they do."[89] Obviously not all ancient practices could be regarded as possessing the force of revealed law. The pragmatic test of reason, therefore, was applied to tradition. Usages were considered binding when they were in accord with the teaching of the Torah and contributed to religious and social welfare. Like the leaders of Hellenistic Judaism, who by means of their allegorical method of interpretation endeavored to reconcile the Torah with the wisdom of Hellas, so the rabbis with the aid of their fanciful exegesis (*midrash halachah* and *midrash haggadah*) sought to explain and to justify the body of traditional practice. Though they proceeded from the conviction that the Torah, coming from God, must never change, they greatly deepened its ethical meaning and widened the scope of its application. In their hands, tradition served as a vehicle of progress. It was not merely *masoret* and *kabbalah*, that which is handed down or received from the past, but also *halachah*, "manner of conduct," "rule of behavior," "law," functioning as an educational guide and discipline. By its very nature, it removed the deadening literalism of Scripture, upon which the Sadducees like the Samaritans insisted; and thus tradition made for the steady advance of Judaism.

While in principle tradition was subordinate to the written word, in reality their relation was reversed. By the process of building "a hedge around the Torah," tradition set itself up as the final arbiter of the Torah. It was tradition that created and preserved the canon of Scripture, established the correctness of its text, and determined the authority of its respective parts and their use in the synagogue and the home. And it was tradition that settled the meaning and the application of the precepts of the Torah. The endeavor to build a hedge around the Torah resulted in the creation of a vast body of oral teaching, consisting of scriptural interpretations, old traditions, popular customs and laws, designed to meet the exigencies of the varying circumstances. The material, composed of religious ideas, moral maxims, exhortations, fanciful tales, legends, parables, etc., is known as *Haggadah*. Its purpose is to edify and to hearten the people in their spiritual and ethical endeavors. The legal portions of the oral teaching constitute the *Halachah*,

[89] *Antiq.* XVIII.1.3.

which is authoritative in character and which has functioned as the bond of union of the Jewish people. From Exodus 34:27, the rabbis inferred that Israel's covenant with God rests upon the acceptance of the Oral Law,[90] for it alone distinguishes Israel from all other peoples.[91] However, the Oral Law was not to be raised to the status of scripture. On the basis of Exodus 34:27, R. Judah bar Naḥmani, the interpreter of R. Simeon ben Lakish, teaches that what has been delivered orally may not be put in writing.[92] The writing down of *halachot, haggadot,* and even of prayers was frowned upon at first, because, in the absence of unanimity among the rabbis on vital matters, the reduction of private opinions to writing might have endangered the unity of Judaism. There was the further fear that in written form, tradition might eclipse the Torah. These fears were neither universally shared nor permanently maintained. In response to the urgent need of providing Judaism with a formidable weapon in its struggle for self-preservation, they were completely set aside. Hermann Strack suggests that "the formation of the New Testament and its growing recognition acted as a spur for the Jews by codifying the oral law to create an authoritative supplementary continuation of the Old Testament."[93] Through the labors of R. Judah Hanasi, the Oral Law, representing the chain of tradition from the men of the Great Assembly down to his own days, was arranged methodically into the six orders of the Mishnah. This great work constitutes a compendium of laws and of legal opinions of the leaders of Judaism, rather than a code in the usual sense of the word. Having been reduced to writing, it was endowed with permanence and with power. In the academies of Palestine and of Babylonia, it was treated as canonical[94] and became the chief subject of study. The results of their painstaking exposition and supplementation of the Mishnah, covering three centuries, are embodied in the Gemaras of Palestine and Babylonia.[95]

---

[90] *Git.* 60b.

[91] Jeru. *Ber.* I.7; Jeru. *Ḥag.* I.8; *Tanḥ., Ki Tisa,* ed. Buber, 17; *Exod. R.* 47.

[92] *Git.* 60b.

[93] H. Strack, *Introduction to the Talmud,* p. 18.

[94] *Letter of Sherira Gaon.* ובימי דרבי בנו של רשב״ג אסתייע מלתיה ותרצינהי וכתבינהו והוי מילי דמתניתין כמשה מפי הגבורה אמרן. I. H. Weiss, *Dor Dor V'dorshav* III.216.

[95] The Amoraim prohibited the issuing of decisions on the basis of the Mishnah itself without the Gemara, i.e., the careful analysis of its content. Those who did so were branded as "world destroyers," מבלי עולם. Rashi *Ber.* 5b and *Sota* 22a.

Principles of Rabbinic Authority

The authority of the rabbis was based upon their claim of being the exponents of a divinely revealed tradition which serves as a hedge around the Torah. Their efforts took the form of (a) religious and legal instruction based on tradition; (b) the laws derived through the exposition of Scripture according to established exegetical rules; and (c) decrees (*gezerot*), ordinances (*takanot*), new rites (e.g., *ketubah*), and customs (*minhagim*).[96]

1. On critical occasions, when the cause of religion demanded it, the rabbis felt themselves empowered to set aside the words of the Torah.[97] Adjustment to new circumstances appeared as a condition of Jewish survival.[98] Among the outstanding examples of this order, we may name the following: Permission to fight on the Sabbath.[99] Finding the well-intentioned law of Deuteronomy 15:1 f., canceling debts at the beginning of the Sabbatical year, worked hardship on the people, Hillel instituted the *prosbul,* consisting in the legal execution of a document whereby the lender retained the right to collect despite the advent of the year of release. The reason for this reform is stated as *mipne tikkun haolam,* general welfare.[100] Similarly, the increase in homicides in the years preceding the war with Rome (66 C.E.) prompted R. Joḥanan b. Zakkai to supsend the antiquated ceremonial of breaking the neck of a heifer in the case of an untraced murder, thus to remove the blood-guilt of the city nearest the spot where the victim was found.[101] He also suspended the ordeal of jealousy in consequence of the growth of moral laxity, justifying his action by Hosea 4:9.[102] On the basis of

---

[96] See I. H. Weiss, op. cit., vol. II, chap. VII, for a detailed survey of the subject.

[97] *Ber.* IX.5, 54a. See I. Schetelowitz, "Konnte das alte Judentum Dogmen Schaffen," *MGWJ* 70 (1926), pp. 434 ff.

[98] Judah Ḥassid interprets: תורה צוה לנו משה מורשה וגו' "צוה לנו שנעשה תקנה שתהא מורשה".

[99] I Macc. 2:40–41. See L. Finkelstein, *Menorah Journal,* 1936, pp. 135–36. Rabban Gamaliel deliberately broke with his day's prevailing luxurious custom of burying the dead in costly shrouds. To relieve the poor of this needless hardship, he ordered that he be buried in a plain linen shroud. *M. K.* 27b, *Ket.* 8b.

[100] *Git.* IV.3, 36a, b; *Sheb.* X.3–4.

[101] Deut. 21:1–9, *Sota* IX.9.

[102] Num. 5:11–31; *Sota* IX.9.

Ezra 10:8, the rabbis claimed the right of confiscation of property when necessary (*hefker bet din hefker*), even if thereby a biblical law is set aside.[103] Their power of abrogation and modification of the law extended not only to business matters but also to matrimonial affairs. Thus they nullified marriages not contracted in conformity with their rulings.[104] In all such cases of abrogation of a biblical law, they "attempted whenever possible, not to abolish it, but to introduce some legal fiction whereby the authority of the law was upheld and yet at the same time rendered null and void for all practical purposes."[105]

2. That their enactments might serve the purpose of safeguarding the Torah, the rabbis invested them with the force of the Torah. The Mishnah clearly stated: "The infringement upon the enactments of the scribes is weightier than that upon the words of the Torah. When one denies the law of tefillin,[106] he goes free; but if he claims that the tefillin must have five compartments, in place of the four required by the scribes, he is guilty."[107] "The rabbinic court," the Talmud states, "smites and punishes without the authorization of the Torah, not in order to contradict its words but to form a hedge around the law. Thus in the days of the Greeks, a man was found riding on a horse on the Sabbath. He was brought to court and stoned, not because he merited such severe punishment but because the hour demanded it."[108] Laws admittedly introduced by the rabbis (i.e., *mitzvot derabbanan,* as

---

[103] *Git.* 36b.

[104] *Yeb.* 90b, 122a.

[105] S. Zucrow, *Adjustment of Law to Life in Rabbinical Literature,* p. 4. A further case in point is טבילה לבעלי קריין. *Ber.* 21b–22b, *Pes.* 67b–68a; Maimonides *H. Keriat Shema* IV.8 and *Kesef Mishneh:* וכבר בטלה גם תקנה זו :H. *Tefila* IV.5: תפלה לפי [של טבילה ל] ולא פשטה תקנה זו שלא פשטה בכל ישראל ולא היה כח בצבור לעמד בה. This case illustrates also the force of *minhag,* of ארח ארעא as the basis of the Halachah. *Meg.* 23b. Cf. *R. H.* 15b. This is the real basis for the number ten required for a מנין. The citation of verse-proofs is only for the purpose of supplying the custom with biblical authority. ואף הוא (ר' יהודאי, גאון) כתב לארץ ישראל בשביל סירכא ובשביל כל המצות שנוהגין בהן שלא כהלכה אלא כמנהג שמד — ולא קבלו ממנו; ושלחו לו: מנהג מבטל להלכה, פרקי רב בבואי, ישראל בגולה, Dinaburg, vol. 2, p. 182. See ספר ראבי"ה, ed. Aptowitzer, p. 322.

[106] Deut. 6:8.

[107] *Sanh.* XI.3.

[108] *Yeb.* 90b; *Taan.* 17b: דברי סופרים בריכין חיזוק. See also Mishnah *R. H.* 2.2 and Gemara

distinguished from *mitzvot deoraita*) were invested with the force of the Torah. Among these are (1) the benedictions for various enjoyments; (2) ablutions of the hands before meals;[109] (3) lighting the Sabbath lamp;[110] (4) the *erub,* i.e., the fiction of joining boundaries to circumvent the law which prohibits walking beyond 2,000 cubits on the Sabbath or carrying things from one court to another, and of blending *yom tob* and Sabbath to permit the preparation of food for the Sabbath on a festival; (5) the recitation of the *Hallel* on holy days; (6) kindling lights on Hanukah; and (7) reading the Scroll of Esther on Purim. These have the force of biblical laws, and are preceded by the formula *asher kiddeshanu bemitzvotav vetzivanu,* "who hath sanctified us by His commandments and hath commanded us to . . ."[111]

3. Rabbinical decrees, prompted by the motive of promoting the social and spiritual welfare of the people, must not become a burden to them. Hence the general rule: "No *gezerot* may be imposed upon the people except when the majority can tolerate them."[112] Consequently, no prohibitory or mandatory statute may be enacted where loss, pain, or serious inconvenience is involved. Where there is danger of transgressing a weighty law of the Torah, the rabbinic "hedge" may be broken.[113] Likewise, where the people are so accustomed to their actions that new decrees would prove of no avail, they should be left alone, on the principle that it is better that they err unwittingly than presumptuously.[114]

4. When the reason for an enactment has been removed, due to altered conditions, the enactment, too, loses its force. Nonetheless, not just anyone may discard it. "Whatever has been decreed by vote of a court requires

---

R. H. 19b, concerning the changing or abolishing of customs, for the sake of safeguarding the basic law. See *More Nebuchim* III, 41:

[109] This innovation formed one of the points of difference between Pharisaic Judaism and Christianity.

[110] The purpose may have been anti-Samaritan and anti-Sadducean, both of which groups interpreted the verse לא תבערו אש וכו' literally. The same can be said about *erub.*

[111] *Sab.* 23a.

[112] *A.Z.* 36a, *B.B.* 60b.

[113] *Sab.* 153a.

[114] *Sab.* 148b.

another vote to be set aside." A court must decide whether or not the reason for the law actually has been removed. In some instances it may seem as if the original ground for a law or practice had disappeared; but upon examination, the contrary may prove to be the case.[115] Following the establishment of the calendar, the Babylonian scholars asked the authorities of Palestine for a ruling regarding the continuance of the second days of the festivals, in view of the fact that there was no further uncertainty regarding the exact dates of the festivals. The reply was that the reason for the practice had not been removed, for there was still danger of persecution by the government which might lead to further confusion. The admonition given them, "Be heedful of the customs of your fathers," made for the continuance of the practice to the present.[116]

5. To prevent conflicts between different courts, the rabbis established the principle that "no court may abrogate the decisions of another court unless it is superior in both wisdom and numbers."[117] This rule applies not only to courts of the same age but also to those of bygone times. During the talmudic period, this principle seems to have been purely theoretical. In practice — as the controversies of the Mishnah and Gemara show — courts did not hesitate to overthrow the rulings of other courts.[118] Subsequently, however, this principle acted as a deterrent to the modification of old laws; for with their excessive veneration of the wisdom and saintliness of the ancients, rabbis generally hesitated to presume superiority of scholarship to their remote predecessors so as to be able to set aside their decisions.[119]

6. Laws which a rabbinical court finds necessary to institute as a "hedge around the Torah," and which have been accepted by all Jewish people, cannot be abrogated by any other rabbinical court no matter how superior.[120] However, in accordance with rules one and five, even an inferior court may

---

[115] For instance, *Megillat Taanit* lists festive days on which fasting and mourning are prohibited. This stipulation was variously abolished or modified; and the rulings were either partially or entirely accepted. See *Meg.* 5b, 7a.

[116] *Beza* 4b–5a.

[117] *Eduy.* I.5; see also I:4, 6.

[118] I. H. Weiss, op. cit., pp. 57 ff.

[119] Zucrow, op. cit., pp. 37 ff.

[120] *A.Z.* 36b.

temporarily suspend such laws if the higher interests of religion clearly require such action. Maimonides adds:

> Similarly, if the rabbinical authorities find it necessary to set aside temporarily mandatory or prohibitory commandments of the Torah in order to restore many to the faith or to save many Jews from stumbling in other matters, they have the right to act according to the need of the hour. As a physician amputates the hand or leg of a patient in order to save his life, so a rabbinical court, when the occasion demands, may break some commandments for a while in order to preserve the rest.[121]

7. During the existence of the Sanhedrin, differences of opinion arising among rabbis or among rabbinical courts were referred to the Sanhedrin. In the absence of the high tribunal, differences arising between two courts or scholars are disposed of by following the strict decision in matters relating to biblical laws and the lenient decision in rabbinical laws.[122] After one authority has declared a thing unclean, no one else may declare it clean; after one authority has forbidden a thing, no one else may permit it.[123] An ordained teacher who dissents from the ruling of the highest court may continue to uphold his opinion; but if he applies it in practice he becomes a "rebellious elder."[124]

8. In their decisions, the rabbis were often guided by the prevailing custom (*minhag*), the fruitful source of law.[125] When in doubt concerning a practice or law, they accounted the common usage among the people as their guide. *Minhag abotenu torah hi.*[126] Where a custom conflicts with an established halachah, the custom often takes precedence. *Haminhag mebatel et*

---

[121] H. *Mamrim* II.4. S. Funk, "Die Kompetenz der Gerichthöfe," *MGWJ*, 1910, pp. 699–722.

[122] *A.Z.* 7a; H. *Mamrim* 1.5.

[123] *Ber.* 63b, *Nid.* 20b.

[124] Deut. 17:12; *Eduy.* V.6; *Sanh.* XI.2, 88a, b. Cf. *R.H.* 2.9.

[125] אין הלכה נקבעת עד שיהא מנהג — *Sof.* XIV.18.

[126] *Ber.* 45a, *Pes.* 66a, Jeru. *Peah* VII.5; *Shulhan Aruch, Yore Deah* 376.4. Rashi, *Sefer Hapardes*, ed. H. L. Ehrenreich, pp. 227f. See Frankel, *Darke Hamishnah*, pp. 68–70. כל הלכה שהוא רופפת בב"ד ואין אתה יודע מה טיבה צא וראה היאך הצבור נוהג ונהוג.

hahalachah.[127] Transgression of an established custom is as punishable as the transgression of a written law.[128] "Man must never deviate from custom."[129] The proverb "Remove not the ancient landmark which thy fathers have set" was interpreted by R. Simeon b. Joḥai to mean: "Do not change a custom established by thy fathers." R. Joḥanan adds: "Thy fathers have set it up not for themselves alone but for all the generations."[130] While emphasizing the binding force of custom, the rabbis differentiated between customs of individuals and of communities, between customs that have biblical support and those that have not, and between useful customs and those that are injurious or that grow out of superstition, ignorance, or error.[131] Particular care was taken to avoid imitating the religious customs of non-Jews (*ḥukot hagoyim*), as being detrimental to Judaism. Moreover, customs which at one time were current among the Jews were abandoned when they were adopted by other religions, as, for example, the practice of kneeling in worship, which is now retained only in the Rosh Hashanah service during the *Alenu* and on Yom Kippur during the *Abodah*. Considerable variation in custom affecting important phases of religious life developed among the Jews of Palestine and Babylonia, and subsequently among the Ashkenazim and Sephardim and among the different communities within these divisions, e.g., Ḥasidim and Mitnagdim, etc.[132] While the custom of each place is binding upon its people, difficulties present themselves when Jews of different communities settle in the same city. The conflicts in *minhagim* often endangered the peace of the communi-

---

[127] *Sof.* XIV.18; cf. *Yeb.* 13b, *Nid.* 66a, *Taan.* 26b; *Jeru. B. Mez.* VII.1. Distinction must be made between an established custom and an unproved one. וזה שאמרו מנהג מבטל הלכה מנהג *Soferim* XIV, 18. Cf. J. ותיקין אבל מנהג שאין לו ואיה מן התורה אינו אלא כטועה בשיקול הדעת Müller, *Masechet Soferim*, p. 202.

[128] *Jeru. Yeb.* XII.1; *B. Mez.* VII.1 and *Jeru. ad loc.*

[129] *B. Mez.* 86b. *Suk.* 38a–39a. *Mas. Soferim* 14.16, ed. Higger, 270–71.

[130] Midrash to Prov. 22:28.

[131] *Jeru. Pes.* IV.1; *M.K.* 27b; *Ket.* 8b; *Bet Joseph, Orah Hayyim* 605. מקום שנהגו לכפל יכפול, לפשוט יפשוט, לברך אחריו יברך *Suk.* III, 11 — הכל כמנהג המדינה. Cf. Isserles, *Orah Hayyim* 690.17: ואין לבטל שום מנהג או ללעוג עליו כי לא לחנם הוקבע. See *Tur*, ibid.; Tos. *A.Z.* 11a ד"ה ואי חוקה. See also Abraham Berliner, *Randbemerkungen zum täglichen Gebetbuche (Siddur)*, 2 vols. (Berlin: M. Poppelauer, 1909–12), vol. II, vii.

[132] *Jeru. Pes.* IV. 1. Levy, art. *minhag. Jeru. Peah* 7:6; *Maas Sh.* 5.3; *Ber.* 7.2; ראבי"ה 69.

ties.[133] In order to extend the authority of the Babylonian schools and the Babylonian Talmud, R. Yehudai Gaon urged Palestinian Jewry to abandon its customs.[134]

Authority of the Talmud and the Codes

With the compilation of the Palestinian and especially of the Babylonian Talmud, the norms of Jewish life were thoroughly regulated. The Babylonian Talmud, as the more comprehensive of the two, at once became the foundation of the Halachah.[135] Embodying the traditions of well-nigh a millennium, and arranged under the supervision of the whole body of scholars of the then (end of fifth century) only center of learning, it took its place by the side of the Bible as the authoritative guide of all Jewish life.[136] Through the wide connections of the Babylonian *geonim*, it was transplanted into Egypt, North Africa, Spain, Italy, France, and Germany, etc., and cherished as the absolute rule of faith and practice.

[133] See Kohut, *Aruk Ha-Salem*, s.v. *nahag*; Levy, *Wörterbuch*, s.v. *minhag*; R. Joseph Kolon; *Responsa* LIV; S. Bernfeld, Intro. to *Kebod Ḥakamim*; Rab Zair, *Hashiloah* IV, pp. 400 ff.; M. S. Antokolsky, *Maamar Tokef Haminhagim*, in Hirshovitz's *Ozar Kol Minhage Jeshurun*; J. Eisenstein, *Ozar Dinim Uminhagim*, pp. 236–37, S. A. Horodetski, *Lekorot Harabanut*, pp. 112–21 (on Isserles and *minhag yisrael*). On the entire subject, see *Pes.* IV and Gemara 50a ff. See Appendix to *Minhagim* in B. Lewin's *Ozar Hageonim*. Aptowitzer, *Sefer Rabiah*, Intro. pp. 436–44. Isserles and Magen Abraham, *Orah Hayyim*, Hil. Pesah 493, Hil. *Meg.* 690.17. On customs introduced by an individual scholar, see *Ket.* 8b. מנהג רבן גמליאל, I. H. Weiss, *Bet Talmud* II, pp. 37–38.; *Dor* IV, 295–96.

[134] L. Ginzberg, *Geniza Studies in Memory of Doctor Solomon Schechter*, II, 9, 535, 540. L. Ginzberg, *Geonica* I, p. 4, n. 1.72–73. A. Guttman, לשאלת היחס מנהג-הלכה בתקופת התלמוד, *Bitzaron* VII, Sivan-Tammuz. For the *ḥerem* of Rabbi Gershom, see F. Rosenthal, "שי למורה", לכבוד ר' עזריאל הילדסהיימר, pp. 37–53. Simhoni, "רבינו גרשום מאור הגולה", *Hashiloach*, v. 28. Graetz, v. 3; A. R. Malachi, *Hadoar* XVII, pp. 202–3. Ginzberg's description of the Pirke ben Baboi, in *Geniza Studies in Memory of Solomon Schechter*, II, 506–8.

[135] Palestinian Jewry followed the teaching of its own Talmud, despite the efforts of the leaders of Babylon to force upon it the authority of the Babylonian Talmud. Only toward the end of the Geonic period did they succeed in their endeavor. See L. Ginzberg, *Geniza Studies*, II, p. 506.

[136] השופט אשר יהיה בימים ההם. Tos *R.H.* 2.3 ff. Only the judge of your own days must be the judge. Rashi, Deut. 17:9.

In view of the halachic controversies contained in the Talmud, rules were adopted for the discovery of the authoritative halachah. Thus, where one *tanna* is opposed by many, the opinion of the many prevails. In most cases the views of the house of Hillel prevail against those of the house of Shammai. When opposed by any other master, the opinon of R. Jose, R. Judah Hanasi, or R. Akiba prevails.[137] Among the *amoraim,* where Rab and Samuel differ, "the halachah is according to Rab in ritual prohibitions [*issure*] whether his decision is lenient or rigorous," and according to Samuel in civil law (*dine*).[138] As a *tanna* could not contradict a biblical law, so an *amora* could not oppose a *mishnah* or *baraita* unless he could support his view with another equally authoritative tradition. Likewise an *amora* could not contradict an opinion of an elder *amora*.[139]

In addition to the rules for deciding the halachah, it became necessary to sift the conflicting discussions of the *tannaim* and *amoraim,* and to formulate definite rules for the regulation of conduct. The external stimulus for the codification of talmudic law was provided by the Karaitic opposition to the supremacy of the Talmud in Jewish life. Protesting against the excessive growth of the Oral Law beyond the literal statement of the Written Torah (thus reverting to the position of the Sadducees), the Karaites raised the cry: "Back to Scripture!" Discarding all rabbinic tradition, they set out to reestablish their religious life upon the foundations of revelation as contained in the Bible. (In course of time, however, they developed a tradition of their own.[140] In response to these attacks, the rabbis intensified their efforts to demonstrate the authoritative nature of tradition by the careful codification of its contents. The author of the *Halachot Gedolot* (probably R. Simeon of Kayyara of the eighth century) endeavored to link talmudic law with the *Taryag Mitzvot,* i.e.,

---

[137] Tos. *Suk.* 2.3; *Erib.* 46a–47a.

[138] *Nid.* 24b, *Bek.* 49b.

[139] *Beza* 9a and Rashi ad loc. A complete compendium of such rules first appeared in סדר תנאים ואמוראים, the *Halakot Gedolot* under the title *Halakot Kezubot,* ed. J. Hildesheimer, pp. 469–70. See also Samuel Hanagid, *Mebo Hatalmud.* Maimonides, Intro. to *Seder Zeraim*; Benveniste, *Kelale Hatalmud.* All three are included in the first volume of the Wilna (Rom) ed. of the Talmud. For a list of works dealing with this subject, see Strack, *Intro. to the Talmud,* ch. XIV.

[140] See *Kuzari* III, 37 ff.

the 613 Pentateuchal commandments, thereby establishing the biblical basis of the halachah.[141] His attempt was followed by other codifiers (*posekim*) like R. Eliezer b. Samuel of Metz in his *Sefer Yereim,* R. Aaron Halevi of Barcelona in his *Sefer Hahinuch,* and R. Moses of Coucy in his *Sefer Mitzvot Gadol (SeMaG).* Maimonides, too, wrote his *Sefer Hamitzvot* on the *Taryag,* as an introduction to his *Mishneh Torah.* Other codifiers proceeded directly to present abstracts on the halachic content of the Talmud. This was the purpose of R. Isaac Alfasi in his *Halachot.* On the basis of this and other halachic works, Maimonides composed his *Mishneh Torah* or *Yad Hahazakah,* the outstanding achievement of rabbinic codification. Among the other codes exercising authority in Jewish life are the *Halachot* of R. Asher b. Jehiel (the *Rosh*), the *Tur* by R. Jacob b. Asher, and above all the *Shulhan Aruch* of R. Joseph Caro. Following the labors of his predecessors, Caro drew up his code on the basis of the Sephardic tradition. Modified by the annotations of R. Moses Isserles, which set forth the Ashkenazic practice, the *Shulhan Aruch* established itself as "the code par excellence of Rabbinic Judaism." L. Ginzberg observes: "Nevertheless, it must always be borne in mind that the really decisive authority is the Talmud, and a reference to a code as authoritative is equivalent to saying that its exposition is regarded as the correct one."[142]

Accordingly, to discover what is binding upon the Jew from the standpoint of Orthodoxy, one must consult the *Shulhan Aruch* and its commentaries, and from them go back to the older codes, to the responsa of the outstanding

[141] According to the *Mechilta,* the *tannaim* of the second century were already familiar with the number of the commandments. Thus R. Simeon b. Elazar refers to the 613. (See *Mek., Yitro, Bahodesh* 5, ed. Weiss, p. 74a.) As the number is not given in the *Yalkut,* Weiss considers it as a later interpolation. The *Sifre* offers more convincing proof, quoting Ben Azzai that there are 365 negative commandments (Deut. 76, ed. Friedman, p. 90b). On the basis of this tannaitic tradition, R. Simlai (3d cent.) built his homily regarding the 613 commandments, 365 negative and 248 positive (*Mak.* 23b). For systematic works on the *Taryag,* see Jellinek, *Kuntres Taryag,* and his additional supplements in the *Kuntres Harambam* and in *Kuntres Hamafteah,* listing in all 176 works. It must be noted that while the *Taryag* was considered the distinguishing element of Judaism, it was not regarded as authoritative for the practical purposes of issuing legal decisions. (See R. Simeon b. Zemah Duran, *Zohar Harakia,* end.)

[142] Art. "Law, Codification of," *JE* VII, 646.

rabbis and of the *geonim,* and to the discussions of the Babylonian Talmud. The Palestinian Talmud is generally followed only when it does not conflict with the Babylonian Talmud. Thus the ultimate authority in Orthodox Judaism is the Babylonian Talmud. The Bible itself ranks second to it in reality if not in theory.

In the rabbinic age, following that of the *geonim,* a line of distinction is drawn between the *rishonim* and the *aharonim* (the "former" masters Aharonim and the "latter ones"). These terms are relative, depending on the person who uses them. Caro, for example, writes: "Upon the completion of the Mishnah it was resolved that the latter generations of scholars shall not oppose the former ones. When the Gemara was completed it was similarly decided that henceforth no one shall be permitted to contradict its teachings."[143] In the Talmud itself, the wisdom and piety of the *rishonim* was contrasted with that of the *aharonim* to the disparagement of the latter.[144] The more ancient the masters, the greater was the weight attached to their teachings. This conservative tendency manifested itself toward the codifiers or *posekim.* The dividing line between *posekim rishonim* and *posekim aharonim* is variously drawn. Some commence the line of *aharonim* with the Tosafists of the twelfth and thirteenth centuries; others with R. Isaac b. Reuben of Düren (1320), author of the *Shaare Dura,* although the Maharil refers to him as one of the *rishonim*; and still others with R. Joseph Caro of the sixteenth century.[145] Despite the great veneration for the *rishonim,* the decisions of the *aharonim* prevail.[146] "The opinions of *rishonim,*" as L. Ginzberg points out, "which are frequently decisions of practical cases, have the same significance as the decisions of a higher court in modern jurisprudence, which are valid until they have been proved to be erroneous."[147]

To safeguard the Halachah, no one was permitted to issue decisions

---

[143] *Kesef Mishne* to *H. Mamrim* II.1.

[144] *Ber.* 35b, *Erub.* 53a, *Sanh.* 94b, *Jeru. Shek.* V.1.

[145] I. Lampronti, *Pahad Yizhak,* Art. "Aharonim"; *Hilkot Eliyahu,* no. 206; I. H. Weiss, op. cit., V, p. 171: M. Steinschneider, *Sifrut Yisrael,* tr. by Malter, p. 108; S. Baeck, "Die Halachische Literatur," in *Winter und Wünsche,* II, p. 497.

[146] *Yad Malaki,* p. 168; R. Asher b. Jehiel, *Sanh.* IV. 6.

[147] Op. cit., p. 646.

(responsa) without securing permission from the proper authorities. Among the Ashkenazim it became customary for leading scholars to issue rabbinic authorizations (*hattarat horaah*) to qualified students, and to invest them with the additional title of *morenu* ("our teacher"). This quasi-*semichah*, authorizing the recipient to be called *rabbi*, conferred no personal powers upon him.[148] It served only as a testimonial of his fitness to act as interpreter of the Halachah. Whatever powers of jurisdiction he possessed, he derived from the consent of the community which elected him, such powers being restricted to the religious sphere of that community. Within the limited autonomy of the Jewish communities, the rabbinic courts helped to maintain the formal unity and the religious character of the Jewish people. In the absence of the arm of the state, as enjoyed by the church, the leaders of Judaism could only appeal to the moral conscience of the people, and reinforce their decisions with the power of the ban.[149] While temporary emergencies were cared for by special synods, all regular matters were governed by rabbinic law as contained in the codes.[150]

Reform Judaism and Authority

Authority in Judaism entered upon a new phase of its development with the rise of Reform at the beginning of the nineteenth century. As long as Judaism constituted a world apart, the Talmud and the *Shulḥan Aruch* ruled its life. Under the force of social pressure and public opinion, Jews readily subjected themselves to the strict and often heroic discipline of rabbinic tradition. Its binding character, as we have seen, was derived from the belief that it is

[148] R. Jacob Berab's attempt to restore the institution of *semichah* in Palestine, in 1538, proved abortive.

[149] H. *Talmud Torah* VI.14; H. *Mamrim*; S. Asaph, *Lechorot Harabbanut, Reshumot* II, pp. 286 ff. I. Wiesner, *Der Bann*.

[150] For further details on this subject, see Art. "Crimes and Punishment (Jewish)," Hastings, *Encyc. Rel. and Ethics*, IV, pp. 288–90. Enforcing authority by means of the ban, Dinaburg, *Yisrael Bagolah* II, 145 ff. Art. "Parnas," *JE*, IX, 541–42. Takkanot and Synods, see Güdemann, התורה והחיים, II, 220–41; I, 211–25.

implicit in the Sinaitic revelation. The Maimondean creed affirms: "The whole Torah, now in our possession, is the same that was given to Moses our teacher, peace be upon him. . . . This Torah will not be changed, and there will never be any other law from the Creator, blessed be He." Whereas the messages of the other prophets were addressed chiefly to their own generations, Moses issued everlasting statutes, binding upon all generations. These can be neither abrogated nor modified. The other prophets only exhorted fidelity to the Mosaic Law. The rabbis, in even greater detail, defined the Written Law and applied it to the changing exigencies of Jewish life. Rabbinic law, therefore, claimed the loyalty and obedience of all Jewish people.[151]

Despite their theoretically immutable nature, neither biblical nor rabbinic law escaped the mutations of time. With the cessation of the sacrificial cult and the dispersion of the Jewish people, the laws pertaining to the Temple and to Palestine ceased to function. Of all the 613 commandments, according to R. Aaron Halevi (13th cent.), only 270 are in force. These he finds to be equivalent to the numerical value of the word *er*, "awake," in Canticles 5:2 ("I am asleep but my heart is awake").[152] It would be instructive to discover how many of them actually have survived the ravages of time. Solomon Schechter suggested that "barely a hundred laws remain which really concerned the life of the bulk of the people."[153] M. Friedländer consoles himself that "the Law is not altered; our circumstances demand a *temporary* suspension of such laws and not their abrogation."[154] In point of fact, it comes to the same thing. The changing seasons have found many branches upon the tree of Judaism withered. To preserve them on the tree means to sap its vitality.

With the composure characteristic of philosophers, Moses Mendelssohn was able to recognize the authority of the whole ceremonial law as divinely revealed, and at the same time to uphold the right of free inquiry. But to him, in the light of his deistic philosophy, "revealed" could have meant only

---

[151] Maimonides, *H. Yesode Hatorah* IX; see also Halevi, *Kuzari* III, 38–53. See Crescas on this point; "The Dogmas in Judaism," in Schechter, *Studies in Judaism*, First Series (Philadelphia, 1938), pp. 167–70.

[152] Preface to *Sefer Hahinuk*.

[153] *Studies in Judaism*, I, p. 248.

[154] *The Jewish Religion*, p. 140.

"reasonable."[155] Applying the test of reason to the ceremonial law, many of his followers could not retain the philosophic calm. The rationalistic attempts to endow them with meaning notwithstanding[156] —many of the rabbinic laws and customs appeared burdensome and unreasonable. They were enforced only by social pressure and by the rabbinical ban. (David Fried-länder petitioned the Prussian government, in 1787, for the abrogation of the ban, with the result that it was abolished in 1792, thereby dealing a serious blow to rabbinic authority.)

For a pragmatic people which, upon receiving the Torah, exclaimed *Naaseh* ("we will do") before *Nishma* ("we shall hear"), the deed often precedes the theory. With the crumbling of the ghetto walls, in consequence of the political and industrial changes at the turn of the eighteenth century, the Jewish people in Germany began to break away from what seemed to them to be the dead hand of the past, without pausing to petition rabbinic sanction. As Caesar Seligmann points out, the Reform movement originated among laymen rather than among rabbis, and in some instances was directed against the rabbis.[157] The strong will to live as Jews in the face of the dawning freedom from Jewish disabilities in politics and occupations and of the dazzling culture of the Occident — which lured many to apostasy — prompted the pioneers of Reform to modernize the modes of religious expression in order to save the younger generation for Judaism.[158] Their first attempts were limited to the aestheticization of the synagogue service, e.g., casting away all that gave the appearance of foreignness and made for

---

[155] See the author's presentation of Mendelssohn in his *The History of the Beginnings of Modern Judaism*, section 1.

[156] See especially Maimonides, *Moreh Nebuchim* III, chs. XXVI-XL. The rationalistic and mystical interpretations of the commandments lie outside the scope of the present essay.

[157] *Geschichte d. juedischen Reformbewegung. Einleitung.* The compilers of the Charleston, S.C., Prayerbook (1830) announced in their introduction that they "act only for themselves, for their children, and for all those who think the period has arrived, when the Jew should break in pieces the scepter of Rabbinical power, and assert his attribute as a free agent, obedient only to the laws of God, and responsible for his thoughts and actions to the merciful Creator alone." The deistic tinge of the declaration is evident. An even more radical position was taken by the Society of Friends of Reform.

[158] Chorin, אגרת אלאסף, especially pp. 29b ff. ילד זקונים.

separateness, introducing instrumental music and choral song, abbreviating the traditional ritual, and adding new prayers and hymns in the vernacular. The spirit of Reform was soon felt in the home, in the discard of either some or all the dietary laws, and in the disregard of certain observances of the Sabbath and festivals. Liberalism and enlightenment spelt emancipation from the burden of external pressure, whether of inherited laws, ceremonials, and customs or of the sometimes irksome rabbinical rules.[159] This inner emancipation from the burden of tradition seemed to hold out the further promise of removing the last barrier to complete civic and social equality of the Jew with the non-Jew.

The deed came first; the theories afterwards.[160] Leopold Zunz devoted his great work, the *Gottesdienstliche Vorträge der Juden,* to demonstrating that there are no grounds for the prohibition of synagogue reforms. The history of Jewish literature reveals the steady growth of the Jewish liturgy, of the use of the vernacular in prayer, and of preaching as a permanent feature of Jewish religious life. Hence the innovations of the Reformers cannot be considered a breach with the past. Lack of system was but natural in the endeavors of the early Reformers. Some of these efforts were frankly opportunistic, but they stemmed from the desire to adjust the Jewish people to the new circumstances which confronted them. Thus, the Hamburg Prayerbook eliminated certain portions of the traditional liturgy which invoked divine aid for the ingathering of the Jewish people from the lands of their sojourn to Palestine, on the ground that these portions clashed with the best interests of the Jews and with their struggle to secure civic equality with their German neighbors. Having been Europeans for well-nigh two thousand years, the Jews felt that they had a right to consider themselves at home in the lands of their sojourn. Gradually, consistent theories of Reform made their appearance, thus justifying the deviations from established usage. R. Aaron Chorin's words to the Hungarian rabbis, in 1844, about the need of differentiating between *permanent* and *unessential* elements in Judaism reappear as the basic idea of Holdheim's,

---

[159] In consequence of the political emancipation of Jewry in France, Germany, England, and the United States, the Jewish civil law, for the most part, became inoperative. And the rabbi ceased to be a judge, and became chiefly a teacher and preacher.

[160] See Eliezer Liebermann, *Or Nogah*; M. I. Bressilau, *Hereb Nokemet*, 1819.

Einhorn's, and Philippsohn's teachings. For instance, Holdheim wrote: "The rabbis have perpetuated as religion the temporary part of Mosaism, the symbolism and *particularism* of the theocracy, and, on the other hand, they misconceived and neglected its *eternal element, the ideal of universalism,* which was the real purpose of the theocracy."[161] Einhorn conceived the task of the Jewish Reformers as being twofold: "First to unchain by the breath of the living spirit the forms that had become rigid and to make them fluid; and, secondly, to sift these forms according to their antiquity and esentiality; and in accordance with such sifting, to reduce their great number, beneath whose burden Judaism, without a doubt, is sighing and panting." Above all, the empty formalism must give way to earnestness, and religion must be restored to its prophetic teaching and purity.[162]

Religious authority was made dependent not merely upon what in the eyes of the pioneers of Reform seemed "the need of the hour," but also upon careful *scientific research.* The movement for the scientific study of Judaism, auspiciously begun by Zunz, thus assumed far-reaching practical signifi- cance. In the hands of its indefatigable and creative exponent, Abraham Geiger, it became the instrumentality of solving vexing communal and spiri- tual problems of the day. He wielded it as a two-edged sword against obscurantism, on the one hand, and radicalism, on the other. Historical criticism demonstrated to him, as he writes,

> that not in violent and reckless amputation of all that has been transmitted to us from the past, lies our salvation, but in the careful investigation into its deeper message; and in striving, even now that we have become organs of history, to continue to develop historically that which has grown up historical- ly, checking here, furthering there, here following the wheel of time and seizing it while in motion and speeding it along with a strong hand.[163]

Geiger's claim of authority for scientifically derived truth implied, first,

---

[161] Cited by David Philipson, *The Reform Movement in Judaism* (1931), p. 42. Holdheim rejected the Halachah on the ground of its dependence on the Jewish state.

[162] Cited ibid., p. 43.

[163] *Das Judentum unserer Zeit,* reprinted in *Nachgelassene Schriften,* I, p. 448.

the right of free inquiry; and second, the right of applying the results of the investigation to life. On both points stout opposition was offered to him and to his followers. Orthodoxy, rallying to the banner of R. Solomon Tiktin, denied the first; the Breslau school, led by the redoubtable talmudist Zacharias Frankel, denied the second. If the first party demurred at all scientific study, the second shrank from its application to life as a *halachah lemaaseh,* a law which can be carried into practice. Nor was it easy for Geiger and the other constructive Reformers to convince all who were interested in the renovation of Jewish life that *evolution* did not mean *revolution,* and that through historical criticism the *shalshelet hakabalah,* "the chain of historical continuity," of Judaism must be secured. The common differentiation between permanent and transitory elements in Judaism led some to identify the first with what they chose to call "Mosaism," and the latter with "Talmudism" or "Rabbinism." The Society of Friends of Reform (1843), on the one hand, recognized "the possibility of unlimited development in the Mosaic religion," and, on the other, resolved that "the collection of controversies and prescriptions commonly designated by the name Talmud possesses for us no authority from either the dogmatic or the practical standpoint."[164] Einhorn united with Frankel in denouncing these articles as a "confession of unbelief." Even Holdheim recognized the danger of the society's declaration. Geiger considered it confused in thought and ill-timed in utterance, especially in its attack on circumcision. Eliminating the talmudic or rabbinic phase of its development, and limiting it to the Bible, would have reduced Judaism to a pale type of Karaism, minus the religious fervor for Scripture and for the Hebrew language that distinguished the Karaites.[165]

---

[164] Philipson, op. cit., p. 122.

[165] It is significant that the Karaites, despite their devotion to the Bible, to the Hebrew language, and to the hope of the restoration of the Jewish people to Palestine, have been repudiated by the main body of Jewry. Expressive of this attitude is the play on the name Karaim: הקראים אינם מתאחים לעולם. (A play on ואלו קרעין שאין מתאחין *M.K.* 26a. See Poznanski, art. "Karaites," Hastings, *Encyc. Rel. and Ethics* VII, p. 670, n. 3; R. Fahn, *Kol Kitve* I, pp. 65 ff.; J. Mann, "New Studies in Karaism," *Yearbook CCAR,* 1934, p. 222; cf. *Texts and Studies* II, p. vii. See also Caro, *Bet Josef, Tur Eben Haezer* IV, end, and Isserles's gloss ad loc. in *Shulḥan Aruch.*) The Reformers, on the other hand, despite their attenuated

The differentiation between "Mosaism" and "Rabbinism" went beyond the ill-advised *Protestantische Juden,* as the so-called Friends of Reform were stigmatized. Its disastrous consequences manifested themselves in the whole field of Reform theology. While the canons of historical research were freely applied to talmudic literature, they were kept away from the Bible and especially from the Pentateuch.[166] For Einhorn, Reform rested unconditionally upon what he considered to be the unshakable foundations of Mosaism and revelation. I. M. Wise, too, agreed in this regard with the Conservatives and even with the Orthodox. He devoted his *Pronaos* to a defense of the Pentateuch against "the science commonly called Modern Biblical Criticism, actually negative criticism." In his belief, "The authenticity of the Mosaic records is the foundation of all Bible truth. The whole system of righteousness, justice, and equity for public government and the conduct of the individual, virtue and holiness as a form of divine worship, monotheism itself with all the doctrines derived from this principle, the entire canon of divinity and humanity depends on the authenticity and veracity of the Pentateuchal records." He was convinced that in the Psalms we find the "Theology of Moses, in Proverbs the Ethics of Moses, in Job and Ecclesiastes the Apologetics of both, in Chronicles, Ezra and Nehemiah the necessary addenda to the ancient canons; so that the entire Book is a logical organism, with every part

loyalty to Hebrew and rejection of the belief in the restoration of the sacrificial cult and the ingathering of the Jewish people under a Davidic Messiah in Palestine, have continued as an integral part of *Kelal Yisrael.* Various reasons may be given in explanation of this fact. Chief among them is the consideration that while the Karaites withdrew from the body of Israel and formed a sect apart, the Reformers have refused to separate themselves from world Jewry and conscientiously share in its burdens. Furthermore, while claiming the right to reinterpret the meaning of both revelation and tradition in the light of science, and to modify practice in accordance with the requirements of the people in the new age, the leaders of Reform have steadily emphasized their attachment to historical Judaism. The attempts to remove the Reformers from the body of Israel met with failure. See, for example, Rabbi Shlomo Zebi Schück in Bernat Schuck's *Dat Vadin* (Temesvar, 1904), pp. 25-29.

[166] While the department of Bible studies at the Hebrew University of Jerusalem operates as part of the school's humanities, thus providing freedom for the critical-historical approach, it has evoked repeated "vociferous" attacks by the conservatives. (Verified by the department chairman, Professor Shemaryahu Talmon, in a letter of Sept. 11, 1967).

in place."[167] As a last resort he strove to rescue the Decalogue from the unhallowed spirit of biblical criticism.[168]

Here, too, Geiger led the way. Imbued with the spirit of the historical sciences, which is the glory of the nineteenth century, and passionately devoted to truth, he beheld Judaism as an unbroken chain of spiritual development, beginning with the fathers of Israel and continuing to our own times. This steady outreaching of the Jewish spirit Godward, he traced in the stratified remains of the Bible no less than in postbiblical literature. The same spirit that came to expression in the prophets revealed itself also in the religious strivings of the Pharisees, and is still at work whenever Jews earnestly strive to read life's hieroglyphs. On this side of the Atlantic, he was followed by a number of scholarly champions of Reform, among whom B. Felsenthal, E. G. Hirsch, and K. Kohler rank foremost. Under the banner of progress and with the aid of the discoveries of science, they labored to furnish Judaism with a sound basis in modern thought, and thereby to regenerate it as a vital force in the life of the Jewish people and of the world.

[167] Preface to the *Pronaos*, 1891.

[168] In his essay "The Law" (1880), he argues that "the Decalogue is the Torah, in letter and spirit, the eternal law and doctrine, the exclusive and adequate source of theology and ethics, the only intelligible categoric imperative. Therefore it is called in the Pentateuch *Had-dabar*, the word or the substance, the only true logos by which the moral world was called into existence, and which, as the Talmud states, existed before the creation of this earth; . . . its laws are categories, its doctrines are fundamental principles; in its logical order it is a unit, and in its totality it comprises the entire substance of theology and ethics; no new category of law can be added to it and none can be taken away from it without destroying its unity and perfection. . . .

"Inasmuch as the Mosaic doctrines were ideally implicit in the Decalogue before they took form in special provisions, and inasmuch as the Decalogue was given to Israel through the agency of Moses (Deut. 5:5) every law of the Pentateuch, whenever, wherever, and by whomsoever written, may justly be termed a law of Moses, as the whole Torah may justly be styled the Law of Moses."

He concludes: "This, I believe, is the historical basis of reform, progressive and law abiding. The only problem to be solved is, who shall decide for the community of Israel which law or custom is an embodiment of a doctrine contained in the Decalogue, which one should be preserved and which amended. For the individual, the Decalogue, conscience, and reason must decide, and guide him to salvation by righteousness." (D. Philipson and L. Grossman, *Selected Writings of I. M. Wise*, pp. 133–35, 151–52.)

Crystallizations of the viewpoints of Reform are embodied in the resolutions adopted by the Reform conferences at Braunschweig, Frankfurt, and Breslau (1843–1846) and in the declaration of principles adopted in Philadelphia in 1869, under the auspices of Samuel Hirsch, David Einhorn, and I. M. Wise, particularly in the Pittsburgh Platform of 1885, under the leadership of K. Kohler,[169] and in the Columbus Platform (1937).[170] The Central Conference of American Rabbis set for itself the task of continuing the labors begun by the previous rabbinical bodies. That the newly won liberty must not be permitted to degenerate into license forms the conviction upon which the CCAR is founded. Since its organization, it has endeavored to create standards for the rebuilding and guidance of the religious life of the American Reform congregations. Its publications (the *Union Prayerbook, Rabbi's Manual, Union Haggadah,* etc.) and its annual deliberations tend to consolidate American Jewry.[171] Its committees on education, social justice, church and state, liturgy, responsa, etc., endeavor to link Reform Judaism, as it faces the tasks of today, with the standards and ideals of historical Judaism. Prior to taking action on any vital issue, it explores the historic position of Judaism on the subject. To keep Reform within the historic channel of Jewish tradition is the aim of the Hebrew Union College in preparing men for the rabbinate. To union with the past and to progressive unfoldment of our faith, every Reform religious school and every house of worship bears eloquent testimony.

In Reform Jewish worship the reading of the Torah still holds the center. Though reserving the right of drawing a line between obsolete regulations and vital ceremonial and ethical precepts, exponents of Reform take their texts and starting points from the Torah. Much of the form and spirit of Reform worship and a considerable part of its contents are in line with traditional standards. Conscientious Reform Jews celebrate — though with less rigor — the festivals prescribed by Jewish tradition. While the social and economic

---

[169] *Proceedings of the Pittsburgh Rabbinical Conference,* published by the CCAR, 1923.

[170] *CCAR Yearbook,* 1937, pp. 94–114. [*Editors' note*: The Columbus Platform was almost completely the work of Samuel S. Cohon.]

[171] A compendium of resolutions and authoritative opinions of the CCAR regarding religious observance is contained in the *Rabbi's Manual,* 1928. [*Editors' note*: Samuel S. Cohon was the unnamed author of the *Manual,* and the editor of the 1923 *Union Haggadah.*]

conditions of our American frontier civilization, playing havoc with our historical Sabbath, impelled some few congregations to assemble for worship on Sundays only, they have not transferred the Sabbath nor uprooted the ethical and spiritual ideals underlying our holy days. Thus far not even the most iconoclastic of our leaders have ventured to alter the dates of our solemn days of Rosh Hashanah and Yom Kippur. These are still the sacred days of all the children of Israel who respond at all to the call of Judaism. Likewise, with but few exceptions, all Reform Jews submit their sons to the Abrahamitic rite. The prohibited degrees of marriage, too, are as binding upon Reform Jews as they are upon the Orthodox.

Principles and Agents of Authority in Reform Judaism

The underlying principles of authority in Reform Judaism have not yet been fully crystallized. However, Reform's rather brief history exhibits certain trends toward such crystallization. To bring these out into the open should prove helpful in guiding the further development.

1. Reform Judaism has unmistakably tended toward the establishment of standards of its own, even though it began by breaking away from certain fixed forms. While it found the *Shulḥan Aruch* inoperative under the changed conditions of Jewish life in Western lands, it has not abandoned all law, ritual, and ceremony. On the contrary, it finds them essential to the preservation of Judaism as a force in the lives of men. If each individual is not to be a law to himself, he must learn to follow standards not of his own making.

2. In line with its fundamental conceptions, Reform presents a revised view of authority. While recognizing the urgency of authoritative guidance in the religious and moral life, Reform cannot support its claims in the manner in which Orthodoxy has done. It cannot prove that God wills this or that practice by citing a verse of Scripture, a saying of the rabbis, or a paragraph from the *Shulḥan Aruch*. The road of faith in modern Judaism, even more than in its past forms, runs along and merges with the paths of reason and human need. Similarly, it is not possible for Reform, under the changed spiritual and intellectual outlook of our day, to impose its authority by threats of punishment in a hereafter or to resort to the arm of the state. Only in countries where religion has the backing of the government can penalties be

employed to bolster its demands. In democracies where church and state are sharply divided, such politics are out of the question. Even if they were feasible, they would clash with the deepest feelings of spiritually minded men. The struggle for religious liberty has deeply impressed the conviction upon the conscience of men that religion is not true to itself unless it comes as the expression of the free personality. The *herem* is a violation of human conscience. We may not look to external restraints to force the modern Jew to conform to the standards of Judaism, at any rate not in free countries. Neither can the weakened force of public opinion be relied upon to exert the necessary pressure. However excellent the beliefs, ethical ideals, and ceremonial observances of Judaism, they can command the heart only if it voluntarily yields itself of them and makes them the rules of its being. The rabbinic ideal of *kabalat ol malchut shamayim beahabah,* "receiving the yoke of the Kingdom of Heaven in love," forms the only basis of authority for us moderns. We must learn to yield ourselves joyously to the divine, and gladly to obey the obligations growing out of this relationship, and to surrender ourselves unreservedly to the dictates of right and of truth as they are interpreted to us by the wisest and the best of our people. By freely assuming the burden of the law, which reveals itself within our own spirits and within the spirit of our people and of humanity, we gain real inward freedom and secure the well-being and the peace which we crave.

As in all former phases of Judaism so in Reform, two factors enter into the nature of authority: (a) the needs of the Jewish people, and (b) their attitude to the divine as expressed in their conceptions of revelation and tradition.

3. The standards of conduct for the individual and the community have ever been prompted and regulated by the sentiments, interests, and ideals that seemed vital to the self-preservation and welfare of our people. *Vehai bahem,* "Live by them," describes the Jewish view of the relation of the commandments to the people. Indeed every religion assumes the power to command the lives of its followers by proving itself useful in their struggle for existence, by aiding them as individuals and as groups to a truer, richer, and purer life.

4. While the welfare of the Jewish people has been the driving force in Judaism, it has been subordinated to the visions of God and of duty, as presented by revelation and tradition. For Reform no less than for Orthodoxy, revelation and tradition constitute permanent elements of religion, though

Reform puts a somewhat different construction upon their nature. Historical criticism has enabled Reform to disengage revelation from the mythological forms which it assumed in the Bible and from the artificial molds into which it was cast in rabbinic literature and theology. It is the primal inspiration of religion, the opening of the eye of the soul to supersensuous reality. In the words of Sabatier, "it may be said to consist of the creation, the purification, and the progressive clearness of the consciousness of God in man — in the individual and in the race."[172] Instead of being the supernatural manifestation of God's will in the distant past, amid the thunders and lightning at Sinai, revelation appears as the progressive disclosure within the souls of godly men of the truths and values most vital for the religious life.

5. Tradition is the means of socializing the inspiration of religious genius. It forms the channel through which revelation comes down to the people. It is the vital process whereby the inspirations of the past continue in the present, whereby the life-forces, social customs, and institutions, the moral and the religious ideals and convictions, hopes, and strivings, experiences, and philosophies of the group, nation, or race are preserved through the ages, and made operative in the present. Without retaining what he has won in the course of his experience, man can make but little progress. It is a mistaken notion that tradition succeeded revelation. As a matter of fact, it operated at the very time when the prophets were at the height of their power and when the Torah was not yet codified. Indeed, as our analysts has shown, much of the Torah continued long as tradition before it became Scripture. "Tradition," Geiger writes, "is the developing power which continues in Judaism as an invisible creative agent, as a certain ennobling something that never obtains its full expression but ever continues to work, transform, and create. Tradition is the animating soul in Judaism, it is the daughter of revelation and of equal rank with her."[173] It has preserved prophecy as a living force, and it has pieced together the broken gleams of the divine vouchsafed to priest, sage, and rabbi. It represents Israel's unbroken aspiration Godward, bridging the generations and linking the ages, and holding out the promise of a future for Judaism.

---

[172] *Outlines of a Philosophy of Religion,* p. 35.

[173] *Judaism and Its History,* pp. 86–87. See R. Ḥananel's comment on Gen. 18:19 in Baḥia b. Asher's Commentary on Genesis.

Single traditions may grow antiquated and lose their worth, but Tradition ever constitutes a creative force by the side of revelation or inspiration. It may be said to represent the oneness of a people's development and "the path of the soul to itself." At no time does tradition become purely static. Beneath its placid surface course the dynamic powers of prophecy, philosophy, and mysticism. Like a mighty stream, it shapes and fructifies the terrain through which it flows. It molds the life of the people and, in turn, expands and grows in response to life's needs.

The progressive nature of revelation and its interrelation with tradition call for the correction of the tendency on the part of some liberals to confine themselves to what they regard as prophetic Judaism. Historical criticism shows that the teachings of the prophets found embodiment in the Torah. Accordingly, what we cherish in the prophets, we treasure also in the Torah. Furthermore, while the prophet's voice speaks to us with authority, it is not confined to the canonical books of the Bible. The *ruah hakodesh* has never wholly disappeared from Judaism. It often manifested itself in rabbinic *haggadah,* in the pure ethical ideals of the *halachah,* in the prayers of saintly souls, in the poems of God-intoxicated singers, and in the *musar* literature.

6. Revelation and tradition must be checked and corrected by reason. In the Bible, as in postbiblical literature, we have learned to distinguish between the temporary and the eternal. Being of human origin, Jewish religious writings are subject to human limitations. Not all that they contain is of equal value. The loftiest ethical and spiritual truths may be found by the side of imperfect interpretations of God, of human nature, and of the motives and forms of obligation. The self-evident character of the one may be absent from the other. Not all that was of value in the past has retained its worth for today, even as not all that seemed true in bygone times continues to be valid in the light of newer knowledge. Accordingly, the prescriptions of the Torah, the Talmud, the codes, etc., while showing the path which the Jewish people have followed toward the realization of the religious life, command our obedience only to the extent to which they aid us in our quest after the divine and help us to maintain ourselves as a united Jewish community. Similarly, past customs can serve us only as means of stimulating our Jewish religious consciousness rather than as absolute standards of conduct.

Seeking to preserve the unity of Judaism and refusing to set itself up as a sect apart, Reform asserts the right of scholarship in each age to interpret the records of both revelation and tradition, to distinguish between their essential and abiding elements and those of secondary and transitory character, and to institute, through concerted action, such modifications in belief and practice as accord with the highest demands of truth and of conscience and with the best interests of the Jewish people and of Judaism. In the best interests of mankind and of religion itself, tradition must be kept as an aid rather than a hindrance to progress. It must be controlled and restrained from turning so rigid and inflexible as to exclude necessary change and possible advance.

7. While Reform takes its position within the intellectualistic stream of Judaism, finding in reason a potent instrument of religious knowledge and life, it does not overlook the fact that there are spheres which remain impenetrable to reason and which may be apprehended only intuitively and felt emotionally. The heart has its reasons as well as the mind. Though placing the ethical and universalistic elements of Judaism in the forefront, Reform recognizes the need of cultivating personal religion and ritual observance in the home and in the synagogue, as well as those distinctive forms which give Judaism its uniqueness. It is learning to take account of individual and social psychology as well as of philosophy in religion. The longings of the soul have no less claim upon men than the demands of the intellect. Symbols, forms, and ceremonies may speak to the heart more forcefully than discursive reason, and offer manna to the hungering spirit. Of such character are the Hebrew language in worship, certain familiar ancient prayers and songs, traditional music, and the Jewish calendar of sacred days. Rich in association and sentiment, they feed the religious consciousness of the Jewish people.

8. Reform Judaism acknowledges further the need of certain agents of authority. No religion can function without the aid of leadership. Reform, like Orthodoxy, while democratic in nature, is dependent upon men specially qualified by virtue of training and character for the presentation of its standards and ideals. The rabbis derive their authority, on the one hand, from the consent of the congregations or communities that entrust themselves to their guidance, and on the other, from their functioning as exponents of the historical Torah, of the authentic ideals, traditions, and needs of the *Keneset Yisrael*. To avoid the chaos that may result from clashing individual interpretations, Reform rabbis have sought to take counsel together and to plan in

concert for the welfare of Jewry and of Judaism. While the rabbinical conferences function as deliberative bodies, their actions and resolutions tend to serve as standards of Jewish practice.[174] To preserve Judaism as "the unifying and creative force" in the life of our people, it becomes imperative for the leaders of Reform to guide themselves consciously by the goal of retaining our historical continuity, refusing to permit the chain of Jewish tradition to be broken through either neglect or irresponsible iconoclasm. The aim of ideal Reform is to foster and develop all that is alive in Judaism and possessed of value, and to remove only that which is dead and which is an impediment to progress. Its further aim is to preserve the pure character of Judaism by guarding against the "strange fires" that a supurious liberalism would offer upon its altar, by introducing ideas and observances derived from alien sources which are subversive of its essential nature.

9. If the development of Reform is to follow the earlier phases of the evolution of Judaism, its beliefs, ideals, and standards will be translated into definite forms. If Judaism is not to evaporate for the modern man into a vague and ineffective sentiment, it is necessary to define not only its principles of belief and moral ideals but also the practices and ceremonies which we deem essential from the standpoint of Reform Judaism, and embody them into a code for the guidance of our people. Avoiding the danger of formalism, i.e., of undue veneration of externals and the consequent disregard of their underlying spirit, such a code would enable us to pay greater regard than we have done hitherto to the concrete ways of living the Jewish religious life. Reform Judaism came to save the modern Jew for Judaism, and Judaism for the modern Jew. It has met the challenge of a changing world by modernizing Jewish life and by beautifying the service of the synagogue. Its appeal has been to reason and to morality. Its next step must be to help the individual Jew recapture the joy of faith. It must touch the emotions as well as the mind if it is to function as a personal force in our lives. In addition to emphasizing social justice and social service, we must revive our faith's poetic and symbolic elements which make for the beauty of holiness.

---

[174] The advisability of establishing a Jewish synod in America was discussed at the Louisville meeting of the CCAR. A collection of opinions on the subject was published by the CCAR under the title *Views on the Synod*, 1905.

Reform no less than Orthodoxy must make demands upon us if it is to evoke the best within us. A religion that does not seek to lead and to correct, that asks for nothing, that is soft and yielding, that is all things to all people is, in reality, nothing to anybody in particular, and consequently of doubtful value to mankind. Only a Judaism rooting itself in the divine, building itself philosophically consistent and ethically exacting, calling for sanctification through self-discipline, probity, and integrity, stressing personal and communal prayer, ceremony, and observance, weaving education and service into the fabric of life, and holding the Jewish people in a strong bond of spiritual brotherhood — only such a religion will bestow blessing on man. Amid the perplexities of our age, such a Reform Judaism must prove a consecrating and regenerative force.

The Unity of God*

A Study in Hellenistic and Rabbinic Theology

The doctrine of Divine Unity climaxed the religious development of the Bible. The teachings of the prophets combine with the commands of the Torah and the wisdom of the sages in affirming the monotheistic faith that the universe was called into existence by the living God, who preserves the highest heavens and sustains the earth, and directs the destinies of men and of nations. This world-embracing creed, proclaimed in the opening words of Genesis, forms the substance of the world-view of the remainder of Scripture and constitutes the foundation of the theocentric view of the Rabbis. By the side of the Creator everything else is a creature. He is the Holy *One*, the Lord of the universe, of humanity, of Israel and of every individual.

Two Biblical documents, in which this crowning achievement of Jewish theology crystallized itself, came to form the basic texts of Rabbinic Judaism: the *Decalogue* and the *Shema*.

The affirmation *anochi adonai elohecha* ("I am the Lord thy God") of the first commandment is completed by the prohibition *lo yihye l'cha elohim aherim* ("Thou shalt have no other gods") of the second.[1] They are the positive and negative forms of the doctrine of divine Unity. God is not truly One if there are other gods besides Him.[2] No nature deities, no man or animal

---

* Published: Hebrew Union College Annual, Vol. XXVI, Cincinnati 1955.

[1] Ex. 20.2–3; Deut. 5.6–7. Josephus, *Antiq.* III.5, 4 combines the two as the first commandment. So, too, R. Ishmael taught that the two were heard from God together. Hor. 8a; Mak. 23a–24b.

[2] Tertullian writes: *Deus si non unus est, non est* — If God is not one, He does not exist. *Against Marcion* I.3.

gods, no creation of man's mind or hand can be placed by His side. He is essentially transcendent, incomparable with anything in existence, high and exalted, eternal and holy.[3]

This doctrine, implicit in the Sinaitic covenant between Israel and God negated — first for Israel, and subsequently for the entire world — the pantheons and the cults of antiquity. It motivated the protracted struggle against Canaanitic Baalism, the astral worship of Assyro-Babylonia and the nature gods of Egypt. It formed the battle cry of Elijah on Mt. Carmel. The response of the assembled hosts to his challenge to choose between YHVH (Lord) and Baal: "The Lord, He is God; the Lord, He is God,"[4] has resounded through the ages. It assumed its classical form in Deut. 6.4, "Hear, O Israel: the Lord is our God, the Lord is one." Hosea had condemned Israel's espousal of other deities as disloyalty to God and as harlotry. "I am the Lord thy God from the land of Egypt, and no other god besides Me shalt thou know, and there is no savior besides Me."[5] Isaiah acknowledged Him as the author and director of the drama of world history and as the Lord of hosts (of heaven) acclaimed by the angel chorus as thrice holy.[6] Jeremiah knew Him as the universal Lord of nature and of humanity, the architect who molds the destinies of nations as a potter molds his clay.[7] "The Lord God is the true God; He is the living God, and the everlasting King." In His name the prophet defied the polytheistic cults: "Thus shall ye say unto them: 'The gods that have not made the heavens and the earth, these shall perish from the earth, and from under the heavens.' He hath made the earth by His power, hath established the world by His wisdom, and hath stretched out the heavens by His understanding."[8] Deutero-Isaiah, confronted by Parsi dualism, protested in God's name: "I am the first, and I am the last, and besides Me there is no god . . . I form the light, and create darkness; I make peace, and create evil; I am the Lord that doeth all these things." As the Master of all

---

[3] Deut. 4.16 ff.; Isa. 57.15.

[4] I Kings 18.39.

[5] Hosea 13.4.

[6] Isa. 10.5 ff.; 6.3.

[7] Jer. 5.22 ff.; 16.19; 18.

[8] Jer. 10.10 ff., reflecting the ideas of Deutero-Isaiah.

creation, He is the hope of all mankind. "Look unto Me and be saved, all the ends of the earth; for I am God and there is none else . . . unto Me every knee shall bow, every tongue shall swear. Only in the Lord, shall one say of Me, is victory and strength. . . In the Lord shall all the seed of Israel be justified, and shall glory."[9]

The prophetic theology served also as a philosophy of history. For the prophets, history formed a continuous whole, with the future growing out of the present and the past. The course of events moved toward a goal, an "end" not merely "of days" but of meaning and purpose. In their minds the popular expectation of the coming day of the Lord, when He would avenge Israel, was transformed into a day of judgment of Israel as well as of the other nations. The consequences of Israel's sinfulness would be her inescapable punishment administered by God in the course of history.[10] The apocalypticists seized upon this belief as the basis for the reign of evil in the world and made it the core of their teaching. For them history is a discontinuity, with the future breaking in upon the present. When God will rise to establish His reign over the world, the power of wickedness will be crushed. The sinful nations will be brought low and God's own people will be vindicated and saved.[11] God will triumph not only over the nations, but also over their gods. He will destroy death itself and wipe away the tears from all faces.[12] With His exaltation, His people will be exalted. All the nations will throng to Mt. Zion to be taught of His ways and to honor His elect.[13] The people, therefore, must prove themselves worthy of their God, who will be a stronghold to the poor and the needy, "a refuge from the storm, a shadow from the heat."[14] Following the judgment and destruction of the wicked nations and their gods, "the Lord shall be King over all the earth; in that day the Lord shall be One, and His name One."[15]

---

[9] Isa. 44.6; 45.7, 22–23, 25.

[10] Isa. 2.12–17; Amos 5.18–20.

[11] Isa. 13.14 ff.; 14.5, 12; 34.2 ff.; 59.15 ff.

[12] Isa. 24.21 ff.; 25.8.

[13] Isa. 2.1–4; 55.5; 56.6–7; 60.3 ff.; Zech. 8.20–23.

[14] Isa. 25.4; cf. Jer. 46.27–28.

[15] Isa. 66.15–16; Zech. 14.9.

The Battleground of Judaism

Having established itself as the central dogma of Judaism, the doctrine of divine unity offered the supreme challenge to heathenism. The unwearying emphasis on this belief by the Jewish masters of post-Biblical literature, can be best understood in the light of the persistent attacks which it drew from anti-Jewish philosophies and competing cults.

In the Graeco-Roman world, the non-Jews were disturbed by the Jewish refusal to acknowledge their gods. As their states rested on community of cult-observances, they looked askance upon anything that threatened to weaken their formal structure.[16] Accordingly, *asebeia*, impiety, was regarded a criminal offense. States like Athens took measures to rid themselves of persons like Socrates who entertained ideas about the gods contrary to those held by the state.[17] The negative attitude of the Jews towards the cults of their neighbors in Egypt and in Graeco-Roman cities could not but evoke resentment. Their aggressive propaganda on behalf of their own religion added fuel to the flames. However, in many instances, the Jewish congregations were, by special grant, immune from persecution for impiety. The attempt to abrogate their immunity and to compel their conformity to the law of *asebeia* ran up against the fact that the immunity was a real grant by the heads of state and was not reachable by local legislation.[18] Consequently, though the Jews gained the enthusiastic approval of some of their neighbors, they did not escape the odium of others. In Egypt, in particular, the feud between the natives and the Jews had been of long standing. From Persian times on, the Jews were identified with the foreign rulers of the land and with a form of worship radically at variance with Egyptian. With the translation of the Torah into Greek, the reputation of the Egyptian Pharaohs was tarnished. The Egyptians retaliated by exposing the Jewish people to ridicule. The Jews were presented by the Egyptian priest Manetho as derived from a race of

[16] Max Radin, *The Jews Among the Greeks and Romans*, ch. XII, pp. 164 ff.
[17] *Against Apion* II.37.
[18] *Antiq.* XIV.10, 216, 241–261.

lepers who worshiped their God in the form of an ass.[19] From Manetho the slander spread to some classical writers.

While their writings have been lost, quotations from them are cited by Josephus in his polemic against Apion. The first of the classical writers quoted is Mnaseas, a rhetorical historian who wrote before the establishment of the Maccabean state. He tells of an Idumean named Zabidius, who duped the Jews by promising to deliver his god, Apollo, into their hands, and contrived to get into the Temple of Jerusalem and remove from there "the golden head of a pack-ass."[20] This calumny reappeared in a variety of forms. It is repeated in a fragment from the writings of Apollonius Molo, a teacher of Caesar and of Cicero, and reiterated in Apion's statement that the Jews adored the head of an ass, and worshiped it with much ceremony. He also circulated the story that Antiochus Epiphanes, on the occasion of his spoliation of the Temple, found there "a head made of gold and worth a high price."[21]

From Apion the libel got to Tacitus, who wrote that the Jews "consecrated an ass in their sacred shrine." He expressly avoids the allegation that the Jews worshiped the statute, thus modifying Apion's words to fit them into the then established fact, which he states, that "the Jews acknowledge one God only, and conceive of Him by the mind alone."[22]

The charge of ass worship was particularly vicious. In Egypt the ass was associated with Typhon, and formed an object of fear and hatred. This slander, therefore, was equivalent to charging the Jews with a kind of "devil-worship," at least of venerating a deity hostile to the Egyptians.[23]

Their imageless worship and their resolute denial of the gods of their neighbors brought upon the Jews the stigma of *atheioi*, "atheists" or *godless*.

---

[19] *Apion* I.25.

[20] *Ibid.* II.9.

[21] *Ibid.* II.7, 5 Posidonius is quoted (Radin, *op. cit.*) to the effect that the innermost shrine of the Temple contained the statue of a long-bearded man, presumably Moses, riding on an ass. So Diodorus (XXXIV. frag.) states that Antiochus found such a statute in the Temple. The charge of ass-worship was transferred to the Christians. See Thackeray's note to *Apion* II.7, 80, p. 325.

[22] *Histories* V. 3 ff. See *J. E.* IV.109.

[23] Radin, *op. cit.*, pp. 170–72; S. A. Cook, note to W. R. Smith's *Religion of the Semites*, p. 690. See also S. Krauss, "Ass-Worship," *J. E.*, II, 222–224.

As thoroughgoing monotheists, the Jews disregarded the gods of the heathen as non-existent, or denounced them as *elilim*, nothings, or *shedim* and *seirim*, demons and satyrs, and as *toebah*, abominations."[24] Molo branded Jews as "atheists and misanthropes."[25] Lysimachus of Alexandria repeats the accusation of misanthropy and charges that they were enjoined "to overthrow any temples and altars of the gods which they found."[26] The elder Pliny denounced them as "a race famous for its insults to the gods."[27]

The forceful measures of Antiochus Epiphanes to win over the Jewish people to Grecian polytheism stiffened their resistance to the point of martyrdom.[28] His claim to being an incarnation of Zeus aroused their abhorrence and branded him as *Epimanes,* the madman. Emperor-worship, like the cults of dying and resurrecting saviors that peopled the pantheons and cults of antiquity, appeared to them as the height of blasphemy.[29] In Roman times, the Jews would not so much as permit the Roman troops to enter Jewish territory with their banners which bore emblems of the Caesars. We hear of Hasidim who would not look upon a coin, because the image of Caesar was engraven upon it.[30]

The national revival which followed the restoration of the state under the Maccabees raised the hope of the fulfillment of the prophetic promise of the conversion of the nations to the worship of the living God.[31] The apocalypticists sounded the theme of the imminence of God's judgment over the nations and the establishment of His reign over them.[32] An unknown author invoked the authority of the mysterious Roman prophetess, the Sibyl, to urge the conversion of the gentiles to the worship of the One God and the pursuit of His laws. In the name of the sovereign and incorruptible Creator, the Eternal,

---

[24] Lev. 17.7; Deut. 32.17; Ps. 106.37; II Chron. 11.15.

[25] *Apion* II.14, 148.

[26] *Apion* I.34.

[27] *Hist. Nat.* XIII. IV, 46, cited Radin, *op. cit.* 195-6.

[28] I Macc. 1-2; II Macc. 6-7.

[29] *Apion* II.6, 73 ff.; *Ant.* XVII.6, 2-4; XVIII.3, 1.

[30] See L. Blau, art. "Worship, Idol," *J. E.* XII, 568-9.

[31] Isa. 2.1 ff.; Mic. 4.1 ff.; Mal. 1.11-12, 14, etc.

[32] Dan. 3.44; 7.13-14.

dwelling on high, who rewards the good and punishes the evil, the Sibyl thundered against the folly of idolatry and the viciousness of immorality. "Be ashamed of making gods of serpents, dogs and cats; ye reverence winged creatures and animals that creep on the earth, and images of stone and statues made with hands, and stones piled together by the roads." Divine judgment will come upon the wicked nations with war and sword and with cataracts of fire and brimstone. "War and pestilence shall come upon all mankind at once, and God shall make the great heaven above frozen" and bring drought over the whole earth. "Hellas, why dost thou put trust in governors, mortal men who are powerless to escape the consummation of death? With what view dost thou proffer vain gifts to the dead and sacrifice to idols? Who has put error in thine heart, that thou shouldst perform these rites and forsake the face of the mighty God? Reverence the name of the Father and forget Him not. Long have the haughty rulers of Greece wrought evil for mankind, holding fast to idols and defunct gods. When the divine wrath will be upon you, ye shall know the face of the great God. And every creature will upraise hands to the broad heavens and shall call for God's help and deliverance from the mighty wrath."[33]

In a calmer mood the author of the Letter of Aristeas utilizes the Euhemeristic philosophy of religion to refute the wisdom of the Greek myth-makers. Euhemerus, a resident at the court of Cassander in Macedonia (circa 316), gave currency to the idea that the gods of the nations were originally heroes who distinguished themselves either as warriors or as benefactors and who, after their death, received divine worship from the grateful people. The author of the Letter turns this theory against the practice of idolatry. Having set up statutes of stone and wood, men acclaim them as the images of inventors of things useful for life, and worship them, despite their being devoid of all feeling. It would be utterly *foolish*, he argues, "to suppose that anyone *became a god* in virtue of his inventions. For the inventors simply took certain objects already created and, by combining them together, showed that they possessed a fresh utility: they did not themselves create the substance of the

---

[33] The Sibylline Oracles, tr. Lanchester in Charles' *Apocrypha and Pseudepigrapha* II, Fragment III.17 ff.; also 1.2 ff.; Bk. III.545–561.

thing, and so it is a vain and foolish thing for people to make gods of men like themselves. For in our times there are many who are much more inventive and much more learned than the men of former days who have been deified, and yet they would never come to worship them." We need hardly speak of the Egyptians and other infatuated people "who place their reliance upon wild beasts and most kinds of creeping things and cattle, and worship them, and offer sacrifices to them both while living and when dead."

In contrast to this folly, the Letter of Aristeas holds out the doctrine of Moes that "there is only one God and that His power is manifested throughout the universe, since every place is filled with His sovereignty and none of the things which are wrought in secret by men upon the earth escapes His knowledge." Not even the evil which man devises escapes God.[34]

The Wisdom of Solomon expands these ideas. The root of idolatry is human folly. From the abundance of good things men do not infer their author. "Neither by giving heed to the works did they recognize the artificer; but either fire, or wind, or swift air, or circling stars, or raging water, or luminaries of heaven, they thought to be gods that rule the world." If the heathen had understanding, "how is it that they did not find the Sovereign Lord of these works?" From the greatness and beauty of created things men should deduce the idea of their creator. Most miserable are they who called the products of human labor gods, artistic creations in gold and silver, in the likeness of beasts, a useless stone, or the carving of a skillful woodcutter in the likeness of a man or animal, painted and set up as an object of prayer.

Modifying the Euhemeristic theory, the author of the Wisdom of Solomon traces idol worship to human error. A father mourning the death of a child orders an image of the child to be prepared, and then honors the image as a god, instituting "mysteries" and solemn rites, which in course of time acquire the force of law. So, too, likenesses of a king are set up to flatter an absent ruler, and are subsequently made the objects of worship. The artificer investing his work with beauty, allures the multitude to worship human beings. Thus a hidden danger is created, because men, in times of stress, invoke "stones and stocks with the incommunicable name."

---

[34] See 132–138, and notes by Andrews in Charles, *Apocrypha and Pseudepigrapha* II, p. 107.

Straying in their knowledge of God, the people live in conflict with His laws, disregarding life and morality, "slaughtering children in solemn rites, or celebrating secret mysteries or holding frantic revels in strange ordinances." They kill one another treacherously, engage in thieving and lying, corruption, faithlessness, perjury, adultery, and wantonness. For the worship of those unnameable idols is the beginning and cause and end of every evil. In the style of Deutero-Isaiah and the Psalmists,[35] the manufacture of idols is derided and their worship mocked. The idols have neither eyes for seeing nor nostrils for drawing breath, for they are made by the hand of mortal man. "Being mortal, he maketh a dead thing with his lawless hands; for he is better than the things he worshipeth. Of the two, he indeed had life, but they never." Special scorn is reserved for Egyptian worship of loathsome, irrational and unclean animals.[36]

The major themes of the propaganda literature, the reality and excellence of monotheism and the delusion of polytheism, the spiritual and moral debasement which idolatry produces and the commercialism which supports its practices and cults, reappear in Philo and in Josephus. Philo grounds his attack on polytheism and idolatry, in his philosophical theology. In his view, it was the true vision of God as a *unity* for which Moses prayed, since the mind may be deluded to conceive of Him as more than one, even as the eye, when it is weak may see double, i.e. one object as two. At the burning bush, Moses was charged by God: "First tell them that I am He who *is*, that they may learn the difference between what is and what is not, and also the further lesson that no name at all can properly be used of Me, to whom alone existence belongs." God is conceived ontologically as "He who truly is," "the truly existent one" and "the cause of all that comes into being." He is also spoken of as "the Mind of the Universe." Philo concludes his treatise on Creation with the five-fold creed: first, "God has been from eternity," thus opposing the atheists who doubt either His eternity or His existence; second, "God is one," contrary to the polytheists who transfer "mob rule" from earth to heaven; third, "the world came into being," opposing the view that the world is eternal, thereby

---

[35] Cf. Isa. 40–41; 44; 46; Pss. 115, etc.
[36] Wisdom 13; 14.12–31; 15.

depriving God of superiority; fourth, "the world, too, is one as well as its Maker," contradicting the ideas of the plurality of worlds: and fifth, "God exercises forethought on the world's behalf." Only the believer in this creed will lead a life of bliss and blessedness because his character is shaped by the truths that piety and holiness enforce.

Philo applies these ideas to his interpretation of the first two commandments of the Decalogue. The major part of humanity, he comments, is under delusion regarding "the transcendent Source of all that exists." "Some have deified the four elements, earth, water, air and fire; others the sun, moon, planets, and fixed stars; others, again, the heaven by itself; others the whole world. But the highest and the most august, the Begetter, the Ruler of the great world-city, the commander-in-chief of the invincible host, the Pilot who ever steers all things in safety, Him they have hidden from sight by the misleading titles assigned to the objects of worship mentioned above. Different people give Him different names: some call the earth Kore or Demeter or Pluto, and the sea Poseidon, and invent marine deities subordinate to Him and great companies of attendants, male and female. They call air Hera and fire Hephastus, the sun Apollo, the moon Artemis, the morning-star Aphrodite and the glitterer Hermes, and all of the other stars have names handed down by the myth-makers, who have put together fables skilfully contrived to deceive the hearers and thus won a reputation for accomplishment in name-giving." So, too, they divided the heaven into two hemispheres, one above the earth and one below it, and called them the Dioscuri.

In contradistinction to these myths Moses forbade the deification of any part of the universe. For the world is in process of becoming, and there was a time when it was non-existent. "But to speak of God as 'not-being' at some former time, or having 'become' at some particular time and not existing for all eternity is profanity."

Intellectual ineptitude prevents many from knowing "the truly Existent because they suppose that there is no invisible and conceptual cause outside what the senses perceive, though the clearest possible proof lies ready at their hand. For while it is with the soul that they live and plan and carry out all the affairs of human life, they can never see the soul with the eyes of the body." Still more difficult it is to behold "the Uncreated and Eternal, the invisible charioteer who guides in safety the whole universe." Anyone who pays to the creatures the tribute due to their Maker is as foolish as he who bestows on subordinates the honor due to their master. It behooves us, Philo pleads, to refrain from worshiping created things, and to devote ourselves with every faculty to "the service of the Uncreated, the Eternal, the Cause of all." "Let us, then engrave deep in our hearts this as the first and most sacred of commandments, to acknowledge and honor one God who is above all, and let the idea that gods are many never even reach the ears of the man whose rule of life is to seek for truth in purity and guilelessness."

Particularly mischievous is the manufacture of idols for worship, of giving shape to stocks and stones and silver and gold, etc., according to human fancy, and filling the habitable world with images and wooden figures and other works of human hands. "For these idolaters cut away the most excellent support of the soul, the rightful conception of the Ever-living God." In their ignorance they fail to comprehend that most "obvious truth which even 'a witless infant' knows, that the craftsman is superior to the product of his craft," both in time and in value. Worst of all some image-makers offer prayers and sacrifices to their own creations. They might well be told that inasmuch as the best of prayers and the goal of happiness is to become like God, they should pray to be made "like their images and thus enjoy supreme happiness with eyes that see not, ears that hear not, nostrils which neither breathe nor smell, mouths that never taste nor speak, hands that neither give nor take nor do anything at all, feet that walk not, with no activity in any parts of your bodies, but kept under watch and ward in your temple-prison, day and night, ever drinking in the smoke of the victims. For this is the one good which you imagine your idols to enjoy." However, "such advice would be received with indignation as savoring of imprecations rather than of prayers."

The Egyptians not only share in general polytheism but have "advanced to divine honors irrational animals, bulls and rams and goats, and invented for each some fabulous legend of wonder." Among them are not only domestic animals, useful for men, but also "the fiercest and most savage of wild animals, lions and crocodiles and among reptiles the venomous asp, all of which they dignify with temples, sacred precincts, sacrifices, assemblies, processions, and the like." They deified also dogs, cats, wolves and among birds, ibises and hawks. Fishes, too, have received divine honors. "What," Philo asks, "could be more ridiculous than all this?" "Indeed," he informs us, "strangers on their first arrival in Egypt before the vanity of the land has gained a lodgment in their minds are like to die with laughing at it," while intelligent people are moved to pity those who venerate these creatures, as men with souls transformed into the nature of those beasts.[37]

Josephus' apologetic of Judaism follows along Philo's lines. Without urging, as Aristobulus and Philo did, that the wisest of the Greeks adopted conceptions of God from Moses, he claims that their teachings bear testimony to the excellence of the Jewish doctrine of the nature and majesty of God. Among them he includes nearly all the philosophers. However, while they confined their philosophy to the select few, Moses had addressed himself to the masses not only of his day but also to their descendants to all future generations in order to make their practice accord with their teaching.

A Greek note appears in Josephus' reference to God as "the blessed being or nature" and in the negative attributes which he applies to God. Divine Unity forms the center of his theology. It is the theme of the first of all the commandments of the Torah. Moses, he writes, represented Him "as One, uncreated and immutable to all eternity, in beauty surpassing all mortal thought, made known to us by His power, although the nature of His real being passes knowledge." He is "perfect and blessed, self-sufficing and sufficing for all, He is the beginning, the middle and the end of all things. By His works and bounties He is plainly seen, indeed more manifest than aught else; but His form and magnitude surpass our powers of description. No materials, however costly, are fit to make an image of Him; no art has skill to conceive and represent it. The like of Him we have never seen, we do not imagine, and it is impious to conjecture." No other explanation of creation is required save His active will; thus dispensing with the idea of the Logos of Hellenistic Judaism. All things issue from Him and exist for Him.

---

[37] *Quaestiones et Solutiones in Genesin* IV.8; *Moses* I.75; *Decalogue* 52–55 and 66–81 (tr. F. H. Colson); *Special Laws* I.1–52; *Allegorical Interpretations* III.97–99; E. R. Goodenough, *By Light, Light*, p. 148; H. A. Wolfson, *Philo*, I, chap. IV.

From God's unity all other unities derive. Like the cosmos, so humanity proceeds from Him who is the Father and determiner of destiny. By virtue of God's unity, Israel, too, is one. Josephus boasts of the homogeneity of religious belief among the Jews, producing "a very beautiful concord in human character" unknown among other peoples. The contradictory ideas about God among the common people and philosophers of other nations, ranging from arguments against His very existence to denials of His providence, are not found among the Jews. "With us," he claims, "all act alike, all profess the same doctrine about God, one which is in harmony with our Law and affirms that all things are under His eye."

The entire Mosaic system centers in the *theocracy*, which makes Israel the servant of God. As the sole ruler of the universe, God assigns the administration of its highest affairs to the entire body of priests under the direction of the high-priest. The constitution by which they are guided is the Torah. By it the whole community is guided. "We have but one temple for the one God . . . common to all as God is common to all."

Josephus' conception of Divine Unity stands in sharpest contrast to all forms of idolatry, whether Egyptian theriolatry or Greek polytheism. He approaches the task of criticizing the foreign cults with reluctance, professing that Moses forbade the Jews to "deride or blaspheme the gods worshiped by others out of respect for the very word God (cf. Ex. 22.27)." However, since the revilers seek "to confute us by a comparison of the rival religions," he is forced to speak out. He gathers courage from the fact that his devastating criticism of the gross and immoral ideas of the Homeric gods was not original with him but was drawn from many writers of "the highest reputation." "Who, in fact," Josephus asks, "is there among the admired sages of Greece who has not censured their most famous poets and their most trusted legislators for sowing in the minds of the masses the first seeds of such notions about the gods?" The fertile imagination of the myth-makers invested the gods with attributes so anthropomorphic and licentious as to evoke the censure and the ridicule of thinking minds. The cause for the spread of these falsehoods Josephus assigned to the legislators who enter upon their tasks without proper knowledge of the nature of God. Hence they allow the poets to invest the gods with all the passions and the painters and sculptors to devise figures of their own imagination.[38]

Liturgic Creed

It is within Jewry that the doctrine of Divine Unity assumed its characteristic expression. As the watchword of Judaism and the bond of Jewish unity, it has evoked the deepest loyalty of the Jewish people. Believing that their very existence depended upon this truth, Jews in all ages have witnessed to it with their lives and often died a martyr's death with the profession of unity on their lips. As a confession of faith, it holds the center in Jewish worship, mornings and evenings.

When the Shema assumed the character of a liturgic creed cannot be stated with certainty. The Mishnah records that together with the Decalogue, the Shema (consisting of three passages: Deut. (a) 6.4–9, (b) 11.13–20, and (c) Num. 15.37–41) served as the core of Jewish prayer-service at the Temple.[39] The Nash Papyrus indicates that the two were joined in the liturgy of Alexandrian Jews in pre-Christian times.[40] To cancel the sectarian claim that the Decalogue represented the entire body of commandments given to Moses at Sinai, it was eliminated from the liturgy of the Synagogue after the fall of the Temple, and the Shema alone was retained.[41]

---

[38] *Antiq.* II.12, 4; *Apion* II.33 ff. (tr. H. St. J. Thackeray). Josephus refers to the Septuagint interpretation of Ex. 22.28, "Thou shalt not revile God." He treats this law also in *Antiq.* IV.8, 10. Philo explains this law on the ground that reviling the gods of the neighbors might lead to retaliation "lest they on their part be moved to utter profane words against Him who truly is." *Special Laws* I.50; *Moses* II.203.

[39] Tamid 5.1; Ber. 11b.

[40] W. F. Albright, "The Nash Papyrus," *Journal of Biblical Literature,* 1937, pp. 145–176. The two passages figuring in the teachings of Jesus may have been used in the worship and instruction of Palestinian Jews outside the Temple as well. See Mt. 19.16 ff.; 22.34 ff.; Mk. 10.17; 12.29–30; Luke 18.18–30.

[41] Jeru. Ber. 1.8; B. Ber. 12a. Philo regarded the Decalogue or the "Ten Covenants" as summaries of the entire Torah. These were spoken by God in person to the people, while the

We are informed that "the pious used to complete the recitation of the Shema at sunrise,"[42] and that it was recited also in the evening, as suggested by Isa. 45.7 and Ps. 72.5. This usage may have been prompted in the first instance by the Parsi practice of hailing the sun at its rising and setting, thus acknowledging Ahuramazda as creator.[43] He is said to have charged the ancestors of the race, who were "created perfect in devotion" by him, to perform devotedly the duty of the law, think good thoughts, speak good words, do good deeds, and worship no demons. Their first act on rising was "to wash themselves thoroughly and their first deeds were to acknowledge that Ahuramazda created the water and earth, the stars, moon and sun, and all prosperity whose origin and effect are from the manifestation of righteousness." Subsequently, enmity entered their minds and they were corrupted, and declared that the evil spirit created the water and earth, etc.[44] The benedictions preceding the Shema (the *yotzer* in the morning and *maarib arabim* in the evening) thus aim to overcome the dualism suggested by the phenomena of light and darkness.

Another factor which probably contributed toward the use of the Shema as a confession of faith was the spirit of martyrdom which came to be the mark of Ḥasidic piety in opposition to Antiochus Epiphanes' forceful spread of pagan worship among the Jews. The Parables (written before 63 B.C.) in the book of Enoch seem to assume such a practice. The pious are assured that their works are known and will be judged by the Lord of Spirits. "Then shall

remaining legislation of the Torah He gave through Moses. A similar view regarding the Decalogue is expressed in Tanḥuma, Vayelech, 2. For other opinions see Mechilta, Baḥodesh, ed. Lauterbach, Vol. II, p. 228 and note; Makkot 23a–24b; Pesikta R., ed. Friedman, p. 111a and notes; L. Ginzberg, *Legends*, Vol. VI, p. 45, note 243.

[42] Ber. 9b; Jeru. Ber. 2.1.

[43] *Sacred Books of the East*: *Pahlavi Texts* I, 15.6 ff. See K. Kohler, *The Origins of the Synagogue and Church*, ch. XIV.

[44] Cf. *Zend Avesta* II.351; III.111 ff.; *Bundahis* XV.6 ff. Ch. XXX.5 states that by Ahuramazda "corn was created so that, scattered in the earth, it grew again and returned with increase [cf. the benediction: המוציא לחם מן הארץ]. . . . when by me a son was created and fashioned in the womb of a mother, and the structure severally of the skin, nails, blood, feet, eyes, ears, and other things was produced." (Cf. Job 10.8 ff. and אשר יצר את האדם בחכמה וכו' Ber. 60b).

they all with one voice speak and bless, and glorify and extol and sanctify the name of the Lord of Spirits." Also the hosts of heaven, the angels, *cherubim*, *seraphim* and *ophanim* will be summoned to "raise one voice, and bless and glorify and exalt in the spirit of faith, and in the spirit of wisdom, and in the spirit of patience, and in the spirit of mercy, and in the spirit of judgment and of peace, and in the spirit of goodness, and shall all say with one voice: Blessed is He, and may the name of the Lord of Spirits be blessed forever and ever." The repentant "kings and the mighty" shall acknowledge: "We have now learned that we should glorify and bless the Lord of kings and Him who is King over all kings."[45]

Josephus considers the recitation of the Shema "twice each day, at the dawn thereof and when the hour comes for turning to repose" as an ordinance of the Torah which goes back to Moses.[46] The Talmud records a difference of opinion regarding the antiquity of the practice. While one view considers it Scriptural (i.e. Mosaic), another regards it of Rabbinic origin.[47] The Sifre states that on his deathbed, Jacob after admonishing each one of his twelve sons separately, addressed them collectively: "Is there perchance a division in your hearts concerning the Creator?" They answered: "Hear, O Israel our father, even as there is no division in your heart concerning the Creator so there is none in ours concerning Him. The Lord is our God, the Lord is one." Jacob responded: "Praised be His name whose glorious kingdom is forever."[48] R. Berechya and R. Ḥelbo cite the opinion of Samuel that this is what the Jewish people say daily, morning and evening: "Hear, O Israel out of the cave of Machpela! That which you commanded us is still observed by us: the Lord is our God, the Lord is one."[49] R. Pinḥas bar Ḥama is of the opinion that Israel obtained the privilege of reciting the Shema at the time of the giving of

[45] Enoch 61.5 ff.; 63.4; see Suffrin, Art. "God," Hastings, *Encyclopedia of Religion and Ethics*, VI, 298.

[46] *Antiq.* IV.8.13 (212–213). The content of the passage indicates that the Shema and not prayer in general is meant.

[47] Ber. 21a.

[48] Sifre, Deut., Vaethanan 3.31 (to Deut. 6.4); Targum Jerushalmi to Gen. 49.2; Pesaḥim 56a.

[49] Gen. R. 98.3.

the Law at Sinai, for God opened His revelation with the declaration: "Hear, O Israel, I am the Lord your God," and the assembled hosts responded: "The Lord is our God, the Lord is one." And Moses spoke: "Praised be the name of His glorious kingdom forever."[50]

Accordingly, the recitation of the Shema came to be styled as "accepting the yoke of the Kingdom of Heaven." Abudraham interprets the recitation of the Shema as bearing witness to one's faith in God's unity. Hence the texts write large the *ayyin* of the word *shema* and the *dalet* of *ehad*, spelling *ed*, witness.[51]

The Rabbinic Defense

Though monotheism established itself as the basic doctrine of Judaism, the danger of the recurrence of polytheism, which pervaded the ancient world, continued to menace the Jewish people not only in the diaspora but also in Palestine and in the Jewish centers of Babylonia. Hence the zeal of the Tannaim and Amoraim to check the inroads of polytheism. Their lines of reasoning are in basic accord with those used by the masters of Hellenistic Judaism.

The Rabbinic attitude toward polytheism was dictated by the logic of monotheism. This may be conveniently noted in the comments of the Mechilta on the first two commandments of the Decalogue.[52] The opening words of the first commandment stress God's oneness amid His varied manifestations. At the Red Sea He revealed Himself as a warrior doing battle against Israel's foes (Ex. 15.3). At Sinai He appeared as an elder full of compassion (Ex. 24.10). Subsequently He showed Himself "like the very heavens for clearness" (ibid.) and "thrones were placed" and "a fiery stream issued and came forth before

---

[50] Deut. R. to Deut. 6.4; see Kasher, *Torah Shelema, Vayehi*, p. 1775, note.

[51] Abudraham cites another explanation of the word Shema as forming an abbreviation of שאו מרום עיניכם, "lift up your eyes on high," and שדי מלך עולם "the almighty King of the universe." *Sefer Abudraham*, ed. Amsterdam, p. 30a.

[52] Bahodesh, 5–6; Shirata to Ex. 15.3; Kaspa, 4 to Ex. 34.23; Sifre, Vaethanan to Deut. 6.4. On the entire subject, see A. Marmorstein, "The Unity of God in Rabbinic Literature," *HUCA*, I, pp. 467–499; and *Rabbinic Studies*, 1950, pp. 72–105.

Him" (Dan. 7.9–10). Not to afford the nations an excuse for the claim that there are two sovereignties, God specified: "I am the Lord thy God." I am He who was in Egypt, and I am He who was at Sinai. I am He who was in the past, and I am He who will be in the future. I am He who is in this world, and I am the selfsame who will be in the world to come (Isa. 44.6).

While the Eternal is "the God of all flesh" (Jer. 32.27), he is in a special sense "the God of Israel," because He conferred His name particularly upon the people dedicated to Him. Having accepted His bounty and His sovereignty, Israel is bound to observe His decrees and to avoid the worship of all deities besides Him. All worship other than His constitutes *aboda zara* "foreign worship" or *akum (abodat kochabim umazzalot)*, "the worship of stars and planets." On the ground of a detailed examination of each word and phrase of the second commandment, the Rabbis prohibited not only the making of idols but also the possession of those already made. Their designation as *elohim* in the face of the Biblical denial of their reality[53] is taken to mean "those whom others call gods." The word *aherim* is interpreted as "holding back" the coming of goodness into the world, also as "turning their worshipers into 'others' [i.e. perverting them] or as those who act like strangers to their worshipers." In the words of the prophet regarding the idol: "Yea, though one cry unto him, he cannot answer, nor save him out of his trouble."[54] R. Jose takes the indefinite way of referring to idols, i. e. without specifying their names, as intended to indicate their worthlessness. R. Eliezer explains the expression "other gods" as signifying that the idolaters manufacture for themselves new gods every day. If one owns an idol of gold and needs the gold, he replaces it with one of silver; if he has a silver idol and needs the silver, he makes another one out of copper. If he has a copper idol and needs the copper, he replaces it with one of iron, of tin or of lead. Hence the expression "new gods that came newly up."[55]

R. Isaac remarks that if we were to enumerate all the idols there would not be enough parchment in the world on which to write out their names.

---

[53] Isa. 37.19.
[54] Isa. 46.7.
[55] Deut. 32.17.

Among idols, R. Ḥanina b. Antigonos includes any fetish whose power is acknowledged, "even if it be a chip of wood or a piece of potsherd." R. Jehuda Hanasi interprets the words *elohim aḥerim* as "gods that are later than the last of creation," i.e. man who calls them "gods."

The expression "before Me" was taken to exclude the thought that the prohibition of idolatry applied only to the generation of the Exodus. The words "before Me" signify that "even as I live and abide forever and for all eternity, so you and your son and your son's son to the end of all generations shall not worship idols."

The further statement, "thou shalt not make unto thee a graven image" was understood as prohibiting not only an image that is engraven, but also a solid one, a plant, a tree, a stone, or an image of any metal or any figure, whether of cattle, beasts, birds, fishes, locusts or reptiles, of stars, of angels, *cherubim* or *ophanim*,[56] even representations of the deep, of darkness, or of reflected likenesses. "Scripture has pursued the evil inclination so as to leave no room for any pretext of permitting idolatry." The words "thou shalt not have them nor serve them" evoked the comment that not only does Scripture condemn the two acts together, but each one by itself.

The objectionable anthropopathism of the words "I the Lord am a jealous God" is removed by R. Jehuda Hanasi's comment that Scripture means to say that "God controls jealousy, not that jealousy has power over Him." Similarly, Ps. 121.4, "Behold, He that keepeth Israel doth neither slumber nor sleep" signifies that He rules over slumber, not that slumber has power over Him. Another explanation is: "I zealously exact punishment for idolatry, but I am merciful and gracious in other matters."

As to God's jealousy toward idols, a philosopher asked R. Gamaliel: Why is God jealous of the idolaters rather than of the idols? The sage replied with a parable: It is like unto a man who had a son who named his dog after his father. With whom is the father angry, with the son or with the dog? The philosopher objected: "You call the idol 'dog.' Has it no substance? Once a fire broke out in our province and destroyed all buildings, but the house of the idol was spared. Was it not because the idol could take care of itself?" Gamaliel

---

[56] Cf. Ezek. 1.5 ff.

answered with another parable: "It is like a king who had to put down a revolt in a province. When he waged war, was it against the living or the dead?" The philosopher retorted: "You call the idol a 'dog,' and you call it 'dead.' If so, why does not God destroy idolatry from the world?" Gamaliel replied: "If men served only useless objects, God might have destroyed them, but they worship the sun, moon and stars and planets, brooks and valleys. Shall he destroy the world because of the fools?"[57]

Idolatry was regarded as the first of the cardinal sins which the Jew must avoid at the very cost of life.[58] Whoever acknowledges idols negates the entire Torah.[59] Departure from the Torah is equivalent to attachment to idolatry.[60] The sin of the golden calf stands out as Israel's gravest offense, the effect of which is still felt. One must not look at images. The very thought of idolatrous worship was prohibited.[61]

While Jews were forbidden to mock at anything holy, it was deemed meritorious to deride idols.[62] Akiba held that the names of idols may be caricatured.[63] This may be the intention of calling Baal Zebub, Baal Zebul in the New Testament.[64] The Talmud speaks of sacrifices to idols as *Zebel*, manure.[65] The Tosephta enjoins that on beholding an idol, one was to say: "Blessed be the long-suffering One." When seeing a place from which idolatry was removed, he was to say: "Blessed be He who plucked out strange worship from our land. May it be Thy will, O Lord our God, that idolatry be removed from our land and from all dwelling places of Israel, and may the hearts of their worshipers be turned to serve Thee."[66]

---

[57] See also the parallel in Ab. Zar. 54ab.

[58] Pes. 25a.

[59] Sifre, Deut., 54.

[60] Sifre, Num., 43.

[61] Tos. Sab. 17.1 (ed. Zuckermandel, p. 136).

[62] Meg. 25b; see Mechilta, Kaspa, 4 to Ex. 23.13.

[63] Sifre, Deut., 61.

[64] See marginal notes in the revised standard ed. of the N. T., to Mat. 10.25; 12.24, 27; Mk. 3.22; Lk. 11.15, 18; T.K.C., art. "Beelzebub," *Enc. Biblica*, I, 514–515.

[65] Jeru. Ber. 9.1; Ab. Zara 18b, 49a.

[66] Tos. Ber. 7.2, cf. Mishnah Ber. 9.1; Sifre, Deut. 61. See above note 38 on the attitude of Hellenistic Judaism.

Practical necessity led the Jews who lived among idolaters to adopt a more tolerant attitude. Thus the command in Deut. 12.2–3, to destroy all heathen objects of worship, was limited by the Rabbis to Palestine. "In the land of Israel thou art commanded to persecute (idolatry), but thou art not commanded to persecute it outside of the Land."[67]

Witnessing to God's unity came to represent the distinguishing mark of a Jew. "Whoever denies idolatry is considered a Jew." *Ish yehudi* is defined as *yehidi*, "one who professes the unity of God."[68] Unity acquired the meaning of *reality*. A haggadah preaches: "From the start of creation, 'the beginning of Thy word is truth.'" The idea is derived from the end letters of the first three words of Gen. 1.1 (*bereshit bara elohim*), which were arranged to spell EMeT — truth. The word *elohim* in this verse is defined as *truth*, as we find in Jeremiah 10.10 "and the Lord God is truth."[69] This verse supports the thought that "God's signet is truth."[70] A late Midrash states: "The Holy One is called truth; the throne which He occupies from of old is truth; His presence faces loving kindness and truth; all His words are truth; all His judgments are judgments of truth; and all His paths are loving kindness and truth."[71]

One opinion explains the first two letters of *EMet* as an abbreviation of E*lohim ḥayyim* M*elech olam*, "the living God and everlasting King." Another view, paralleled by comments of Philo and of Josephus states: "*Aleph* is the first letter of the alphabet, *Mem* the middle and *Tav* the end, thus teaching: "'I (God) am the first,' I have not derived My divinity from another; 'and besides Me there are no gods,' I have no partner; 'and with the last one I am the same One,' for I shall not hand over My divinity to another."[72]

God's eternity is an aspect of His unity. In sharpest contrast to the mystery religions which centered in the belief in dying and reviving gods,

---

[67] Meg. 13ab.

[68] Esther R. to Esther 2.5.

[69] Gen. R. 1.10, the text as given in the Yalkut Gen. 1.

[70] Gen. R. 81.2; Deut. R. 1.10; Cant. R. 1.9; Sanh. 64a; Jeru. Sanh. 1.1.

[71] Alpha Beth of R. Akiba in Eisenstein's *Ozar Midrashim* II, 408. The proof texts are: Isa. 16.5; Ps. 89.15; 119.160; 19.16; 25.10.

[72] Isa. 44.6; 41.4.

Judaism affirmed that God is from everlasting to everlasting. A Rabbinic prayer reads: "Thou wast ere yet the world was created. Thou has been since its creation. Thou art in this world and Thou wilt be in the world to come."[73] He transcends time as He transcends space. He is without beginning and without end. "All things decay but God does not decay."[74] He is not merely the living God but He imparts life or being to the Universe.[75] He has created and preserves it; and should the world pass away, He will continue to endure. The words in Hannah's prayer, *"en biltecha"* — "there is none besides Thee"[76] are read *"en lebalotecha"* — "There is none to wear Thee out." Human beings are outlasted by their works. God outlives His work. "An artist dies and his painting remains. Not so God! His creations die and He lives and abides forever and ever."[77] With deified emperors in mind, the following parable is advanced: A king came to a province. Pleased with the praise accorded him by its residents, he promised them public works, bath houses, and a water conduit. He went to sleep and did not wake again. Where is he and where are his promises? It is not so with God. "The true God, He is the living God, and the everlasting King."[78] The exclamation "Who is like unto Thee, O Lord, among the gods!" is explained: Who is like unto Thee among those who serve Thee in the heavens;[79] who is like unto Thee among those who call themselves gods — Pharaoh, Sennacherib, Nebuchadnezzar, the prince of Tyre![80] Who is like unto Thee among those who are deified by others and in whom there is no substance, of whom it is said: They have mouths but they speak not![81] He is not only *one* but *unique*. Reference to other gods is simply a concession to human speech.

[73] Yalkut Vaethanan 836. See also Mech., Shirata, 4; Sifre, 31 to Deut. 6.4, end.

[74] Lev. R. 19.2.

[75] Neh. 9.6.

[76] I Sam. 2.2.

[77] Ber. 10a; Meg. 14a; Tanh. Tazria, 3; Midr. Ps. 18.26; Midr. Sam. 5.

[78] Jer. 10.10; Lev. R. 26.1.

[79] Ex. 15.11; Ps. 89.7-9.

[80] Ezek. 29.9, 3; Isa. 36.20; 14.14; Ezek. 28.2.

[81] Ps. 115.5.

Gnostic Dualism

The doctrine of Divine Unity encountered the opposition of the Gnostic sects which appeared as a threat to Judaism as well as to Christianity in the early centuries of the common era. Gnosticism was not primarily an intellectual system aiming to reconcile philosophical reflection with religion, but a body of knowledge claimed to have been based on revelation and was to be accepted on faith and guarded as a secret. Its ultimate goal was personal salvation or the assurance of a fortunate destiny of the soul after death. The central object of Gnostic cults was "a redeemer-deity who has already trodden the difficult way which the faithful [one] has to follow."[82]

The esotericism of Gnosticism partly accounts for the obscurity of its origin and of its chracter. Its extant expression shows the syncretistic nature of the movement, combining elements of Babylonian, Persian and Greek thought with Egyptian magic. These were variously merged with Jewish teaching. Stray evidence points to a pre-Christian type of Gnosis in Judaism itself. It is probably against the danger of engaging in its hidden knowledge, that Ben Sira warned his pious readers.[83] The Essenes seemed to have possessed some of its secret lore. The Apocalypticists, as evidenced by Enoch and its kindred literature, were attracted by its secrets. The mystic lore concerning Creation and the Throne Chariot, the divine Name, angelology, etc. preserved in Rabbinic literature and forming the basis of the Kabbalah is of this character. The Rabbinic adepts of this type of *Gnosis* included R. Johanan b. Zakkai and some of his leading disciples.[84]

As a mysterious doctrine it was imparted only to initiates.[85] The Mishna interdicts the exposition of Creation before as many as two disciples and of the Chariot before even one unless he be specially endowed with wisdom and with an intuitive understanding.[86] Like magic formulae, so this mystic lore was

---

[82] W. Bousset, art. "Gnosticism," *Encycl. Brit.,* 11th ed. Vol. XII, 153.

[83] Sirach 3.21–22.

[84] See "Maase Bereshit" and "Maase Merkaba," Eisenstein's *Ozar Midrashim* II, 311–319.

[85] Cf. Sifre to Deut. 13.7 on בסתר.

[86] *Hacham u-mebin midaato.* (Cf. *Gnostikos*) Hag. 2.1; Tos. Hag. 2.3.

believed to possess the power of initiating action in the upper and lower spheres. Hence Johanan b. Zakkai refused to expound the Chariot before his disciple Eleazar b. Arach. When the disciple surprised the master by discoursing on the subject before him, the *Shechinah* and the ministering angels descended, and a heavenly flame surrounded the trees of the field, which burst forth with song. When two other scholars discussed the Chariot, clouds covered the bright summer sky, the likeness of a rainbow appeared, and the ministering angels thronged to listen.[87]

There were further reasons for withholding this mysterious lore from all save the specially endowed. The Mishna admonishes that "whoever pries into four things would better not have been created: what is above [creation], what below, what aforetime, and what hereafter." Such investigations were on a par with "disregarding the honor of the Creator."[88] They "produce jealousy, enmity, and strife between Israel and God."[89]

The very basis of Gnosticism lay in dualism. The world of good and the world of evil are sharply contrasted, the divine world and the material world, the world of light and the world of darkness. In many Gnostic systems no attempt was made to derive one from the other. Men like Basilides, Valentinus and Bardesanes were thorough dualists in their theology. The fall of God into the world of matter was a favorite theme of Gnostic systems. Thereby insensate matter was animated with life and activity. Then arose the powers, both partly and wholly hostile, who held sway over the world. Such figures of fallen deities are Sophia (i.e. Aḥamoth = Ḥochma?) among the Ophites, Helena among the Simmioni, or the *Primal Man* among the Naaseni. In the Valentinian system the fall of Sophia takes place within the godhead, and Sophia, inflamed with love, plunges into Bythos, the highest divinity. The lower world is thus derived from the suffering and passions of fallen divinity.

An approach to a monistic philosophy appears in the system of emanations of Basilides. It assumes that from the highest divinity emanated a somewhat

---

[87] B. Hag. 14b ff.; Jer. Hag. 2.1; Sukka 33b. See Blau, art. "Gnosticism," *J. E.*, V, 683.

[88] Hag. 2.1.

[89] B. Sab. 116b; Jer. Sab. 16.1; Tos. Sab. 14.4. The word for scrolls (gilyonim) may signify *evangelion*. See Levy, *Wörterbuch*, under אָוֶן, I, 41.

lesser world, from this world a second, and so on, until the divine element of life became so weakened and attenuated as to have made possible the appearance of the wholly evil world. The nineteenth and the twentieth books of the Clementine Homilies represent the devil as the instrument of God. Christ and the devil figure as the two hands of God, Christ the right hand and the devil the left. The devil has power over this world epoch, and Christ over the next. The characteristics of the devil are very much like those of the God of the Old Testament.[90]

The Gnostic world of evil is full of active energy and of hostile powers derived from Persian dualism. This idea of two hostile powers within the world combined with the Greek dualism of the opposition between spirit and matter into the notion of the corporeal world as the seat of evil, constantly treating the bodily existence of mankind as essentially evil and the separation of the spiritual from the physical as the object of salvation. "Out of the combination of these two dualisms," Bousset concludes, "arose the teaching of Gnosticism, with its thoroughgoing pessimism and fundamental asceticism."[91]

Gnostic speculation was particularly dangerous since a dualistic trend appeared in Judaism as an expression of piety. Thus the Essenes associated only the good in nature and in human experience with God, accounting for evil as the action of demonic powers.[92]

Of the four rabbis who entered the realm of Gnosis (the *Pardes*) only Akiba came out unhurt. Ben Azzai beheld the mysteries and died. Ben Zoma lost his reason. Elisha b. Abuya became an apostate.[93] What led him to

[90] Irenaeus writes that the Ophites affirmed that "the serpent cast down had two names, Michael and Samael." *Haer.* I.30, 9.

[91] *Op. cit.*

[92] K. Kohler and E. G. Hirsch, art. "Dualism," *J. E.*, V, 5; I Enoch, 15; G. F. Moore, *Judaism*, Vol. 3, note 110; cf. Ber. 5.3; B. Ber. 33b; Meg. 25a; I Cor. 9.9–10.

[93] Cf. Ascension of Enoch and of Paul. II Cor. 12.1–4; Hag. 2.1; Cant. R. on Cant. 1.4. The name *Aḥer* that was attached to Elisha may express the idea of *dualist* as distinguished from מיחד for one who confesses the unity of God. Thus the Midrash observes that if you change the letter *dalet* of the word *eḥad* in the Shema into a *resh*, thus reading *aḥer*, you destroy the world. Tanḥ., Bereshit I; Lev. R. 19.2. The expression דרך אחרת stands for *Minut*, Gnostic heresy. Tos. Ber. 7.20. Z. Frankel takes it to connote Christianity. See his commentary Jeru. Berachot 9.1.

apostasy, according to the Palestinian Gemara, was his concern with the problem of evil. He noted one man who disregarded the law of Deut. 22.7, without suffering ill effects, while another who fulfilled the law scrupulously was killed by a serpent. Again he beheld the bleeding tongue of a martyred scholar dragged by a dog. "Is this the tongue that uttered words of Torah, and this be its reward?" he protested. "It seems," he concluded, "that there is no reward for righteousness and no resurrection of the dead" (i. e. he rejected the belief in a final balance in the hereafter).[94] The Babylonian Gemara accounts for Elisha's defection from Judaism on the ground that on his ascent to Paradise he beheld Metatron seated while recording the merits of Israel. This independent behavior of Metatron in the presence of the Holy One led Elisha to conclude that there are "two sovereignties."[95]

The Christian Gnostics derived their ideas from Jesus himself and from his disciples with whom they claimed to have been connected by a secret tradition. While Jesus was in complete agreement with Pharisaic Judaism in affirming the unity of God,[96] his identification in the minds of his followers with the supernatural Messiah or with the Son of Man of the book of Enoch furnished the basis for dualistic teaching in the early church. He was quoted as saying: "We know that we are of God, and the whole world is in the power of the evil one." He was further reported to have stated: "Now is the judgment of this world, now shall the ruler of this world be cast out; and I when I am lifted up from the earth, will draw all men to myself."[97] Paul speaks of his ascent to heaven in a moment of ecstasy where he beheld the Christ. The figure of Christ represented for him "the likeness of God." He acknowledged God the Father "from whom are all things and for whom we

---

[94] Jeru. Ḥag. 2.1.

[95] Ḥag. 15a. See Levy, *Wörterbuch* III.87, under מטטרון. See below notes 132–137. Metatron's recording Israel's merits seems to identify him with Michael.

[96] According to Mark 12.29, Jesus quoted the Shema, Deut. 6.4–5, as the greatest commandment and based upon it the command of Lev. 19.18 to love one's neighbor. While the parallel passages in Matthew 19.16 ff., 22.34 ff. and Luke 18.18–30 omit the Shema, they record his belief in the unity of God. It forms the foundation of his preaching regarding the Fatherhood of God and of His Kingdom. See Sermon on the Mount. Mat. 5–7.

[97] I John 5.19; John 12.31.

exist, and one Lord, Jesus Christ, through whom are all things and through whom we exist." Opposing him is "the prince of the power of the air, the spirit that is now at work in the sons of disobedience." The Christian struggle, he assured his followers, was not "against flesh and blood, but against the principalities, against the powers, against the world rulers of this present darkness, against the spiritual hosts of wickedness in the heavenly places." He is ever aware of the "flaming darts of the evil one."[98] The faith and mission of the early Church crystallized themselves in the formula of Matthew 28.19: "Make disciples among the nations, baptizing them in the name of the Father and of the Son and of the Holy Spirit."[99]

The Christian Gnostics make these dualistic elements the basis of their mythologies. Particularly instructive is the example of Marcion. His interest was not theoretical but practical, viz. faith in Jesus Christ and in his Father as a means of salvation. That faith issued in an ascetic life which demanded the rejection of the work of the Creator as much as human conditions allowed. Only celibates were admitted to baptism. The resurrection of the body was denied, since matter is inherently evil. Salvation was only for the spirit.

Marcion differed from the Gnostics in excluding any doctrine that could not be derived from his interpretation of the Jewish or Christian Scriptures. His lost work, named *Antitheses,* containing proofs of his theology, derived from Old Testament statements about God, placed side by side with the opposing utterances of Jesus and Paul. His exegesis combined a high estimate of the objective truth of the Old Testament as a historical document — avoiding allegorical explanations such as were current among the Gnostics — with a startlingly audacious criticism of the New Testament, ruthlessly cutting away such books and portions of books as did not fit his preconceived notions, and re-editing the text on subjective grounds. Finding Luke best suited to his theology, he adopted this gospel, though in mutilated and altered form, as the sole reliable portion of the historical writings of the New Testament. Of the apostles he singled out Paul as the only master, accepting ten of his epistles as

[98] II Cor. 12.1–4; I Cor. 8.6; II Cor. 4.4; Ephesians 2.2; 6.12, 16. See also Col. 2.9; Phil. 2.6–11.

[99] Another trinitarian statement appears in I John 5.6–8.

genuine, with the usual deletion and alteration of portions that did not fit into his system.[100]

The basic discrepancy between the two Testaments, Marcion found in the doctrine of God. Following the Syrian Cerdo, who had some connection with the Gnostics, he maintained that the just God of the Old Testament was other than and inferior to the New Testament God of goodness and of lovingkindness. According to Tertullian, Marcion arrived at his dualistic theology by "morbidly brooding over the question of good and evil. He was further stimulated by a saying of Jesus, reported in Luke 6.43 ff., that "the good tree bringeth not forth corrupt fruit, neither the corrupt tree good fruit." Finding further that Isa. 45.7 declares in the name of the Creator, "I am He that createth evil," Marcion "applied to the Creator the figure of the corrupt tree bringing forth evil fruit, that is, moral evil, and then presumed that there ought to be another god, after the analogy of the good tree producing its good fruit. Accordingly, finding in Christ a different disposition, as it were — one of a simple and pure benevolence — differing from the Creator, he readily argued that in his Christ had been revealed a new and strange divinity." The One deity is "judicial, harsh, mighty in war; the other mild, placid, and simply good and excellent.[101]

For all their antagonism to the Torah, the anti-Jewish Gnostics, in keeping with their syncretistic tendencies and through their alliance with Christianity, recognized —if only for argument sake — the validity of the Torah and utilized some of its teachings in constructing their heretical systems. They turned to it also for weapons with which to fight Judaism. They used the opening chapters of Genesis as the framework of their emanationist cosmogonies. The numerous divine names in the Bible served them as arguments for the plurality of gods or of persons in the Godhead and for a dualistic view of the world. They distinguished between the supreme God and the God of Israel. The latter, they contended, could not be the supreme God since much that is credited to Him in the Torah cannot be reconciled with such a being. They, therefore, insisted that while *elohim*

---

[100] N. McLean, art. "Marcionism," Hastings, *Encycl. Rel. and Ethics,* VIII, 408.

[101] Irenaeus, *Haeres.* I.27,1; Tertullian, *Against Marcion,* I.2,6.

(theos) designates the Supreme God, who is the source of goodness, YHVH is
the God of this world, i. e. the *Demiurgos,* who fashioned the material
universe, the satanic cause of evil and of rigid justice. Attaining its most
radical expression in Marcionism, this anti-Jewish viewpoint underlies all
Gnostic systems.

Rabbinic theology countered these Gnostic doctrines by careful reinterpretation of the significance of the divine names. The Gnostic distinction
between *elohim* and YHVH may account for the Rabbinic emphasis on the
two as expressions of the attributes of justice and of mercy by which God rules
the world. Their elevation of *elohim* above YHVH is probably the reason
which led the Rabbis to minimize its use. We have noted the attempt of the
Jewish authorities to reintroduce the Tetragrammaton in personal greetings
in order to overcome the opinions of the "impious" (Peruzim), a term referring to Jewish Hellenizers and other sectarians whether Gnostic or Christian.[102] This may also account for the avoidance of the use of *Elohim* "in the
schools and the synagogues of the first four centuries of Palestine except in
quotations from the Bible, in prayers and magic."[103]

The Gnostic contention further explains the shift in Rabbinic interpretation of *Elohim* and YHVH. A. Marmorstein has shown that originally the
Rabbis identified YHVH with the attribute of justice and *Elohim* with the
attribute of mercy.[104] This view underlies the teaching of Philo. *Theos* =

---

[102] See "The Name of God," (this volume, p. 152).

[103] A Marmorstein, *Old Rabbinic Doctrine of God,* pp. 67–72. It is used in combination
with the Tetragrammaton, in the first person possessive, with the patriarchs and with Israel.
See Kassovsky, *Concordance Totius Mischnae,* I, 151, sub *El.* For the significance attached to
the use of these names see Tos. Ber. 7.20. הפותח ביוד ה' וחותם יוד ה' הרי זה חכם, באלף ולא בדלת
וחותם ביוד ה' הרי זה בינוני, ביד ה' וחותם באלף ולא בדלת הרי זה בור, באלף ולא בדלת וחותם באלף ולא
בדלת הרי זה דרך אחרת   Cf. Jeru. Ber. 9.1 and comment of Z. Frankel.

L. Finkelstein claims that "the contemporaries of R. Gamaliel II never used the term 'ה
אלהינו in their prayers" and makes its presence or absence one of the criteria in dating prayers
— "Development of the Amida," *JQR,* n. s. 1925, p. 4 f. For a criticism of this view see
Marmorstein, *op. cit.,* pp. 70–71.

[104] Mech. Pisḥa, 7, 10a, ed. Lauterbach I, p. 55: אני ה' בשבועה אני נפרע מהם. קו"ח ומה אם
מדת פרענות מעוטה אמר הקב"ה לעשות ועשה, מדה מרובה על אחת כמה וכמה. The Tetragrammaton is
used here in connection with punishment: "I am YHVH — Under oath I declare that I shall

Elohim represents *Euergetes* the good, the God of love and of benevolence and *Kyrios* = YHVH (*Adonai*) denotes lordship, rulership, judgment.[105] However, a reversed norm appears in the Sifre to Deut. 3.24: "Wherever the term YHVH occurs, it represents the attribute of mercy (as in Ex. 34.6); wherever *Elohim* is used, the attribute of justice is meant" (as in Ex. 22.8, 27).[106] This reinterpretation of the meanings of YHVH and *Elohim* stems from the desire to emphasize that the distinguishing characteristic of the God of Israel is not strict justice but benevolence and compassion. Hence the designation of God as *Raḥamana*, the Merciful One.[107] The Rabbis found support for their view in Ps. 145.9: "YHVH is good unto all and His mercies are over all His works." R. Joshua b. Levi interprets this verse: His mercies are over all because they are His works. R. Samuel b. Naḥman takes it to mean: His mercies are over all, for such are His works or attributes. He is compassionate. R. Levi takes it to signify: He endows His creatures with His compassion. The difficulties arising from verses supporting the older interpretation of the divine names are solved in this wise: Commenting on Gen. 8.1: "And *Elohim* remembered Noah," R. Samuel b. Naḥman said: "Woe unto the wicked who turn the attribute of mercy into the attribute of judgment, for wherever YHVH occurs it represents the attribute of mercy, yet it is written (Gen. 6.5–7): 'and YHVH beheld the wickedness of man that it was great,' etc. 'And YHVH regretted that He made man on the earth; and YHVH said, I shall blot

exact punishment from them," etc. On the other hand the Mech. Shirata, III, 45a; ed. Lauterbach II, p. 28 states: [זה אלי ואנוהו אלהי אבי וארוממנהו]. במדת הדין. ומנין שאין אלי אלא מדת רחמים, שנאמר (תהלים כב, ב) אלי אלי למה עזבתני, ואומר (במדבר יב, יג) אל נא רפא נא לה, ואומר (תהלים קיח, כז) אל ה' ויאר לנו. "With me He dealt according to the attribute of mercy, while with my fathers He dealt according to the attribute of justice." See also Targ. Jerushalmi, Gen. 8.1. ויזכר אלהים את נח. ואדכר ברחמי טבא דאית עמו ית נח ואעבר ה' רוחא דרחמין.

[105] *Moses* II, 99–100; *Quaestiones et Solutiones in Exodum* II, 66; *Cherubim*, 27 f.

[106] כל מקום שנאמר ה' זו מדת רחמים, שנאמר (שמות לד, ו) ה' ה' אל רחום וחנון. כל [אדני יהוה] ה'. מקום שנאמר אלהים זו מדת הדין. שנ' (שם כב, ח) עד האלהים יבא דבר שניהם ואומר (שם, שם, כז) אלהים לא תקלל. Sifre Deut., 27; also Eccl. R. 7.17; Tanḥuma Lev., 39. Mid. Ps. 56, ed. Buber 294, ascribes this thought to R. Nehorai (=R. Meir, see Erub. 13b). The older source uses מדה טובה and מדת פרענות. The earliest use of מדת דין and מדת צדקה is referred to R. Jose the Galilean and R. Akiba. Hag. 14a; Sanh. 38b. See Marmorstein, *op. cit.*, 43 ff.

[107] Levy, *Wörterbuch*, under רחמנא.

out man,' etc. Happy are the righteous who turn the attribute of judgment
into the attribute of mercy; for wherever *Elohim* occurs the attribute of
judgment is meant" (as in Ex. 22.27, 8; 2.24).[108]

To remove all possible misunderstanding, Onkelos in his Aramaic version
of the Pentateuch regularly translates *Elohim* with YHVH. The same practice
is followed by the Targum of the Prophets. Simeon ben Azzai teaches: "Come
and see that in all the laws regarding sacrifices in the Torah neither *Elohim*
nor *Elohecha, Shaddai* or *Zebaot,* is used but only YHVH, the distinctive
Name, in order to afford the heretics no ground for their contentions," viz.
that the God who commanded the sacrifices is not the same one who rules on
high.[109]

Opposing the Gnostic distinction of persons and attributes in the godhead,
a Tannaitic source teaches: "Why was Adam created alone? That the Minim
(Gnostics) may not be able to claim that there are many Powers in heaven."
The fact that Adam was created single refutes the Gnostic doctrine of *syzygies*
(*zugot*) or "pairs," representing opposites (i.e. that diverse moral characters
are fixed), so that the righteous might not claim that their righteousness came
to them by virtue of their descent from righteous parents, nor the wicked that
their wickedness derived from their parents.[110]

R. Joḥanan contradicts the Gnostic claim that dualism is supported by the
text of the Torah: "Wherever the Minim seek proof for their heretical teaching there, too, they have their refutation. The plural in Gen. 1.26: "Let *us*
make man in our *image*" is corrected by the sequel: "And *Elohim* created man
in *His* image." The plural in Gen. 11.7: "Come, let *us go down* and let *us
confound* their (men's) language," is corrected by the previous singular form
of the verb in verse 5: "And YHVH *went down* (וירד) to see the city and the
tower." The plural verb in Gen. 35.7: "For there the *Elohim* revealed themselves* (נגלו) to him" (Jacob), is righted by the singular form in vs. 3: "I will

[108] Gen. R. 33.3; 73.3. Also Num. R. 9.16.

[109] Sifre Num. 143.

[110] Sanh. 37a. Elisha b. Abuya's argument for "pairs" on the ground of Eccl. 7.14 is
brushed aside by R. Meir. R. Akiba admitted it within limits. Hag. 15a. The Gnostic doctrine of
fixed moral types ruled out repentance. The Rabbis refuted it by pointing to Manasseh. Tanḥ.,
Naso, 30, Pesikta R. K., Shuba; Num. R. 14.1; Yalkut Ps. 739.

make there an altar unto *El*, who *answered* (הענה) me in the day of my distress." Similarly the plural form of the adjective modifying *elohim* is followed by a singular pronoun in Deut. 4.7: "What great nation is there, that hath *Elohim* so *near* (קרבים) unto it as YHVH our God whenever we call *upon Him* (אליו)," and in 2 Sam. 7.23: "And who is like Thy people, like Israel, a nation one on earth, whom *Elohim went* (הלכו) to redeem unto *Himself* (לו) for a people." The dualism implied in Dan. 7.9: "(I beheld) till *thrones* (כרסון) were placed and One that was ancient of days took His seat" is accounted for by R. Joḥanan on the ground that "God does naught without consulting His heavenly family (פמליא של מעלה) i. e. the angels,[111] as it is said (Dan. 4.14) 'the matter is by the decree of the watchers (angels) and the sentence is by the word of the holy ones.' Why the two thrones? One for Himself and one for David (the Messiah). Another explanation is: one for justice (*din*) and one for charity (*tzedakah*)."[112] R. Simlai made for a similar reply to the Gnostics who asked him: "How many gods created the world?" "Do you ask me? Why not inquire of Adam, as it is said (Deut. 4.32): 'For ask now of the days past, which were before thee, since the day that God created man (Adam) upon the earth.'" The Hebrew verb "created" is written not in the plural (בראו) but in the singular (ברא). To their retort that the word *Elohim* in the opening verse of Genesis indicates a plural, he pointed out that the verb "created" is in the singular.[113]

To overcome the Gnostic claim that the order of the Hebrew words in Gen. 1.1. indicates that God Himself was created, the Gemara reports that all the seventy-two elders who translated the Torah into Greek for Ptolemy Philadelphus were inspired to rearrange the words in this order: God created in the beginning.[114]

The Midrash asks: Why is the first book of the Torah called "Bereshit"?

[111] The final decision, however, is His own. Thus He overrules their objection to the creation of man. Gen. R. 8.4.

[112] Sanh. 38b; Tanḥ. Buber, Kedoshim 1.4.

[113] Jer. Ber. 9.1. Gen. R. 8.9; Ex. R. 29; Deut. R. Vaethanan 2.33; Tanḥ. B. Kedoshim; old Tanḥ. Bereshit 1.3; Mid. Ps. 1; Sanh. 38b; 63b.

[114] Meg. 9ab; Jeru. Meg. 1.9; Soferim 1.7; Mech. Pisha, 14; Gen. R. 1.12 and notes by Theodor. The text of the LXX does not bear out this report.

Because it tells the whole account of creation, and records that God was before all, so that all the generations may know that the Holy One existed before the world and that by His good counsel He created the world and all its creatures and not by the counsel of any of His creatures, and that He Himself rules the world.[115]

The Rabbinic rejection of Gnostic doctrine is sharply stated in the Sifre to Deut. 32.39: "See now that I, even I, am He." "This is the response to those who say that there is no sovereignty in heaven (i. e. that the high God is above human contacts). To him who asserts that there are two sovereignties in heaven the reply is: 'And there is no God with Me.' Should one maintain that God can neither revive nor kill, do neither evil nor good, it is affirmed: 'I kill and make alive,' etc. And it is stated by the prophet: 'Thus saith the Lord, the King of Israel, and his Redeemer the Lord of Hosts: I am the first, and I am the last, and besides Me there is no God.'"[116]

Christian Trinitarianism

The polytheistic inferences drawn by the Gnostics from the numerous terms for deity in the Bible met with criticism on the part of some Church Fathers as well as of the Rabbis. Thus Irenaeus rejects the claim that the diverse names occurring in the Hebrew text of the Scriptures, "such as *Sabbaoth, Eloe, Adonai,* and all other such terms . . . are different powers and gods." He emphasizes that "all expressions of this kind are but announcements and appellations of one and the same Being. . . All other expressions likewise bring out the title of one and the same Being, as for example, the Lord of Powers, the Father of all, God Almighty, the Most High, the Creator, the Maker, and such like."[117]

At the same time the Church Fathers adapted the dualistic claims of the

[115] Midrash Tadshe, XX.

[116] Isa. 44.6; Sifre, Haazinu, 329. R. Jonathan said: When Moses was writing down the Torah, he said to God on reaching Gen. 1.26, "Lord of the universe! Why dost Thou offer the heretics a loophole?" Said God: "Write! He who desires to err will err." Gen. R. 8.8.

[117] *Haeres.* II.35, 3. See Jude vss. 5 ff.

Gnostics to their doctrine of Jesus as the second deity. They based their argument on Ex. 23.20-21,23 where God says of His messenger who should lead the Israelites into Canaan, "My name shall be upon him." "The messenger's name was Joshua, the same in the original as Jesus. Starting from this and assuming, rather than admitting, that much which was narrated could not be understood of the Supreme Being, they alleged an idea nowhere even hinted in the New Testament, that the God who had appeared to the Patriarchs and spoken with Moses, was a subordinate being and was none other than Jesus in a pre-existent state."[118] Justin Martyr tells Trypho: "I will endeavor to prove to you from the Scriptures, that he who is said to have appeared to Abraham, to Jacob, and to Moses, and is called God, is another god (that is, divine being), different from God who created all things, another, I say, numerically, not in will, for I affirm that he never did anything at any time, but what it was the will of Him who created the world, and above whom there is no other god, that he should do and say." Justin continues: "Scripture mentions another god and lord, subordinate to the Maker of all things, who is also called angel (i. e. messenger) because of his announcing to men whatever the Maker of all things — above whom there is no other god — wishes to announce." "Only this very person called an angel, but being in reality a god — was seen by, and conversed with, Moses."[119] "Do not suppose," he argues further, "that the unoriginated God either descended or ascended; for the ineffable Father and Lord of all neither comes anywhere, nor walks, nor sleeps, nor arises; but remains in His own place, wherever that may be."[120]

---

[118] Huidekopper, *Judaism at Rome,* pp. 349-51. While the Gnostics ranked Jesus as superior to the God of the O. T., the Christians conceded that the Son is inferior to the Father. See John 10.15-38.

[119] *Dialogue with Trypho* 56, 60.

[120] Cf. Ezek. 3.12; also the saying of R. Jose b. Ḥalafta מעולם לא ירדה שכינה למטה וכו׳ Suk. 8a; Sab. 89a. Justin Martyr argues that when fighting Amalek, with Jesus (Joshua) the son of Nun leading the battle, Moses prayed with his arms extended in the form of a cross. If his arms were lowered, thus destroying the figure, the battle went against the Israelites, but as long as the figure was preserved they prevailed. Their final victory was due not to the prayer of Moses but because, while the name of Jesus was in the van of the battle, Moses standing or sitting with his arms extended exhibited the figure of a cross. The rock on which he sat, Justin takes as a symbolic reference to the Christ. See Huidekopper, *op. cit.,* p. 345; n. 36.

Following the description of the greatness, omniscience, and omnipresence of the Supreme God, Justin proceeds: "How, then, can He speak to anyone, or be seen by anyone, or appear in a little portion of the earth, when the people could not behold on Sinai even the glory of him whom He sent? Neither Abraham, therefore, nor Isaac, nor Jacob nor any other man, ever saw the Father, the ineffable Lord of all, even of Christ himself; but they saw him who, through the will of the Father, was a god, His son, and likewise His angel, ministering to His purpose."[121]

Adjusting Prov. 8.22–36 to his Christian theology, Justin writes: "God has begotten as a *Beginning* before all His creatures a kind of Reasonable Power from Himself, which is also called by the Holy Spirit, the glory of the Lord, and sometimes Son, and sometimes Wisdom, and sometimes Angel, and sometimes God, and sometimes Lord and Word." He repudiates the Jewish suggestion that Gen. 1.26 means that God merely said *let us make* to Himself, as well as the opinion that the words were addressed to the angels, and maintains that "this offspring, which in reality was put forth from the Father before all His works, was with the Father, and with him the Father conversed."[122]

A curious line of argument appears in Tertullian. He strongly condemns idolatry on grounds of Old Testament teaching. His treatise "On Idolatry" (written about 200 C.E.) contains numerous points of kinship with the Mishnah *Aboda Zara*.[123] His refutation of Marcion proceeds from what he calls "the Christian verity" that "God is not, if He is not one." "The conscience of all men" acknowledges that "God is the great Supreme, existing in eternity, unbegotten, unmade, without beginning, without end." "That Being which is the great Supreme, must needs be unique (unicum —alone of His Kind), by having no equal." "How, therefore," Tertullian asks, "can two

---

Tertullian follows Justin's interpretation of the battle with Amalek. The brazen serpent set up on a tree by Moses was an exhibition of the devil on the Lord's cross. *Adversus Judaeos*, 10. Rosh Hashanah 3.8 may be the Rabbinic answer to these claims.

[121] *Ibid.* 127.

[122] *Ibid.* 60, 61, 62. See A. Lukyan Williams, *Adversus Judaeos*, pp. 36–37.

[123] See W. A. L. Elmslie, *The Mishna on Idolatry, Aboda Zara*, 1911.

great Supremes co-exist, when this is the attribute of the Supreme Being, to have no equal — an attribute which belongs to One alone, and can by no means exist in two?" "Nature itself, therefore, if not an Isaiah, or rather God speaking by Isaiah, will deprecatingly ask: 'To whom will ye liken Me? (40. 18, 25)'" Furthermore, on what principle, he demands, "did Marcion confine his supreme powers to two?... If there be two, why not more? Because if *number* be compatible with the the substance of deity, the richer you make it in number the better. Valentinus was more consistent and more liberal; for he having once imagined two deities, *Bythos* and *Sige*, (depth and silence), poured forth a swarm of divine essences, a brood of no less than thirty Aeons, like the sow of Aeneas.[124] Now, whatever principle refuses to admit several supreme beings, the same must reject even two, for there is plurality in the very lowest number after one. After unity, *number* commences. So, again, the same principle which could admit two could admit more. After two, *multitude* begins, now that *one* is exceeded."[125]

The argument that Scripture applies the name god to beings besides God[126] is dismissed by Tertullian as frivolous, for the question at issue is not that of words but of essence.[127]

On the other hand, as an apologist of Christianity, Tertullian takes the position that "the designation of God as one in the prophetic Scriptures is intended as a protest against heathen idolatry, but does not preclude the correlative idea of the Son of God, with whom 'He stretched out the heavens alone.'"[128] In his polemic against Praxeas, he writes that sometimes the devil aims "to destroy the truth by defending it." Out of the doctrine of the unity of God the heresy has been fabricated "that the Father Himself came down into the Virgin, was Himself born of her, Himself suffered, indeed was Himself Jesus Christ." In opposition he sets forth the "rule of faith" that "there is one only God, but under the following dispensation, or οἰκονομία as it is called, that this one only God, has a Son, His Word, who proceeded from Himself, by

---

[124] Virgil, *Aeneid*, VIII, 43, etc.
[125] Tertullian, *op. cit.* ch. 5.
[126] Ps. 82.7, 6.
[127] *Against Marcion* I.3–6.
[128] Isa. 44.24.

whom all things were made, and without whom nothing was made. Him we believe to have been sent by the Father into the Virign, and to have been born of her — being both Man and God, the Son of Man and the Son of God, and to have been called by the name Jesus Christ." In the face of the claim that one can believe in God's unity only by assuming that "the Father, the Son, and the Holy Ghost are the very selfsame Person," Tertullian maintains that "the mystery of the dispensation (οἰκονομία) is still guarded, which distributes the Unity into a Trinity, placing in their order the three Persons — the Father, the Son, and the Holy Ghost: true, however, not in condition, but in degree, not in substance, but in form; not in power, but in aspect; yet of one substance, and of one condition, and of one power, inasmuch as He is one God, from whom these degrees and forms and aspects are reckoned, under the name of the Father, and the Son, and of the Holy Ghost."

Tertullian defends himself against the charge of dualism or tri-theism by taking refuge in the concept of monarchy as applied to God. His possessing sole government does not preclude Him from having a son or from entrusting the administration to hosts of angels. On the basis of 1 Corinthians 15.24–28, he establishes (against Praxeas) that the "Father and the Son" are "two separate persons" or "Beings." The spirit is the "third from God and the Son, just as the fruit is third from the root, or as the stream out of the river is third from the fountain, or as the apex of the ray is third from the sun."

With the Trinity as his basic doctrine, Tertullian proceeds to reinterpret the Old Testament along the lines followed by Justin. It is the Son of God that spoke to Moses and said to the people: "Lo, I send my messenger before thy face" who shall guard thee in the way and introduce thee into the land which I have prepared for thee. "Attend to him . . . for my name is upon him." The Son or the Logos was the minister of God in creation and in all His subsequent works. Whatever actions are ascribed to God in the Old Testament refer to him. It is he who descended to converse with men, from the time of Adam to that of the patriarchs and prophets.[129]

The references to the Messenger in Justin and Tertullian throw light upon the following dialogue reported in the Talmud. Rab Idit was asked by a *min* (i. e. a Gnostic or a Christian) regarding Ex. 24.1: "And unto Moses He (God)

---

[129] *Against Praxeas* 1–8; *Adv. Judaeos* 9; *Marcion* I.12, 14; III.16; *Praxeas* 16.

said: Go up unto YHVH." This seems to indicate that the God who spoke must be distinguished from YHVH. Otherwise the verse should have read: "Come up unto Me." He replied: "Metatron spoke these words, for his name is the same as his Master's, as it is said of the angel who was to *guide* Israel on the way to the promised land (Ex. 23.21): 'for My name is in him.'" "In that case," the *min* continued, "he should be worshiped." "It is written (vs. 21): 'Do not exchange Me for him (literally, 'be not rebellious against him').'" "Why, then, does Scripture state 'for he will not pardon your transgression'?[130] 'By our faith! Even as a messenger, we refused to accept him, for it is written (Ex. 33.15): If Thy presence go not, lead us not up hence.'"[131]

Rashi explains the words "for his name is the same as his Master's" by pointing to the numerical equivalent of the letters מטטרון and שדי.[132] More likely the words אל יהוה in Exodu 24.1 suggested the reading יהואל (The verse would mean: "Yahoel said unto Moses: Go up.") In the Apocalypse of Abraham Jaoel (Yahoel) figures as the teacher of the patriarch, explaining to him the mysteries of the *Merkabah* and of the last judgment.[133] He tells Abraham: "I am Yahoel . . . a power in virtue of the ineffable Name that is dwelling in me."[134] After Enoch's transformation into Metatron, he was identified in mystic circles with Yahoel, whose name leads the list of seventy-two names of Metatron that came down from Gaonic times.[135] The name

---

[130] That is, He knows that I am a God of vengeance. See R. Hananel, Sanh. 38b.

[131] Sanh. 38b. The Gemara reports further arguments of this character, based on Gen. 19.24; Amos 4.13, etc.

[132] Kohler, Art. "Angelology," *J. E.* I, 594; Frank, *Kabbalah*, p. 43; Jellinek, *B. H.*, II.30.

[133] The angel Jaoel also taught Abraham the "Song of Unity" based on "a midrashic development of the divine attributes and character as deduced from the various names of God (El, Shaddai, Elohim, Jahweh, Sabaoth)." G. H. Box, *Apocalypse of Abraham*, p. 61.

[134] *Ibid.* ch. 10. G. Scholem cites a ms. in the possession of the British Museum and originating among the Jewish mystics in Germany of the 12th century to the same effect that Yahoel taught Abraham the entire Torah and that he invited Moses to ascend to heaven, "to that angel whose name is like that of His Master. EL YHVH contains the letters of Yahoel." In the Hechalot literature Metatron plays this role. *Major Trends in Jewish Mysticism*, p. 362, n. 107.

[135] Alphabet of R. Akiba, ed. A. Wertheimer, 1953, pp. 352 קראתיו בשמי יו"י הקטן שר הפנים, also ידוד הקטן. Jacob Mann, *Texts and Studies* II, p. 85, n. 91 cites Kirkisani, the Karaitic critic of Judaism to the effect that the Rabbis interpreted ה' אלהיך of the first commandments as וקאלו פי אלתלמוד אן מטטרון הו י"י קטן; יוי קטון ויוי גדול. So, too, Benjamin of Nahavend, *ibid.*, p. 88.

"lesser Yaho" figures in Gnostical writings and has been retained also in *Merkabah* literature.[136] Kirkisani claims that the text in Sanhedrin 38b referred to Metatron as the "lesser YHVH." G. Scholem suggests that the name was deliberately eliminated from the Talmudic text because of its heretical connotation.[137]

The offices of Yahoel-Metatron seem to have been claimed by the Church Fathers for Jesus. In this light the dialogue of R. Idit rejects the thought of any demiurge as inadmissible in Judaism.[138] The answers which the Rabbis gave to the claims of the Gnostics also served their purpose in dealing with Christians. Specifically, R. Abahu seems to be answering the Christians in his interpretation of the words, "I am the Lord thy God" in the first commandment: "A reigning monarch has a father or a brother. Not so God. 'I am the first' for I have no father; and 'I am the last,' for I have no brother, 'and besides Me there is no God,' for I have no son."[139] R. Abahu explains Num. 23.19: "If a man should tell you 'I am God,' he lies; if he says 'I am the Son of Man,' he will regret it; (if he says) 'I will go up to heaven,' of him it is said: 'He has asserted something which he will not make good.'"[140] R. Elazar Hakappor comments on this verse: "God foresaw that a certain man born of a

---

[136] See Odeberg, *Third Book of Enoch,* Introduction, ch. 3, for an analysis of the "lesser Yaho" in the Coptic *Pistis Sophia.*

[137] "It is quite possible," Scholem writes, "that the word Metatron was chosen on strictly symbolical grounds and represents one of the innumerable secret names which abound in the Hechalot texts no less than in the Gnostical writings or in the magical papyri. Originally formed apparently in order to replace the name Yahoel as a *vox mystica,* it gradually usurped its place." While Metatron holds high rank in heaven, no suggestion appears in the classical Merkabah literature that he is to be regarded as being one with the glory that appears on the throne. He even "remains in the position of the highest of all created beings, while the occupant of the throne revealed in *Shiur Komah* is, after all, the Creator Himself." *Ibid.,* p. 69. On the etymology of Metatron see Kohut, *Aruch Hashalem,* under מטטר and מיטטרון III, 118–120; Levy, *Wörterbuch* III, 86–87; Krauss, *Lehnwörter,* p. 331; L. Ginzberg, *Legends,* V, 163 f. finds a relationship between Enoch-Metatron and the Babylonian Nebo.

[138] *Ibid.,* Alphabet of R. Akiba, p. 353.

[139] Ex. R. 29.5; Deut. R. Vaethanan 2.32–33; see also Aggadat Bereshit, Buber 31.3; Tanhuma Beha'alotecha, 9; ed. Buber, *ibid.,* 16.

[140] Jer. Ta'an. 2.1.

woman would arise and seek to set himself up as God. He, therefore, endowed the voice of Balaam with power to travel from one end of the earth to the other that all the nations may hear, warning them against being led astray by that man, for God is not a man that He should lie; and if he says that he is God, he lies. He will further deceive by saying that he will die and then reappear. Of that it is said: 'He asserts that which he will not fulfil.'"[141] R. Simlai counters the claim of the Christians that the repetition of the three names "*el elohim YHVH*" in Josh. 22.22 indicates a trinity by pointing out that the pronoun and verb following them are in the singular (הוא ידע). To his disciples he added: "The three are one name as one says Basileus Caesar Augustus." The appearance of the same three names in Ps. 50.1 (אל אלהים ה' דבר ויקרא ארץ) he explains similarly, as one says: "The craftsman, builder and architect." The plural אלהים קדושים הוא in Josh. 24.19 is explained as "holy in all the ways of holiness" (קדוש בכל מיני קדושות), referred to in Scripture: "His way is in holiness; He speaks in holiness; His dwelling is in holiness; the baring of His mighty arm is in holiness; He is revered and glorified in holiness." Likewise the plural form of the adjective "near" as applied to God in Deut. 4. 7 (מי גוי גדול אשר לו אלהים קרובים אליו) is explained as near in every way of nearness (קרוב בכל מיני קרובות).[142]

The Rabbinic doctrine regarded the divine names as synonymous, and descriptive of His actions.[143] R. Abba bar Mamal says that, in response to Moses' request that he be apprized of the Divine Name (Ex. 3.13) the Holy One told him: "Dost thou desire to know My name? I am named according to My deeds ... when I judge My creatures I am called *Elohim*; when I wage war against the wicked I am called *Zebaot*; when I defer punishment of man's sins I am called *shaddai*; and when I manifest compassion upon My world I am called *YHVH*."[144] The three times that the word "*ehye*" is used in Ex. 3.14, indicate that He is the God of the past, the present, and the future.

---

[141] *Yalkut Shim'oni*, ed. Saloniki, 1526–7, Balak, 765, deleted from later editions. It is given by Jellinek, *Beth Hamidrash*, V, 207–208.

[142] Jer. Ber. 9.1; Tanḥuma, Buber, Kedoshim 4.

[143] See "The Name of God," in this volume, pp. 161–6 ff.

[144] Ex. R. 3.6; Tanḥ., Shemot 20.

While He is eternally the same, He reveals Himself to the people in accordance with their varying needs.[145] In the words of the *Shir Hakabod,*

"They have envisioned Thee in many likenesses,
Thou art One in all presentations."

A late Midrash comments: As the *aleph* is written as one letter and pronounced as three, so God is called One and is praised in threes. The Shema reads: "The Lord our God, the Lord (is One)." Likewise: "The Lord, the Lord, Merciful God," "Holy, holy, holy (is the Lord of hosts)," and "great is the Lord, and mighty to be praised, and His greatness is unsearchable."[146]

Angelology

The doctrine of Divine Unity was endangered by certain developments within Judaism itself. The Bible indicates the embarrassment caused by the belief in the existence of angels. Thus, with a few exceptions, the pre-exilic literary prophets and Deutero-Isaiah, the Deuteronomic and Priestly Codes consistently avoid references to angels. On the other hand the E document and to a lesser degree J, Isa. 6, and the post-exilic books of Ezekiel, Haggai, Zech. 1–8, Malachi, Isa. 14, a few Psalms, 1 Chron. 21 and above all Daniel assigned great prominence to angels in their theological conceptions.[147] While the Hasidim and the Pharisees adopted the belief, the conservative Sadducees persisted in negating it.[148]

The belief in angels derived from several causes. First, there was the need of harmonizing the lingering survivals of defunct polytheism with the pure faith of monotheism. Accordingly, the gods of the nations and the deified

[145] See note 52. Pes. R. Kahana 98a לא שאתם רואים אותי דמינות הרבה יש אלוהות הרבה אלא אני הוא שבים אני הוא שבסיני.

[146] Alphabet of R. Akiba, I, ed. A. Wertheimer, p. 350.

[147] On the general subject in the Bible, see J. Morgenstern's art. "Angels" in the *Universal Jewish Enc.*

[148] Acts 23.8.

forces of nature were subordinated to YHVH, the universal God. Stripped of their independence, they reappeared as the guardian princes of nations and of individuals, and as angels of fire, rain, snow, wind, healing, death, etc.[149] Second, with the growing transcendence of God, it became necessary to bridge the gap between Him and the world. From His throne on high, He intervenes in the affairs of men by means of a *malach* or messenger.[150] Whereas God is presented as speaking directly to the pre-exilic prophets, His messenger acts as the agent of revelation for the post-exilic apocalyptic prophets.[151] Third, the requirements of the monarchic conception of God, which represented an aspect of His transcendence, called for an entourage of ministering angels. Foreign religious influences contributed further to this conception. In the Babylonian panethon the chief deity was attended by numerous subordinate deities. Persian dualism surrounded Ormuzd and Ahriman with retinues of good and evil spirits or angels. As the King of Kings, YHVH rules over all. Even Satan in the prologue of Job, as in Zech. 3.1–2, while acting as "the district attorney of heaven," operates under God.[152]

Rabbinic angelology carries forward the Biblical ideas on the subject. The Mishnah, as the authoritative code of normative Judaism, follows the pre-exilic Prophets, the Deuteronomic and Priestly Codes in avoiding all reference to angels.[153] Other Tannaitic compilations, too, are reserved with regard to them.[154] On the other hand, the Haggadah, presenting much of the mystic lore of the Rabbis, abounds in angels. The angelology cultivated by the Essenes and Ḥasidim and which reached fantastic proportions in the books of

---

[149] Dan. 10.13; 21; 12.1; cf. Deut. 4.19; Ps. 58.2, 82; also Gen. 32.25; Ps. 91; Dan. 3.28; 6.23; Tobit 3.17.

[150] Ex. 23.20–23; 32.34.

[151] Ezekiel makes use of *kabod* and *ruaḥ* as well as of angels.

[152] For a picture of the monarchic court see Isa. 6; I Kings 22.19; Zech. 3.1–2; Dan. 7.10; 10.5 ff.

[153] D. Neumark, *Toledot Ha'ikkarim* II, pp. 3 ff.

[154] The Tosephta mentions Michael who appears in the Bible. Other references to angels are similarly of biblical character. Tos. Sota 3.9, 18; 4.6, 9; cf. 13.8. Also Sifre, Naso 47; Haazinu 338, 343; Mek., Shirata 8, where the four angels standing before the face of God lead four troops of angels glorifying God, who is seated in the midst of them.

Enoch, Jubilees and the Testament of the Twelve Patriarchs and other apocalypses, found adherents among leading Pharisaic teachers. Akiba and Ishmael b. Elisha were adept in the esoteric lore of the "Chariot" and the *pamalia shel maala*. The lore dealing with "Creation" — as part of the Jewish Gnosis — originally confined to initiates, came to be shared by wider circles and was even imparted in popular homilies, as the speculations regarding angels in the Midrashim indicate.[155]

With all the popularity of the belief, some Rabbis recognized that the elaborate development of angelology with personal names of angels was something new in Judaism. R. Simeon b. Lakish states: "The names of the angels were brought from Babylonia. Before the Exile, Isaiah spoke merely of *seraphim* or fiery angels (i. e. they were nameless). After the Exile we have 'the man Gabriel,' 'Michael Prince.'"[156] Historical criticism corroborates the correctness of this observation. It is in Daniel that names of angels first appeared. From Babylonia came the distinction between the upper and lower spirits, and the "four angels of the presence of the Lord," who stand near the crystal throne of God, which is encircled by fire and surrounded by *Seraphim, Cherubim,* and *Ophanim.* They seem to correspond to the Babylonian rulers of the four parts of the earth.[157] The seven archangels,[158] too, may correspond to the Babylonian seven planetary spirits or possibly to the Parsi *Amesha Spentas* and the *Fravashis.*[159] Under Parsi influence the fallen angels of Gen. 6.1–4 and Isa. 14 and Azazel of Lev. 16.10[160] combine with popular animism to form the hosts of destructive angels (מלאכי חבלה) or demons, headed by Satan or Samael, who is identified with the angels of death, Asmodeus and Lilit.[161] The good angels are of numerous kinds. Ben Sira had anticipated the book of Daniel in teaching that "for every nation He (God) appointed a ruler" (17.17, cf. Deut. 4:19–20). As Gen. 10 names seventy nations, the

[155] Cf. בית דין של מעלה, Mak. 13b.

[156] Jeru. R. H. 1.2, based on Isa. 6.2, 6; Dan. 9.21; 10.21.

[157] Ezek. 1.15; Enoch 21; 40.2; see Pirke de R. Eliezer IV; Hechalot 6; Num. R. 2.10.

[158] Ezekiel sees seven angels in human form (9.2). Tobit 12.15.

[159] A. V. W. Jackson, *Zoroastrian Studies*, 1928, ch. V.

[160] See Jeru. Targum and Naḥmanides *ad loc*.

[161] Deut. R. 11.10.

belief arose that there are seventy guardian princes in heaven.[162] During the
building of the Tower of Babel, God called the seventy angels that surround
His throne of glory and asked them to join Him in confounding men's speech.
Hence the text reads (Gen. 11.7) not "*I shall go down*" but "*Let us go down.*"
Having divided humanity into separate nations possessing diferent languages,
He then cast lots for them.[163] In consequence, Abraham and his seed fell to
the portion of God Himself, whereas each of the seventy angels became the
guardian of a separate nation.[164] While Ben Sira and the Book of Jubilees
(15. 32) similarly speak of God as the guardian of Israel, the example of
Daniel who names Michael in this capacity, is also followed in the Haggadah.
As his name is linked with God (*mi-cha-el*, "who is like God?"),[165] he is considered the *sar zaba* or captain that came to Joshua (5.15) to help him.fight
Israel's battles, who smote the hosts of Sennacherib (2 Kings 19.35), and who
will arise to help Israel in the future.[166] The destiny of the nation is inter-
linked with that of its heavenly guardian. God does not punish a nation before
He punishes its heavenly guardian.[167] As in Dan. 10.20, the guardians fight
against each other in the interest of their peoples. The hostility of the nations
toward Israel is reflected by the hostility of their guardians toward Michael.
They side with Egypt against Israel, but God takes Israel's part. Jacob saw
them in his dream, ascending and descending the ladder, and feared that they
would ever oppress Israel.[168] With the council of the seventy-one, God sits in
judgment over the nations.[169]

Michael who is described in Dan. 12.1 as "the great *sar*" is not only the
head of the guardian angels but also the Prince of the Divine Presence, *sar*

[162] So Enoch 89.59. Cf. Deut. 32.8 which according to LXX, L. and S. the reading is יצג
גבולות עמים למספר בני אל(יד). See Kittel-Kahle's edition and Jeru. Targum *ad loc.*
[163] *Ibid.*
[164] Pirke R. Eliezer 24 and Jeru. Targ. Gen. 11.7.
[165] Num. R. 2.10.
[166] *Zohar* Num. 148a; Lekaḥ Tob, Ex. 23.20; *B. H.* II, 56. Cf. Dan. 12.1.
[167] Cf. Isa. 24.21; Cant. R. 8.14; Mech. Shirata, II.
[168] Ruth R., Introduction; Jeru. Targ. Ex. 24.10; Pesikta R. 23, 150b; also Ex. 4.15.15;
Pesikta R. 150a.
[169] That is the 70 plus Michael.

hapanim (cf. Isa. 63.9) and the *sar haolam,* the Prince of the World. The same titles were appropriated for Metatron. Not only is "his name like that of his Master," but like God, he has seventy (or even ninety-two) names corresponding to the seventy nations, and God calls him "Lad" (נער).[170] He calls himself both "Lad" and "Elder" (based on Ps. 37.24).[171] Metatron is further identified with Enoch, who was taken up to heaven and raised to the highest rank of vice-regent, *sar hapanim.* Among the seventy names of Metatron are: Yahoel, Yehadriel, Akatriel, Yefefiel and Yeshaiah.[172]

As there are "Princes" over the nations so there are "Princes" over the elements: Gabriel of fire, Yurkemi of hail, Ridia of rain, Rahab of the sea, Ben Nez (cf. Job 39.26) of the winds, Lailah of the night and of conception, Dumah of death and of hell (also of fire).[173] The names of these princes are often formed by the Hebrew name for a nature force or element of life with the addition of *el.* Thus we have names like Baradiel, Ruhiel, Barakiel, Zaamiel (*zaam*-storm), Zikiel (comet), Raashiel (earthquake), Shalgiel, Matariel, Shamsiel, Lailael, Kochbiel, etc.[174]

The vastness of the angelic hosts may be estimated from the saying of R. Simeon b. Lakish: "There are 12 *mazzalot* (signs of the zodiac), each *mazzal* has 30 armies, each army 30 camps, each camp 30 legions,[175] each legion 30 cohorts, each cohort 30 corps, and each corps 365,000 myriads of stars under

[170] Yeb. 16b; Sanh. 94a; Hul. 60a.

[171] Jellinek, A., *Bet Hamidrash* II, 16.56; *Yalkut Reubeni,* Gen. 110–111. See Wertheimer, *Bate Midrashot,* revised, ed. Jerusalem, 1953, pp. 351 ff. for the transformation of Enoch into Metatron and his seventy names.

[172] Jeru. Targ., Gen. 5.24; Midrash Agada, ed. Buber *ad loc.* Hebrews 11.51. Enoch and Elijah are the two heavenly witnesses of Rev. 11.3. In kabbalistic tradition Elijah is identified with Sandalfon, the "angel who ties bands for his Master" (*Emek Hamelek,* 152, col. 4). The *Yalkut Hadash,* pp. 115–116, no. 9, 38 refers to three angels who receive Israel's prayers and weave them into crowns for God. They are: Akatriel, Metatron and Sandalfon; Pes. 118a.

[173] Ta'an. 25b; B. B. 74b; Sanh. 96a; Nid. 16b; Ber. 18b. A prince of Gehinnom is mentioned in Aruch. 15b. See Cohen, *Everyman's Talmud,* p. 55, and S. S. Cohon, "Angel of Death," *Univ. J. E.,* I, 302–303.

[174] *Sefer Hanoch, B.H.,* V, p. 176; Kohler, *J. E.,* I, 594.

[175] Cf. Mat. 26.53.

its care."[176] Still another opinion estimates their number at 496 myriads, corresponding to the numerical value of the Hebrew word מלכות or at 499 myriads, the equivalent of צבאות.[177] At Sinai sixty myriads of angels descended to crown each Israelite with two crowns, one for the pledge "we will do" and the other for "we will hear" (Ex. 24.7).[178] Maimonides tried to arrange them into ten classes in accordance with their Biblical designations and their rank: the *holy ḥayyot, ophanim, erelim, ḥashmalim, serafim, malachim, elohim, bene elohim, cherubim and ishim.*[179]

To check the possible notion of dualism, the Rabbis taught that the angels did not exist before creation. Neither were they among the six things decided upon before creation. In the view of R. Joḥanan they did not come into existence until the second day when the winds were created (cf. Ps. 104.4), and in the opinion of R. Ḥanina not until the fifth day, when the winged beings were fashioned. R. Isaac adds: "All agree that they were not created on the first day that it may not be claimed that Michael was stretching the heavens to the north and Gabriel to the south, while God was fastening them in the middle, but 'I am the Lord that maketh all things; that stretched forth the heavens alone; that spread abroad the earth by Myself' (Isa. 44.24). 'By Myself' is written: מי אתי, meaning 'who was with Me as partner' in the world's creation?"[180] Though He consulted them regarding the creation of man, He did not follow their advice.[181] Still another view is expressed that from every utterance issued by God an angel is created, as it is said: "By the word of the Lord the heavens were made, and by the breath of His mouth all their hosts" (Ps. 33.6).[182] (Philo similarly conceived of angels as Logoi.)[183] It was believed

---

[176] Ber. 32b.

[177] Seder Eliyahu Rabba, XVII, XXXI; Seder Eliyahu Zutta, XII; ed. Friedmann, pp. 32, 34, 193.

[178] Sab. 88a.

[179] H. Yesode Hatorah II.7; cf. Enoch 61.10.

[180] Gen. R. 1.3; III, 8; Mid. Ps. 24.4 adds: שלא יאמרו המינים וכו׳.

[181] Sanh. 38b; Gen. R. 8.5. Tertullian, *Against Praxeas* 16, suggests that this idea was intended to contradict the Christian claim that the plurals connected with God indicate a Trinity. See Ginzberg, *Legends*, V, p. 3.

[182] Ḥag. 14a.

[183] Philo regards angels as a kind of immanent powers or *logoi* in the world. They are pure

that angels are composed of the same elements as the heavens. An angel consists half of water and half of fire and has five aspects (i.e. a harmony of opposing elements).[184] Unlike men, angels do not propagate themselves and are not subject to the evil inclination, but they feed on Manna, and, according to another view, on the radiance of the *Shechinah*, as it is said: "And Thou preservest them all; and the host of heaven worshipeth Thee" (Neh. 9.6).[185]

As the Hebrew word *malach* indicates, angels are not independent divine beings but messengers of God, created to carry out particular tasks. From these tasks they derive their names.[186] In the words of the *Yotzer*: "He is the creator of the ministering angels who stand in the height of the world and together proclaim in fear the words of the living God and the universal King. All of them are beloved, all of them are pure, all of them are mighty, and all of them do in awe and in fear the will of their Master. And all of them open their mouths in holiness and in purity, with song and hymn, blessing, praising, glorifying, revering, sanctifying and enthroning the Name of God, the great, mighty, and awful King, blessed be He! And all of them take upon themselves the yoke of the kingdom of heaven, one from the other, and they give permission one to the other to sanctify their Creator in tranquil spirit, with pure speech and holy melody. They respond in unison and exclaim in awe: Holy, holy, holy is the Lord of Hosts; the whole earth is full of His glory."[187] They join Israel in crowning God with their adorations.[188] To emphasize still further that angels exist only for the glory of God, the belief was expressed that a new body of celestials is created each day to sing God's praises. Only the archangels Michael and Gabriel remain unchanged.[189]

disembodied souls serving as instruments of Providence in caring for men. "God not condescending to come down to the external senses, sends His own words or angels for the sake of giving assistance to those who love virtue" (*On Dreams* I.12). They are "lieutenants of the Ruler of the Universe, as though they were the eyes and ears of the Great King, beholding and listening to everything" (*ibid.*, 22). See Wolfson, *Philo* I, pp. 366 ff.

[184] Jeru. R. H. 2.4. See Cant. R. 3.11, and Wolf Heidenheim's comment in Wilna (Rom) ed.
[185] Gen. R. 8.11; Ex. R. 32, 48.11; Yoma 75b.
[186] Num. R. 10.5, based on Judg. 13.18: לפי השליחות ששלח הקב"ה אותנו קורא לנו שם.
[187] Morning Service, cf. Enoch 61.11.
[188] Thus the Sephardic Musaf Kedushah: *Keter Yitnu*. See also Ex. R. 21.
[189] Ḥag. 14a; Gen. R. 78.1.

The "cult of angels" referred to by Paul in Col. 2.18 is not Jewish but Gnostic.[190] Angel worship was determinedly opposed by the masters of the Synagogue.[191] Making images of angels, *ophanim* and *cherubim* is included by R. Ishmael in the prohibition of idolatry.[192] Offering a sacrifice to "Michael the great Prince" is branded as an idolatrous act equivalent to sacrificing to the sun, moon, stars and planets.[193] Instead of receiving the worship of men, Michael himself stands like a high priest in the Temple of the heavenly Jerusalem and offers up sacrifices to God.[194] When in trouble one should turn neither to Michael nor to Gabriel but cry to God who will answer him immediately. This is taken to be the meaning of Joel 3.5: "Whosoever shall call on the name of the Lord shall be delivered."[195] R. Johanan teaches that

[190] See Kohler, art. "Angelology," *J. E.* I, 595a.

A characteristic feature of the Gnostic conception of the universe is the role of the seven world-creating powers. In the Valentinian school the Demi-urge takes the place of the seven. These are half-evil, half-hostile powers frequently named "angels." They are reckoned as the last and lowest emanations of the Godhead. Below them — and frequently considered as derived from them — comes the world of the actually devilish powers. The Mandean speculations present a different and perhaps more primitive conception of the seven, according to which they, together with their mother Namrus (Ruha) and their father (Ur) belong entirely to the world of darkness. They are regarded as captives of the god of light, who pardons them, sets them on chariots of light, and appoints them as rulers of the world.

While in Babylonian religion the planetary constellations are reckoned as the supreme deities, in Gnosticism they are subordinate half-demonic powers, or even completely the powers of darkness. This development Bousset ascribes to the victory of Parsism over the Babylonian religion, reducing its deities into half demons or into demons. These seven are the creators of the material world, which is separated from the light-world of the good God. (See *Bundahis* III.25; V.1; Bousset, *op. cit.*).

[191] See *JQR* o. s. IV, 247. R. Jehuda b. Yakar, a teacher of Naḥmanides writes: ויש שאומר
מיושב מכניסי רחמים הכניסו רחמינו . . . ודעות חלושות הן שהרי לא מצאנו בכל המקרא בצרת ישראל
שהנביאים בקשו רחמים למלאכים ולמתים לבקש רחמים עליהם רק שהיו הולכים לחסידים להתפלל
עליהם . . . ובודאי התפלה קרויה עבודה . . . וכתוב זובח לאלהים יחרם בלתי לה' לבדו, ואין ספק שאסור
לזבוח לשום מלאך כדי שיבקש הוא רחמים עליו וגו'.

[192] Mech. Yitro 10; Jeru. Targ. Ex. 20.2 f.

[193] Ḥulin 40a; Ab. Z. 42b. On Michael and Gabriel see Horodetzki, *Hamistorin B'yisrael*, 161 ff.; *MGWJ*, 1928, 499–506; Num. R. 2, 10 end.

[194] Ḥag. 12b; cf. Test. Levi. VIII.

[195] Jeru. Ber. 9.1 (13a). Cf. Rev. 22.8–9.

"the following three keys have not been entrusted to the keeping of any angel: of birth, of rain and of resurrection." That is, God Himself takes care of them, as is borne out by Gen. 30.22; Deut. 28.12 and Ezekiel 37.13. On the basis of Ps. 145.16, the key of sustenance was added to the above. Prayers for these bounties must be directed to no angel but to God.[196]

These admonitions were necessitated by popular practice. Indeed the miracle-working Essenes and Hasidim and subsequently the Kabbalists put their angelology to practical uses to enlist the celestials as man's helpers. Names of angels even found a place in the public liturgy of the Synagogue despite the protests of rationalistic leaders.[197]

Angels serve in Rabbinic thought as the agents of God's revelation, providence, and retribution. They communicate knowledge to chosen individuals. Only to Moses God spoke directly without the mediacy of an angel or a messenger.[198] They guard and protect men, intercede in their behalf and carry their prayers to the throne of God. They also record men's evil deeds, and act as instruments of divine wrath. "Angels of peace" accompany the righteous dead to their resting place (as in Isa. 57.2; 58.8), while "destructive angels" follow the wicked (as in Job 33.22 and Ps. 35.6).[199] Despite their supernatural character, R. Johanan voices the opinion that "the righteous are superior to angels." Though subject to the *Evil Yetzer* they do God's will. The ministering angels do not begin their song of praise in heaven until Israel offers homage to God on earth.[200]

The Rabbinic endeavor to defend the doctrine of monotheism on Scriptural grounds holds a significant place in man's struggle for a pure vision of God. The Rabbis scrupulously guarded the faith of the Torah and the prophets, and devotedly preserved its light for future generations. Divine Unity connoted for them, as it does for all monotheists, not merely God's

---

[196] Ta'an. 2a; Jeru. Targ. Gen. 30.22; Deut. 28.12. Kohler, *op. cit.*, citing Gefrörer, *Jahrhundert des Heils*, I, 377.

[197] Zunz, *Synagogale Poesie*, pp. 149, 501 ff. See Appendix.

[198] Mech., Shabbata I, ed. Lauterbach, III, p. 197.

[199] Num. R. 11.7.

[200] Hulin 91b. Mid. Ps. 103.18; cf. I Cor. 6.3; Heb. 1.13-14; 2.5. See Ginzberg, *Legends*, V, p. 24, n. 66.

numerical oneness, excluding divisions and distinctions in His personality, but also His spiritual oneness, absolute completeness and perfecton. Only·such a God satisfies the quest of the soul for unity amid the multiplicity and chaos of things, and for the unifying goal and purpose toward which humanity must strive if it is to attain spiritual soundness.

To the minds of the Rabbis as to those of the masters of the Bible, God appeared as unique, incomparable to anything in human experience. All similes used to picture Him must be taken as mere figurative devices to make Him real to men. While He may not be touched by the senses, He is near to the heart that longs for Him and to the spirit that reaches out after Him. The term which, since Tannaitic times, has come to designate Him in Jewish usage, is *Hakadosh baruch hu* — "the Holy One, praised be He." Beyond all other designations, He is "the Holy One," removed from all impurity, imperfection, and evil, and embodying within His character all goodness, truth, righteousness, and compassion. In the words of Hannah's prayer: (1 Sam. 2.2) "There is none holy as the Lord, for there is none besides Thee; neither is there any rock like our God."

Appendix

Midrash Otiyot R. Akiba, Aleph, states that when God saw the wickedness of the men of the generation of the flood, He removed his Shechinah from their midst and ascended to heaven, amid shouting and the blast of the shofar (as in Ps. 47.6). He took Enoch from among them and raised him up amidst the sound of the shofar to act with the four *Hayyot* of the *Merkaba* as guardians of His treasures in heaven, and transforming him into Metatron, apointed him chief of the princes in heaven, minister of God's throne.

This legend shows the connection between Metatron and the blowing of the shofar on Rosh Hashana. A private prayer recited during the ceremony reads:

> "May it be Thy will, O Lord my God and God of my fathers, that the blasts of the *Tekia, Shebarim, Tekia*, which we blow this day be wrought [by the angel Tartiel] into Thy throne of glory, [even as Thou didst receive — i. e. Israel's

prayers — through Elijah of blessed memory and *Jeshua Sar Hapanim* (Prince of the Presence) and the Prince Metatron]. And mayest Thou be filled with mercy toward us. Blessed be Thou, O Lord of mercy."

The composite nature of this prayer is quite apparent. Like the other Kabbalistic additions to the Shofar Service, it comes from the school of Isaac Luria (1534-1572), and is based on the angelology of Sefer Raziel, in the German-Polish rituals, but in no Sephardic or oriental ritual. Its earliest appearance, as far as I have been able to trace, is in Herz Treves' kabbalistic prayer book (Thiengen 1560), where the words which I have bracketed are omitted. In a note, Herz utilizes an older kabbalistic interpretation of the shofar blasts, presenting the numerical value of their Hebrew names as equivalent to the names of certain angels. Among others, it reads: "The numerical value of *Elijahu Hanabi Zachur Latob* corresponds to the numerical value of the abbreviations KRK (*Tekia Terua Tekia*), i. e. קר״ק = 400 (אליהו = 52 + הנביא = 68 + זכור = 233 + לטוב = 47] = 400). It also equals Jeshaiah (ישעיה with the addition of a ה for God, which is a component part of names for angels), which is the name of Metatron. With slight variations this note is printed in most of the later editions which include the prayer.

None of the other early editions of the Ashkenazic liturgy, which I have been able to examine (viz. Pesaro, 1517; Augsburg, 1536; Bologna, 1540; Sobieneto, 1552; Cracow, 1585; Thanhausen, 1594, etc.), contains kabbalistic additions to the Shofar Service. The Venice edition of 1567, in the possession of the Hebrew Union College Library is most instructive. Like the other early prints, it is free from the kabbalistic additions. A former owner of the copy, whose name is given as Lewa of Bonn but whose dates are not indicated, inserted a page in handwriting, supplying the prayers which had come into use after the publication of the volume. The text of the prayer follows that of Herz Treves. In a distinctly different hand there was added later, above the line, the part which I bracketed. Next I find the Prague ritual of 1612 (3rd ed.) presenting the entire text, but it reads *Joshua* (יושע). The subsequent edition (4th), which appeared soon thereafter, corrects the name to *Jeshaiah* (ישעיה״ה). The Sulzbach ed. of 1699 has Jeshua (ישוע) and the Venice ed. of 1711-15 reads Joshuaiah (יושועיה). In course of time the reading *Jeshua* was standardized. In all of these and in subsequent editions, the explanatory note to which I referred above remains the same, viz. that Jeshaiah is a name of Metatron.

The name Jeshua is the shortened form of Jehoshua, as is clearly shown in Neh. 8.17. The variations, which I have detailed, may be due either to some printer's manipulation or to some kabbalistic vagary. Obscurity, it must be rememberd, is the very atmosphere of kabbalah. Since Metatron was believed to have shared God's seventy or ninety-two names, Jehoshua-Jeshua may have been one of them. The ground for my conjecture is the fact that both Metatron and the conquering hero are called by the same name *Naar*-youth. While one fights Amalek, the other resists the forces of Samael or Satan. Thus the Zohar to Exodus 17.9. In the mystic Sefer Raziel the name of Joshua ben Nun is classed with celestial saints (ed. Wilna, 1881, p. 6). Their union in the prayer during the blasts of the shofar, which are intended to frighten away Satan, is thus understandable.

The identification of Jeshua Sar Hapanim with Jesus is pure conjecture. A. Berliner, for example, speaks of the "Sehr verdaechtigte Jeshua Sar Hapanim." Another scholar suggests that some unscrupulous fellow of Christian leanings smuggled the name of Jesus into the Jewish ritual. The zealous Bodenschatz fulminates against the "blindness" and the "stubbornness" of the Jews who failed to recognize that the conceptions which they entertain concerning the fictitious Metatron and Jeshua Sar Hapanim are worthy only of Jesus, and adduces proof from Matt. 11.10; Mark 1.2; Luke 1.7, 7.6; 7.27, 28; I Tim. 6.15; Rev. 16.14; 19.15, 16. What he and others, whether Christians or Jews, fail to grasp is that common elements (viz. Logos, mediacy, etc.) underlie the conceptions of both Enoch-Metatron and Christ, and that these received different development in the Church and the Synagogue.

The kabbalistic insertions have been eliminated not only from the Reform rituals (see Union Prayer Book) but also from some modern Orthodox rituals as well. See, for example, Michael Sachs, *Festgebete der Israeliten, Neujahrsfest*, Berlin, 1855, pp. 135–6; and Adler-Davis, *Service of the Synagogue, New Year*, London and New York, 1906, pp. 126–7, and notes on pp. 240–42; Philip Birnbaum, *High Holy Day Prayer Book*, N. Y., 1951.

The Name of God,
A Study in Rabbinic Theology*

I

Divine names embody the conceptions of God of a particular religion. Coming down from a distant past their meanings often are obscure. The personal name of a deity thus represents an epithet the meaning of which has been forgotten.[1] The epithet generally derived from some function, characteristic or relation of the deity to the tribe, its members or surroundings. Acquiring the distinction of a personal name, it is identified with the deity and invested with *mana*, i.e. with power and mystery. Being sacred, it is guarded by tabus against profane use and is reserved for magic rites and tribal mysteries by medicine men or priests. For ordinary relations new epithets are created denoting the relation of the deity to the life and destiny of the people and to nature. These newer appellations, expressed in more transparent language, in turn become the titles by which the deity is invoked, sometimes independently and often in combination with the original personal name. The formation and use of new epithets for the deity constitute milestones in the progress of religion.

The use which the Rabbis made of the divine name and its related expressions reveals the intensity of their effort to reach out after a fuller and firmer comprehension of the divine. In their quest after God they walked humbly with Him. Though certain of His reality and ever conscious of His presence,

* Published: Hebrew Union College Annual, XXIII, Cincinnati, 1950–51.
[1] J. A. MacCulloch, art. "Nameless Gods." Hastings, *Encycl. Rel. and Ethics*, IX, 179.

they spoke reservedly of His nature. They often resorted to the words of Isaiah 45.15: "Verily Thou art a God that hidest Thyself, O God of Israel, the Savior."[2] They were aware of the challenging words addressed to Job:

"Canst thou find out the deep things of God?
Canst thou attain unto the purpose of the Almighty?
It is high as heaven; what canst thou do?
Deeper than the nether-world; what canst thou know?"[3]

Being unlike anything in existence, mysterious and transcendent, He is beyond human grasp. The Rabbi interpret Ex. 33.20, "Man shall not see Me and live" (האדם וחי), to mean: "Man shall not see Me nor angel." In evident opposition to the Gnostics, who claimed direct knowledge of God, R. Akiba, who was versed in their doctrines, adds that not even the angels that bear God's throne can behold Him. R. Simeon b. Azzai supplements Akiba's statement: "Not even the ministering angels who live eternally see God."[4] When Moses prayed: "Show me Thy Glory,"[5] he meant: "Show me the attribute wherewith Thou guidest the world."[6] Even that was ruled out as impossible. "It is God's glory to conceal" His nature.[7] In the words of Solomon's prayer: "The Lord said that He would dwell in thick darkness."[8] "He dwells in the highest secrecy, seeing all things and is Himself unseen."[9]

Though God is shrouded in mystery, the questing spirit strives to draw

[2] Cant. R. 4; Mid. Psalms 94.1.

[3] Job 11.7-8. Jer. Ber. 9.1; Tanhuma, Kedoshim 15; Mid. Ps. 106.2; 139.1; Yalkut Job 906.

[4] Num. R. 14.22. The Marcosian Gnostics took Ex. 33.20 to refer to the ignorance of the highest divinity, whereas the Demiurge, whom they identified with Yahveh, was seen by the prophets. Some Gnostics claimed that by virtue of their spiritual natures they were acquainted with the spiritual Pleroma. Iranaeus, *Against Heresies* I.19, 1-2; II.19, 2. Cf. Matthew 11.27; John 5.20; 10.15.

[5] Ex. 33.18.

[6] Mid. Ps. 25.6.

[7] Prov. 25.2.

[8] I Kings 8.12.

[9] Mid. Ps. 91.1; Num. R. 12.3.

near to Him, to behold His graciousness and to perceive something of His relation to man and to the world. The whole endeavor of religion may be said to consist in bridging gap between the finite and the infinite and thus to endow human life with sanctity and spiritual purpose.

In view of this polarity of the religious experience, the development of the Jewish idea of God exhibits a twofold trend. On the one hand, Judaism strove to discover the essential being and nature of God, which, in the idiom of the ancients, meant to find His true name. Accordingly it persisted in ascertaining the significance of the divine names in general and of the Tetragrammaton in particular. On the other hand, in its steady spiritual advance it sought to divest itself of the thought that the Divine may be named as men or objects are named. Popular piety clung to the first. Advanced theological thought tended toward the other position.

While this problem is present in all religions, it assumed a somewhat different form in Judaism. The pantheons of the polytheistic religions employ names of deities to differentiate them from one another. Monotheism, with its emphasis on the uniqueness of the Holy One, requires no names wherewith to distinguish Him from others. According to R. Levi, when Moses and Aaron came to Pharaoh and asked him in the name of "the God of the Hebrews" to send forth Israel to serve Him, the monarch consulted his directory of deities. Reading off the names of the gods of Edom, Moab, Sidon, etc., he said: "I do not find here the name of your God." To which Moses and Aaron replied: "You will not find Him among these, for they are dead, but 'the Lord God is the true God, He is the living God, and the everlasting King.'"[10] This comment may be related to Philo's interpretation of God's answer to Moses' request for His name: "First tell them that I am He who is, that they may learn the difference between what is and what is not, and also the further lesson that no name at all can properly be used of Me, to whom all existence belongs."[11] In another connection, he adds: "God indeed needs no name; yet,

[10] Jer. 10.10. Tanhuma, Vaera, 5; ed. Buber, 2. Cf. Philo., *Life of Moses,* I, xv, 8 (Loeb ed., p. 320).

[11] *Ibid.,* 1.75. Cf. Josephus, *Against Apion,* II, 167, 190–191. Justin Martyr states in this spirit that "to the Father of all, who is unbegotten, there is no name given. For by whatever name He be called, He has as His elder the person who gives Him the name. But these words, Father, and God, and Creator, and Lord, and Master are not names, but appellation derived

though He needed it not, He nevertheless vouchsafed to give to humankind a name of Himself suited to them, that man might be able to take refuge in prayers and supplications and not be deprived of comforting hopes."[12] God is essentially nameless, transcending any designation that man can apply to Him. Within this limitation, however, names of God are spiritual necessities. They stem from human habits of thought and of speech. An emotion, experience or idea is incommunicable unless it is verbalized. Only when expressed in a fitting word or name does it acquire power. Names of God have retained their place in advanced Jewish monotheism not merely as survivals of earlier and less developed religious views but also as indispensable designations of the personality of the Divine and as compact attributes of His nature.[13] Instead of being proper names of God, in the customary sense of the word, they simply point to His reality and to His effects.[14] They awaken the devout and searching mind to the awesome mystery and meaningfulness which environ the soul.

1. The Tetragrammaton.

The recognition that God transcends all names is paradoxically coupled in Jewish thought with the persistence to invoke Him by the right name. This is the case in both Hellenistic and Rabbinic Judaism. According to Josephus, Moses besought God not to deny him the knowledge of His name that he might know how to invoke Him to be present at the sacred rites. "Then God

---

from His good deeds and functions. . . Also the appellation 'God' is not a name, but an opinion implanted in the nature of man of a thing that can hardly be explained." (The Second Apology, 6).

[12] On Abraham, 51. Clement of Alexandria, sharing the doctrine of the Alexandrine schools of the namelessness of God observes that high names like "Father," "God," etc. are employed "because of our incapacity to find a true name, so that the mind may have something to rest on and steady it. None of these names taken separately expresses God." (Stromata V, 81 ff., cited by J. A. MacCulloch, op. cit., 179). The Martyrdom of Isaiah 1.7 declares that God's name "has not been sent into the world."

[13] Lekah Tob Ex. 3.13 ואמרו לי מה שמו, כלומר עוצם גבורתו. While personality is conceivable in nameless beings, it is greatly crystalized by a name.

[14] Philo, On Abraham 24.121.

revealed to him His name, which ere then had not come to men's ears, and of which I am forbidden to speak."[15] We have here the same reserve to utter the Ineffable Name, YHVH (= Yahveh), which forms a characteristic feature of Rabbinic theology. By a play on the word לעלם in Ex. 3.15 — written defectively — the rabbis teach that the divine name must be kept secret.[16] It must not be pronounced in the way in which it is written, but by a substitute word. Jewish piety, from post-Exilic times on, withdrew the four lettered name YHVH (= Yahveh), the specific designation of the God of Israel, from ordinary usage and invested it with awe and mystery. The third commandment and the related prohibitions of using the divine name in vain rendered it sacrosanct.[17]

The avoidance of the use of the Tetragrammaton — שם בן ד' אותיות, which figured as a proper name — in some of the later books of the Bible, is due to the growing sense of God's transcendence, a tendency which shows itself in the older books as well. The editorial revisions of the second and third books of the Psalter employ Elohim as the general appellation for Deity — in place of Yahveh.[18] Job avoids the Tetragrammaton in favor of other names and particularly of the archaic Shaddai (31 times). Ecclesiastes makes exclusive use of Elohim. The same is true of Daniel, with the exception of the interpolated prayer in Ch. 9. The total avoidance of all mention of divine names in Esther may stem from the same motive rather than from the supposedly secular nature of the book.

The substitution of other names for the Tetragrammaton continued in both Hellenistic and Rabbinic literature. The LXX invariably renders it with ὁ χύπιος = Adonai.[19] The same idea underlies the Masoretic pointing of the

---

[15] Antiq. II, 275-6.

[16] Pes. 50a לעלם כתיב. Rashi comments לשון העלמה. Ex. R. 3.7. Cf. Eccl. 3.11; Kid. 71a.

[17] Ex. 20.7; Deut. 5.11; Lev. 18.21; 19.12; 20.3; 21.6; 22.2, 32; 24.16; Ezek. 20.39; 36.20.

[18] The third book of Ps. (73–89) uses אלהים צבאות in place of the usual יהוה צבאות. Ps. 80.5,20 combines the two; cf. vss. 8 and 15. See Wellhausen, Book of Psalms, p. 82.

[19] See Wolf Wilhelm Graf Baudissin, Kyrios als Gottesname im Judentum u. seine Stellung in der Religionsgeschichte, p. 9 ff. Elohim is translated Θεός. The distinction is carried out most consistently in the Psalms and fairly so in the Pentateuch. Kyrios is used also for El, Adon, and Adonai. Aquila, in his literalism, rejected the LXX usage as being inexact and intro-

Tetragrammaton with the vowels of *Adonai* and with those of *Elohim* when the word *Adonai* itself precedes it. Onkelos, by identifying Elohim with Yahveh, removes all possible misunderstanding.[20]

The motive of reverence combined with the dread of breaking the third commandment underlies the use of "the Name" for Yahveh and subsequently even for its substitute *Adonai*.[21] This usage derived from the general tendency to identify the name with the person of its bearer.[22] As in magic so in ancient religion, knowledge of the name of a spirit or deity was believed to give one power over him and the means of securing his help.[23] However, improper mention of the name might spell disaster. Hence caution was required in its employment. Persons and objects belonging to God were designated as "called by His name."[24] Owned by Him, they were entitled to His protection. Deutero-Isaiah expressed the thought of Israel's consecration to God by the words: "Every one that is called by My name, whom I have created and formed and made for My glory."[25] Jeremiah spoke of himself as having "*the name* of the God of Hosts called upon" him, and referred to Jerusalem and the Temple, even as Shiloh was aforetime, as a place over

---

duced the word bodily into his translation, "writing it IIIIII, a form which is found in the Hexaplar manuscripts of the Septuagint and is the representation in the Greek alphabet of the letters of יהוה read from left to right." W. Bacher, *J. E.* XI, 263, referring to Swete, *Introduction to the O.T. in Greek*, p. 30; Nestle, in *Z.D.M.G.*, XXXII, 468, 500, 506.

[20] Onkelos leaves *Elohim* only where it accompanies the Tetragrammaton. Where the word is used for foreign gods Onkelos translates דהלתא (Gen. 31.32) and מעות עממיא for אלהים אחרים. Deut. 7.4; cf. 4.28. In Ex. 30.3 he uses אילה אוחרן. See Luzzatto, *Oheb Ger*, p. 2. Sheftel, *Biure Onkelos*, Gen. 1.1.

[21] Ex. 20.24 בכל המקום אשר אזכיר את שמי. Ex. 23.20–23 speaks of an angel in place of Yahveh moving before the people, and demands reverence for him on the ground that Yahveh's name is within him כי שמי בקרבו. For this tendency in the Apocrypha, see W. Bousset, *Religion d. Judentums*, p. 302, n. 1.

[22] *E.g.* Isa. 30.27; 42.8; 56.6; 59.19; Ps. 102.16; I Kings 3.2; 5.17,19; 8,17,20. Like "the Name" so "the glory" and "the face" appear in place of Yahveh. Ex. 33.14, 15, 18, 20, 23; Ps. 34.17; cf. Ex. 23.21; 32,34 and Isa. 63.9, where מלאך is associated with "the face of Yahveh."

[23] Cf. Judg. 13.17–18; Gen. 32.30; Ex. 33.12. See G. Foucart, "Names, Egyptian," Hastings, *Encyc. Rel. and Ethics*, IX, 151; A. H. Gardiner, "Magic, Egyptian," *Ibid.*, VIII, 265b.

[24] Am. 9.12; II Sam. 6.2; cf. I K. 16.24.

[25] Isa. 43.7.

which Yahveh's name was called, or where He caused His name to dwell.[26] Deut. 28.10 assures the people of Israel that when the other nations "will see that Yahveh's name is over you, they shall be afraid of you."[27] His power is communicated to the possessors of His name.

At the same time care was exercised not to limit Yahveh or His name to any locality. While popular usage persisted in referring to Him as "He that dwells at Zion[28] — a belief that gave the people ground for confidence in times of stress[29] —advancing Jewish thought made it clear that He was confined to no earthly habitation. 2 Sam. 7.11 rejects His need of a dwelling that human beings might erect for Him. Solomon's prayer at the dedication of the Temple — in line with Prophetic teaching[30] — repudiates the popular notion that the sanctuary is the seat of the Deity. He is the God of the universe. "The heaven is My throne and the earth My footstool. Where then is the house that ye may build unto Me, and where is the place that may be My rest."[31] High and exalted, inhabiting eternity, He yet dwells with those of a contrite and humble spirit. His transcendence combined with His nearness forms the favorite theme of numerous psalms.[32]

Similarly Yahveh's early identification as the God of Israel was modified by the Prophetic doctrine that He is the universal God of humanity. The Creator of the world is also the father of all men. He is the King of the nations who rules them by His unfailing justice and mercy.[33] Accordingly, Rabbinic usage requires that His kingship over the universe be combined with the acknowledgment of Him as personal God in the standard form of benediction.[34] Monotheism spells universality.

[26] Jer. 15.16; 7.10, 12, 14 etc.

[27] Driver, *International Critical Commentary*, Deuteronomy, p. 310. See also Isa. 63.19. Amos 9.12 speaks similarly of other peoples.

[28] שוכן בציון יי ושב ציון, and as השוכן בהר ציון. Ps. 9.12; Joel 4.17, 21; Isa. 8.18.

[29] Cf. Ps. 46.48.

[30] Jer. 7.4; 26.6; I Kings 8.27; II Chr. 6.16.

[31] Isa. 66.1; 57.15.

[32] Pss. 36.6 ff.; 66.4 ff.; 68.5 ff.; 89.6 ff.; 113 etc.

[33] Jer. 10.7, 10 ff.; Pss. 65.3; 66; cf. Isa. 6.3; 2.1–4, 9; 40.28; 44.6; Ex. 34.6, etc.

[34] Ber. 12a; cf. Jer. Ber. 9.1, ed. Zechariah Frankel and note. Hence every benediction begins with the six words: ברוך אתה יי אלהינו מלך העולם.

2. Liturgic Uses of the Name

The chief use of "the Name" in place of Yahveh was in ritual. Ex. 20.21 states: "In every place where I cause My name to be mentioned I will come unto Thee and bless Thee." The name is linked with the altar and with the ark,"[35] with Mt. Zion[36] and Jerusalem.[37] "The name of Yahveh" represented a most ancient formula of worship. The Yahvistic account traces it back to the days of Enosh.[38] Its liturgical usage is indicated in Deut. 32.3: "I invoke the name of Yahveh, ascribe ye greatness to our God."[39] Knowing His name, in which the essence of His being was believed to inhere, gave ground for trust, for invoking it brings help.[40] He makes His name known by responding to His people's prayers. Hence His name is a protection.[41] In blessing the people, the priests placed Yahveh's name upon them.[42] On the other hand those that do not invoke His name are His enemies who are fated for His wrath.[43] "The Name" served also as a formula of oath-taking. Deut. 10.20 commands: "By His name shall ye swear," i.e. in place of the names of foreign deities. Lev. 19.12 warns against swearing by His name falsely.[44] In prophecy the name of Yahveh "served as a mark of authenticity." The true prophet speaks "in the

[35] The patriarchs, building altars, invoke the name of Yahveh. Gen. 12.8; 13.4; 23.33; 26.25; cf. 28.18 f.; 33.20; 35.7; II Sam. 6.2. Similarly Ps. 113.1; 135.1: הללו את שם יי; 148.5, 13: יהללו את שם יי. 34.4. and the call: הללויה.

[36] Isa. 18.7.

[37] Deut. 12.5, 11; I Kings, 8.16; also II Chr. 6.33.

[38] Gen. 4.26.

[39] Also Ps. 72.19; cf. 113.2; Job 1.21; Neh. 9.5. See further Ex. 33.12; 34.5; Deut. 21.5; II Sam. 6.18; I K. 18.24, 25,32 (cf. vs. 26 ויקרא בשם הבעל); II K. 5.11; Zeph. 3.9; Ps. 116.4, 13, 17; 129.8; I Chr. 16.2 etc.

[40] Zech. 13.9; Ps. 9.11; 91.15.

[41] Isa. 52.6; cf. Isa. 64.1; Ps. 20.2.

[42] Num. 6.27.

[43] Jer. 10.25//Ps. 76.6.

[44] Cf. Amos 8.14; Jer. 12.16. God Himself swears "by His great name" Jer. 44.26; cf. Amos 8.7.

name of Yahveh."[45] Thus Jehoshaphat orders Micaiah to speak to him the truth in the name of Yahveh only.[46] Jeremiah complains that he was not permitted to speak in the name of Yahveh.[47] The "name of Yahveh" figured also in personal greetings, as in Judges 6.12, "Yahveh be with thee" and Ruth 2.4, "Yahveh bless thee." It is paralleled by the benediction, "The Lord bless thee out of Zion,"[48] and by the interchange of greetings between the lay worshipers at the Temple and the Levites entering upon their night service.[49] The response to this greeting, as given in Ps. 129.8, is: "We bless you in the name of Yahveh." Tradition reports that after the death of Simon the Just (probably the contemporary of Ben Sira), whether out of considerations of reverence or possibly because of Hellenistic persecution, the use of the divine name was withheld from greetings. With the passing of the danger, the old usage was reinstituted.[50] We are informed further that, bent on the Hellenization of the Jews, the Greek government forbade them to mention God's name (שם שמים) in documents. Following the Maccabean victory the old practice was restored. The formula ran: "In the year .... of Johanan the High Priest of the 'Most High God.'" This use of the divine name in secular documents displeased the sages (Pharisees), who, upon gaining the upper hand, abolished the practice on the ground that the notes, when cancelled, would be thrown away and the name would thus be defiled.[51]

[45] Deut. 18.22.

[46] I K. 22.16//II Chr. 18.15.

[47] Jer. 11.21; 26.9; 16.20. See further Jer. 23.25; Zech. 13.3; I Chr. 21.19; II Chr. 33.18.

[48] Ps. 128.5.

[49] Ps. 134.3; cf. I Chr. 9.33.

[50] Bertinoro comments: ולא אמרינן מזלזל הוא בכבודו של מקום בשביל כבד הבריות להוציא שם שמים עליו. See Geiger, *Urschrift*, p. 263. Ber. 8.5; Yoma 39b. Marmorstein's argument in *The Old Rabbinic Doctrine of God*, Ch. 1, fails to carry conviction. See Tos., ed. Zuckermandel, *Sotah* 13.8, p. 319, l. 24. Ms. W: משמת שמעון הצדיק פסקו מלברך בשם. Graetz considers this injunction to use יהוה in place of אדני = ζύρτος as "a measure taken at the time of Bar Kochba to distinguish Jews from Judeo-Christians who regarded Jesus also as Lord. *Geschichte*, 2nd ed. IV, 458. The dating fits into the statement of Abba Bar Kahana (Mid. Tehil. on Ps. 36, end) that two generations used the שם המפורש, the Men of the Great Assembly and those of the period of the *Shemad* (Hadrianic persecution)." Bacher, *J.E.* XI, 263.

[51] Meg. Taanit VII; R.H. 18b.

It is noteworthy that "the name of Yahveh" nowhere figures as a separate divine being, but is generally equivalent to Yahveh. Such a phrase as "Ashtorteh, the name of Baal"[52] has no analogue in Hebrew writings. While Isaiah 30.27 contains the startling expression "the name of Yahveh cometh," the context shows that Yahveh Himself is meant, and in the parallel passage 59.19 "the name" alternates with "the glory of Yahveh." So, too, the combination of "name" with "glory," as in "the name of His glory" or "His glorious name," refers to God.[53]

While "the Name" is invariably combined with Yahveh or with a possessive pronoun, in three Biblical verses it appears by itself with the definite article: *Hashem*, e.g. in Lev. 24.11, 16; Deut. 28.58. The Deuteronomic passage marks the culmination of the use of "the Name" as a substitute for Yahveh. It is given as "the glorious and awful Name," thus conveying the doxological connotation associated with it in the minds of the people. "Hashem" became the standard usage among both Samaritans[54] and Jews, displacing both the Tetragrammaton and its substitute Adonai for uses other

---

[52] עשתרת שם בעל *Corpus Inscriptionum Semiticarum*, Paris '81, pt. I, no. 3, 1, 18.

[53] Ps. 72.10; 29.2; 96.8. Cf. Ex. 33.18 f. T.K. Cheyne, *E.B.*, art. "Name," III, 3268 and כבוד in Brown, Driver and Briggs, *Hebrew and English Lexicon*, and Lewy, *Neuhebräisches und Chaldäisches Wörterbuch*; Marmorstein, *The Old Rabbinic Doctrine of God*, p. 88. שם כבד מלכותו corresponds to שמיה רבא in the Kaddish. Thus the Targum Jerushalmi to Gen. 49.2 and Deut. 6.4 states that Jacob on his death bed, hearing his sons recite the Shema and thus professing the unity of God, responded יהי שמיה רבא מברך לעלמו ולעלמין. Pes. 56a, repeating this Haggadah, reports that he said ברוך שם כבד מלכותו לעולם ועד. (For variants see Kasher, *Torah Shelemah* to Gen. 49.2). Both expressions stand for שם אדנות, the Tetragrammaton. Cf. Gen. R. 93.1 קבל מלכותו ואדנותו. Thus the Shema is referred to as מלכות שמים. (Deut. R. 2.31 איזה מלכות שמים, שמע ישראל ה' אלהינו ה' אחד ... כבדי אחר ומיזחד בעולם. The recitation of the Shema is referred to as קבלת עול מלכות שמים (Ber. 13a).

[54] שמא Kirchheim, *Karme Shomron*, pp. 17, 94, 99; Geiger, *Urschrift*, p. 262. They substituted שמא for Yahveh. Abraham Ibn Ezra's report that the Samaritans translated the first verse of Genesis with ברא אשימא with a reference to 2 Kings 17.30, is groundless. See the introduction to his commentary on Esther. The Samaritan Targum reads: בקדמתא טלמם אלהה ית שמיה. It retains the word השם in Lev. 24.11. Verse 16 is rendered: ומקסם שם יהוה. In Deut. 28.58 השם is translated with the Tetragrammaton, *e.g.* למדחל מן יהוה יקירה ונוראה הדן מן יהוה אלהך.

than worship.[55] The Tetragrammaton became the שם מהיוחד and שם המפורש, the *Ineffable Name* "ἄρρητον, unspoken, unutterable."[56]

The Tetragrammaton was originally spoken by all the priests in the Temple in pronouncing the benediction. In the synagogues the substitute name Adonai was employed in worship.[57] (This practice has prevailed in

[55] Sanh. 60a. Thus למען השם, חלול השם, קדוש השם and in still later usage השם יתברך and ברוך השם.

[56] The term permits of two interpretations. One is: "expressed distinctly" (as in Shek 1.5; תקנה גדולה; Git. 36a וכן הוא מפורש על ידי עזרא; Tamid 3.7; Mid. 4.2 ועליו הוא מפורש על ידי יחזקאל; המגדף אינו חייב עד התקינו שיהיו עדים מפרשין שמותיהם בגיטין. Thus the Mishnah teaches that שיפרש השם a blasphemer is not condemned until he has clearly pronounced the name. (Rashi comments: שיזכור את השם). Sanh. 7.5; 55b. In this case שם המפורש has to be taken in the opposite sense of the ineffable or the unspoken name of God. The Targum of Judg. 13.18 renders פלאי with מפרש. Similarly Onkelos and Jonathan translate פלא (Ex. 15.11) with פרישין. This would give the term שם המפורש the meaning of the mysterious or ineffable name. See Levy, *Wörterbuch*, sub פרישא. The Syriac שמא פרישא is interpreted by Bar Bahlul as גניזא. See Geiger, *Urschrift* p. 264, note. Another possibility is to derive the word מפורש from the root meaning of פרש "to separate," "to set aside," as in Lev. R. 24.4: כשם שאני פרוש כך תהיו פרושים. Whatever the etymology, the name is used in the sense of שם המיוחד. Thus Jonathan employs שמא דמייחד in Lev. 24,16. Sotah 38a (also Sifre to Num. 6,27) interchanges the two: כה תברכו את בני ישראל, בשם המפורש. אתה אומר בשם המפורש או אינו אלא בכינוי ת"ל ושמו את שמי, שמי המיוחד לי. Similar usage is found in Sanh. 60a,b; Sab. 36a "The incommunicable name" appears in *Wisd. Solomon* 14, 21.

Bacher suggests that "since the Tetragrammaton is called also 'Shem Hameyuhad' it may be assumed that 'meyuhad' is used elsewhere in the terminology of the Tannaitic schools as a synonym for 'meforash,' both words designating something which is distinguished by a characteristic sign from other objects of its kind." (See Bacher, *Die Exegetische Terminologie der Jüdischen Traditionsliteratur*, I, p. 159), *J.E.* XI, p. 262, art. "Shem Ha-meforash." See Kohut, *Aruk Hashalem*, art יחד II, p. 123.

It is instructive to note that theophorus names, with יהו, either as a prefix or as a suffix, so common in pre-exilic times underwent a change in post-exilic times. From the prefix the ה or הו is dropped and from the suffix the ו or the י, e.g. יורם = יהורם, יקים = יהויקים, ישוע = יהושע. מיכה = מיכיהו, ישעיה = ישעיהו, ירמיה = ירמיהו, חניה = חנניה = חנניה and.

[57] Tamid 7.2; Sotah 7.6; 38a; Mek. Bahodesh 11; Sifre, Num. 39; Hag. 16a. Outside of the Bible it became customary to write יי, ייי, or יי (i.e. two yods with a vav over them, numerically equivalent to הויה). ה' for השם or ד' for אדני. The word אלהים was generally written without change. (See J. Z. Lauterbach, "Substitutes for the Tetragrammaton." *Proceedings of the*

worship to the present. In study and conversation *Hashem* is used.) Following
the death of Simon the Just —which was marked by the spread of Hellenism
and its heretical trends — the Tetragrammaton ceased to be spoken even in
the Temple by the ordinary priests. The High Priest alone pronounced it on
Yom Kippur while reciting Lev. 16.30 during the confessional.[58] R. Tarfon
reports that even the high priest uttered it cautiously under his breath.[59] The
rest of the time both he and others invoked God as *Hashem*.[60] The LXX interprets Lev. 24.16 as threatening with death any one who mentions the Tetragrammaton. Onkelos understands the verse in the same sense. On the other
hand, the Jerusalem Targum adheres to the plain meaning of the text, forbidding the employment of the Tetragrammaton in abusive speech.[61] The
Gemara preserves both meanings, basing the first one on the derivation of the
word ויקב from the root נקב "to point out," "to designate," as in Num. 1.17,
and the second one by deriving the word from קבה "to curse," as in Num.
23,8. A third meaning is added by relating it to another connotation of the
root נקב "to pierce," as in II Kings 12.10, *i.e.*, using the divine name for
magic purposes.[62]

The third interpretation of Lev. 24.16 sheds light upon the awesome
sanctity with which the Rabbis surrounded the Tetragrammaton. It was a
cardinal Gnostic doctrine that the Creator God of the Bible was an inferior
deity, whose name was known and used in their formulas, whereas the highest
divinity remained unknown and inexpressible.[63] To overcome this heretical

---

American Academy for Jewish Research, 1930–31, pp. 39–67.) During the last century it
became customary to write אלקים for אלהים, אלוק for אלוה and קל for אל. J. D. Eisenstein
denounces this practice on the part of preachers and journalists as blasphemous. *Hadoar*, Vol.
XXI, no. 40, p. 689, Oct. 16, 1942.

[58] Tos. Yoma 2.2 reports that the name was spoken ten times by the high priest on Yom
Kippur. For the continued use of אנא השם in liturgic compositions, see Davidson, *Ozar
Hashirah*, I, p. 287, nos. 6295–6302.

[59] Jeru. Yoma 3.7, end.

[60] Ber. 4.4; Yoma 3.8; 4.2; 6.2.

[61] Rashi combines both meanings. Ibn Ezra takes the word in the sense of pronouncing, as
in Isa. 42.2 and Num. 1.17.

[62] Sanh. 56a.

[63] Iranaeus, *op. cit.*, I, 5.

teaching, the Rabbis stressed the ineffable nature of the Tetragrammaton as representing the one and only God, and withdrew it from ordinary use.

3. Theurgic Uses of the Names.

Hillel's saying וְדִישְׁתַּמַּשׁ בְּתַגָּא חֲלָף points to the theurgic use of the Name.[64] More definitely Abba Saul denies future bliss to anyone who pronounces the Tetragrammaton with its actual consonants. The context of the Mishnah relates this statement to the prohibition of plying the magic art for purposes of healing.[65] We seem to be confronted with Gnostic practice in which sacred names and formulas were employed. The knowledge of the names of the demons or gods was essential to the Gnostic scheme of salvation. Bousset writes: "We constantly meet with the idea that the soul, on leaving the body, finds its path to the highest heaven opposed by the deities and demons of the lower realms of heaven, and only when it is in possession of the names of these demons, and can repeat the proper holy formula, or is prepared with the holy oil, finds its way unhindered to the heavenly home." Accordingly Gnostic books (like the II Coptic Jiu) are filled with such names and symbols. "This system again was simplified, and as the supreme secret was taught in a simple name or a single formula, by means of which the happy possessor was able to penetrate through all the space of heaven.[66] It was taught that even the redeemer-god, when he once descended on to this earth, to rise from it again, availed himself of these names and formulas on his descent and ascent through the world of demons." In such ideas Anz finds the central doctrine of Gnosticism.[67]

---

[64] Abot 1.13; Ab. R.N., I, ed. Schechter, p. 56.

[65] Sanh. 10.1. According to Ab. Zarah 17b Hanina b. Teradion met with a martyr's death as a punishment for teaching the pronunciation of the Tetragrammaton to his disciples. From the Samaritans Theodoret learned that it was pronounced Ἰαο. See Levy, *Wörterbuch*, under אגה, I, 17: Hastings, *Encycl. Rel. and Ethics*, art. "Charms and Amulets," III, 424–5.

[66] Cf. the use of "Caulacau" among the Basilidians, Iranaeus, *op. cit.*, I, 24, 5.

[67] Art. "Gnosticism," *Encycl. Brit.*, 11th ed., XII, 155. For Jewish parallels see Hekalot Rabbati, 22, in Jellinek's *Bet Ham.*, III, 90 ff.; Gershom G. Scholem, *Major Trends in Jewish Mysticism*, pp. 48 ff., 358, no. 50, *et al.*

The use of the Tetragrammaton and other divine appellations for magic purposes by Gnostics led to the *halachah* that the writings of the Minim must not be saved from conflagration despite the *azkarot,* the divine names, occurring in them.[68] R. Jose taught that on week days one may read the divine names in them and store away or burn the rest. R. Tarfon, indignantly, avowed that should the books of the Minim fall into his hands he would burn them together with the divine names, because "they would inject enmity, jealousy and envy between Israel and the Heavenly Father."[69] They offended monotheistic belief.

The Rabbinic opposition to the theurgic uses of the name notwithstanding, the practice spread among the Jewish people. The belief in the almighty potency of the name, which may go back to Egyptian magic,[70] gained strong hold on the Jewish mind both as a subject of mystic speculation and of practice. The Hasidim, Essenes, and Pharisees were attracted to it. Enoch 69.13–25 speaks of the "hidden name" as having been guarded by Michael and employed in the oath wherewith God created the whole universe.[71] The Jewish variety of Gnosticism as preserved in the mystic Haggadah utilized it. The four sages who entered the *Pardes,* i.e., Gnostic speculation, resorted to the *Shem Hameforash* to gaze into the divine mysteries.[72] The mystic *Pirke de*

---

[68] For the use of אזכרה and הזכרה (Aramaic אדכרתא) in place of שם in Rabbinic literature see Bacher, *op. cit.,* 187. The usage goes back to the Bible, where זכר appears several times in place of שם (Ps. 30.5; 97.12; 102.13; Hos. 12.6) or as a synonym of שם (Ex. 3.15; Isa. 26.8; Ps. 135. 13; cf. Job 18.17).

[69] Tos. Sab. 13.5; 116a. Cf. Ber. 8a; Gen. R. 20.6; Tanh. B, I, 71b. See Anz, *Zur Frage nach dem Ursprung des Gnosticismus,* p. 6 ff. et passim. Ἰάω Σαδαώθ and Ἀιλεῖν figure in Greek magical papyri. In Egyptian magical papyri, too, Jewish and heathen names appear in juxtaposition or combination. Sanh. 60a, Yoma 3.7 and Eccl. R. 3.11 refers to the use of the Name by gentiles as a magic formula. See Marmorsteing, *Old Rabbinic Doctrine of God,* pp. 18,30. Scholem calls attention to the predilection on the part of Jewish mystics to use Greek formulas, *op. cit.,* pp. 358–9, notes 50, 57, 58. For example see Hekalot R., 12.

[70] The Egyptian origin of Jewish magic is attested by the books of Hermes and by the Greek and Coptic magic papyri. See L. Blau, art. "Magic," *J.E.,* VIII, 255 f. M. Gaster, art. "Magic, Jewish," Hastings, *Encycl. Rel. and Ethics,* VIII, 303.

[71] See also *Prayer of Manasseh*; K. Kohler, *Origin of Synagogue and Church,* I, ch. 1.

[72] For a discussion of the entire theme see Scholem, *op. cit.,* pp. 39–78. Hag. 12a and commentaries of Rashi and R. Hananeel (Hag. 14b).

Rabbi Eliezer teaches that the great Name existed by the side of God before-creation.[73] The opinion persisted that the Name served as an instrument wherewith God created the world. The thought is further expressed that He fashioned both this world and the world to come by means of the first two letters of the Tetragrammaton[74] The *Sefer Yezirah*, the classic text of Kabbalistic speculation, teaches that the world was created through the combination of the letters in the Divine name. Such knowledge, we are told, enabled Rab Hanina and Rab Oshaiah to create a living calf every Friday for Sabbath use, an act of which the Rabbis disapproved as magic.[75] God wages war by means of the Name. It also served as the sword of Moses and as the weapon with which the generations of Hezekiah and Zedekiah fought. The Name was revealed to Moses that he might redeem Israel. R. Simeon b. Yohai says that God gave Israel a weapon at Sinai in which the name is inscribed. With its aid demons are dispelled.[76] The occult character of the Name is further apparent from the saying of R. Johanan that the sages transmitted it to their disciples once in seven years. This refers particularly to the twelve and forty-two lettered names of God. We read: "At first the twelve-lettered Name was given to any man. When the impious (פרוצים, sectarians, gnostics?) multiplied, it was entrusted only to the discreet ones (צנועים) among the priests, and they blended it in the chant of their brethren during the priestly benediction. R. Tarfon says. Once I went up to the dais (where the benediction was pronounced) with my maternal uncle. I inclined my ear and heard the high priest blend it in the melody of his brother priests. R. Jehudah cited Rab's teaching

---

[73] *Pirke de Rabbi Eliezer,* 3.

[74] Hag. 2.1; Men. 29b; Gen. R. 12.10 and notes by Theodor; Kasher *Torah Shelemah* II, no. 73; Midr. Alpha Betha of Rabbi Akiba II, letter Shin, *Bet Ham,* III, 54; Mas. Hekalot, Ibid., II, 46; Pesikta R. 21, ed. Friedmann, 104a (ז ,מב 'יש) הוא שמי [אני ה'] מה אני אמר הקב״ה בונה עולמות ומכריב עולמות אף שמי בונה ומחריב עולמות.

[75] Sanh. 7.11; 65b; 67b; Ber. 55a יודע מים בצלאל לצרף אותיות שנבראו בהן שמים וארץ; Gen. R. 1.1, where the Torah figures as the instrument of creation (cf. Logos).

[76] Midr. Tehillim 36.8; Tanhuma, Buber, Vaera 5; Gaster, *The Sword of Moses;* J. D. Eisenstein, *Ozar Midrashim* I, 201, חרב של משה; Ascoli, "Sifre Hafalashim," in *Sinai,* 1941, IV, 236–39. See Targum Jeru. Num. 31.8; Sanh. 106ab; מעשה ישו in L. Ginzberg, *Ginze Schechter* I, 324 ff., תולדות ישו, in Samuel Krauss, *Das Leben Jesu nach jüdischen Quellen,* pp. 40, 47, 79, 118, 128, 147; Jeru. Yoma 3.7; Git. 68a; Num. R. 12.3; Tanh., Buber, Balak, 23.

that the forty-two lettered Name may be entrusted only to one who is discreet and humble, and in his middle years, who is not given to anger and to drunkenness and is not stubborn. He who knows it and is careful about it and who guards it in purity is beloved above and is liked below, and he is respected by his fellowmen and he inherits both this world and the world to come."[77] The Haggadah knows also of a seventy-two lettered Name. It is believed to be the name wherewith God delivered Israel from Egypt.[78] The twelve lettered Name is supposed to be composed of the three words אהיה in Ex. 3.14. The forty-two lettered Name is represented by the abbreviations of the forty-two word prayer ascribed to the first century tanna, R. Nehunya b. Hakanah, אנא בכח, arranged in three letter words: אב״ג ית״ץ קר״ע שט״ן נג״ד יכ״ש בט״ר חק״ב טנ״ע יג״ל פז״ק שק״ו צי״ת צת״ג.[79] It is also explained as the combination of the letters of אדני הויה אהיה יהוה, written in full, viz., אלף דלת נון יוד הא ואו יוד הא אלף הא יוד הא יוד הא ואו הא. The seventy-two lettered Name is derived from the three verses, Ex. 14.19-21 (ויסע ויבא ויט), each of which contains seventy-two letters. The letters of these verses are fantastically arranged in three lettered words by reading the letters of ויסע and ויט forward and of the middle verse ויבא backward.[80] According to the Hebrew book of Enoch the mysterious great name of God was confided to Metatron, who entrusted it to Moses, and Moses to Joshua, and Joshua to the elders, and the elders to the prophets, and the prophets to the men of the Great Synagogue, and the men of the Great Synagogue to Ezra, and Ezra to R. Abbahu, and R. Abbahu to R. Zeera, and R. Zeera to the men of faith (אנשי אמונה = mystics) and the

---

[77] Kid. 71a. Cf. Eccl. R. 3.11; Hekalot R., 13; *Bet Ham.* III, 93. Scholem, *op. cit.*, 46ff.

[78] Gen. R. 44.19 and notes by Theodor; Pesikta R. 15, 78b. Alpha Beta of R. Akiba, letter He, *Bet Ham*, III, 23–25.

[79] I. Davidson, *Ozar Hashirah V'hapiyyut* I, 285, no. 6242; *Nehora Hashalem*, p. 12. These speculations bear a strong relationship to the teachings of the Marcosian Gnostics regarding the names of deity. "The unoriginated and inconceivable Father," they held, enunciated his whole name as consisting of thirty letters, which correspond to the names of the Aeons and figured as instruments of creation. Irenaeus, *op. cit.*, I, 14.

[80] Lekah Tob, ad loc.; Responsum of R. Hai Gaon, *Ozar Hageonim*, Hag. p. 23 and art. "Names of God" in *J.E.* IX, 164, where a table of the 72 tri-lettered names is given. See also שעור קומה in Eisenstein's *Ozar Midrashim* II, 562a.

men of faith to their disciples (אנשי אמונה לבעלי אמונות) to guard it and, with it, to cure all sicknesses.[81]

Rationalists looked with disfavor upon the extravagant speculations regarding the Name. Maimonides considers the twelve lettered name inferior in sanctity to the Tetragrammaton. In his opinion it was "not a simple noun, but consisted of two or three words, the sum of their letters being twelve." These words were employed as a substitute for the Tetragrammaton in the manner of the substitute Adonai, but of more distinctive character. Similarly the forty-two lettered name, he maintains, could not possibly constitute one word but rather "a combination of words of metaphysical character conveying a correct notion of the essence of God." "*Shem hameforash* applied neither to the Name of forty-two letters nor to that of twelve but only to the Tetragrammaton." Whereas all other names for God are homonyms, the Tetragrammaton is the distinct name of God, denoting something peculiar to Him which is shared by no one else.[82]

Maimonides warns against the theurgic uses of the Divine names. "You must beware of sharing the error of those who write amulets (*kameot*). Whatever you hear from them, or read in their works, especially in reference to the names which they form by combination, is utterly senseless; they call these combinations *shemot* and believe that their pronunciation demands sanctification and purification, and that by using them they are enabled to work miracles. Rational persons ought not to listen to such men, nor in any way believe their assertions."[83]

Kabbalists, on the other hand, found a fertile field for their activities in the occult manipulations of the letters of the divine names. Through such combination they believed themselves able to work miracles. Various uses of this type are enumerated in the question concerning the Name addressed to Rab Hai Gaon. Excepting the Talmudic reports of the miraculous uses of the

[81] Sefer Hanok, *Bet Ham.*, II, 117.

[82] *Guide* I, 62; *Biur Shemot Kodesh Vehol*, ed. Gaster, *Debir* I, 194 f.: וזהו שאומר עצמו שמו ושמו עצמו cf. *Kuzari* IV, 3.

[83] *Guide* I, 61, tr. Friedlander, p. 90 f.

Name, he categorically rejected all subsequent claims as based on mere hear-say and credulity and denounced them as sheer nonsense.[84]

4. God's Attributes

While the Tetragrammaton was revealed by God to Moses,[85] it was also believed to have been discovered by the unaided reason of man. Human intelligence expressing itself in naming objects, found also the name God. R. Aha says that when the Holy One was about to create man, the angels dissuaded Him. "What is man that Thou rememberest him?"[86] "His wisdom will exceed yours," God replied. While the angels proved unable to find the names of animals, beasts and birds, "the man gave names to all cattle and the fowl of the air, and to every beast of the field."[87] Himself he called Adam because of his origin out of the earth (*Adamah*). "And what is My name?" The Holy One asked him. "It is fitting to call Thee Yahveh (= Adonai), for Thou art the Lord of all Thy creatures," Adam replied. R. Aha adds: "The Holy One said, 'I am Yahveh; that is My name;[88] that is the name which Adam gave Me; that is the name which I specified for Myself; that is the name which I agreed upon with the ministering angels.'"[89]

To reconcile this belief with the statement of Gen. 4.26 that in the days of Enosh men began to call upon the name of Yahveh, the Rabbis interpret the

---

[84] *Ozar Hageonim*, Hag. pp. 16–17: אלו וכיוצא בהם דברים במלים . . . וכל אלה דברי רוח. Albo, *Ikkarim* II, 28, ed. Husik, Vol. 2, pp. 285–6. Cf. *Sefer Raziel Hamalak*, Amsterdam, 1701, p. 2b. The term *Baal Shem* came to figure prominently as a theurgist and folk healer, particularly after the spread of Lurianic Kabbalah. See Abraham Kahana, *Sefer Hahasidut*, pp. 20 ff. Reference is made to חסידים בעלי שם in ס' מלחמות ה', Mahzor Vitri, p. 738.

[85] Ex. 6.2–3.

[86] Ps. 8.5.

[87] Gen. 2.20.

[88] Isa. 42.8.

[89] Pesikta R. 14, pp. 59b–60a, on I K. 5.11. Gen. R. 17.4 cites the additional saying of R. Aha in the name of R. Hiyya.

latter to mean that in the days of Enosh men began to call their idols by the name of Yahveh.[90]

The other names of God are all of human origin. R. Johanan cites R. Simeon b. Yohai's teaching that Abraham commenced to call the Holy One by the name of *Adon* = Lord (אדני יהוה במה אדע וכו').[91] Hannah was the first to call Him *Zebaot*.[92] The other designations of the Holy One represent human efforts to make His being real to themselves. They are descriptive of His nature and actions and may be classed as *divine attributes*. The *Mechiltah* regards them as terms of praise, and lists among them: "God," "Judge," "Almighty," "[Lord of] Hosts," "I am that I am," "gracious and merciful," "long-suffering and of great kindness and true," and "Almighty Lord."[93] The Talmud includes the following seven among the sacred names that may not be erased: אל, אלהים (אלהיך אלהיכם), אהיה אשר אהיה, אדני, שדי, צבאות.[94] The *Sefer Yezirah* enumerates thirteen names (probably corresponding to the thirteen attributes in Ex. 34.6–7: יה, יהוה, צבאות, אלהי ישראל, אלהים חיים, ומלך עולם, אל, שדי, רחום, וחנון, רם ונשא, שוכן עד, מרום וקדוש שמו.[95]

The Midrash knows of seventy names of God of Biblical origin.[96] The late

---

[90] Thus Targum Onkelos reads חלו. Jonathan states: הוא דרא דביומוהי שריאו למטעי ועבדו להון. Gen. R. 23, 16 interprets the word הוהל as מרד לשון. טעוון ומבנין לטעוותהון בשום מימרא דיי. Midrash Aggada, ad. loc. states: נעשה שמו של הקב"ה מחולל שעשה ע"ז והנעו עצמם מלקרא בשם ה'. Rashi explains הוחל as ד"א הוהל, התבטל, כמו לא יהל דברו (במדבר ל,ג,9 בתרגומו לא יבטל לשון חולין). לקרא את שמות האדם ואת שמות העצבים בשמו של הקב"ה לעשותן ע"ז ולקרותן אלהות See Kasher, *Torah Shelemah*, n. 159.

[91] Gen. 15.8; Ber. 7b; cf. Sifre. Deut. 317 and *Yalkut Hamakiri*, Ps. 22.12: עד שלא בא אברהם אבינו לעולם כביכול לא היה הקב"ה מלך אלא על משמים. משבא אברהם אבינו מהליכו על השמים ועל הארץ.

[92] I Sam. 1.11. Ber. 31b, and Tosafot.

[93] Ps. 89.9. Tractate Kaspa, tr. J. Z. Lauterbach III, 181.

[94] Shabuot 35a, b; Soferim 4.1. Maimonides presents these seven with some variations: ושבעה שמות הם, השם הנכתב יו"ד ה"א וא"ו ה"א והוא השם מהפורש או הנכתב אדני, ואל, אלוה, ואלהים ואלהי, שדי וצבאות. Joseph Caro refers to a different text which omitted אלהי. He also cites the reading of the Venice ed.: השם הנכתב ... ואלה, ואלהים, ואהיה ושדי וצבאות (ed.. Wilna) *H. Yesode Hatorah* 6.2 and *Kesef Mishneh., Yoreh Deah* 276, 12.

[95] *Sefer Yezirah* 1.1.

[96] Num. R. 14.12; an incomplete list is given in Mid. Zutta to Canticles, ed. Buber, p. 8; *Yalkut Hamakiri*, ed. Buber, Psalms, 24.35. Mid. Hagadol to Gen. 46.8 gives the full list. See Konovitz, *Haelohut*, 1.5, where 71 names are listed.

Hebrew book of Enoch refers to ninety-two names without listing them.[97] Marmorstein discusses ninety-one terms for God in Rabbinic literature.[98] To these may be added numerous creations of the Kabbalists, *Payyotanim* and philosphers.[99] The above quoted Midrash comments that the seventy names are those expressed directly, but the indirect names are numberless.[100] The Zohar regards the whole Torah as composed of God's names.[101]

Upon examination, some of the names in the Midrash and in Marmorstein's study can be admitted only by a most liberal stretch of the imagination. We refer to such designations as אדם, איש, אש, אריה, עופר האילים, צבי, נשר. Some of them are dynamic symbols of life, light, power, truth, justice, etc. serving to intimate God's nature. Others are metonyms derived from some association with God in the text of Scripture. Still others express His relation to the world and to man. We may group them into terms expressing God's:

a) reality: אהיה אשר אהיה, היה הוה ויהיה, אחד, יחיד, אמת, חי, חי וקים, אלהים חיים.

b) personality: אני, אתה, הוא, פנים, איש, אדם.

c) mystery: נורא, נפלא, מסתתר, קדוש, הקדוש ברוך הוא, רואה ואינו נראה, יושב בסתרו של עולם.

---

[97] *Bet Ham.* II, 116.

[98] *Op. cit.,* Ch. III.

[99] Zunz, *Synagogale Poesie,* pp. 498–500 presents a number of rare names. See *Midrash Talpiyyot,* art. כנויי המדות, pp. 407 ff. for Kabbalistic, and J. Klatzkin, *Ozar Hamunahim Hapilosufiim,* 4 vols., for philosophical additions.

[100] Sefer Hanok, *Bet Ham.* II, 114.

[101] *Zohar,* III, 73. See Nahmanides, Com. Gen. 1.1. Muhammad, while stressing the unity of God, refers to many names of God. In Quran 20.7 he declares: "God, there is no god but He! His are the excellent titles." According to a tradition of Abu Huraira, he taught: "Verily there are ninety-nine names of God, and whosoever recites them shall enter Paradise." These names all express some quality of God, such as Merciful, Creator, Clement, Majestic, etc. The reason offered for this multiplicity of epithets is that God may be ever addressed by a name most suited to the needs of His petitioner. In confessing sin, a man addresses God as "The Forgiving" or "The Acceptor" of repentance; when in need of sustenance he may invoke God as "the Provider." In perplexity he may turn to God as "the Director," etc. "To assist in the repetition of these names, a rosary of one hundred beads is used. The Wahabites, however, use their fingers, believing that to have been the custom of Muhammad. The name of *Allah* is recited first or last to make up the hundred." (Edward Sell, art. "God, Muslim," Hastings, *Encycl. Rel. and Ethics* VI, 301.)

d) eternity: ראשון, אחרון, עתיק יומין, שוכן עד (ש' עדי עד), קדמונו של עולם, עתיקו
של עולם.

e) sublimity: נשגב, נשא, רם, עליון, בחור, דגול מרבבה.

f) beauty: צח ואדום, הדר, חור.

g) wisdom: חכם, מבין, בעל מחשבות, יודע מחשבות, חוקר לבבות, בוחן לבבות, בוחן
כליות.

h) moral excellence: תמים, צדיק, חסיד, טוב, ישר, הטוב וממטיב, הרחמן, רחמנא,
חנון ורחום, ארך אפים, ורב חסד, נוקם ונוטר, נאמן, הימנותא. בעל הנחמות, ב' הפקדון, ב'
הרחמים, ב' השבועה, ב' המשפט, מי שענה.

i) might: אביר, אדיר, גבור, הגבורה, עזוז, צבאות, שדי, אל, אלהים, גאוה, חזק, מגדל
עוז, [הצור].

j) nature symbols: אש, אריה, נשר, צבי, צור, עופר האילים.

k) relations to

 (1) space: שכינה, מקום, שמים, גבוה, גבהות העולם, רומו של עולם [רם ונשא,
עליון], מעון, מרום, מעלה.

 (2) world: בורא, יוצר, פועל, קונה, ורגע, בעל הבית, בעל הבירה, בעל מלאכה,
צור עולמים, רבון העולם (ר' העולמים),
רבש"ע, יישרו של עולם, צדיקו של עולם, גדול העולמים, אלופו של עולם, מי
שאמר והיה העולם, כבשונו של עולם, כבודו של עולם, יחודו של עולם, מזנא
דעלמא. מרותיה של עולם, עשירו של עולם, שלום העולמים, הי העולמים, מרן די
בשמיא.

 (3) Israel: אלהי ישראל, שומר ישראל, צור ישראל, לבו (לבן) של ישראל, אביר
יעקב, (א' ישראל), תוקפיהון של ישראל.

 (4) Man: אב, אח, דוד, ידיד, גואל, שומר, רועה, עד, דיין, שופט, מרי (מרן),
אדון, מלך ממ"ה, קורא הדורות, אב לכל באי עולם.

These and the numerous other designations of God clearly convey the meaning of God in the life and thought of the Jewish people. The freedom with which they are used indicates that the Jewish religious consciousness was clear regarding their symbolical significance and was not troubled by fear of their being possibly misunderstood. To the Jewish mind they conveyed provisional and figurative but nonetheless real presentations of the deepest truths of religion, of God's being, His transcendence and His nearness, His baffling mysteriousness and His clear light and accessibility. The conviction was firm

— though not philosophically demonstrated — that while God is one and unique, nameless and inscrutable, He acts outward upon the universe, revealing attitudes and ways to which names may be given. But these are human creations and consequently apply to God only provisionally. Hence great caution must be exercised in their use. We are told that a certain man invoked God in these terms: "The great God, the mighty, the awe-inspiring, the strong, the powerful, the feared, the omnipotent, the forceful, the true and the revered." When he finished praying, R. Haninah rebuked him: "Have you exhausted the praises of your Master? Why all these attributes? Even the first three, had they not been spoken by Moses in the Torah[102] and fixed by the Men of the Great Synagogue in the *Tefillah*, we would hesitate to speak them. And you heap up all these! It is like a person who owned myriads of golden dinars and was praised for possessing some silver coins. Is not such praise an offense to Him?"[103] "'Who can express the mighty acts of the Lord? Who can proclaim all His praise?'[104] Rabba bar Bar Hana said in the name of R. Johanan: 'He who details the praises of the Holy One more than is proper will be extirpated from the world.' . . .[105]" R. Judah of Kefar Giburiyah (or of Gibbor Hayyil) interprets the words of Ps. 65.2 לך דומיה תהלה (literally: "praise befitteth Thee") as "for Thee silence is praise."[106] Since God's praises cannot be expressed adequately, it is most becoming for man to remain silent before Him.

Despite these exhortations, the praises of God in Jewish worship reached the extravagant. Both the formal liturgy and the *piyyutim* abound in them. In many instances they assume the form of wearisome enumerations of divine

[102] Deut. 10.17.
[103] Ber. 33b. The parallel account in Jeru. Ber. 9.1 reports this incident as having occurred to R. Johanan and R. Jonathan. In Ket. 8b Judah bar Nahmani approvingly praised God as "the great in the abundance of His greatness, mighty and strong in the abundance of His fear, reviving the dead by His word, doing great things beyond searching out and wondrous things without end."
[104] Ps. 106.2.
[105] Referring to Job 37.20.
[106] Meg. 18a; Jeru. Ber. 9.1; Midr. Ps. 19.2. For the use of these passages in support of the doctrine of negative attributes see Maimonides, *Guide* I, 59.

honorifics, strung together alphabetically. However, at times — as in portions of the Rosh Hashanah and Yom Kippur services — they rise to ecstatic heights, producing an overpowering sense of mystery and awe before the supreme majesty and glory of the Holy One.

Love, Human and Divine,
in Post-Biblical Literature*

Introduction

Since the days of Paul and John, the view has prevailed that the originality of the Christian religion consists in its proclamation of a new doctrine of love. In place of God, the stern Judge, Christianity—it is asserted—enthroned the God of Mercy; and, instead of "an eye for an eye, and a tooth for a tooth," it promulgated the great commandment of forgiveness. Hence this antithesis, drawn by most Christian theologians: whereas Judaism rests on rigid justice, Christianity lives on the milk of human kindness.[1] Gradually this belief has filtered through our own theological reasoning, with the result that one of our own teachers[2] has ventured to discover the foundation of Judaism in the "Moral Indignation" as expressed in the *lex talionis*.

All such views ignore the basic truth that Judaism, besides being a *corpus juris*, is a living faith. A civil code must repose on the firm rock of justice; but a religion draws its life breath from the atmosphere of Divine love. Through

---

* Published: Central Conference of American Rabbis Yearbook, XXVII, 1917.

[1] The "American Israelite" recently reported a sermon by a Methodist minister in which he "proved to his congregation that the whole trouble with the Kaiser is that he 'has discarded the New Testament God as exemplified by Jesus Christ and adopted the Old Testament Jehovah, making Germany the exclusive favorite of God as Israel was formerly supposed to have been.'" The minister having found the disease, advanced "a remedy: 'Power and war, the old Testament methods of progress, must give way to the New Testament program of brotherhood and love.'"

[2] C. C. A. R. Yearbook XXVI, p. 360.

the influence of religion on the civil code, the very law of retaliation was transformed in the Bible into the golden rule: "Thou shalt not take vengeance nor bear any grudge against the children of thy people, but thou shalt love thy neighbor as thyself."[3] On account of its religious nature, the entire system of life in the Bible, says Dr. Kohler, "is permeated by the principle of love, and the relation between God and man, as well as between man and man is based upon it."[4] This is especially true of Hosea, Jeremiah, and Ezekiel, of Deutero-Isaiah and Malachi, of the Psalms, Deuteronomy, and the Priestly Code. In striking fashion it is emphasized in the parable of Jonah and in the institution of the Day of Atonement. Even Amos,[5] Micah,[6] and Isaiah[7] ever fall back on God's mercy.

Our post-Biblical literature is begotten of the same spirit that produced the Bible. The Apocrypha and the Pseudepigrapha, the Talmud and the Midrashim, the ethical, philosophic, and Kabbalistic works, and the various prayerbooks, represent the Bible in a re-written form, re-adapted to the needs of the changed ages.[8] Indeed, due to the historical fluctuations, the

[3] Leviticus XIX:18.

[4] Art. "Love" in *Jewish Encyclopedia*, VIII.

[5] Amos VII:1-3.

[6] Micah VII:18-20; see also Joel II:13.

[7] As evidenced by his doctrine of the "Survival of a Remnant" *(Shear Yashub)*; also Isaiah XXVIII:23-29; XXIX:22-24; XXX:19ff; XXXII:15-XXXIII:6.

[8] Professor Solomon Schechter has characterized the Pseudepigrapha as the product "not of the Synagog, but of the various sects hovering on the borderland of Judaism, on which they may have left some mark by a few stray passages finding their way even into the older Rabbinic literature. The Hebrew works, however, which are especially conspicuous for the affinity of their contents or the larger part of their contents with the Pseudepigrapha, are of later date. They make their appearance under disguise, betraying sufficiently their origin by their bewildering contents as well as by their anachronisms. They were admitted into the Synagog only under protest, so to speak. The authorities seem to have been baffled, some disavowing them, while others are over-awed by their very strangeness, and apologize for their existence or reinterpret them." *(Some Aspects of Rabbinic Theology*, p. IX.) These remarks of Dr. Schechter suffer from the equal force with which they apply also to the philosophic writings of our foremost masters. Neither the *More Nebuchim* nor the *Ani-Ma'amin* were admitted into the synagog without protest. It matters little how late these writings entered into the sacred precincts of Judaism. The fact remains that, freed from their sectarian coloring, they have

literary forms and religious doctrines of our post-Biblical literature have, as do all living things, undergone many modifications and, in some instances, even transformations. However, the scattered, disconnected and often mutually contradictory homiletical and exegetical comments, upon careful examination, reveal a common tendency and purpose. In our post-Biblical, as well as in our Biblical writings, the tendency prevails to regard "Love, Human and Divine" as an essential element in the Jewish conception of life and duty. To establish this fact, through the testimony of our literature, and thereby to vindicate the right of Judaism to the doctrine of Love, are the pleasant tasks before us in this essay.

Love, the imperious passion under whose influence man is raised from his narrow self to solicitude for others, to the sacrifice of self for others, and to joy in objects, persons and principles for their own intrinsic value—this spark of celestial fire was deemed by our masters worthy of God Himself. Thus love became the regulative force not of the affairs of man only, but of the divine government of the world as well. It traces "with its wings a bridge" of union

grown into the Jewish consciousness. And while it is undeniably true that some of the Apocryphal and Pseudepigraphic works have exerted little influence on Rabbinical literature, ("The Rabbis were either wholly ignorant of their very existence, or stigmatized them as fabulous or 'external'—a milder expression in some cases for heretical—and thus allowed them to exert no permanent influence upon Judaism." Schechter: *Aspects,* p. 5), when carefully examined it will be found that, though emanating from non-Rabbinic and even heterodox centres of Jewish life and thought, these various writings reflect much of the same basic Jewish convictions. The Jewish spirit, with the Torah as its parent source, called both classes of literature to life. We must make this claim also for Kabbalah, in which certain tendencies of the Apocrypha and the Pseudepigrapha appeared in resurrected form. "It is totally wrong," writes Abelson, "to follow Graetz in regarding the mediaeval Kabbalah as a thing *per se,* as something quite apart from its Talmudic antecedents, as an unnatural child of the darkened intellects of the Jewish Middle Ages. Neither is it right to judge of its merits and demerits by the rationalistic standards which Graetz and his school adopt towards it. The mediaeval Kabbalah is a direct descendent of the Talmudic Kabbalah; and by the Talmudic Kabbalah one means all those mystic pronouncements which lie scattered and dispersed throughout the extensive realms of the Talmudic literature." *(The Immanence of God in Rabbinical Literature,* p. 2.) Far from being an exotic growth in Judaism, it is "an integral portion of Talmudism, . . . part of its flesh and blood." (Ibid.) In it, the suppressed "mythology" of the Jewish people found a voice.

between earth and heaven, between finite, mortal man and the Immortal and Infinite God."[9]

I. God is Love

Man's love of God corresponds to his mental and spiritual endowments.[10] The rationalist seeks to find God through the careful workings of reason, and, with Philo,[11] gives primacy to the conception of Him as Absolute Being. Those of more emotional or mystical temperament cannot be satisfied with such a philosophic abstraction. They wish to discover His relation to the cosmos and to man, and to bask in the radiance of His glory. Instead of a far-off, transcendent Being, God appears to them as the ever-present, all pervading, immanent spirit that quickens all things and sustains all things. Through the regularity of the operation of law everywhere in the universe, He reveals Himself in the attribute of King-ship; as the life-giving, indwelling Spirit of all existence, He manifests Himself as the loving Father, the Bene-factor, and the Guardian of the world.

Divine Goodness

Far from divorcing the conception of God as Reason from that of God as Love, the Jewish mind welcomed both conceptions as windows of the Infinite,

---

[9] While a distinction is sometimes made—and by no means a rigid one—principally in the Bible, between "love" and "mercy," reserving the latter to describe the relation of God to man, these terms being used interchangeably in post-Biblical literature, are, for the purpose of our study, treated together. Concise and helpful presentations of the subject may be found in articles on "Love" by Dr. K. Kohler in the *Jewish Encyclopedia*, and by Dr. G. Deutsch in Hasting's *Encyclopedia of Religion and Ethics*; also in Dr. E. G. Hirsch's articles "Compassion" and "Golden Rule" in the *Jewish Encyclopedia*.

[10] For delightful amplification of this thought, see *Pesikta*, ed. Buber XII:187. cf. Midrash *Adonoi B'hochma Yosad Erez*, in Eisenstein's *Ozar Midrashim*, p. 106 and the *Shir Ha-Kovod*.

[11] *De Abr.* XXIV-XXV; Bentwich: *Philo*, p. 161–162.

as fit avenues of approaching God. The love of God offered to our masters a solution to the riddle of the universe. Ben Sirach, who imputes a very definite personality to God, declares that "He is All," and ascribes to Him the attributes of Creation, Eternity, and Holiness, also of Fatherhood and of Mercy.[12] From Him, proceed good and evil, as do life and death.[13] History attests that He never fails those that trust in Him.[14] The Letter of Aristeas voices Sirach's belief that evil as well as good comes from God,[15] and declares that "It is necessary to recognize that God rules the whole world in the spirit of kindness and without wrath at all."[16] Samuel Holmes characterizes the theology of the Wisdom of Solomon in these words: "God created the world by means of wisdom, and as wisdom is *philanthropos*,[17] the motive of Creation, though not explicitly stated, can be assumed to be God's love to man."[18] The Essenes, in their belief in the love of God, held, as Philo informs us, "that God causes only the good and no evil whatsover."[19] In this instance, Philo shared their view. Regarding God as the free, self-determining mind, he makes divine goodness the cause of creation. "If anyone were to ask me," says Philo, "what was the cause of the creation of the world, having learned from Moses, I should answer that the goodness of the living God, being the most important of His graces, is in itself the cause."[20] Furthermore, His benevolence is due not to any incapacity of His for evil, but to His free preference for the good.[21] Here the philosopher himself does not think of God in terms of Absolute

---

[12] *Sirach*, XLIII:27; cf. XXI:1; XV:13, 14 (v. Psalm XC:10).

[13] Ibid XV:11.

[14] Ibid II:10, 11.

[15] *Letter of Aristeas*: par. 197.

[16] Ibid: par 254. cf. *Syb. Oracles* I:3–5, 8, 15, 17, 35; II:1–8, 42.

[17] *Wisd.* I:6; VII:28.

[18] Introduction to Wisdom of Solomon in Charles' *Apocrypha* and *Pseudepigrapha* I:528–9. v. Baruch XIV:18; 4 Ezra VIII:1, 44 for the view that the world was created for mankind. Cf. *Assumption of Moses* I:12; 4 Ezra VI:55, 59; VII:11; 2 *Baruch* XIV:18 (note), 19; XV:7; XXI:24. *Hebrew Testament of Naphtali* I:6b.

[19] *De Vita Contemplata*, ed. Conybeare, p. 53, cited by Kohler, art. "Essenes" in *Jew. Encyc.*

[20] On the Changeableness of God, XXIII—cited by Abelson: *Immanence*, p. 62.

[21] *De Plantatione Noe*, par. 20, referred to by E. G. Hirsch, art. "God" in *Jew. Encyc.*

Being. The instant he brings God into relation to the world, he looks upon Him from the standpoint of goodness and beneficence. Elsewhere, the Jew in Philo asserts himself even more strongly. He writes: "The fifth lesson that Moses teaches us is, that God exerts His providence for the benefit of the world. For it follows of necessity that the Creator must always care for that which He has created, just as parents do always care for their children."[22]

The Rabbis were at one with their predecessors in regarding goodness, beneficence and mercy, as the very essence of God. Like Philo, they regarded Creation as a manifestation of mercy. The Sabbath morning prayer voices the best Rabbinic sentiment in praising God for the light which He causes to shine upon the earth and its inhabitants which He created with the attribute of Mercy.[23] And the daily prayer adds: "Through His goodness, He renews each day the work of creation."[24] The Rabbinic doctrine which is avowedly teleological and homocentric may clash somewhat with Philo's view that the goodness of God is in itself the cause of creation. It is in perfect harmony with the idea of the Wisdom of Solomon that the motive of calling the universe into existence was God's love for man.

Fatherhood of God

The plenitude of God's love is manifested in His attribute of Fatherhood.

---

[22] *On the Creation of the World,* par. LXI, edited by J. Abelson, *Immanence,* p. 62.

[23] *Hakol Yoducho.*

[24] *Yozer Or.* Commenting on Gen. II:2: "And God finished His work on the seventh day," Philo states: "God never ceases from making something or other. But as it is the property of fire to burn, and of snow to chill, so also it is the property of God to be creating. And much more so, as He Himself is to all other beings the author of their workings. . . . For He makes things to rest which appear to be producing others, but which in reality do not affect anything. But He Himself never ceases from creating." (The Allegories of the Sacred Laws, par. III, VII, cited by J. Abelson, *Immanence,* p. 64.) The Midrash, on the other hand, while following the verse in its literal sense, and at the same time desiring to show God's ceaseless activity in the world, teaches that, on the seventh day, God ceased from creating the physical world, but not from guiding the moral order. "He ceased neither from creating the wicked nor from creating the righteous. He ever works with both." *(Gen. R.* XI. Abelson takes this passage to mean that God's labors are limited "to the creation of the variegated characters of man." Ibid.) The prevailing Jewish doctrine, as embodied in the Morning Prayer, is in agreement with Philo.

Rabbinic as well as the older Jewish literature views God not only from the aspect of Creator, Judge, and Sovereign of the whole world, but also from that of loving Father of every soul. He is the third parent of each human being; for, while the father and mother supply the child with a body, God endows it with the spirit of life and with all the intellectual and moral faculties.[25] God's indwelling in the soul of man makes for the majesty and the sacredness of human life. "Beloved is man," exclaims Akiba, "for he is created in the image of God."[26] This is the proud distinction of all men, and especially of Israel. "Beloved are the Israelites, for they are called the children of God."[27] From the verse, "Sons are ye to the Lord your God," R. Judah deduces the moral truth that divine sonship can be claimed only by those who obey the will of the divine Father. R. Meir refuses any limitations upon this ennobling claim. The sinners and the saints of humanity alike are sons of the living God.[28] God is grieved by the execution of even wicked men;[29] He mourns over the drowning Egyptians,[30] for, though sinful, they are still His children. Israel's sins justly caused the destruction of the Holy Land and Temple. Nevertheless, God weeps over the ruins and over the lowly state of His children that were exiled from His table.[31] As a father, God is with man in suffering. In the parables of the Midrash and the Talmud, He frequently figures as the royal Father of an only son or daughter, carrying the sorrows of His child in His heart.

The Rabbis were conscious of the danger of applying the word Father to God, for thereby a human-like personality is ascribed to Him. They were, therefore, careful to explain this and all other anthropomorphisms, as subjective rather than objective, holding to the principle that "the Torah employs man's mode of speech."[32] In naming Him Father, they sought to express the

---

[25] *Nidda* 31a; v. Guttman's *Maphteah Ha Talmud*, vol. I:71-72.

[26] *Abot* III:14.

[27] *Ibid.*

[28] *Kid.* 36a; *Ab. Z.* 3a; *Ber.* 7a; *Yoma* VIII:9 and 5b.

[29] *Sanh.* VI:5 and 46a.

[30] *Mechilta B'shalah.*

[31] *Ber.* 3a, 59; *Hag.* 5, 14.

[32] *Ber.* 31b; *Sanh.* 64b, 90b; *Erakim* 3. v. I. Hamburger, "The Philosophy of the Religion of the Jews." *Hebrew Review*, vol. I, p. 238.

idea of tenderness, devotion, solicitude, compassion, and love, which they associated with God. To express the idea that God sustains the intimate relation of Father to man, and is at the same time exalted above man, the Rabbis used the appellations: *"Abinu Malkenu*—our Father, our King," and *"Abinu Shebashomayim*—our Father who is in Heaven." Transcendence blends with immanence.

Divine Love Contrasted
with Human Love

Divine love, though understood only in the light of human love, is intenser and purer. It does not forsake God even in times of anger.[33] A human being seeks to destroy the person that angered him. But God, although He cursed the serpent, yet supplies it with food. He cursed Canaan, yet sustains him. "He cursed woman, and yet (permits her to be so attractive that) all run after her." Though He cursed the earth, He made it fruitful.[34] In His love, God is not only ministered to, but He ministers. "Come and see," states a Midrash, "that the ways of God are not like those of man. When a man walks by night, his servants carry lights and torches before him; and, by day, they make a sunshade for him, to spare him pain. But God, in His abounding love for Israel, went before them in Person. And were it not for the expressed Scriptural verse, it would be blasphemy to utter it. For it is written: 'And God went before them by day with a pillar of cloud, and by night with a pillar of fire, to lead them by day and by night.' Hence it is said: 'Thou hast led in Thy love this people which Thou hast redeemed.'"[35] R. Ḥanina draws this contrast between God and man. "A human king stays within (the palace), and is guarded by his servants from without. God's way is different. His servants stay within (their homes), and He Himself stands sentinel for them. For it is said: 'The Lord is Thy Keeper; the Lord is thy shade upon thy right hand.'"[36] The same *Tana* teaches that man does not so much as hurt his finger, unless it

---

[33] *Ex. R.* 3. *Pes.* 86.
[34] *Yoma* 75; cf. *Pesikta* ed. Buber III:18.
[35] *M. Vayosha*, Eisenstein's *Ozar Midrashim*, p. 154.
[36] *Men.* 33.

is so decreed above,[37] i.e., in His love, God looks after every deed of man. This idea is implied in the doctrine of Providence which, whether in general or in a special sense, is an accepted article in Judaism.

When God proclaimed His thirteen attributes, Moses bowed down and worshiped.[38] The Talmud asks: What did Moses see that overwhelmed him thus? R. Ḥanina b. Gamla answers: He beheld the largeness of God's mercy.[39] According to another tradition, Moses, on ascending to heaven, found God writing the attribute *Erech-apayim*—"long suffering." "Sovereign of the world," said Moses, "long suffering with the righteous!" "No," God corrected him, "also with the wicked."[40] He is gracious and merciful even with the undeserving.[41] That vision of the divine essence is the most radiant yet perceived by the eye of mortal man. In its light, our masters could call God *Raḥamana*—"the Merciful One," a most frequent name for God in the *Halachic* as in the *Aggadic* passages of the Babylonian Talmud.[42]

Attribute of Mercy:

The Rabbis, who believed that both justice and mercy are the pillars of the earth, devoted much thought to the nature and function of these attributes, and to their relation to each other. Philo had already contrasted the divine attributes of Goodness and Power, which he finds expressed in the Biblical names of God. To quote from Siegfried, Philo "interpreted *'Elohim'* (Septuagint, *Theos*) as designating the 'cosmic power'; and, as he considered the

---

[37] *Hul.* 7.

[38] Ex. XXXIV:6–8.

[39] *Sanh.* 111b.

[40] *Ibid.*

[41] *Ber.* 7.

[42] "In the tractate *Pesaḥim* alone," writes S. Schechter, "it occurs about forty-one times, but always in the Halachic controversies." *Aspects*, p. 34, footnote. "Diese Bezeichnung Gottes als des 'Barmherzigen' ist nun von den Juden zu den Christlichen Syrern uebergegangen, gerade wie auch Mohammed אל רחמן aufgenommen hat, sei es dass er unmittelbar aus der juedischen oder mittelbar aus der Syrisch-Christlichen Quelle geschoepft hat." A. Geiger, *Nachgelassene Schriften.* Bd. III:323.

Creation the most important proof of divine goodness, he found the idea of goodness especially in *Theos*."[43] And, in keeping with his general philosophy, he held that God's "pity is older than His judgment."[44] Like Philo, but with greater consistency, the Rabbis identify the divine attributes with the Hebrew names for God. In the tetragrammaton, *Yahweh*, they find the attribute of Mercy; in *Elohim*, the attribute of Justice.[45] When Moses inquired after the divine name, God replied: *"Ehye asher Ehye"*—"I am that I am."[46] Explaining this enigmatic expression, R. Abba Bar Mamol observes: "The Holy One said to Moses: Dost thou wish to know my name? I am called after my works—*Elohim*, when judging my creatures; *Zebaoth*, when waging war against the wicked; *El-shaddai*, when suspending the punishment of man's sins (until he repent); *Yahweh*, when showing mercy to the world. 'I am that I am'—I am called after my works."[47]

The attribute of Mercy, it appears from Rabbinic writings, is a greater favorite with God than the attribute of Justice. *Midda tobah merubbah mimiddat pur'oniyot*—"the measure of divine goodness exceeds that of punishment."[48] The second commandment proclaims that God visits the iniquity of the fathers upon the children unto the third and fourth generation of them that hate Him; and shows mercy unto thousands of them that love Him.[49] From the use of the word "thousands" in the plural number, meaning at least two thousand, the Rabbis infer that the grace of God lasts five hundred times as long as His punishment, for the visiting of the iniquity

---

[43] Art. Philo in *Jew. Encyc.*, referring to "De Migratione Abraham," par. 32. Siegfried adds that "Philo's exposition here is not entirely clear, as he sometimes conceives the powers to be independent hypostases and sometimes regards them as immanent attributes of the Divine Being." He also refers to his book on Philo, pp. 214–218. v. further Bentwich, *Philo*, p. 159ff; Bousset, *Die Religion des Judentums in Neutestamentlichen Zeitalter*, p. 428 ff.

[44] *Quod Deus Sit Immutabilis*, par. 16; *Ibid*.

[45] *Gen. R.* 33; *Pesikta*, ed. Buber XXIIB 4 p. 149a. *Targum* to *Psalm* LXI:11.

[46] Ex. III:13.

[47] *Ex. R.* 3.

[48] *Sanh.* 100; *Sotah* 11a; *Yoma* 76a; *Mechilta B'shalah* 49; v. M. M. Eichler's art. "Grace" in *Jew. Encyc.* VI:60–61. *Tanhuma Nizabim*, par. 5.

[49] Ex. XX:5–6.

extends only to the fourth generation at the utmost.[50] Moreover their fine conception of individual responsibility, led them to believe that the children suffer for the guilt of their fathers, only if they themselves are wicked. However, in case they are righteous, the chain of punishment is broken, and their fathers, too, are delivered from judgment.[51]

This belief that God's mercy lasts longer than His punishment, by no means conflicts with the doctrine of divine justice. R. Joḥanan explains the verse: *"Elohim Elohecho Ani"*[52] in this sense: By the use of *'Elohim,'* God announces: 'I am a Judge'; and by the second phrase *'Elohecho Ani,'* He proclaims: 'I am your Patron.'[53] God is long-suffering, but He collects His debt in the end.[54] He declares: "I am the Merciful One; I am also a Judge to punish."[55] While justice has its anger, it has also its pity. Pity is, indeed, as Victor Hugo remarks, "only a more exalted justice." Justice and mercy are not mutually exclusive ideals. They rather supplement and complete each other. Thus R. Akiba, while teaching that a net is spread for all the living and that judgment is meted out to all, also teaches that "the world is judged by grace."[56] The Mercy of God springs not from weakness or indulgence but from His benevolence and goodness.

According to Rabbinic fancy there are times in the divine government of the world when God is forced to deal with man after the rule of strict justice. Such occasions cause God grief. For example, in connection with the destruction of the generation of the deluge, the Scriptural narrative uses the tetragrammaton *YHVH,*[57] though as a term expressive of the attribute of mercy, it hardly belongs there. This incongruity prompted the rabbis to exclaim: "Woe

[50] v. Schechter's *Aspects,* p. 181; also Midr. *Hashkem* in *Ozar Midrashim* p. 139. *Yalkut Shimeoni* 292, 399, 814, 815.

[51] *Sanh.* 27b. Midr. *Hashkem,* Ibid.

[52] Ps. L:7.

[53] *Pesikta,* ed. Buber XII:170.

[54] *B. Kama* 3a, 50a; *Yeb.* 121b; *Zeb.* 116b. *Midr. Tanḥ.* ed. Buber, 8, 10; *Midr. Petirat Moshe, Ozar Midr.* p. 370.

[55] *Gen. R.* 16:6.

[56] *Abot* III:19-20 and commentaries; also *Pesikta* ed. Buber IX:2, XXV:91-96; *Kid.* 39-40a; *Eccl. R.* 10:1.

[57] Gen. VI:5.

unto the wicked who turn the attribute of mercy into that of judgment."[58]
Isaiah's rebuke, "A sinful nation . . . they have forsaken the Lord,"[59] is given
this interpretation: God says: "They have made Me forsake Myself; I am
called the 'Merciful and Gracious,' but through their sins I have been made
cruel, and have converted My attribute (of Mercy) into that of strict judgment; as it is said, 'The Lord was an enemy.' "[60]

On the other hand, God delights when He can turn the attribute of justice
into that of love.[61] The school of Hillel intrepreted the phrase *verab hessed*—
"abundant in mercy"[62] as *Mateh kelape hessed*—"He inclines towards
mercy."[63] Rab (Abba Areka) is quoted by R. Zutra bar Tubia to the effect
that God Himself prays thus: "May it be My will that My mercy restrain My
anger, and that My mercy assert itself (literally: 'be rolled upon') over My
(other) attributes; and may I deal with My children according to the attribute
of mercy, and go with them beyond the line of judgment."[64] R. Judah, quoting Rab, says that God devotes three hours each day to judging the world.
"Seeing that it merits destruction, He rises from the throne of judgment, and
seats Himself upon the throne of mercy."[65] Other aggadists, too, state that
"when the *Shofar* is sounded on *Rosh Hashanah,* God rises from the throne of
judgment, and seats Himself upon the throne of mercy . . . He takes pity (on
the people of Israel) and turns, for them, the attribute of justice into that of
love."[66]

---

[58] Gen. R. 33:3.

[59] Is. I:4.

[60] *Tan. B.* 3:55a. Cf. *Yalkut Machiri* to Isaiah p. 7, quoted by S. Schechter, *Aspects,* p.
239–240. v. *M. Vayosha, Ozar Midr.* p. 149.

[61] *Song of Songs, R.* 2:17; 4:6.

[62] Ex. XXXIV:6.

[63] *Pesikta* in *Ozar Midr.* p. 495.

[64] *Ber.* 7a; *Jer. Ta'an.* ch. 2. An older tradition puts this prayer in the mouth of R. Ishmael
ben Elisha. He is said to have offered it when, while offering incense, he was asked by God for a
blessing.

[65] *Ab. Z.* 3. The *Massechet Hecholot* discusses the number of God's thrones, and mentions a
throne of *Hesed* and a throne of *Rahamim.* v. *Ozar Midr.* p. 108.

[66] Pesikta, ed. Buber, XXIII:30–33 and notes, 62–64, 69, 81. XXVI:6. Pesikta in *Ozar
Midr.* p. 495–496; *D'rash Liptirat Moshe,* Ibid. p. 315. v. also the Piyut *"Mi Ya'aroch elecho
Ma'aneh"* in the Mussaph service for Yom Kippur.

Rab declares further that loving-kindness and mercy are among the means (or categories) by which God called the world into being.[67] Thus love figures, in aggadic speculation, as a cosmic principle. It appears in its most fascinating form in the following poetic Midrash to Psalm LXXXIX: "Ethan was asked: 'Whereon does the world rest?' Said he: 'Upon mercy, for it is said: "And the throne (i. e. the world) is set firm through mercy." It is like unto a chair one of whose legs was a bit too short. To render it stable, a chip of wood had to be placed under that leg. Even so was the throne of the Holy One, blessed be He, shaky until God supported it. And wherewith? With mercy. Hence the Psalm says: *Olam ḥesed yiboneh*—"the world is built on love."'"[68] Another Midrash states that when God was about to create the world, He had intended to create it in accord with the attribute of mercy. Seeing that, in that case, its sins would be numerous, He wished to create it in accord with the attribute of justice. But He saw that such a world could not abide. In order to make it enduring, He tempered justice with mercy.[69]

R. Simon says: When God was about to create Adam, the ministering angels divided themselves into groups, some approving of God's plan, and others disapproving. "Mercy argued: 'Let him be created, for he will perform deeds of loving kindness.' Truth objected, foreseeing that man will be full of lies. . . . What did God do? He cast Truth to the ground. Affrighted, the angels cried: 'Sovereign of the world, dost Thou despise Thine own ornament? Let Truth arise from the ground!' Taking advantage of this commotion, God hastily created Adam."[70] (And man still shows the effects of that haste!) It is by virtue of God's mercy and grace that mankind could arise and flourish.[71]

---

[67] *Ḥag.* 12.

[68] The ordinary translation is: "Forever is mercy built." v. the New Translation. v. *Yalkut Shimeoni* to Ps. LXXXIX; also *Abot* I:2; and *Abot de Rabbi Nathan* IV:5, and Leeser's Bible translation.

[69] *Gen. R.* 12. *Alpha Betha De Rabbi Akiba*, letter Gimmel, *Ozar Midr.* IX, p. 411; *Adonoi Beḥochma Yosad Erez*, Ibid. p. 104, 105; *Midr. Chonen*, Ibid, 259.

[70] Ibid; Ginzberg's *Legends of the Jews* I, 51ff. v. poem *"Middat Ha-Mishpot"* in Heidenheim's *Maḥzor* for Yom Kippur.

[71] *Shoḥar Tob* to Ps. XXV:8. Gerald Friedlander remarks: "There may be an attempt here to counteract the un-Jewish doctrines of the Paulinian School, which taught that, owing to Adam's sin, God's grace was withdrawn, and only through the advent of a second Adam (or Christ) could this divine grace be restored to the world. The theologians who suggest that

These passages show the tendency in Rabbinic literature to hypostatize Mercy, as the other divine attributes, and to assign to it mediatorial functions.[72] The attribute of Mercy is often represented as helping man. Occasionally the Holy Spirit or the Torah takes its place as paraclete.[73] A penitential hymn in the *Neilah* service reads: *"Attribute of Mercy,* reveal thyself for us; make our supplications to fall before thy Creator; and, on behalf of thy people, implore mercy." Another *Seliḥa* addresses itself to the *"Angels of mercy,* ministers of the Most High," asking them to intercede in behalf of the afflicted people. It must be noted, however, that these personifications were never hardened into a dogma. In some respects they present a striking simi-

Judaism has something to learn from the Paulinian doctrine of grace must be unaware of the Jewish teaching on this theme." *Pirke de Rabbi Eliezer* p. 136, note 2. A few illustrations will suffice: In the *Pirke De Rabbi Eliezer,* we are informed that God first disclosed His plan of creating man to the Torah. "Sovereign of the world!" said the Torah, "The man whom Thou wouldst create will be limited in days, and full of anger; and he will come into the power of sin. Unless Thou wilt be long-suffering with him, it would be well for him not to come into the world." God quieted the fears of the Torah, saying: "And is it for nought that I am called 'slow to anger' and 'abounding in love'?" (Chap. XI.) Further on in the same work, Israel appears in the role of advocate of humanity. When the world was completed, Israel (i. e. the Heavenly prototype of Israel) petitioned God not to withhold His mercy and loving-kindness, for without them the world cannot exist. (Chap. XIX.) "With love abounding did the Holy One, blessed be He, love the first man, inasmuch as He created him in a pure locality, in the place of the Temple, and He brought him to His palace." As an act of special mercy, God created Adam out of the dust that was gathered from the four corners of the earth, so that wherever man dies the earth may have no right to refuse to receive his body. (Chap XI and Rashi to Gen. II:6.) When the earth learned that God intended to supply Adam with a help-mate, she suffered a Malthusian shock and registered her objections: "Sovereign of the worlds! I have not the power to feed the multitude of mankind." God removed her complaints by entering into an agreement whereby she was obliged to feed mankind only by day, while He would sustain it by night. "What did the Holy One, blessed be He, do? He created the sleep of life, so that man lies down and sleeps whilst God sustains him and heals him and gives him life and respose." To spare Adam the pain, God cast a deep sleep upon him while "He took one of his bones from his side and flesh from his heart, and made it into an help (meet for him) and placed her opposite to him." (Chap. XII.)

[72] v. further, *Seder Din in Ozar Midr.* p. 289; *Perek Gan Haḥavim,* Ibid. p. 91; *Adonoi Beḥochma Yosad Erez,* Ibid. p. 105.

[73] Songs of Songs, R. 8:12.

larity to Philo's doctrine of the *Logos,* or rather the *Logoi,* to which he gives the following description: "For God, not condescending to come down to the external senses, sends His own *Logoi* or angels for the sake of giving assistance to those who love virtue. But they attend like physicians to the diseases of the soul . . . offering sacred recommendations like sacred laws, and inviting men to practice the duties inculcated by them."[74] Like the *Logoi,* the attribute of Mercy, though pictured as a person, is not separated from God, and may be regarded as chiefly denoting God's attitude towards the universe. It may be best characterized as an offshoot of Divinity, ceaselessly energizing the eternal drama of creation.

The Kabbalah, which represents an extension, though occasionally a distortion of Talmudic and Midrashic thought, assigns an even more commanding place to this doctrine of love as a cosmic principle. There the divine attributes appear under the guise of the ten *Sefirot* (literally "digits" or "numbers").[75] The *Sefer Yezirah*—the authorship of which Dr. Neumark ascribes to the school of Rab—explains the emanation of the visible world from the God-head, through the instrumentality of the *Sefirot.* Whereas all matter was produced by means of the twenty-two letters, the form to all things was given by the ten *Sefirot.* The *Masseket Azilut* names the *Sefirot,* and invests them with human feeling, calling one of them *Hesed.*[76] Later Kabbalah went a step further and invoked the "mystery of sex"—a survival of an old Semitic belief—to explain the birth of the world. The *Sefirot* are,

[74] On Dreams Being Sent by God, XII, XIX, cited by J. Abelson, *Immanence,* p. 7. For the definition of the Philonian Logos, v. Zeller, *Die Philosophie der Griechen* III:2, p. 378, referred to by Schuerer, *History of the Jewish People* II:3, p. 375.

[75] These are conceived as divine emanations, employed as tools in the creation of the world. *Massechet Azilut, Ozar Midr.* p. 68. For a discussion of the *Sefirot,* v. Ginzberg's art. "Cabala" in *Jew. Encyc.* and Abelson's "Mysticism," pp. 114–115.

[76] *Keter* contains "the thirteen gates of wisdom and pity which Moses mentions in the Torah" (referring to Ex. XXXIV:6–7). *Hesed* is named the attribute of Abraham (referring to Micah VII:20). *Nezah* is the attribute of Moses, through whose merit the Manna came down for the righteous. *Hod* is the attribute of Aaron, through whose merit the clouds of glory surrounded Israel in the desert. *Yesod,* the attribute of Joseph, includes all the emanations, the Mercies and the Compassion and the Might of the Holy One with which He feeds and sustains the congregation of Israel. v. *Massechet Azilut,* Ibid.

therefore, divided into triads, each consisting of a "father," a "mother," and a "child" or "son."[77]

Thus God called the world into existence. At first, He created worlds and destroyed them,[78] because they were full of strife. Only when, in this world, harmony prevailed, He let it abide. The unbridled imagination of the Kabbalists produced the *Hekalot* or Heavenly Halls and consecrated one of them to Love.[79] In the Palace of Love, *Hechal Ahabah,* according to the *Zohar,* "the deepest mysteries are enacted. There are all the souls that are beloved of God. God Himself dwells with them there, and unites with them through kisses of love, *Nishikin direḥimu.*"[80] For, while in life the human soul may unite with the Oversoul in occasional moments of ecstasy, the perfect union with God can be attained only through death.[81] Then the cerements of the flesh are removed, and the soul soars home to God. Divine love thus deprives

---

[77] From the first *Sefirah, Keter* (Crown), emanate *Hochmah* (Wisdom), masculine, active; and *Binah* (Intellect), feminine and passive. From their union proceeds *Da'at* (Reason). This triad forms a unity in itself, "that is, knowledge, the knower, and the known, are in God identical, and thus the world is only the expression of the ideas or the absolute forms of intelligence." (Some Kabbalists do not consider *Da'at* an independent *Sefirah;* hence they complete the triad by including *Keter* among the Sefirot. v. Ginzberg, Ibid, III:474.) The second triad, which emanates from the first one, interprets the world as the expression of God's moral nature. *Ḥesed* (Mercy) appears here as the masculine, active principle, mated to the feminine and passive *Din* (Justice), also called *Paḥad* (Awe) and *Geburah* (Might); and begets *Tiferet* (Beauty). Ginzberg writes: "The concepts, justice and mercy, however, must not be taken in their literal sene, but as symbolical designations for expansion and contraction of the Will, the sum of both, the moral order, which appears as beauty." The last triad represents dynamic nature. The masculine *Neẓaḥ* (Triumph) is coupled with the feminine *Hod* (Glory). Their offspring is *Yesod* (Foundation), i. e. "the reproductive element, the root of all existence." In the last *Sefirah, Malkut* (Dominion), "the will, the plan, and the active forces become manifest. It is the sum of the permanent and immanent activity of all *Sefirot.*" Ibid, p. 474–475. The *Sefirot* are reproduced in the Sabbath Hymn *"El Odon,"* Singer's ed. Prayer Book, p. 129. However, v. Israel Abrahams' note (Ibid). v. also the *piyut* "*Hoaderet Weho-emunoh.*"

[78] Cf. Gen. R. 89.

[79] *Massechet Azilut,* Ibid, p. 81–82.

[80] *Zohar, Mishpotim* 97a; Franck, *Kabbalah,* German ed., p. 181.

[81] The same view, though for different reasons, is held by Leo Abravanel. v. *Vikuaḥ al HoAhavah,* p. 10a.

death itself of its horror. Death is the home-coming of the divine child, the soul, from the school of this world's experience—an occasion for special festivities by the Royal Father in Heaven, and the Queen Mother (the *Shechina* or Holy Presence).[82]

Not only in Rabbinic and Kabbalistic thought, but also in the speculations of several of our philosophers, Love illumines, with its glow, the whole pageant of cosmic as well as of human life. The Mediaeval Jewish philosophers, especially of the Aristotelian school, viewing all the universe as the manifestation of Reason, tended to the idea of God as Law. But they were faithful heirs to Jewish tradition; and, while striving to harmonize it with the accredited philosophy of their day, firmly clung to its doctrines. As disciples of Aristotle, they refused to admit positive attributes to the divine Essence. As Jews and theologians, they found a loophole in their logic for attributes descriptive of God's actions. Hence, following Biblical, Talmudical, and Kabbalistic examples (several of the philosophers wrote commentaries to the *Sefer Yezira*, the classic of the Kabbalah), they continued to speak of the attributes of Mercy and Love. Like Philo, they emphasized God's beneficence. Bahya[83] recognizes God through the abundance of goodness in the world, through its display of order, wisdom, light, and joy. Judah Halevi, in his poems[84] and in his *Kuzari*, revels in the overflowing goodness and mercy of God. Maimonides and Gersonides clear God of the suspicion of evil by denying its reality.[85] Judged by His actions, God appears good and kind.

Hasdai Crescas, who was free from the hypnotic spell of the Stagirite, struck out a bold path by reclaiming the propriety of using positive attributes in describing the nature of God, and by asserting that the unifying principle of the world is not Intelligence, as Maimonides and the other Aristotelians among the Jewish philosophers believed, but Goodness. "The infinite goodness which is essential to God, comprehends all the attributes, rendering them

---

[82] *Zohar, Vayechi*, p. 245b; Abelson, Mysticism, p. 161ff.

[83] *Hobot Ha-lebobot.*

[84] Harkavy's ed., vol. II, p. 121.

[85] *Moreh Nebuchim* III:8, and *Milhamot* IV:3. v. H. Zeitlin: *Hatob wehora*, p. 71ff. cf. 50ff.

one. . . . His substance is simple in an absolute sense, and goodness in general follows from Him essentially."[86] "God," he declares, "is the absolute good; and the purpose He aims at is to do good, since indeed the Purpose of Creation and Revelation was nothing (else than to do good)."[87] As a logical corollary, love becomes "the essential quality of God,"[88] whose nature is goodness.

Love, as a cosmic force, dominates the philosophy of Don Judah ben Isaac Abravanel, who is known also as Leo Hebraeus or Medigo. His work *Dialoghi d'amore, "Dialogues of Love,"* which Graetz aptly terms "a philosophical idyll," combines the Platonic and pantheistic tendencies of the Italian renaissance, reechoing, now and then, the doctrines of Empedocles.[89] While identifying God with intelligence,[90] he recognizes, in love, a force which lies "at the root of the whole world, not only in the material, but even more so in the spiritual spheres. . . . From the first cause to the very last of the creatures, there is not a thing without love."[91] It holds the world together, and draws it

---

[86] *Or Adonoi* I:3:3, p. 24b, cited by Wolfson, "Crescas on Divine Attributes," *Jewish Quarterly Review* VII, p. 207, note 111. v. also E. G. Hirsch art. Crescas, in *Jew. Encyc.* IV:352.

[87] Ibid., p. 64, cited by D. Neumark, *Crescas and Spinoza*, C. C. A. R. Yearbook, vol. XVIII, p. 299.

[88] Kohler, art. "Love," *Jew. Encyc.*

[89] Graetz fails to do him justice when telling that "he did not penetrate to the true spirit of Judaism" and that "therefore his work was valued by Christians more than by Jews." *(History of the Jews,* IV:480–481.) The cause of this book's greater popularity with Christians than with Jews is due to the precarious condition of Jewish literature—resulting from incessant persecution—that caused the Jews to neglect the Apocryphal and Pseudepigraphic literature, the writings of Philo, the Fons Vitae of Gabirol, and a host of other works written in Greek, Arabic, Spanish, etc. Even original Hebrew compositions have suffered neglect. The poems of Halevi—not to mention the works of lesser masters—have not yet been printed in full. Naturally, Abravenel's book, written in Italian, gained greater circulation among the Italian Christians than among the Jews, a small number of whom spoke or understood the language of the book. That this book was not neglected by the Jews may be seen from the fact that R. Gedalia b. Yaḥia translated it into Spanish, and Judah of Modena into Hebrew. Under the title *"Vikuaḥ al Ho-ahabah,"* it was published by Mekize Nirdamim, Lyck, 1871. That his book is conceived in the true spirit of Judaism, we venture to claim this paper sufficiently proves.

[90] *Vikuaḥ al Ho-ahabah,* p. 9a.

[91] Ibid., 12b ff.

to God. Divine love has created the world, and makes for the perfection of all things, especially of man.

The teachings of Abravanel, as well as of Crescas, with certain modifications, reappear in Spinoza's system. Stripping love of all earthly passion, and with Abravanel employing for it the epithet "intellectual," Spinoza too applies it to God, whom he identifies with the universe. He writes: "God loves Himself with an infinite intellectual love"; and "it follows that God, insofar as He loves Himself, loves men, and consequently that love of God toward men, and the intellectual love of the mind toward God, is one and the same thing."[92]

II. God's Love of Man

Signs of Benevolence

God as love forms a part not alone of our literature and philosophic speculations. It is a conception which runs through the whole fabric of our faith, and colors all our theological doctrines. The author of the Wisdom of Solomon declares: "Thou lovest all things that are, and abhorrest none of the things that Thou hast made."[93] Hence he views suffering and evil in the light of this doctrine. In His love, he says, the Creator fashioned man in His own image. Therefore He expects from man conduct worthy of his privileges, viz., wisdom and righteousness. When he attains to goodness, he receives the rewards of holiness and the prize of a blameless life; but when he falls short of the divine ideal, he receives his due penalty. Thus justice itself is a manifestation of divine love.[94] Divine judgment is not merely disciplinary, but also remedial in its purpose. With the Prologue to the book of Job, the Wisdom of Solomon holds suffering as a means of testing the righteous. "As gold in the furnace, He proved them."[95] His motive throughout is love to man. Ben Sirach holds

[92] *Ethics,* Prop. XXXV-XXXVI.
[93] Wisdom of Solomon, XI:24.
[94] *Midr. Hashkem, Ozar Midr.,* p. 140.
[95] Wisdom of Solomon, I:6; VII:28.

the same ground. He points to the extent and to the all-inclusiveness of divine mercy as manifested in His

> "Reproving and chastening and teaching,
> And bringing them (all flesh) back as a shepherd his flock.
> He hath mercy on them that accept (His) chastenings,
> And that diligently seek after His judgments."[96]

The author of II Maccabees regards the afflictions that came upon Israel as intended not for the destruction, but for the chastening of the race, and as "a sign of benevolence." If the heathens have escaped them, it is to the end that they may be punished "when they have attained to the full measure of their sins."[97]

"Punishment," writes Abelson, "was never considered by the Jew an act of a vindictive Judge. It was a pledge of God's merciful interest in him, a sinner, urging him to abandon his evil course."[98] Pain and sorrow, in the view of the rabbis, are the arena "for the exercise of Love's invincible charms."[99] A term of their coining, *yisurim shel ahabah*—"chastisements of love"— indicates that in their thinking, as in the thought of the masters of the apocryphal writings, undeserved suffering is sent upon man out of the fulness of God's love, for thereby man is purged of every vestige of sin and is led to the higher life. "Beloved are *yisurim* (chastisements)," declares R. Nachman, "for as sacrifices atone, so do *yisurim* atone for sin."[100] "Seekest thou life?— Wait for suffering." God says: "I shall punish thee in this world in order to cleanse thee from thy sins in the world to come."[101] Thus the eye of faith beheld the sign of God's love, even in affliction. Firm in this conviction, the Rabbis taught: *Kol deabid Raḥamana letab abid*—"all that the Merciful

---

[96] Sirach XVIII:13, 14.

[97] II Maccabees V:17-20; VII:12-16; cf. Judith VIII:11-27.

[98] *Immanence*, p. 31.

[99] *Ibid.*

[100] *Yalkut Shim.* 837.

[101] *Pesikta*, ed. Buber, XXIII:27, 29, 41-42; Maimonides: *Moreh Nebuchim* III:24 and I. Aroma, *Akedat Yitzchok* XIX.

One does is for the good."[102] Nahum Ish Ginsu is remembered for his opti-
mistic saying, *gam zu letobah*—"this too is for the best,"[103] welcoming everything that befell him as a sign of divine goodness. In this spirit, a marginal
note in R. Meir's Torah Scroll to the verse "And behold it was very good,"
read *zeh mowet*—"that refers to death." Another interpretation of the quali-
tative adverb "very" in the above cited verse, takes it to refer to the *yezer
hora*—"the evil passions"; for were it not for the passions, no man would
build a house, marry, beget children or engage in business. Other explanations
of the adverb "very" make it include suffering, punishment and even
Gehenna and the Angel of Death.[104] That which in the popular mind is considered evil, serves a higher good. To the beclouded eye of man, this may not be
clear. But God looks upon it and pronounces it "very good."

However, though suffering and evil are good in their place, they shall have
no room in God's future kingdom. On the basis of the future tense in the verse
yehi shem Adonoi Mevoroch (literally): "God's name will be praised," the
Rabbis said: "In this world, God is praised for good and for evil. When good
betides us, we say: *hatov wehametiv*—"Praised be the All-good who causes
good things to come to pass." When evil befalls us: *Boruch Dayan Ho-
emet*—"Praised be the truthful Judge." In the world to come there will be
only the one blessing over the good, for the curse of death shall vanish, as
Scripture says: "He hath destroyed death forever."[105] The angel of death
shall be slaughtered, and men shall eternally rejoice in the glory of God, free
from the fear of mortality. This world which God "has created with the attribute of mercy,"[106] and which He sustains in His kindness, moves toward
goodness in its most perfected form, where sorrow and sighing shall be no
more.

Even in this world of suffering, God's purpose of love is manifest to man.
Before smiting, He creates the remedy wherewith to heal the wound *"makdim*

---

[102] *Ber.* 6ob.

[103] *Sanh.* 108b. This saying is met with also on the lips of Akiba and of other Jewish
masters.

[104] *Gen. R.* 89; *Yalkut Shim.* 16.

[105] *Midr. Hallel, Ozar Midr.,* p. 127.

[106] Sabbath Morning prayer: *Hakol Yoducho.*

refu'oh lemakko."[107] Man suffers from sin. In order to enable him to free himself from its thralldom, God created for him the power of repentance. *Teshubah* was indeed called into existence before Creation.[108] The underlying philosophy of repentance is that a change in the human heart and mind bring about a corresponding change in God's attitude toward man. This change of heart is not brought about through man's own powers. He takes the first step, but the final defeat of the evil *yezer* takes place through the grace of God. "Every day the *yezer* of man assaults him, and endeavors to kill him, and but for the Holy One, blessed be He, who helps man, he would not resist him."[109] Thus repentance is a shield against punishment.[110] "After God thought of creating the evil *yezer,* He began to regret it, but prepared the cure before the affliction, and created repentance."[111] A passage in *Pirke De Rabbi Eliezer* states: "The world could never have existed but for the fact that repentance was created (first), and the Holy One, blessed be He, stretches out His right hand to receive penitents each day."[112] Whenever man repents, God's mercy asserts itself.[113] Through the repentance of one man the whole community may be forgiven.[114] Repentance, as an aspect of divine love, is well illustrated by the parable of R. Yochanan about the prince who was carrying a heavy beam. The king, seeing it, asked that the burden be laid upon his own shoulders. So God, in His love for even His sinful children, invites them to cast their sins upon Him.

Like repentance, so is prayer a remedy prepared by God, to free man from

---

[107] *Midr. L' Hanukah, Ozar Midr.,* p. 193.

[108] *Pes.* 54a; *Pirke De R. Eliezar,* ed. G. Friedlander, III, p. 11-12; *Pirke Rabbenu HaKodosh,* VII in *Ozar Midr.,* p. 512. One of the finest bodies of rabbinic teaching on Repentance is found in the *Pesikta* for Yom Kippur in *Ozar Midr.,* 496-498.

[109] *Sukka* 52b. v. Schechter, *Aspects,* 279-280; also 4 Ezra VII:135-137.

[110] *Abot* IV:11; v. further Apocalypse of Baruch LXIV:8; Prayer of Man.; Apostolic Constit. II:22; Synh. 103a; Gen. R. 18:20; 52:7; Ex. R. 21; Pes. 119a; *Tana Debe Elijah Zutta* XXII-XXIII; *Pirke De R. Eliezer* XLIII; I. H. Weiss, *Dor Dor Wedorshov* III:274; *Jew. Encyc.* art. Repentance; and Schechter, *Aspects,* p. 279ff; also Yom Kippur ritual.

[111] Cited by Schechter, *Aspects,* p. 314.

[112] Ibid.; also v. different version in Pirke de Rabbi Eliezer XLIII:337.

[113] *Pesikta,* ed. Buber, 164a.

[114] *Yoma* 86b. v. whole section from 85b through 87b; also *Sanh.* 111a.

sinfulness. Through confession of sin man slays his evil *yezer*,[115] and effects a reconciliation between himself and God. While God desires neither sin-offerings nor burnt-offerings, He delights in man's words of prayer, springing from the sincere heart.[116] He reciprocates man's love for Him, and longs to commune with His creatures.[117] Abelson writes: "Humanity heaves twoards God, and God responds with a counter-heaving towards humanity. It is the essence of what is implied in divine love."[118] Albo rightly considered prayer as an aspect of Providence.[119] The belief in its efficacy has, on this ground, been deeply rooted in the Jewish consciousness. "Prayer avails a man both before and after the signing of the divine decree,"[120] changing the divine disposition from wrath to mercy.[121] In its purest form, prayer puts man in a frame of mind which makes him feel the nearness and the love of God.

Still greater love was shown to man by God's revelation of the Torah. Like Repentance, the Torah had a premundane existence.[122] Though the choicest of His treasures—for the sake of which He created the world[123]—God, in His love, entrusted it to man. Through its merits, Israel is saved from suffering and from the power of the evil *yezer* and is filled with the Holy Spirit.[124] It has brought light[125] to the world, and it has brought peace.[126]

When the words "I am the Lord thy God" were thundered forth at Sinai, the Israelites fainted. Thereupon the angels embraced them and kissed them and called unto them: "What ails you? Fear not; 'Ye are children unto the Lord your God'!" And God Himself softened His speech and soothed them,

---

[115] *Lev. R.* IX:1.

[116] *P. R.* 198b. Schechter, *Aspects*, p. 338.

[117] *Num. R.* 13:6.

[118] *Immanence*, p. 302.

[119] *Ikkarim* IV:16.

[120] *Rosh Hash.* 16a.

[121] *Yebam.* 64a.

[122] *Zeb.* 116a; Sab. 88b; Midr. *Shemuel* V:2 (13).

[123] *Gen. R.* 1.

[124] *Midr. Gadol u-Gedulah, Ozar Midr.*, p. 79.

[125] *"Torah zu Orah—Torah is light."* Megil. 16. "The sun lights only by day, and the Torah by day and by night." v. Abudraham, ed. Warsaw, p. 45.

[126] *Zebah.* 116; cf. *P. R.* 95a; *Sifre* 142b.

saying: "Are ye not My children? I am the Lord your God; ye are My people, ye are beloved before Me." Thus He comforted them until their spirits were restored.[127]

Theologians of the anti-Jewish bias may say what they will about the burden and the curse of the Torah. The Jew has always felt that *Hesed zu hatorah*—"Mercy is a synonym for the Torah," for it is written: *wetorat hesed 'al leshonah*[128]—"and the law of kindness is on her tongue."[129] He has further believed that a "cord of mercy"—*hut shel hesed*—encircles those that study the Torah.[130] In his prayers the Jew declares: "With everlasting love, Thou hast loved the House of Israel, Thy people; a Law and commandments, statutes and judgments hast Thou taught us. . . . Yea, we will rejoice in the words of Thy law and in Thy commandments forever, for they are our life and the length of our days."[131]

The institutions ordained by the Torah, too, were regarded as the expression of God's overflowing love. The *Kiddush* praises God because He "has sanctified us by His commandments, and taken pleasure in us, and *in love* and favor has given us the holy Sabbath as an inheritance.[132] The Rabbis and poets extolled this "delight of days"—*Hemdat yomim*—and pictured it as the bride of Israel.[133] The other festive seasons are likewise looked upon as signs of God's love for Israel.[134]

"Special love," says Akiba, "was manifested to Israel, in that to them was given the precious instrument (the Torah) by which the world was created." In these words, we catch the echo of Akiba's polemics with the rising Christian faith. *Whereas the New Testament writers assert that God's love was manifested through His sacrifice of His only begotten Son, the Christ, for*

---

[127] *Song of Songs R.* 5; cf. *Sab.* 88.

[128] Prov. XXXI.

[129] *Adonoi Behochma Yosad Erez, Ozar Midr.,* p. 106.

[130] *Hag.* 12b.

[131] Prayerbook, ed. Singer, p. 96. With slight verbal variations, this prayer appears also in the Reform Prayerbooks.

[132] *Ibid.,* p. 124; cf. Prayer of R. Zadok, *Tos. Ber.* III:7; v. Schechter, *Aspects,* p. 153.

[133] *Gen. R.* 11:6. Israel is the mate of the Sabbath. cf. Shelomo Halevi's (alkabets) hymn *Lecho Dodi,* in the Friday eve services. *Ibid.*

[134] *Ibid.,* p. 230.

mankind,[135] *this master of Judaism declared that God's special love for humanity has been shown through the revelation of the Torah, which is His will to man.* It is here that we must find the roots of whatever difference there may be between the Christian and the Jewish doctrines of divine love: the one in the process of showing the intensity of God's love for mankind succeeds in turning Him into a monster who appeases His wrath only by devouring His own Son; the other demonstrates the extent of God's love through His instruction and guidance of erring humanity. The Torah, as the rabbis understood it, was revealed for the purpose of leading us Godward and to render us pure from sin. Its study makes man "a lover of the Allpresent, a lover of mankind, and clothes him in meekness and reverence."[136]

It is true, in the Talmud we meet with an apparent objection to the consideration of Mercy as the chief aim of the Torah. The Mishna speaks disapprovingly of prayer prefaced by the declaration: "To the bird's nest Thy mercies extend."[137] Just what was in the mind of the authors of the Mishnah is not clear. The Amoraim in the Palestinian Talmud record their opinions to the effect that such a declaration appears like a complaint against God's justice, as if to say: "Thy mercies reach to the bird's nest but not to man, for Thou allowest him to suffer";[138] or it "sounds as if the divine mercy were limited to the bird's nest alone."[139] Similarly the Babylonian Talmud reports the view of one Amora that such a statement instead of praising God casts a reflection of partiality upon Him, "creating jealousy among God's creatures," as if suggesting that He deals mercifully with some of His creatures and not with others.[140] Another Amora holds that it misrepresents God's relation to His creatures, rendering His attributes (or the laws dictated by them) mercy, while they are decrees.[141]

---

[135] Epistle to the Romans and I John, passim.

[136] *Abot* VI:1.

[137] *Ber.* V:3. The reference is to the law in Deuteronomy XXII:6-7, which prohibits the taking of the mother-bird together with its young from the nest.

[138] *K'kore tagor al Middotov shel Hakodosh Boruch Hu.*

[139] *K'noten kizbah l'middotov. Jer. Ber.* 9c.

[140] *Shematil Kinah bema'aseh bereshit.*

[141] *She'oseh Middotov shel Hakodosh Boruch Hu Rahamim Weenon elo geserot. Ber.* 33b; *Megil.* 25a and *Rashi* ad loc.

The attitude of the Mishnah may perhaps be explained in the light of R. Ḥanina's rebuking the man who strung up a long chain of divine attributes, in offering a prayer, saying to him: "Hast thou exhausted the praises of the Lord?" One may as well imagine himself praising a king of inexhaustible wealth for displaying a small silver coin. Is not such praise insulting to him?[142] In this spirit the Mishnah may have objected to basing the praise of the All-merciful One on a small manifestation of kindness.

Such remarks may have been called forth as protests against allegoristic interpretations of the Law, as Professor Lauterbach suggests,[143] or against

---

[142] *Ber.* 33b and *Meg.* 25a.

[143] Professor Lauterbach—to whom I am grateful for several suggestions in this paper— takes these explanations as unsatisfactory guesses at the meaning of the Mishnah. "The fact is," he writes, "that the Mishna did not mean to forbid a man to appeal in his prayers to the divine mercy, by referring to the law of Deut. XXII, 6, as an expression of His love for His creatures, and there is no harm in seeing in the laws of God merely expressions of love. And when a rabbi once uttered the prayer: 'Thou hast shown mercy to the bird's nest, show Thy mercy and Thy compassion to us also,' he gained the admiration of Rabbah, who expressed himself thus: 'How well this rabbi knows how to plead with his Master.' These words were said in all sincerity, not merely to sharpen Abaye's wits and to rouse his protest against this prayer, as explained in Talmud Berakot 33a. [However, Rabbah's words may perhaps be taken in the sense of R. Hanina's remarks.] The Mishnah here refers to the people who deny that God meant us to fulfill the law of Deut. XXII, 6, in declaring it to be beneath God to extend His mercies to such insignificant creatures as birds in a nest. We can find similar interpretations by Philo and by Paul. Philo (De somnis, 1, 16) explains the law in Exod. XXII, 26, in an allegorical way. He says, it cannot mean a real garment, as God would not concern Himself about a garment, and would not think of prescribing a law for it. And Paul, in I. Corinthians IX, 9–10, in explaining the law (in Deut. XXV, 4), says: It is written in the law of Moses, 'Thou shalt not muzzle the mouth of the ox that treadeth out the corn.' Doth God take care of the oxen? or doth He say it altogether for our sakes? For our sakes, no doubt this is written.

"He therefore explains the law to mean that the teachers of religion be supported and provided for, for it would be unworthy of God to concern Himself with oxen and take care of them. To such allegoristic interpretations of the law the Mishnah refers in the saying האומר על קן צפור יגיעו רחמיך? Whosoever says: 'Do God's mercies extend to the bird's nest? Can God concern Himself with such trivial things?' is to be silenced. We should not listen to such interpretations of the law, which deny the necessity of fulfilling it and observing it practically.

"This resentment against the allegoristic method grew greater in Palestine, where there were frequent disputes with the Jewish Christians, who used such allegoristic interpretations of some heretical sectarians who tended to exalt a special doctrine at the cost of essential principles of faith. "The Synagog, through its interpreters," observes Dr. Schechter, "recognized the true nature of this apparent repudiation, and continued to give the objectionable doctrine its proper place and proportion among the accepted teachings of Judaism."[144] thus the above warnings were put aside by the Synagog "which continued the tradition of Pseudo-Jonathan to Leviticus XXII:28,[145] and never hesitated to explain such laws on the principle of mercy."[146]

God's Love of Israel

The Torah, with all its commandments and institutions, even as Repentance and Prayer, was intended for all humanity. Only when the other nations refused to accept this boon of divine grace, was it thrust upon Israel.[147] The universalistic nature of God's love is clear. As the nation that became the standard bearer of the Torah, or God's revelation to man, Israel became, to borrow Goethe's phrase, God's "elective affinity."[148] R. Judah bar Simon, in the name of R. Joshua ben Levi, teaches: "Before you received the Torah, says God, your name was *Israel,* even as the other nations are called *Soba, Habila,* etc. But since you received the Torah, you are called 'My people'; as it is said:[149] 'Hear My people, and I shall speak; Israel, and I shall testify against thee.'"[150]

the Scripture in their arguments for the superiority of their new religion. The later Palestinian teachers rejected its use, and tried to suppress it." Ancient Jewish Allegorists in Talmud and Midrash. *Jewish Quarterly Review,* New Series. Vol. I, pp. 529–530.

[144] *Aspects,* p. 10.

[145] Berliner's *Targum,* 2:85.

[146] Schechter, *Ibid.,* note. cf. *Gen. R.* 75:13; *Deut. R.* 6:1; *Tan. B.* 3:48a; also *Gen. R.* 33:13, with reference to Ps. CXLV:9.

[147] v. Byalik and Rabinitzki, *Sefer Ha-Aggadah* I, p. 70ff, and *Midrashim* to Ex. XIX. Ginzberg's *Legends of the Jews,* III, p. 8off.

[148] For Ben Sirach's views of God's love for Israel, v. XVII:17; XXIV:8–12; also XLIV–XLIX, and Box and Oesterley's Introduction to Sirach in Charles' A. P. E. vo I. v. *Tana Debe Elijah* XXV, XXVI.

[149] Ps. L:7.

[150] *Pesikta,* ed. Buber, XII:168.

All the vocabulary of love was exhausted in the description of God's devotion to Israel. He called Israel "My daughter" and "My sister." In ten instances Israel is said to be called God's bride."[151] The relation between God and Israel is pictured as being that of man for woman.[152] It is significant that the Song of Songs, the finest love poem in literature, was deprived of its human import and turned into a sacred song, singing of God's mystic love for Israel. Because of this interpretation this poem was acclaimed by Akiba as the Holy of Holies of the Temple of Song.[153] The preachers of the *Midrashim*[154] never wearied of explaining every relation between God and Israel in the light of the Song of Songs. The *Paitanim,* too, attuned their harps to its melody,[155] so that many of their compositions received an erotic tone. This rapturous spirit is felt also in Halevi's numbers,[156] and in the Songs of Israel Najara. Of the latter, Dr. Israel Abrahams writes: "He did not hesitate to put the most passionate words of love for Israel into God's mouth. He was strongly attacked, but the saintly mystic, Isaac Luria, retorted that Najara's hymns were listened to with delight in Heaven—and if ever a man had a right to speak of Heaven it was Luria."[157]

These passages from our post-Biblical literature which, but for the limitation of space, might have been multiplied indefinitely, these passages representing God as the Heavenly Father who showers His goodness and His love upon all mankind and especially upon Israel, show that the Jew need not purloin the doctrine that God is love from other religions; for his whole faith is built on it. The Prayerbook, or rather the Prayerbooks of Israel, in which Jewish theology appears in its most crystallized form, repeatedly refer to God as the Heavenly Father who abounds in mercy and graciously leads the world towards ever greater perfection. The belief in God's over-arching love per-

---

[151] Ibid., XXII:25.

[152] *Yoma* 54b.

[153] v. *Midrash R.* to Song of Songs, which is a veritable storehouse of mystic love.

[154] v. *Pesikta,* ed. Buber, passim; and *Pesikta Rabbati* passim.

[155] cf. *Ahot Ketanot*; *B'rach Dodi.*

[156] v. Section II in vol. I of Harkavi's ed. of Halevi's poems.

[157] *The Book of Delight,* p. 239; v. his entire essay on "Hebrew Love Songs," Ibid., pp. 184–241.

meates all Jewish ideas about God's relation to the world, about Creation, Providence, Revelation, and even Retribution.

III. Man's Love of God

The Great Commandment of Love

Man's love of God—the core of all religion—represents the response to God's love for man. "Deep calleth unto deep"! It springs not from a sense of external obligation, but—as Abelson so well remarks about worship in general—"from an impulse of the Holy Spirit, that emanation of Himself which He had deposited in the finite heart."[158] The rabbis, philosophers, and mystics, whether they view it from the standpoint of pure intellect, or from that of filial confidence and faith in God, unite in their belief that the love of God is the underlying motive of all pure morality and ritual. Their teachings on this subject cluster round the golden text: "Thou shalt love the Lord thy God with all thy heart, with all thy soul, and with all thy might."[159]

In their characteristic style, the Rabbis lay stress upon the applications of each word. Conscious of the fact that religion is often born out of the sense of fear, the Rabbis emphasized love as a higher motive of worship.[160] "Greater is he who follows God's precepts out of love than out of fear."[161] This love must come from the *whole heart,* i. e., from both *yezers,* the evil as well as the good inclinations of the heart, or in singleness of purpose;[162] *whole-souled,* it must be a love unto death.[163] It must not stop short of sacrifice of one's *might* or substance, which many people prize more than their hearts and souls.[164]

---

[158] *Immanence,* p. 287.
[159] Deut. VI:5.
[160] *Sifre* 32; *Yalkut Shim.* 837; v. Bentwich: *Philo,* pp. 162–164.
[161] *Sota* 31.
[162] *Ber.* 61; cf. Ps. LXXXVI:11.
[163] *Yalkut,* Ibid.
[164] Ibid.

Martyrdom

In the view of the saintly teacher, Akiba, the phrase "with all thy might" indicates[165] that it is man's duty to love God even in chastisement. He found support for his belief in the Psalms and in the sublime example of Job's unfalttering devotion to God in suffering. And he offered most eloquent expression of his conviction by his own life. When arrested on the charge of teaching the Torah in violation of the Roman edict, and subjected to inexpressible torture, he cheerfully recited the *Shema*, Israel's confession of the divine Unity. To his disciples who stood amazed at his action he said: "All my life I have worried about the way to love God *'with all the soul'*; at last the opportunity has offered itself." No sooner had he uttered the word *Eḥod* (One) than his soul departed. Thereupon, says the *Midrash*, the angels exclaimed before God: "Is this the reward of the Torah, that men die at Your hands?"[166] "But their portion is among the living," rejoined God.[167] And a *Bath Kol*, "the divine voice," proclaimed: "Happy art thou, Akiba, for thou art immortal!" (literally: Thou art ready for the life of the world to come).[168] Josephus writes that in the last days of Herod, the Pharisees, whom he calls the Sophists, taught their followers "that it was a glorious thing to die for the laws of their country, because the soul was immortal, and an eternal enjoyment of happiness did await such as died on that account, while the mean-spirited and those that were not wise enough to show a right love of their souls, preferred death by disease to that which is a sign of virtue."[169] Removing its Hellenistic wrappings, this statement reveals the true spirit of martyrdom—*mesirat hanefesh*—that animated Akiba and hundreds of thousands of other saints who

---

[165] By a play on the word *"Meodecho—Bechol Middo u-middo shehu moded loch, ben bemiddat hatob uben lemiddat puroniot*—No matter by what measure He metes out to you, whether by the measure of goodness or by that of chastisement."

[166] The reference is to Ps. XVII:14 ממתים ידך יי, literally: "From men by Thy hand, O Lord."

[167] A continuation of the verse. חלקם בחיים.

[168] *Yalkut*, Ibid.

[169] Cited by Bentwich, *Josephus*, p. 114.

died *al ḳiddush ha-shem*—"for the sanctification of God's name."[170] These martyrs of faith went to their death joyfully, conscious that thereby they were fulfilling the commandment of loving God. Thus they indeed attained the higher immortality! Theirs was a love that laughed at death. The many waters of tribulation could not quench the love of God that burned in their hearts.

Intellectual Love

To the philosophers, man's love for God appeared in the light of the finest flower not only of faith but also of reason. Philo, who, with the Stoics, regarded the human intellect as connected with divine Reason, "being an impression of a fragment or ray of that Blessed Nature,"[171] urged: "Let every one on whom God has showered good things pray to God that he may have, as a Dweller within him, the Ruler of all things, Who will raise this small house, the mind, to a great height above the earth, and will connect it with the bounds of heaven."[172]

Saadia, the philosopher of the practical, is of the opinion that man's love for God should not lead him to other-worldliness. His worship should not make him neglect his daily affairs.[173] Baḥya, however, would have man, in his love for God, set his heart upon God, and devote himself exclusively to meditation upon Him. Thus man partakes of the cup of love for God. Baḥya cites the Midrashic comment to the verse in the Song of Songs which reads: "A bundle of myrrh is my beloved unto me; he lieth betwixt my breasts,"[174] i. e., even if He brings me into distress and embitters me (a play on the words, "*ẓeror hamor*," reading them *"Meẓar li umemar li"*), He shall live in my

---

[170] *Aggadat Abraham* in *Ozar Midr.*, p. 8, *Asoroh Haruge Malchut*, Ibid., p. 240ff; *Sanh.* 72; *Yalkut* 838; Maim. *Mishneh Torah* Bk. I, chap. 5. v. also II Macc. VIII:29; and Kohler's art. "Didascalia" in *Jew. Encyc.* IV:588ff (on Bk. V).

[171] On the Creation of the World, LXI.

[172] On Fugitives.

[173] *Emunot vedeot* X:16.

[174] Song of Songs I:13. v. *Midr. R.* to the verse and *Yoma* 88b.

heart. With Job, Baḥya calls: "Though He slay me, yet will I trust in Him."[175] Our love for God should be prompted neither by fear of punishment, nor by expectations of reward. It should be the expression of our pure joy in His pure and exalted Being.[176] Maimonides, like Baḥya, tempers his rationalism with mysticism when speaking of man's love of God. According to him, the man that serves God out of love cannot be moved by any worldly considerations. "He follows truth because it is truth." He is aware of the fact that not all persons are capable of such love. "Ignorant men, women and children are taught to serve Him out of fear, that in the end they may learn to worship Him out of love." True love of God is like the love of man for woman, only much more intense and refined. It is an attachment of soul to His Being, and a constant meditation upon Him. This love of God is not sensuous but intellectual. It is generated by knowledge.[177] The *Zohar*, too, justifies worship prompted by fear, only because it leads to love, wherein "is found the secret of divine unity. It is love that unites the higher and the lower stages and that lifts everything to that stage where all must be one."[178] Abravanel grapples with the difficulty of man's love of God, since man cannot fully know God, and knowledge forms the prime condition of love. And he answers in true Maimonidean fashion that "God, blessed be He, is loved only in the degree in which He is known. Inasmuch as His true nature cannot be fully perceived by man, and as His wisdom cannot be attained, He cannot be loved in the degree of which He is worthy, but only according to the human power to love."[179] Man when good "is God-loving as well as God-beloved" and his "love of God leads him to eternal bliss, which is identical with divine love."[180]

Spinoza, in this as well as in many other matters, remained true to the noblest traditions of the Synagog, from which he was excommunicated. He writes: "Whosoever clearly and distinctly understands himself and his own mental affections, loves God, and all the more in proportion as he better

[175] Job XIII:15.
[176] *Ḥobot Halebabot*, chap. X:1–2.
[177] *Mishneh Torah*, Bk. I. H. Teshubah, chap. 10. v. also *Sefer Ḥasidim* 14.
[178] *Zohar*, Va-Yakhel, II:216a.
[179] *Viku'aḥ al HoAhabah*, p. 6b ff.
[180] Cited by Dr. Kohler, art. "Love," *Jew. Encyc.*

understands self and its affections."[181] When the dark veil of ignorance is removed from the eye of man, God becomes manifest as the source of all the joy of existence. Man can then "look beyond himself to the glory of the sum of things. The glow of feeling with which such a man responds to the universe" is what Mr. Picton understands Spinoza to mean by "the intellectual love of God."[182]

Ritual a means of Love

Man's love of God, we said, has been the guiding motive of all ritual and morality. With reference to the commandment of love,[183] one rabbi observes: "I know not which way one should love the Holy One, blessed be He; therefore Scripture specifies: 'And these words which I command thee this day shall be in thy heart,'[184] which means: place these words upon thy heart, for through them thou wilt know the Holy One, blessed be He, and cleave unto His ways."[185] Schechter finds in these words a warning against "idle spirituality" into which the mystic and his confreres, who delight in revelling in God's love, may lapse—a spirituality which disregards all ritual obligations. The Jewish mystics were at one with the whole house of Israel in regarding the Torah as a special manifestation of God's love, and therefore believed that one can best commune with God through the Torah and its duties. They indeed vested all the *Mizwot*—duties—with special *Kawanot*—intentions— but did not break them. Hence the somewhat strange union of legalism with mysticism, in the Kabbalistic systems.[186] The verse "to love the Lord your God, and to serve Him with all your hearts" is taken to mean prayer.[187] In this sense prayer is regarded in almost all the theological works of the Jewish

[181] *Ethics* V, prop. XV; cited by J. A. Picton "Spinoza," p. 187.
[182] Ibid. In this connection, see Jacob Dubno: *Sefer Hamiddot*, chap. III.
[183] Deut. VI:5.
[184] Ibid., verse 6.
[185] *Sifre* 74a; *Yalkut* 839; cited by Schechter, *Aspects*, pp. 78-79.
[186] H. Vital, *Sha'are Kedusha*.
[187] *Ta'an.* 2. v. the whole section "Ben Odom la-Mokom and Tefilah" in Byalik and Rabinitzki's *Sefer Ho-Aggadah*, II:3, pp. 193-205.

masters. Thus Maimonides classifies all ritual laws under the heading
"*Ahabah*" (Love).[188]   When man's service of God is free from mixed
motives, God Himself delights in it. Says R. Azariah, in the name of R. Judah
bar Simon: "When the righteous do the will of God, they add strength to the
Almighty, as Scripture says:[189] 'May the strength of God be increased.'"[190]
Judah bar Simon quotes R. Joshua ben Levi to the effect that Israel's service
increases God's strength.[191] God does not delight in isolated grandeur. He
longs for all nature and men to act in tune with Him. He reigned supreme
before the world was created, yet was not His throne firmly established until
the children of Israel proclaimed His kingship.[192]

Morality, an Expression of Love

While God delights in man's worship, He is even more pleased with man's
ethical conduct. He even makes man a co-worker in the task of creation. Thus
the commandment, "And thou shalt love the Lord thy God," was also construed to mean that the name of God be loved through you.[193] Someone has
stated that "the true object of religion, the real goal of spiritual progress, is to
make every soul reflect the divine." Through his commendable actions the
God-loving man leads others to love God. According to another interpretation, this commandment teaches "be loved by men, and remove yourself from
transgression, and from robbery whether of a Jew or of a heathen, or of any
man, for he who steals from a heathen will in the end steal from a Jew.
Robbing a heathen may lead to robbing a co-religionist. Swearing (falsely) to
a heathen results in a similar offense against a fellow-Jew. Deceiving a
heathen may lead to the deception of a Jew. He who sheds the blood of a

---

[188] *Mishneh Torah*, Bk. II.

[189] Num. XIV:17.

[190] *Pesikta*, ed. Buber, XXVI:10–12 and note. כל זמן זהצדיקים עושין רצונו של מקום הם מוסיפים
כח בגבורה.

[191] Ibid. (referring to Ps. LX:3).

[192] *Ex. R.* 23:1.

[193] *Yalkut* 838; *Tana Debe Elijah*, R. XXVIII. *Yoma* 86.

heathen will also shed the blood of a Jew. And the Torah was given only for the purpose that God's great name may be sanctified."[194]

IV. Man's Love of Man

The doctrine of brotherly love which, in the Bible, gradually asserted itself above that of retaliation,[195] retained its commanding position in the ethical thought of post-Biblical literature. The duty to love God reached its culmination in the love of one's fellow men; so that the author of the Wisdom of Solomon could summarize the whole matter in this pointed sentence, "Thou didst teach Thy people by such works as these (referring to God's mercy) that the righteous must be a lover of men."[196]

Christianity claims the credit for conjoining the commands to love God and to love one's neighbor. But as this passage in the Wisdom of Solomon clearly indicates, this was the trend of the entire body of Jewish religious thought. Mr. Charles, who shows very little partiality towards Judaism, is compelled to admit that the Jewish masters anticipated the founder of Christianity in this respect. He finds the earliest literary authority for it in the Testament of Dan, written more than a century before the Christian era,

"Love the Lord through all thy life,
And one another with a true heart."[197]

[194] *Tana Debe Elijah, R.* XXVIII.

[195] This primitive law (Ex. XXI:24–25) growing out of the instinctive desire on the part of man to avenge wrongs done to him, was raised to a law of "divine procedure." As Judges I:6, 7, indicates, the belief was shared by the people that in the divine economy, man is dealt with by God as he deals with his own fellows. (So also in II Macc., Jubilees, and in the Talmud.) This conscienciousness, in turn, led to the radical transformation and finally to the abrogation of the original law. cf. Ps. XVIII:25 sq. Hence, the book of Proverbs' counsel against vengeance (XXIV:29; XX:22; XXV:21, 22, also Job XXXI:29ff). The legalists as well as the moralists enjoin forgiveness; v. Ex. XXIII:4, 5; Deut. XXII:1–3. Punishment is left to God. (Deut. XXXII:35, 43.)

[196] Wisd. Sol. XII:19.

[197] *Testament of Twelve Patriarchs, T. Dan* V:3.

The whole of the Testaments of the Twelve Patriarchs—a book of Pharisaic origin—is conceived in the same spirit. Issachar commands his sons to keep the law of God in singleness of heart and in guilelessness, and to "love the Lord and your neighbor," also to have compassion on the poor and weak.[198] Zebulun, likewise, orders his children "to keep the commands of the Lord, and to show mercy to your neighbor, and to have compassion towards all, not towards men only, but also towards beasts.[199] . . . Have compassion in your hearts, my children, because even as a man doeth to his neighbor, even so also will the Lord do to him."[200] According to Philo, the Essenes emphasized this three-fold doctrine: "Love of God, love of manhood (self-control), and love of man."[201] Philo, too, taught that "he who loves God but does not show love towards his own kind, has but the half of virtue."[202]

The Golden Rule

The duty to love one's fellow man is emphasized not only in the Testaments of the Twelve Patriarchs,[203] by the Essenes and by Philo,[204] but also by the much maligned teachers of legalistic Judaism. Akiba regarded the commandment, "Thou shalt love thy neighbor as thyself," as a leading principle of the Torah.[205] This conviction of his doubtlessly grew out of his belief that man is created in the image of God.[206] Before Akiba, Hillel taught, "Be of the disciples of Aaron, loving peace and pursuing peace, loving thy fellow creatures, and drawing them near to the Torah."[207]

---

[198] *Ibid., T. Issach.* V:1; also in VII:6.

[199] On compassion towards animals, Rabbinic ethics is most insistent.

[200] *Ibid., T. Zebul.* V:1–3; also VII:2 and VIII:1; *T. Benj.* III:3, X:3.

[201] *De Vita Contemplata*, ed. Conybeare, p. 53ff. Cited by Kohler, art. Essenes; *Joseph. B. J.* II:8, par. 2.

[202] *De Decal.* XXIII.

[203] *T. Reub.* VI:9; *T. Sim.* IV:7.

[204] v. Bentwich: *Philo*, pp. 117–118.

[205] *Sifra* to Lev. XIX:18, and *Yalkut Shim.* 614, and Rashi (ed. Berliner) to Lev. XIX:18. v. also *Jer. Nedar.* 8:9. cf. *Gen. R.* XXIV:5.

[206] *Abot* III:14; also *Gen. R.* XXXIV. This was also the view of Ben. Azai, Ibid.

[207] *Abot* I:12.

Hillel, while teaching the positive duty of loving one's fellow creatures, also summarized the intent of the whole Torah, to the impatient Roman, in the words: "What is hateful to thee, do not to thy fellowman."[208] Much emphasis has been laid on Hillel's negative formulation of the Golden Rule. Many Jewish teachers as well as Christian scholars have sought to find in it the peculiar tendency of Judaism toward justice, in contradistinction to the positive statement of the Golden Rule by Jesus,[209] typical of the Christian emphasis of love. The trouble with this sophistry is that it overlooks the fact that this saying was given to the Roman while he stood on one foot; and that, had he been endowed with a more generous share of patience, he would undoubtedly have heard Hillel's other doctrine, stating as a positive duty for man to "be of the disciples of Aaron . . . loving thy fellow creatures."

Furthermore, this distinction between the positive and negative forms of the Golden Rule was of small importance to the early Christians. In their writings, the negative form appears by the side of the positive. The recently recovered Apology of Aristides, in giving a summary of Christian belief and practice, states, "Whatever they do not wish to be done to them, they do not do to another."[210] Neither were the Jewish teachers conscious of a radical distinction between the two. Thus Tobit states the positive duty to love one's brethren, and then also the negative form of the Golden Rule. He says to his son: "My child, *love thy brethren,* and scorn not in thy heart thy brethren and the sons and daughters of thy people so as not to take one of them, for in scornfulness is destruction and much trouble. . . . Take heed to thyself, my child, in all thy works, and be discreet in all thy behavior. And what thou hatest, do to no man."[211] The *Didache*—a first century manual of instruction

---

[208] *Sab.* 31a; following a current Targumic construction of Lev. XIX:18. It occurs also in the Armenian version of the *Story of Aḥikar,* chap. II:88 (in Charles, *A. P. E.* and *Hebrew Test. Naphtali* I:6b.

[209] Matthew VII:12, and in a somewhat briefer form in Luke VI:31.

[210] W. A. Spooner, art. "Golden Rule," Hastings, *Encyc. Rel. and Ethics.* VI:310–312.

[211] Tobit IV:15–21. Graetz assigns the book of Tobit to the time of Hadrian. Mr. Simpson believes that it was written about 170 B. C. E. v. his introduction to the Book in Charles, *A. P. E.,* vol. I:185. The Aramaic version of the Golden Rule, as given in the book, is דסנאי לך לחורני לא תעביד.

for Proselytes, which, according to Dr. Kohler, was "adopted from the Synagog by early Christianity, and transformed by alteration and modification into a Church manual"[212]—likewise presents both the positive duty to love one's fellows, and the negative form of the Golden Rule. Its distinctly Jewish part is summarized thus in the opening two verses: "There are two ways, one of life and one of death; and wide is the difference between them. The way of life is this: thou shalt love God thy Maker;[213] second, thou shalt love thy neighbor as thyself.[214] Now the teaching of these two words is this: whatsoever thou wouldst not have done unto thee, neither do thou to another."[215] This manual, Jewish in origin and Christian by adoption, fairly represents the two positions of both Judaism and Christianity. Whatever difference is drawn between Jewish and Christian ethics on the basis of the positive and negative formulations of the Golden Rule, is mere hair-splitting. Both forms grow out of the older Jewish commandment, "Thou shalt love thy neighbor as thyself."[216] This commandment, contrary to the claims of non-

---

[212] Kohler in art. Didache, *Jew. Encyc.* IV:585–587. v. also Harnack, art. Didache in the *New Schaf-Herzog* III:422.

[213] After Deut. VI:5.

[214] After Lev. XIX:18.

[215] Cited by Kohler, art. Didache, *Ibid.* v. his art. "Didascalia" *ibid.*, p. 588–594.

[216] v. also E. G. Hirsch's art. "Golden Rule," *Jew. Encyc.* VI:21–22, and Kohler's art. "Brotherly Love," *Jew. Encyc.* III:397–398. Professor Lauterbach writes (The Ethics of the Halachah, *C. C. A. R. Yearbook* XXIII:255–6): "It is well known that, when Jesus declared the commandment, 'thou shalt love thy neighbor as thyself' (Lev. XIX:18) to be the second greatest commandment of the law (Matt. XXII:39), he merely repeated what every Jewish teacher before and during his time had taught. There was, however, a great difference between the Jewish conception and application of this noble principle and the Christian understanding of the same. The Jewish teachers in declaring this principle to be the fundamental principle of the religion, the whole Law, taught at the same time that the rest of the Law also had its legitimate place; that the other commandments leading up to this consummation of the Law must also be observed. As Hillel expressed it, 'all the rest is merely a commentary,' but a commentary which one must know, 'Go and study it,' in order to learn from it how to apply correctly the one principle, the golden rule. Christianity has accepted the text of Leviticus XIX:18, without the Commentary, the golden rule without the whole system of its practical application. The Law was declared as abrogated. Paul said, 'All the law is fulfilled in one word.' (Galatians V:14.)

Jewish scholars, was understood by the Jewish masters to apply not to the Jewish neighbor alone, but also to all other men. Hillel and his followers, by the use of the phrase *ehab es haberiyot*—"love all creatures," clearly include all mankind under the law of love. Furthermore, Hillel taught the Golden Rule to a heathen, which proves that he in no wise restricted its application to Jews.[217]

Hatred Towards the Enemy

The writings of the New Testament which are not exceedingly complimentary to the Pharisees, contain a calumnious statement in regard to the Jewish doctrine of love. In the Sermon on the Mount, we read these words of Jesus, spoken to the multitude: "Ye have heard that it was said, 'Thou shalt love thy neighbor, and hate thy enemy,' but I say unto you, Love your enemies."[218] The whole range of Jewish literature has been ransacked in search of the law that ordains the duty to hate one's enemy; but thus far, it is not yet in sight. Several Christian scholars have endeavored to uphold, at all hazards, this groundless assertion. Charles points to the infelicitous expressions in the Psalms,[219] about the enemies; and insists that these "more than justify our Lord's summary of the teaching of the Old Testament on this question in Matthew V:43: 'Ye have heard that it was said: Thou shalt love thy neighbor, and hate thy enemy.'"[220] Bousset, showing the class divisions in Jewish life,

But the result was that the so-called fulfillment of the Law remained merely a word. The Love preached by Christianity did not prove to be that love which 'worked no ill to his neighbor.' (Romans XIII:10.) Quite to the contrary, it wrought great harm. The principle, 'love thy neighbor as thyself,' was for many centuries upon the lips of Christian nations without any influence upon their character and conduct. They even committed the most horrible crimes and perpetrated the most cruel acts of hatred in the name of that very religion of love. The voice was the voice of Jacob, repeating the Jewish teachings of brotherly love, but the hands remained the bloody hands of Esau inflicting injury and evil."

[217] cf. *Jew. Encyc.* art. "Golden Rule."

[218] Matt. V:43.

[219] Psalms XLI:10; LIV:4, 5, 7; CXII:9, 8; CXXXVII:9.

[220] *Religious Development between the Old and the New Testaments*, p. 141.

and what he calls "the churchly character of Jewish ethics," says that the word of Jesus "though very sharply pointed, is not unjust."[221]

Schechter, however, has well observed that "after the declaration made by Jesus of his attachment to the Torah, it is not likely that he would quote passages from it showing its inferiority." He further suggests that the only way to get over the difficulty is to assume that Jesus used the formula current in Rabbinic exegesis: *Shome'a ani . . . talmud lomar*—I might hear so and so; therefore there is a teaching to say that, etc." As applied to the passage in question, Jesus may have meant to say: From the commandment, "Love thy neighbor," you may be led to infer that you are to hate your enemies. Therefore I say unto you that Scripture teaches: love also your enemies.[222] The Rabbinic idiom in the original saying of Jesus, mistranslated into Greek, gave rise to the perverted view of Pharisaic ethics.

Forgiveness

The most convincing refutation of this charge of the New Testament writer is supplied by Jewish teaching on the question of forgiveness. Ben Sirach counselled:

"Forgive thy neighbor the hurt that he has done thee,
And then thy sins shall be pardoned when thou prayest.
Man cherishes anger against man,
And does he seek healing from the Lord?
Upon a man like himself he hath no mercy,
And does he make supplication for his sins?"[223]

On the same grounds the ungrateful Nadan asks Aḥikar's forgiveness.[224] Still

[221] *Die Religion des Judentums in Neutestamentlichen Zeitalter*, p. 113.
[222] Schechter, *Studies in Judaism*, 2d Series, p. 117.
[223] Sirach XXVIII:2–3. This rendering by Schechter (*Studies in Judaism*, 2 Series, p. 94) is better than Box and Oesterley's in Charles, *Apocrypha and Pseudepigrapha*.
[224] *Aḥikar*, Syr. VIII:34; Arab. VIII:29; Armen. VIII:24b.

loftier heights are reached in the Testament of the Twelve Patriarchs,[225] which according to Charles' admission anticipates the teachings of Jesus on many subjects. The whole book is filled with the loftiest sentiments of love and forbearance. Joseph is pictured as the saint who bore no malice to those that hated him. He did not afflict them in the least; and did all in his power to help them. His example is commended to all, "Do ye also love one another, and with long suffering hide ye one another's faults, for God delighteth in the unity of brethren and in the purpose of a heart that takes pleasure in love."[226] Gad urges upon his children to remove hatred from their hearts, "for as love would quicken even the dead, and would call back them that are condemned to die, so hatred would slay the living, and those that have sinned venially it would not suffer to live, for the spirit of hatred worketh together with Satan, through hastiness of spirit, in all things to men's death. But the spirit of love worketh together with the law of God in long-suffering, unto the salvation of men."[227] . . . "He that is just and humble is ashamed to do what is unjust, being reproved not of another, but of his own heart, because the Lord looketh on his inclination. . . . Fearing lest he should offend the Lord, he will not do wrong to any man, even in thought."[228] . . . "And now, my children, I exhort you, love ye each one his brother, and put away hatred from your hearts; love one another in deed and in word and in the inclination of the soul. . . Love ye one another from the heart, and if a man sin against thee, speak peaceably to him, and in thy soul hold not guile. And if he repent and confess, forgive

[225] Charles writes: "There is a genuine Jewish work of the second century in which a doctrine of forgiveness is taught that infinitely transcends the teaching of Sirach, and is almost as noble as that of the New Testament. Moreover, this doctrine of forgiveness does not stand as an isolated glory in the Testaments of the Twelve Patriarchs as in other Jewish writings, but is in keeping with the entire ethical character of that remarkable book, which proclaims in an ethical setting that God created man in His image, that the law was given to lighten every man, that salvation was for all mankind through conversion to Judaism, and that a man should love both God and his neighbor." *Ibid.*, p. 153.

[226] *T. Jos.* XVII:2-3; cf. *T. Zeb.* VIII:5; *T. Benj.* IV:1-4; V:4b; VIII:1-2.

[227] *T. Gad.* IV:6-7.

[228] Ibid. V:1-5. cf. *T. Benj.* III:4b-5.

him.[229] But if he deny it, do not get into a passion with him lest, catching the poison from thee, he take to swearing, and so thou sin doubly. . . . And though he deny it, yet have a sense of shame when reproved, give over reproving him, for he who denieth may repent so as not again to wrong thee. Yea, he may also honor thee, and fear and be at peace with thee. And if he be shameless and persist in his wrongdoing, even so forgive him from the heart, and leave to God the avenging."[230]

The noble sentiments of these passages found expression also in other Jewish writings. Philo speaks of the Law's "teaching men by remote examples not to be delighted at the unexpected misfortunes of those that hate them." He also shows that, through conferring a favor on an enemy, there "follows of necessity a dissolution of the enmity."[231] The Rabbis teach: "From the commandment, 'Thou shalt not hate thy brother in thy heart,' you might infer that you may not strike him, slap him in the face, or curse him. Therefore Scripture specifies 'in thy heart,' i. e., you may not hate him even in thought."[232] "Judge every man favorably;"[233] or still better, "Judge not your fellow man until you have come to his place."[234] He who causes his fellow man to suffer punishment is excluded from the immediate presence of God.[235] The Day of Atonement does not remove a man's sin until he has obtained his neighbor's forgiveness.[236] Even if he wronged his neighbor in word of mouth only, he should endeavor to propitiate him.[237] The neighbor in turn must not

---

[229] Another version of the last verse reads: "Love ye, therefore, one another from the heart; and if a man sin against thee, cast forth the poison of hate and speak peaceably to him, and in thy soul hold not guile; and if he confess and repent, forgive him."

[230] T. Gad. VI:1–7. See Charles' discussion of the Ethics of forgiveness in Judaism and Christianity, in his Introduction to the Testaments of the Twelve Patriarchs, A. P. E., p. 293, where he misrepresents Judaism. v. also Fragments of a Zadokite Work IX:50–X:6.

[231] De Humanitate, 15; cited by Charles, Rel. Development bet. the Old and the New Testaments, p. 149; cf. 2 Enoch L:4(a).

[232] Arok. 16; cf. Yoma 23.

[233] Abot I:6.

[234] Abot II:5.

[235] Sab. 149.

[236] Yoma VIII:7.

[237] Yoma 87a.

nurse his wrong, but should be ready to forgive even as God forgives offenses against Him.[238] They who forgive their fellow men may expect to be forgiven by God, but they who show no mercy to others cannot expect the mercy of God.[239]

The Jewish Ideal of Conduct

In the Jewish ideal of conduct, love and forgiveness, not hatred nor vengeance, hold the foremost place, as is evident from this frequently used passage: "They who though offended do not offend, though insulted do not reply, who do God's will out of love and rejoice even in chastisement, of them Scripture says,[240] 'His beloved ones are as the sun rising in might.'"[241] The same spirit is voiced in the Talmudic prayer, which forms part of our rituals: "O my God! Guard my tongue from evil and my lips from speaking guile; and to such as curse me, let my soul be dumb, yea, let my soul be unto all as dust. . . . If any design evil against me, speedily (do Thou) make their counsel of none effect, and frustrate their designs, in order that Thy beloved ones may be delivered."[242]

Forgiveness and love purge man of the weakness of pride and vainglory, and endow him with saintliness. Hatred, on the other hand, is condemned as the equivalent of bloodshed.[243] He who hates an Israelite hates Abraham, Isaac, and Jacob, the grand-sires of Israel.[244] In the spirit of Hillel and Akiba, the Jewish masters felt that he who hates any man hates God, in whose likeness man is made. Ḥayim Vital, emphasizing the belief that all souls root in God, taught: "Let man love all creatures, including gentiles, and let him envy none."[245] Dr. Schechter, calling attention to the fact that this is the distinct

---

[238] Abba Shaul in *Mechilta Beshalaḥ* 3; *Sab.* 133b.
[239] *Megil.* 28; cf. *Sab.* 151; *Yoma* 87b.
[240] Judges V:31.
[241] *Yoma* 22a; *Sab.* 88b; *Yalkut Shim.* 613.
[242] *Ber.* 17a; *Prayerbook*, ed. Singer, p. 54.
[243] *Derech Ereẓ* XII.
[244] Cited by Schechter, *Studies in Jud.*, 2d Ser., p. 168.
[245] *Ibid.*; *Shaare Kedusha*, chap. I:5.

precept of the Jewish saint of the sixteenth century, adds that he knows of no Christian saint of the same period who "made the love of the Jew a condition of saintliness."[246] Claude Montefiore notes a further observation of this scholar that, "while St. Francis spoke of his 'brother wolf' and of his 'little sisters, the doves,' he would hardly have spoken of his brother Turk, heretic, or Jew."[247]

An eighteenth century commentator of Hayim Vital's *Shaare Kedusha* (Gates of Holiness), declares that true brotherly love recognizes no barriers of nationality or language, and is directed solely to man as man. If it is withdrawn from the savage or criminal, it is for the good of society as a whole; for social welfare may demand the execution of a criminal even as the health of a man's body may call for the amputation of a diseased limb. Brotherly love minimizes the dangers of social misery, and improves the chances of social happiness. He concludes that, whether viewed "from the standpoint of nature, reason, or tradition, love of one's neighbor appears as a permanent duty, taking precedence over the search after truth, and scientific pursuits; it is even more precious than wisdom and the honor of the holy Torah". . . . "And do not wonder that there is anything superior to the Torah; for inasmuch as the Torah ordains and commands it, love is not extraneous to, but a part of the Torah."[248]

"The love of your neighbor shall be literally as of 'thyself,' i. e., as each limb of your body responds to the needs of the other, so shall you conduct yourself towards your neighbor. It is, therefore, not sufficient for you to abstain from harming him yourself, but you must strive to ward off all evil from him, even when threatened from other sources."[249] Thus the negative form of the Golden Rule is supplemented by the positive. The one asks that no evil be done to one's neighbor, the other demands that good be done him.[250]

---

[246] *Ibid.*

[247] *Hibbert Lectures*, p. 426, note 1.

[248] *Sefer Haberit hasholem*, by R. Phineas Elijah b. Meir of Wilna, part II, chap. XIII:1–12.

[249] *Ibid.*, 13.

[250] Our author argues that, in its negative form, the Golden Rule admits of no difference between oneself and one's neighbor: "What is hateful to thee, do not to thy fellowman." In the positive form, however, a certain difference between oneself and one's neighbor has to be

Mercy is a distinguished characteristic of the children of Abraham.[251] They are *Rahamanim bene Rahamanim*—"merciful sons of merciful fathers." This trait was formed by the long training of the Jew in the principle of *Imitatio Dei,* morality's highest goal. Schechter writes: "It is to be remarked that his Godlikeness is confined to his manifestations of mercy and righteousness, the Rabbis rarely desiring the Jew to take God as a model in His attributes of severity and rigid justice, though the Bible could have furnished them with many instances of this latter kind."[252] Jealousy, revenge, and punishment are left to God; but man must do justice and follow mercy. Men should not insist upon the letter of the law, for on account of this sin Jerusalem was destroyed.[253] They should endeavor ever to act according to the law of goodness.[254] "Be careful not to be unmerciful, because he who keeps back his compassion from his neighbor is to be compared to the idolator and to the one who throws off the yoke of heaven from himself."[255]

Gemilut Hasodim

Thus the commandment of brotherly love, in itself the outgrowth of the

recognized. While in duty bound to do good to his neighbor, a man cannot, by the very nature of things, be expected to do as much for his neighbor as for himself. Except for rare instances, one's own life precedes that of the neighbor. (*B. Mez.* 62a.) Consequently the duty of love towards one's fellowman assumes a somewhat restricted form: You must do for your neighbor what you expect him to do for you; i. e. love him sincerely, respect him, sympathize with him, receive him kindly, judge him favorably, help him at the cost of sacrifice to yourself, never be overbearing with him. (*Sefer Haberit,* Ibid. 18.) Moses Hayim Luzzato would recognize no such distinction: "The Torah teaches the all-inclusive principle: 'Thou shalt love thy neighbor as thyself,' i. e., as thyself without difference, as thyself without divisions, evasions, or devices." *Mesilat Yesharim,* XI. Though differing in degree, the love of oneself and the love of one's fellowman do not differ in kind, for true love must be in consonance with justice and self-respect. (v. Mendelsohn's *Commentary to Lev.* XIX:18.)

[251] *Beza* 32; *Ket.* 8b; *Yeb.* 79; *Gen. R.* 58:9; *Sefer Hasidim* 11, 20ff. v. Schechter, *Aspects,* p. 201ff.

[252] *Ibid.*

[253] *B. Mez.* 13b.

[254] v. Schechter, *Ibid.,* p. 215–216, 226–227.

[255] *Sifre* 98b; cited by Schechter, *Ibid.,* p. 231ff.

duty of loving God, leads us back to its parent source. Love of God and love of man, according to Jewish construction, are two sides of the same shield, but two expressions of one and the same religious spirit. From this spirit emanated the whole system of *Gemilut Ḥasodim* (loving-kindness), which is by far more comprehensive than *ẓedaḳah*. Originally expressing the idea of righteousness, *ẓedaḳah* came to stand for charity or almsgiving to the poor. *Gemilut Ḥasodim* expresses the personal care that one takes of his fellowman, be he rich or poor. It also includes the respect paid the dead. While the very practice of charity or *ẓedaḳah* fills the world with love,[256] charity is valuable only according to the loving spirit that prompts it. Rightly, therefore, did R. Simlai declare that the Torah begins and ends with loving-kindness.[257]

This loving spirit permeated the criminal code. Akiba teaches: the doctrine "Thou shalt love thy neighbor as thyself," as applied to the criminal, means that it is your duty to find for him a humane form of execution.[258] "This," writes Dr. Kohler, "became the guiding principle for the entire penal law in the Rabbinic Halachah, as one who reads the Mishnah, the Gemara, and the Sifre, can see."[259] Therein did the Pharisaic Code distinguish itself for its leniency as compared with the older Sadducean Code which it replaced.

Reflection of Divine Love upon Human Love

Divine love casts its reflection also upon human sexual love. In the light of religion, passion's putrid flowers could not thrive. Jewish literature celebrates chaste conjugal love, and extols the virtues of fidelity and purity. Unlike the Essenes and the early Christians, the Pharisaic masters did not encourage celibacy. "Neither was the cult of virginity considered a desirable element in

---

[256] Suk. 49b.

[257] *Sota* 14. Excellent summaries of rabbinic doctrine on Charity may be found in *Pirke De Rabbi Eliezer*, ed. Friedlander, XII, XVII, XXIV: in Byalik and Rabnitzki's *Sefer HoAggadah* III: 109ff. and in Dr. Kohler's essay on "The Historical Development of Jewish Charity," *Hebrew Union College and Other Addresses*, pp. 229-252.

[258] *Yalkut Shim.* 613; *Tosefta San.* IX:11; *B. Sanh.* 45a.

[259] *Sanh.: Mish.* IV:1; *Tos.* IX:7; *Gen.* 46b. Halachic Portions in Josephus' Antiquities, *Hebrew Union College Monthly*, vol. III, p. 112ff.

religion, as was the case in the Christian Church." Gerald Friedlander adds that the emphasis laid on the divine participation in Adam's nuptials may have been intended "to counteract the attitude of the Church[260] towards marriage."[261] The traditional marriage ceremony praises God, in whose image man is made, for creating a help-mate for man.[262] To the Jewish teachers marriage, as the means for the preservation of the human race, was a divine institution.[263] The very term for marriage Kiddushin—"consecration"—expresses the idea of holiness. Maimonides arranges in his code all the laws of marriage under the heading kedushah—"holiness."[264] Nachmanides, in his "sacred letter," tries to show "how even such functions as were declared by other religions as distinctly animalic can, with the saint, be elevated into moments of worship and religious exaltation."[265] Other moralists likewise treat the most intimate moments of sex life not so much from the standpoint of hygiene as from that of holiness.

Marriage being divinely ordained, we can understand the view of the Aggadists that since the completion of creation, God has been employing His leisure time in the role of Shadchan (marriage-broker).[266] This conviction was coined into the popular proverb: Marriages are made in Heaven.

Curiously enough, Rab prohibited the marrying of a woman whom the groom had not seen, on the basis of the Golden Rule, for he might dislike her, and break the commandment of the Merciful One: "Thou shalt love thy neighbor as thyself." All Jewish idealism tended towards making the love between husband and wife the sanctifying force in the home. In the light of its sacred flame, the family life of the Jewish people received a lustre all its own. The tender relations of husband and wife had a beneficent influence on the children. In their love for the child, the parents are duty-bound to lead it to

---

[260] Corinth. VII:8; Matt. XIX:10, 12.

[261] Pirke de Rabbi Eliezer, p. 107, note 2.

[262] Ket. 8a; Prayerbook, ed. Singer, p. 229.

[263] Sefer HoAggadah III:5, p. 47ff.

[264] Kohler, art. Ethics, Jew. Encyc. V:251.

[265] Schechter, Studies in Jud., 2d Ser., p. 176.

[266] Gen. R. 68; Lev. R. 29; Pesikta. v. Israel Abrahams' "The Book of Delight and Other Papers," pp. 172–183, 307.

the Torah, i. e., to the knowledge of God and to noble deeds. The child, in turn, honors God by loving and respecting its parents.[267]

Divine love also ennobles and strengthens the ties of friendship. In Jewish literature, the highest place is assigned not to emotional nor even to intellectual, but to religious friendships. To the Jewish teachers, friendships are what Lazarus aptly calls "ideals of spiritual fellowship,"prompted by unselfish disinterested motives. The finest example of true friendship, the Rabbis find in the love of David and Jonathan. Such love, depending on no material object, springing freely from pure souls, is endowed with the qualities of endurance.[268] The ends and motives of friendship should be mutual improvement. "Love him that correcteth thee; and hate him that flattereth thee." "Love that stops short at reproving a man for his evil doing is not true love."[269] Friendship should be fed on mutual loyalty and respect: "Let the honor of your friend be as dear to you as your own." "Love the friend that is true to thee," says a medieval author, "and let his companionship be kept by thee. Devote thyself to him with might and main, when he stands in need of thy help, for this is the most generous form of love; it is the most glorious kind of affection, resulting from companionship."[270]

Conclusion

In the Pirke De Rabbi Eliezer, we read about the two ways which God set before Israel. "The good way," says the author, "has two byways, one of

---

[267] *Sefer HoAggadah* III:5, p. 68-80. Moritz Lazarus writes: "The love of parents for their children is nature, the love of children for elders is ethics. Hence we find that the Ten Commandments and other passages in the Torah make filial love a legal bidding; parental love need not be commanded. Accordingly, in the ethics of Judaism a long chapter is devoted, not to love for children, but to spiritual caretaking of them, to the cherishing and transmitting of culture, the instruction and discipline of the young." *Ethics of Judaism*, Part II, p. 213.

[268] *Abot* V:19.

[269] *Ab. R. N.* XXIX.

[270] *The Foundation of Religious Fear*, translated by H. Gollancz chap. XVIII, par. 183. v. also Guttmacher's art. on "Friendship" in *Jew. Encyc.* V:520-521; and Lazarus, Ibid., p. 299.

righteousness and the other of love; and Elijah, be he remembered for good, is placed exactly between these two ways. When [Israel] comes to enter (one of these ways), Elijah, be he remembered for good, cries aloud concerning him, saying: 'Open ye the gates that the righteous nation which keepeth truth may enter in.'[271] And there cometh Samuel the prophet [who, like Elijah, sought to reconcile God and man] and he places himself between these two byways. He says: 'On which of these (two byways) shall I go? If I go on the way of righteousness, then (the path) of love is better than the former; if I go on the way of love, (the way) of righteousness is better; but I call heaven and earth to be my witness that I will not give up either of them."[272]

Judaism, as the survey of its literature demonstrates, takes the second position. Resting on the faith that sees in God a beneficent Sovereign of nature and a universal Father of mankind, whose attribute is *Rahamana,* the Merciful One, Judaism recognizes in Justice and in Mercy sister-voices, guiding the destinies of man, and calling moral order out of the chaos and confusion resulting from selfishness and hatred. In its view, *justice and mercy do not supplant, but supplement each other.* Aḥad Ha'am finds the difference between the two to consist in this, "that justice measures the cause by the effect; mercy, the effect by the cause. That is to say, justice regards only the character of the deed, and judges the doer accordingly; mercy considers first the character of the doer at the moment of the deed, and judges the deed accordingly."[273] In the process of moral development, justice precedes mercy. "Children and nations in their childhood, distinguish only between deeds, not between doers. They exterminate evil by rooting out the evil-doers and all that is connected with them; they do not discriminate between the sin of compulsion and the sin of free will, between the sin committed with knowledge and that committed in ignorance. The angry child breaks the thing over which he has stumbled; nations in the stage of childhood kill the beast 'through which hurt hath come to a man.' It is only at a later stage and by gradual process that mercy finds its way first into the human mind, to refine

---

[271] Is. XXVI:2.

[272] *Pirke de Rabbi Eliezer,* chap. XV.

[273] *Selected Essays,* translated by Leon Simon, p. 46.

our moral ideas, and then also into the human heart, to purify and to soften the feelings."[274] Thus Judaism tempers justice with love, thereby saving justice from hardness; and it keeps love within the restraint of justice, thereby saving love from degenerating into vapid sentimentalism.

No one religion, happily, can lay claim to an exclusive monopoly on either justice or love. These are the oxygen and the hydrogen of which every religious stream is composed. All hearts pine for love and thirst for righteousness. They all, even if it be in somewhat differing ways, quench their thirst at God's fountain. Hence without minimizing or denying the right of Christianity to the ideals of love and of forgiveness, we firmly maintain that, both before and after entering Christianity, these ideals formed essential parts of Judaism—

---

[274] From the premises of Aḥad Ha'am, we may be warranted in assuming that in his view, the Jewish idea of justice, not in its origin but in its final development, is inseparable from that of mercy, for both the late Biblical and the Talmudic law never judge an act without reference to the particular circumstances that led to its performance; i. e., it regards the sinner as well as the sin. Further in his essay, however, he writes: "Mercy stands high on the ladder of moral development; but justice is the moral foundation on which the ladder stands." This position of Elijah, he supports by Adam Smith's rather dubious definiton of "conscience," as being "nothing but the echo of a man's own pronouncement on the sin of others." He writes: "So long as the feeling of justice predominates, men become accustomed from their youth to hate abstract evil as such, and to loathe evildoers, without much inquiry into the distant causes that have led to the evil act; and, by a further development, they learn to gauge their own actions also by the measure with which they gauge the actions of others. It is not so when the atmosphere is one of mercy only. Then it is not the evil deed, but the evil *will* that awakens the moral feeling; then a man is absolved from justice, if he can be excused by an appeal to the hidden facts of his spiritual life. Such an atmosphere as this does not encourage the utterance of 'man's pronouncement on the sins of others'; and therefore the inward echo of this voice—conscience—is also silent." *(Ibid.,* pp. 49–50.)

At least the Jewish conception of conscience is at variance with Adam Smith's. It is expressed in the mystic phrase, which Ahad Ha'am mentions, but passes over, "the voice of God moving in the heart of man." It is not—as he holds—the echo of man's judgment over the sins of others, but the spark of the divine ideal glowing in the human heart, illumining man's path to holiness, to kindness, to generosity, to forgiveness, and to love. In other words, instead of being a purely sociological phenomenon, conscience, in Jewish ethics, appears rather as a religious expression of man's nature, drawing its vitality from the central principle of *Imitatio Dei,* of modelling one's actions after the divine pattern. v. M. Gaster's art. "Conscience" in Hastings, *Encycl. Rel. and Ethics,* IV:41–46.

flesh of its flesh, spirit of its spirit! Its complete world-view is colored by them. God is the Merciful One, and He demands the service of mercy and loving-kindness. We approach Him "not in reliance upon righteousness or merit in ourselves," "but trusting in" His *"infinite mercy* alone."[275] All duties of man culminate in the great commandment, Thou shalt love thy neighbor as thyself.

Philosophers have indeed tried to show how impracticable it is to command man to love, and how utterly impossible it is for man to love his neighbor as himself.[276] Despite its practical difficulties, the command is one of the loftiest ever given to man, one of the purest echoes of the Divine Voice in the human heart. Like the stars, it is high above the clod. Nevertheless, with the sage of Concord, we must believe in hitching the wagon to the star. For the religious soul, the course of love "runs smooth." The mystic, Moses Cordovero, teaches Love your neighbor as yourself because the souls of both of you are interrelated and united in their essence as in their origin.[277] The modern Jewish philosopher, Moritz Lazarus, states, "The Torah demands in simple words: 'Thou shalt love thy neighbor as thyself.' And why 'as thyself'? Because he is as thou art—a human being, the child of God, thy brother of virtue of the most exalted relation sustained by man."[278] Love of one's neighbor, respect for his person, vital and disinterested concern about his honor, station and wellbeing, should be the guiding passion and principle of man's conduct.

Our sages spoke wisely: *olam ḥesed yiboneh*—"the world is built on love."

---

[275] *Tana Debe Elijah*; Prayerbook, Morning Service.

[276] v. Rabbinic Commentaries of Nachmanides and Samuel b. Meir to Lev. XIX:18; especially that of Moses Mendelsohn.

[277] *Tomer Deborah.*

[278] *Ethics of Judaism*, Part II, p. 238. Lazarus writes: "Before this impregnable barrier of his finite nature, man must tear down the barrier of egotism; love should step into the breach made by adverse fate, and the wounds dealt by destiny should be healed by loving-kindness and charity. But not for the feeble and the unfortunate alone should our benefactions be reserved; to the happy we must be equally ready to offer ungrudging sympathy, friendly feeling, warm devotion. The pathos of sorrow should evoke our sympathy, and in the joy of the happy we should rejoice. It should be our effort not only to lessen the affliction of the sad, but to increase the gladness of the favored sons of men." (Ibid., pp. 236–237.)

The divine throne rests upon it. It is the foundation of all hope in the humani-
zation of man, in the true progress of humanity. Though nature be "red in
tooth and claw," though man maddened with lust of strife reject God and rage
against his brother, we believe—we *must* believe—that Goodness is at the
heart of all, that love is "creation's final law." This belief is our pole-star. For
us as for our fathers, human love is still the golden chain that binds us to the
Mercy-throne of God.

Original Sin*

The doctrine of original sin, which in varying forms figures in Jewish as in Christian thought, derives its vitality from the raw facts of life, and involves both the nature of man and the justice of God. The Bible exalts man as the child of God, stamped with His image and likeness, He is but a little lower than the angels, crowned with glory and with honor. He is capable of deeds of mercy and compassion to the point of complete self-effacement. He often sacrifices himself upon the altar of truth and of goodness. He also shows himself base and cruel, exhibiting traits of savagery that would shame the beasts, and sinking to abysmal depths of degradation. His self-centeredness and his antagonism to others blight his own life and fill the world around him with sorrow. He delights in sadistic pleasures, and employs his gifts of mind to inventing fiendish instruments for the torture of his fellowmen. He aspires after God, and he goes the way of the devil. He strives after freedom of the spirit, and seeks to widen the horizon of truth and of justice. He builds centers of light and of healing to redeem the helpless and the forlorn. He also erects prisons for the human intellect, and darkens the world with falsehood. He constructs torture chambers and horror camps for the extermination of his fellowmen. He uses the richest fruits of knowledge for the "scientific" destruction of the minds and bodies of infants and greyheads.

How can we account for the frightful malignity which appears to fester at the core of human nature? How does man come to create yawning pits of hell in the heart of civilized society? And why are his finest intellectual achievements turned into threats to his own existence, and his hopes perpetually

* Published: Hebrew Union College Annual, XXI, Cincinnati, 1948.
Published in Yiddish translation: Yivo Bleter, New York, XXIX, 95–114, 1947.

blasted? Why does he, the child of God, erect barriers between himself and his Father, and blind himself to the visions of truth, of goodness and of holiness? Being so general in every age and in every country, human depravity, it is claimed, cannot be charged to individual guilt. Some condition common to all mankind must be responsible for the corruption of human nature. Parsiism and Manichaism resolved the difficulty by their dualistic conception of the universe. The principle of evil ever contests the principle of good for the government of the world. Man's depravity is the natural effect of the struggle between Ahriman and Ormuzd. From the standpoint of monotheistic religion, seeking to establish the unitary rule of creation, the problem is more difficult. Is not God, the author of all existence, responsible for His creatures? Does not the evil nature of man reflect upon the goodness and omnipotence of God?

Christianity, following certain trends in Judaism, advanced the view that the moral taint which mars human nature is not in reality the work of God, but the result of a tragic error committed by the first parents of the race. Through the teachings of Paul and Augustine, this view was crystallized into the doctrine of the Fall and Original Sin, which, despite some opposition, became pivotal in Western Christianity. Judaism similarly grappled with the problem of the universality of guilt, without assigning to it the importance which it occupies in Christianity.

1. The Paradise Story

The focus of all theological speculation on this subject is Genesis chapter three, which may be regarded as one of the most influential Biblical chapters in human thought. Contrary to the uses made of it by Paul and his followers, the Paradise story contains no doctrine of the fall of the race through Adam, of the moral corruption of human nature, or of the hereditary transmission of the sinful bias. It represents an etiological myth, accounting for the origin of human labor, for man's natural abhorrence of the serpent, for the consciousness of sex, for the pains of parturition, for the subjection of woman to her husband, and for human mortality. It seems to form part of a legendary history of civilization from the Yahvistic viewpoint, and must be read in connection with Genesis 4 and 11, which deal with the invention of the arts, the progress of civilization, the building of the tower of Babel and the variation of the languages of man. The interest of the ancient thinker centers primarily in the physical ills of mankind, and he seeks their explanation in religious causes. He links the pains of life with the thirst for knowledge of the beneficial and the hurtful, i.e., the knowledge that gives man mastery over nature, from the standpoint of the nascent ethical religion of Israel.

The story is related to the myths of primitive peoples in various parts of the world, dealing with the mystery of death, and, like them, assumes that man would have been deathless if he had not committed a disastrous blunder. In some instances the most trivial incident suffices to explain the origin of death.[1]

Yahveh's jealousy and his apprehension lest man become like "one of us," imply a polytheistic background of the Paradise story. We naturally turn for parallels to Semitic mythology. While no exact parallels have come down, there are some elements in old Babylonian literature that are instructive.

A very slight resemblance to it appears in the Etana legend, which tells of a hero who sought to obtain something that would ease the pains of parturition of his wife. He was carried by an eagle to the heaven of Anu. On the way he changed his mind and decided to go back to earth. Both he and the eagle fell down together to their death to the ground.[2] The only resemblance to the biblical story consists in dealing with the pain of childbirth. As to whether the indecision of the hero, which brought death upon himself and the eagle, also initiated the mortality of all men is not indicated in the legend.

The Sumerian legend of Tagtug comes closer to the biblical tale. It contains a description of the primeval paradise, Dilmun, which included Eridu in the mouth of the Euphrates. (Some interpreters consider it to be a description of the earth prior to the bestowal of civilization upon mankind by Enki.) Enki "decreed forever the fate of the plants" of Dilmun. A list of trees is named which Tagtug may eat. S. H. Langdon supposes that a line followed

---

[1] For an analysis of Gen. 3 and 6.1-4 in the light of primitive lore see Samuel S. Cohon, "Origin of Death," *Journal of Jewish Lore and Philosophy*, 1919, pp. 371-396.

[2] R. F. Harper, *Assyrian and Babylonian Literature*, pp. 318-23.

regarding a forbidden tree from which he was not to eat. Tagtug broke the taboo, and brought upon himself the same curse as Adam did by partaking of the tree of knowledge. The problematical nature of this interpretation is apparent, and Langdon himself warns that it must be accepted with caution.[3]

Somewhat more definite and closer to the Biblical narrative is the myth of Adapa. One version of it figures as an incantation for the healing of the sick. It implies that the disease, which the magician endeavors to heal, was caused not by the sin of the patient, but by Adapa, who brought death and pain into the world in an age when sorrow was unknown in Paradise. The story runs that Adapa of Eridu, famed as a sage, was endowed by Ea with godlike wisdom, enabling him to "perceive the things of heaven and earth," and with a cunning mind, to "give names to all concepts on earth"; but Ea withheld immortality from him. One time as he went fishing, the south-wind drove his sailing boat into the wide sea, ducked him under, and made him sink to the dwelling of the fishes. In his anger Adapa broke the wings of the south-wind so that it did not blow for seven days upon the land. Thereupon Anu, the king of the gods, ordered that Adapa appear before him. Ea clothed him in mourner's garments, and counselled him that on arriving at the gates of Anu, he should explain to Tammuz and Ningishzida that he mourns the dying gods of fertility. They will look at each other in astonishment and pleasure, and speak kind words on his behalf to Anu and thus win for him Anu's good favor. At the same time Ea impressed upon him that when standing before Anu, he will be offered "bread of death" to eat and "water of death" to drink, which he must refuse. Thus Ea's jealousy showed itself. He does not wish Adapa to obtain immortal life, and therefore deceived him by misrepresenting the food and the drink, which were in reality the magic food of eternal life. Ea also advised Adapa that when the gods offer him a garment he shall put it on, and with the oil that they shall offer him he shall anoint himself. Consequently, when Adapa refused the food which would have made him an immortal, Anu ordered him back to earth, deprived of eternal life.

Langdon remarks that this doctrine regarding the way in which mortality

[3] *The Mythology of all Races*, Vol. V. Semitic, p. 200.

became the lot of mankind "arose in the orthodox priesthood as a defense of divine providence, when a Babylonian school of philosophers challenged the ancient teachings of the Sumerians, who held that the gods are good and just. It·was not they who sent disease and sorrow into the world, not they who created man to die, but pain and mortality originated in the ignorance of a great ancestor, tricked by the jealousy of a god, and so passed forever the great opportunity of mankind."[4]

Though the two stories are markedly different in form, they combine a number of common features. The jealousy of a god is the motif in both. The gods of fertility, Ningishzida and Tammuz, figure in one, and the serpent, which in Sumerian mythology serves as the symbol of fertility and is associated with the fertility gods, in the other. Finally both of them exonerate the gods from creating the evils which plague life and trace them to a blunder on the part of an early hero.

Obvious similarities to these stories are found also in the Greek legend of Prometheus. The form, in which it came down in Hesiod and in Aeschylus, represents a fusion of a number of stories. The account of Prometheus, deceiving Jove's wisdom and stealing fire from heaven for the benefit of man, and bringing him only evil, is combined with the independent tale of Pandora, the first woman, from whom descended the "pernicious race, and tribe of women." Jove gave women as "an evil" to men, "helpmates of painful toils."[5] Aeschylus pictures Prometheus as stealing the fire from the cruel Zeus out of sympathy for the wretched lot of men, and teaching them many arts whereby they might advance from their savage animal life to civilization. Though completely different from the Paradise story, it shares with it the thought that the ills of human life stem from man's overstepping the bounds of humanity and invading the domain of the gods. Both stories consider knowledge as wrenched form the deity, jealous of human encroachment, whether by a superhuman being or by a crafty animal. Both of them further imply that human knowledge is a kind of arrogance, and "see in ὕβρις the primal sin."[6]

[4] *Ibid.*, p. 183.
[5] "Theogony," *Bohn's Classical Library*, pp. 585 ff.; "Work and Days," pp. 52 ff.
[6] F. R. Tennant, *The Sources of the Doctrine of the Fall and Original Sin*, p. 52.

The Pandora legend bears obvious similarity to the story of Eve in picturing the first woman as the source of human woe.[7]

These remote parallels throw some light upon the Genesis story. What was Adam's sin? It consisted not merely in his breaking the divine command, but breaking it in such way as to overstep the limits of his humanity and to encroach upon the domain of Yahveh, an idea which recurs in the Bible. It reappears in the story of the building of the tower of Babel (Gen. 11.1–9) and in the prophets (Isa. 2.7–22; 10.12 ff., 33; 14.13 ff.; 22.11; 37.23 ff.; Ezek. 28.2 ff.). Deut. 29.29 voices the thought that some secret things pertaining to the future may be known only by God. Job 28.12–28 exalts wisdom as "hid from the eyes of the living" (Cf. 21.22; 38.16 ff.). The author of Proverbs glorifies it as the possession of God, His special delight and the instrument of His creation, which, at His pleasure, He discloses to men (3.19–20; 8.22–32; 2.6).[8]

The breaking of the taboo led to no fundamental alteration in the moral condition of Adam and Eve, but only to their acquisition of a sense of shame at being naked in place of their original state of blissful ignorance and child-like innocence. Furthermore, this sense was awakened in them not in consequence of their new born consciousness of guilt, but as the magic effect of partaking of the fruit of the tree of knowledge. The transgression, we are told, was followed by the pain of childbirth, of labor, etc. No mention is made of any loss of the spiritual capacity of communion with God or of the perversion of Adam's nature. On the contrary Yahveh admits that the disobedience made them godlike. "The man has become like one of us." He attained the condition that exclusively belonged to the gods. While the Biblical story does not specifically state that Adam was created immortal, it implies that he was capable of becoming immortal. To forestall his appropriation of the next attribute of deity —immortality — by eating of the tree of life, Yahveh expelled him together with Eve form Eden, and inflicted punishment upon all three

---

[7] It is instructive to find elements of the Pandora legend in Haggadic illustrations of Eve's offense. Gen. R. 19.10 and notes by Theodor; Abot of Rabbi Nathan, I.1, II.1, p. 6; Pirke de Rabbi Eliezer, 13.

[8] See C. H. Toy, *International Critical Commentary, Proverbs*, p. 128; Tennant, *op. cit.*, p. 16, n. 7.

participants in the offense. The story does not suggest that Adam's sin was transmitted to his descendants or that it in any way accounts for their tendency to sin. The Yahvist source indeed emphasizes the general diffusion of moral evil (Gen. 4; 6.5–8, 12; 8.21; 9.20–27; 11.1–9). However, this condition prevailed at a particular time, and did not permanently vitiate the nature of man.

The Yahvist concerns himself with the origin of death and suffering rather than with the origin of human sinfulness. That he also reflected upon the gravity of sin is not to be denied. He conceives of sin as a power external to man, and personifies it as a beast "crouching at the door" (of the heart?). Sin is trailed by suffering. It is not an isolated act, but a state of consciousness, so that one sin leads to others. The author's despairing view of human nature is reflected in his statement that "Yahveh saw that the wickedness of man was great in the earth, and that every imagination of the thoughts of his heart was only evil continually" (Gen. 6.5); and again that "the imagination of man's heart is evil from his youth" (8.21). He does not assume the responsibility for his offsprings' disposition to evil, but only states it as a sorrowful reflection on human nature. These verses subsequently served the Rabbis as Biblical support for their doctrine of the Yezer, but they establish no connection between the sin of Adam and the disposition to evil. Generally the Yahvist document treats sin as "a voluntary act or a habit resulting from such acts."[9]

What use was made of the Paradise story in the rest of the Bible? The answer is: hardly any. The Yahvist himself does not seem to have connected it with the rest of his narrative. Cain's sinfulness is not treated as an inheritance from his parents, for his brother Abel was pleasing to Yahveh. His guilt and responsibility are distinctly his own. He is warned that "sin croucheth at the door, and unto thee is its desire." While it lurks for its prey, "thou mayest rule over it" (Gen. 4.7). So too the curse of Lamech followed his own guilt rather than the hereditary taint of his forefather. Likewise, the increase of wickedness, which brought on the flood, was not linked with the transgression of Adam. All that may be said is that Adam's transgression was the first manifestation of sin, but not the cause of the sinfulness of his offsprings. The

---

[9] Tennant, *ibid.*, p. 98.

Elohist portrays Noah as perfect and righteous, who, like Enoch, "walked with God," indicating that the corruption which spread before the flood represented a bad condition of the time rather than the normal state of humanity derived from Adam (Gen. 5.24; 6.9-12). The Priestly document, too, nowhere intimates that the divine image, with which Adam was marked, vanished at the fall. All sources present Abraham as a man of stainless character. The prophets denounce sin, not as a hereditary infection, but as the fruit of man's moral vacillation and failure to recognize the sovereignty of God and to do His will. Jeremiah bemoans the weakness of the human heart and its deceitfulness (17.9; cf. 7; 31.26 ff.; Ezek. 18). The suffering of the people during the Exile accentuated the consciousness of guilt, both of the nation and of the individual, in view of the growing recognition of the solidarity of the community, on the one hand, and of personal responsibility on the other. Job stresses the impurity of man, the creature, by the side of God, the Creator (4.17; 14; 15.14-15; 25.4). Prov. 20.9 muses that "there is no man that sinneth not" (also 1 Kings 8.46; 2 Chron. 6.36; Eccl. 7.20). The Psalmist meditates: "If Thou, O Lord, shouldst mark iniquity, O Lord, who shall stand?" (130.3; also 143.2). Ps. 51.7 confesses the frailty of human nature:

> "Behold, I was shapen in iniquity
> And in sin did my mother conceive me."

He does not suggest the sinfulness of the act of generation, but rather the general instability of the race of humans, who are prone to sinfulness from the very womb (Cf. Isa. 6.5; 43.27; 48.9; 57.3).[10] That he does not imply that an ineradicable taint attaches to human nature is evident from the sequel in which he assumes that man may enjoy the state of spotless purity. Hence he prays for divine forgiveness, and pleads: "Create in me a clean heart, O God, and renew a steadfast spirit within me."

The allusions, which some commentators found to Adam's sin, in Hos. 6.7; Isa. 43.27; Job 31.33 and Ps. 82.7, are without scientific foundation.[11] A

---

[10] T. K. Cheyne, *The Book of Psalms, ad loc.*; Z. P. Hayyes, *Perush Madai: Tehilim, ad loc.*

[11] Equally groundless is the supposed reference to Adam's wisdom in Job 15.7 f. It probably

vague tradition about the Garden of Eden and its guarding cherubim figures in Ezek. 28, which like the Genesis story, reflects Babylonian mythology. It is referred to as a "divine abode" and a "garden of God," i.e., a private reserve of God on some mountain in the North (also 31.8, 9; cf. Isa. 14.13; Ps. 48.3). Ezekiel's Eden, it has been suggested, resembles the mountain of Mashu in the Gilgamesh epic, which contained a tree, bearing costly stones, "dazzling the eye" (cf. Ezek. 28.13–16, also Gen. 2.12):

"Diamonds (?) it bore as fruit,
Branches were hanging (down?), beautiful to behold.
Crystal (antimony?) the branches bore."[12]

Ezekiel compares the prince of Tyre, boasting of his divinity, proud of his wisdom, riches and glory, to a legendary dweller of the Garden of God, whose clothing was adorned with precious stones, and who, on account of his overbearing, was expelled from the divine abode. While the phraseology of this chapter contributed to the later portraiture of Adam and of Eden, it indicates no direct dependence upon Gen. 3.

Furthermore, the theodicy of the Bible completely ignores the fall. The suffering of the righteous is nowhere justified on the ground of the sinfulness transmitted by Adam to his posterity. Job, dealing with the relation of sin to divine retribution, ignores the Paradise story, indicating that at the time of the composition of the book no theological inferences were drawn from it.

---

refers to a legend about the first man acquiring wonderful knowledge by virtue of his access to the council of God; cf. Jer. 23.18; Ps. 89.8. The name Garden of Eden, in Isa. 51.3 and Joel 2.3, the figure "tree of life" in Prov. 3.18; 11.30; 13.12, and the related "fountain of life" in Ps. 36.10; Prov. 10.11; 13.14; 14.27 are mere verbal elements coming from the same stock as the folk tale in Genesis. Similarly Job 34.15; Ps. 90.3; Eccl. 12.7, which speak of man's return to dust, and Isa. 65.25; Micah 7.17, which allude to the serpent's eating dust, express common beliefs and do not necessarily point to the Genesis story. Neither does Eccl. 7.29 point to the change of character that set in because of the fall.

[12] Tablet IX in Harper, *op. cit.*, pp. 344–45; Tennant, *op. cit.*, p. 63.

2. The Fall and Original Sin in the Apocrypha

Only in Apocryphal and Pseudepigraphic Jewish writings does the Paradise story begin to figure as the basis for speculation regarding the origin of death and of sin.[13] The first discussions of this subject appear in the book of Ecclesiasticus. Sirach hews to the line of Biblical teaching, emphasizing the universality of human guilt (8.5), and stressing the fatal character of sin. Sometimes he personifies sin as a serpent and as a lion, and sometimes he speaks of it as a two-edged sword, which slays the souls of men (21.1–3; 27.10). He treats sin as an external force, and definitely links it with Eve. "From a woman did sin originate, and because of her we all must die" (25.24). However, this idea is completely isolated, and contrasts with the general trend of the book to regard mortality as a law from everlasting (14.17; 17.1–2; 40.11). The full consequences of this statement are not drawn by him nor formulated into a doctrine of original sin, i.e., of the transmission of sinfulness from the first parents of the race. Instead, Sirach advances the doctrine of the Yezer as the source of human sinfulness. After restating the Biblical account of the creation of Adam and Eve, he adds:

"He clothed them with strength like unto Himself
   And made them according to His own image.
He put the fear of them upon all flesh,
   And caused them to have power over beasts and birds.
With insight and understanding He filled their heart,
   And taught them good and evil.
He created for them[14] tongue and eyes, and ears,
   And He gave them a heart to understand,

[13] All citations of this literature are from Charles's edition of the *Apocrypha and Pseudepigrapha*, 2 Vols., Oxford, 1913. The New Testament quotations are from Edgar J. Goodspeed's translation. Univ. of Chicago Press.

[14] The Greek reads ζιαβούλιον (Yezer). Moses Z. Segal, *Hochmat Ben Sira* and A. Kahana, *Hasefarim Haḥizonim*, III, read: *Yezer v'lashon*, etc.

To show them the majesty of His works,
  And that they might glory in His wondrous acts. . .
He set before them the covenant;
  The law of life He gave them for a heritage. . .
And He said unto them, beware of all unrighteousness"

(17.1–14).

Sirach continues:

"Their ways are before Him. . .
Their iniquities are not hid from Him. . .
Nevertheless to them that repent doth He grant a return
And comforteth them that lose hope"

(vss. 17–24).

His reference to the Yezer in vs. 31 ("the inclination of flesh and blood") does not imply that man is morally corrupted because of Adam's fall or of God's punishment. Sirach conceives of the Yezer in a neutral sense, containing the power to do right or wrong, i.e. free will.

Repudiating the earlier belief that God was the cause of man's sin,[15] Sirach teaches:

"Say not from God is my transgression,
  For that which He hateth made He not.
Say not: '(It is) He that made me to stumble,'
  For there is no need of evil men. . .
God created man from the beginning,
  And placed him in the hands of his Yezer.
If thou (so) desirest, thou canst keep the commandment,
  And (it is) wisdom to do His good pleasure.
Poured out before thee (are) fire and water,
  Stretch forth thine hand unto that which thou desirest.

---

[15] E. g., Ex. 4.21; 7.3; II Sam. 24.1; Jer. 6.21; Ezek. 3.20.

Life and death (are) before man,
   That which he desireth shall be given to him.
Sufficient is the wisdom of the Lord. . .
He commandeth no man to sin"

                                                        (15.11–20)

Instead of being an inheritance from Adam, sin is the result of man's own wrong choice. "He that keepeth the Law controlleth his natural tendency" or Yezer (21.11). Thus Sirach avoids concluding in the same manner as the Rabbis subsequently did, that sin is hereditary, by stressing the doctrines of freedom, of the saving power of the Torah and of repentance.

A different approach appears in the apocalypse of I Enoch. Like Sirach, the author of this mystic work opposes the idea that God causes man to sin, but instead of ascribing sin to man's free will, he — under Parsi influence — charges it to Satan. As the ruler of the counter kingdom of evil (which is nonetheless a kingdom subject to the Lord of spirits) Satan misguided the angels and made them his subjects (54.6; 69.5). The fallen angels or satans misled the sons of God by means of the daughters of men (Cf. Gen. 6.1–4). One of them led Eve astray and showed men all the blows of death and the weapons of war. Another satan taught men pleasure and all the secrets of wisdom. He instructed mankind in the art of writing, "and thereby sinned from eternity to eternity and until this day. For men were not created for such a purpose, to give confirmation to their good faith with pen and ink." This is the mystic's version of the Biblical story of Adam's partaking of the fruit of the tree of knowledge. He continues: "For men were created exactly like angels, to the intent that they should continue pure and righteous, and death, which destroys everything could not have taken hold of them, but through this their knowledge they are perishing, and through this their knowledge they are being consumed." The author further charges all sinfulness to Azazel, who "taught all unrighteousness on earth" and disclosed all heavenly secrets to men (8.1 ff.; 9.8; 10.8).

A contrary view is expressed in other portions of the book of I Enoch. Sin is sent neither by God nor by His lieutenant, Satan. All sin is of one's own devising. It is neither inherited from Adam nor unavoidable, but voluntary, and, therefore, subject to punishment (98.4; 9.14).[16]

Elements of the first view of 1 Enoch are fused with the rationalized version of the Genesis story in the Wisdom of Solomon. Originally death formed no part of God's plan of creation (1.13), and man, fashioned in God's likeness, was destined for a deathless existence. "But the ungodly by their hands and words called him unto them," i.e., the apostate Jews taking part in the pagan mysteries threw themselves into the arms of death. "They made a covenant with him (cf. Isa. 28.15) because they are worthy to be of his portion" (2.13–14, 16). Sin and death were introduced from without.

"God made man for incorruption (i.e., for immortality)
And made him an image of His own proper being;
But by the envy of the devil, death entered into the world,
And they that belong to his realm experience it"

(2.23–24).

As in 1 Enoch, the serpent of the Biblical story is replaced with the devil. The connection between the two, in which the devil makes use of the serpent or incarnates himself in it, suggested by a Parsi source, became a commonplace of both Jewish and of Christian lore (cf. Rev. 12.9; 20.2).

What of those who do not belong to the realm of the devil? The fact of physical mortality is ignored, and attention is focused upon spiritual death or sin. The wicked were dead as soon as they were born. "But the souls of the righteous are in the hands of God, and no torment shall touch them. In the eyes of fools they seemed to die." However, "their hope is full of immortality" (31.–4; 5.3; 10.3).

While the elements of a doctrine of hereditary depravity are present in the book, it was left to the author of the Hellenistic Book of the Secrets of Enoch to teach definitely that sin is transmitted from Adam. Under the influence of Plato, he finds the origin of death in man's dual nature. The soul was created

---

[16] Charles, op. cit., II, p. 269, note on vs. 4.

pure, and was not predetermined by God (as the Wisdom of Solomon 9.15 claims) either for good or for evil. It was also endowed with freedom of choice, and was shown the ways of light and darkness, of the good and the bad, and was left to shape its own destiny. But through its incorporation into the corruptible body, the soul's power of choice was narrowed and biased toward evil. Accordingly sin derives not merely from voluntary preference, but from the limitations imposed upon the soul by its connection with the body and from wrong education. Ignorance (as in Plato's teaching) is an evil in itself, which produces death (30.15–16).[17] These Hellenistic ideas are loosely combined with the Biblical story. The devil, envious of Adam's high position as lord on earth, seduced his wife Eve, but did not touch Adam himself. In consequence God cursed man's ignorance and sin. Adam is told: "Earth thou art, and into the earth whence I took thee thou shalt go, and I will not ruin thee, but send thee whence I took thee. Then I can again take thee at My second coming," i.e., for the purpose of judging the earth (31–32).

The author of IV Ezra, who lived through the catastrophic fall of Jerusalem in the year 70 C.E., despairs of human nature. He finds an explanation of the sorrows of his time in the fall of Adam, in consequence of which God appointed death for him and for his descendants. The generation of the flood shared the fate of Adam, and, like him, was swept away by death. Only Noah and his righteous offsprings were spared from destruction. When their descendants resumed the practice of ungodliness, God chose Abraham and formed with him an everlasting covenant. Out of his line, Jacob was set aside. To his children God showed His special favor, and gave them the Law. Resorting neither to the serpent nor to the devil, the author finds the source of evil within the human heart itself. Without explaining why this cor malignum or Yezer was implanted in man, he traces to it the self-propagating life of sin. Not even the Law does away with the infirmity. "The Law was indeed in the heart of the people, but (in conjunction) with the evil germ; so what was good departed, and the evil remained" (3.4 ff., 20–22, 26). "The grain of evil seed was sown in Adam from the beginning," and has produced an abundant harvest of ungodliness. The "innate evil thought" leads "astray from life to

---

[17] Ibid., note by Forbes and Charles, p. 450.

death" (4.30–31; 7.92). Taking a gloomy view of human nature, in line with the School of Shammai, this apocalyptist believes that it were better had Adam not been created altogether than to have been formed without a curb on his freedom to sin.[18] What is the good of the promise of happiness and of immortality as reward of faithfulness, when man is doomed because of his Yezer, to grief in this world and to punishment in the hereafter? "O thou Adam, what has thou done! For though it was thou that sinned, the fall was not thine alone, but ours also who are thy descendants!" While the Law is imperishable, it is impotent to save the sinners. Indeed, it is but a mockery to a race that is doomed to sin (7.116–131; 9.32–37). The utmost that may be expected from the Law is that while the many are born to perish, the precious few shall be saved through the grace of God (8.3 ff.). In his admission of the insufficiency of the Law as the means of redemption, IV Ezra dangerously approaches the Paulinian position.

II Baruch, which has been characterized as "the most Rabbinical and accurately theological of all the pseudepigrapha," was concerned chiefly with combating the notions of human sinfulness set forth in IV Ezra and possibly in the Epistles of Paul.[19] In opposition both to the dualistic view of the origin of evil and to the hereditary nature of sin, he stresses man's personal responsibility for his actions. While Adam "brought death and cut off the years of those who were born from him," Moses provided the means for overcoming the evil. He "brought the Law to the seed of Jacob, and lighted a lamp for the nation of Israel." It is given to each individual to choose the light of the Torah, which bestows life rather than the darkness of Adam (i.e., sin) which brings death (17–19). While Adam first sinned and brought premature death upon the race, his descendants have not been deprived of the freedom to prepare for their souls torments or glories to come.

"Adam is therefore not the cause, save only for his own soul,
But each one of us has been the Adam of his own soul"

(54.15, 19; 56.6).

---

[18] Erubin 13b.
[19] Tennant, *op. cit.*, p. 212.

Man's sin is derived not from Adam, but from his own spiritual nature. His inclination turns evil through his own determination. Man is the captain of his soul.

3. The Christian Doctrine of Original Sin

The New Testament was produced in close connection with the circle of ideas in which the writers of the Apocryphal books moved. Nonetheless, with the exception of Paul, the authors of the New Testament pass over the subject. Jn. 3.17 speaks of the redemption of the world through the Son of God, but offers no opinion of the way in which sin entered the world. The Book of Revelations utilizes the scenery of Gen. 3 and holds out the hope of the restoration of Paradise (2.7; 22.2, 14) and of the destruction of "the great dragon, the ancient serpent who is called the devil and Satan, who deceived the world" (12,9; cf. Rom. 16.20), but does not speculate about the fall and the sin of Adam.

Paul, on the other hand, not only makes use of the Paradise story (11 Cor. 11.3), but elaborates a theory of the fall and of original sin, which serves as the foundation of his entire religious system. His ideas are developed in two passages. The earliest of them, 1 Cor. 15, concerns itself with death rather than with sin. (Sin is only hinted at in verse 3). As in the Wisdom of Solomon 2.23 ff., the apostle's interest centers in the way in which mortality entered the world and in which manner it may be overcome. "The first Adam is of the dust of the earth." Like him all earth-born creatures are perishable. The second Adam, i.e., the Messiah, is from heaven. Those who are of heaven are, like him, heavenly, imperishable, immortal. The corruptible natures of the earthly creatures must clothe themselves with the incorruptible by sharing in God's kingdom. The mortal must invest himself with immortality. Then death will be destroyed (Cf. Isa. 25.8). Adam is the head of the old humanity, which is mortal; the Christ heads the new community, which is deathless. Mankind's connection with Adam, involving it in death, is the affair of heredity, and admits of no choice. The connection with the Christ is a matter of faith. Only those who, by their faith, share in God's kingdom through the Christ will be saved from destruction. Immortality is not man's portion by virtue of his being a child of nature — which is subject to decay — but purely as the fruit of faith, and is strictly supernatural.[20]

The second passage, that of Rom. 5.12 ff., deals with sin as the cause of death and with redemption from its power, and forms part of Paul's discussion of God's justice and grace. Adam's transgression marked his fall from grace. In consequence, sin as a malignant force was let loose upon the world with death as its effect.[21] Sin and death originated together, and they have been propagated side by side. Adam's sin was transmitted to all his descendants, i.e. all of them have been infected with the tendency to sin. Without indicating in which way the effects of Adam's sin were transmitted or defining precisely what was transmitted, Paul stresses that all men inherited from their ancestor: (1) the liability to sin as well as (2) the consequent liability to die as a punishment of sin. The Torah, which, according to Judaism, delivers from sin, in Paul's opinion only increases it, since in the absence of the Law, men are not charged with transgression, or, as he expresses it in 1 Cor. 15.56, "It is the Law that gives sin its power." Only the effect of divine grace, as manifested in the Christ, will offset the Law, cancel the evil consequences of the fall, and bring salvation to mankind. The evil ushered in by the first Adam will be remedied by the second Adam, or the Christ.[22]

Paul's teaching regarding original sin implies the imputation of Adam's sin to his posterity, thus holding posterity responsible for the sin as its own; and similarly attributing the righteousness of the Christ to his followers so as to be regarded as their own, and hence justifying them. The Roman Church formulated this idea into a doctrine. Schoolmen defended it on the ground that Adam was the moral as well as the natural head of the human race. His sin was imputed to mankind on the same principle as the actions or commitments of the head of a family or of a state are imputed to his family or state,

---

[20] A. Robertson and A. Plummer, *Intern. Critic. Commentary: First Epistle of St. Paul to the Corinthians*, pp. 330 ff.

[21] For Paul, sin is not an isolated act nor an accumulation of acts, but a force which gained lodgment in man (Rom. 7.17), enslaving and paralyzing his will. See Bernard, art. "Sin," Hastings, *Dictionary of the Bible*, III, 535.

[22] S. W. Sanaday and A. C. Headlam, *Intern. Crit. Com., Romans*, pp. 130 ff. See also Rom. 6.3–11; 8.9.

despite the fact that they had no share in those actions or commitments. When Adam broke the covenant with God, all his descendants were involved in the transgression. In the same way the Christ took the place of all men, so that his actions were imputed to them.

The man who more than any other transformed Paul's teaching on original sin into a basic dogma of the Church is Augustine (354–430). As a former Manichaean he was prejudiced in its favor. He developed it not only out of the teachings of Paul but also out of the ideas of IV Ezra 3.21 and 4.30. As a brand plucked from the burning by what appeared to him as an act of God's grace, he stressed the two poles of his own experience, the extreme sense of depravity and the absolute sense of God's free grace. Despairing of his own weakness, he cast all his hope upon God. While fighting Manichaeism, he never wholly shook off its effects upon him. This accounts for the pessimistic tinge of his mind. The Manichaean view that man is the creature of the devil, and its hatred of human generation and of the conversation of the race, shaped his thinking. The doctrine of original sin offered him the explanation for what he considered as the radical evil of human nature. He assumed the solidarity of the race with Adam, sometimes asserting the seminal existence of the race in Adam and sometimes claiming that Adam's personality and not merely his nature was shared by his posterity. Then, accepting the Greek idea of universals or generic concepts existing apart from their individual or particular cases, he spoke of sin which our nature committed (in Adam). By incorporating our nature in Adam, Augustine sought to establish our guilt for Adam's sin and thus overcome the Pelagian objection that there can be no sin without a person's will. He thus treated Adam as an individual and at the same time as a generic idea. Inasmuch as original sin involved guilt, the unbaptized — even unbaptized infants — incurred and would receive damnation. Commenting on Ps. 51.7, "I was shapen in iniquity, and in sin did my mother conceive me," he exclaims: "Where, I pray thee, O my God, where, Lord, or when was I, Thy servant, innocent?" He prays: "Before Thee none is free from sin, not even the infant which has lived but a day upon the earth."[23]

Original sin constitutes "an infection which propagates itself from father

---

[23] Confessions, I, 11; see also City of God, XIII, 14; On Original Sin, 31.

to son through the act of generation, which being an act of organic trouble caused by sin, is sin itself and determines the transmission *ipso facto* of the sin to the new creature." It impresses itself upon the human body through the persistent stimulus of unreasonable sensuality, and also upon the soul. "Mankind is thus an agglomeration of condemned creatures which cannot acquire any merit before God, and whose hopes for forgiveness and atonement are only in the benevolent grace of the Father and the infallible decree of his predestination."[24] Rufus Jones remarks: "So complete is the havoc of the fall, in St. Augustine's view, that all human free will is lost, and the very faith by which a man accepts the grace won through Christ's merits is a divine gift. Those who have received the gift of such saving faith are the 'elect'; those who have not received it are the non-elect, which means 'damned.'"[25]

Objections to the doctrine came from various sources. The distinguished exegete Theodore of Mopsuesta (4th cent.) denied that the sin of Adam originated death, maintaining that had Adam not sinned, he would have died just the same. The strongest opposition came from the British monk Pelagius (c. 370–420) and his disciples Celestinus and Julian of Eclenum. Pelagius regarded the scandalous moral laxity, which he found in Rome at the beginnng of the fifth century, as due partly to the prevailing belief that man lacked within himself the power or capacity to do good. Averse to theological speculation and interested chiefly in practical matters, he was nonetheless drawn into controversy against the type of Christianity preached by Augustine. The passage in the Confessions, which excited him to heated objection, was the prayer: "Verily, Thou commandest that I should be continent from the 'lust of the flesh, and the lust of the eyes, and the pride of life.' (I John 2.16). . . Give what Thou commandest, and command what Thou wilt."[26] This seemed to encourage man to sit back lazily and to wait for virtue until it might please God to confer and bestow it. The warm sympathy of Pelagius and his followers with Stoic philosophy inclined them to emphasize the direct relation-

[24] Ernesto Bonaiuti, *The Genesis of St. Augustine's Idea of Original Sin*, Harvard Review, Vol. X, p. 163.

[25] *The Church's Debt to Heretics*, p. 129.

[26] X. 41, 45.

ship between the human and the divine. Religion and moral goodness they considered as inherent in human nature, and they set themselves in opposition to the extreme view of the fall, of man's depraved and abjectly sinful condition and his absolute need of divine grace, doctrines which Augustine was forging out at the time. They also stood out as defenders of human nature. Pelagius took the call of Jesus upon men to be perfect as the Heavenly Father is perfect as an indication that the goal is within human reach. His favorite maxim was: "If I ought, I can." Man may live free from sin, and attain a state of purity and perfection, if he but desires it. Human nature being God's creation, cannot be as black and as vitiated as Augustine and his followers made it out to be. Each new born child enjoys the same condition in which Adam found himself before the fall, with no bias either for good or for evil, and now as then each person's fall is due to the sins which he commits. He thus follows the teachings of II Baruch. We are uninjured by Adam's sin save in so far as the evil example of our ancestors misleads and influences us. In fact there is no such thing as original sin. Sin is a thing of the will and not of nature, for if it were of nature it would be chargeable to the Creator. In a letter which he addressed to the See of Rome along with his confession of faith, he wrote: "We maintain that free will exists generally in all mankind, in Christians, Jews, and gentiles; they have all equally received it by nature, but in Christianity is it assisted by grace. In others this good of their original creation is naked and unarmed. They shall be judged and condemned because, though possessed of free will, by which they might come to faith and merit the grace of God, they make an ill use of their freedom; while Christians shall be rewarded because, by using their free will aright, they merit the grace of the Lord and keep His commandments."[27]

The Pelagian views were condemned by the Church, and Augustinianism upheld as the official doctrine on the subject. Its extreme position was tempered by Thomas Aquinas. He denied that natural goodness was forfeited at the fall, that free will was more than impaired, and that concupiscence is of

---

[27] Marcus Dods, *Encycl. Britannica* 11th ed., XXI, 63; Hastings, *Encycl. Rel. and Ethics*, Art. "Pelagianism," IX, 703 ff.

the nature of sin. In his view, original sin was a disordered condition which followed the dissolution of the harmony in which original righteousness essentially consisted. Negatively, it represented the loss of original righteousness or of superadded grace. Duns Scotus went beyond Aquinas in his dissent from Augustine. In his tendency to minimize the first sin, he maintained that it had not affected human nature at all, but only the supernatural gifts that were bestowed upon man. Duns Scotus strongly emphasized fallen man's free will, and refused to identify original sin with concupiscence, insisting that concupiscence belongs to man's unwounded nature. Abelard went still farther. He revolted at the thought that Adam's sin was so serious as to be the adequate cause of the condemnation of all mankind. He considered appetite as both natural and innocent and the conflict between sense and reason as the characteristic of man as God created him. The word "sin" is misused when it is said that we sinned in Adam.[28]

The scholastic idea of sin, especially in the form which it received from Aquinas was declared as official doctrine of the Roman Church at the Council of Trent (1545–1563). Luther and other Reformers of the 16th century inclined toward the elements of Augustinian teaching which the schoolmen rejected. Calvin took over Augustine's doctrine almost unchanged. Sharing the positive teachings of the Roman and Anglican Churches, the Reformers stressed the total depravity of human nature, employed the strongest language in describing the fallen state of man, and explicitly affirmed concupiscence as partaking of the nature of sin. Arminianism strongly reacted to Calvinist teaching, insisting that the inherited bias to evil, which came with the Fall, was met and neutralized by the free and universal grace of God communicated to the race through the Christ, the second Adam. Consequently, original sin does not mean absolute reprobation.[29]

[28] Tennant, Art. "Original Sin," Hastings, *Encycl. Rel. and Ethics* , IX, 561 ff.

[29] Art, "Original Sin," *Catholic Encycl.*, XI, 312 ff.; art. "Confessions," Hastings, *Encycl. Rel. and Ethics*, III, 838 ff.; *Book of Common Prayer of the Protestant Episcopal Church*, Articles of Religion, ix and x, pp. 565.

4. Rabbinic Ideas of the Fall and Original Sin

About the time of the beginning of Christianity three main conceptions of sin struggled for recognition in Judaism. The first regarded the corruption of the race as hereditary. The second vaguely asserted a connection between Adam's sin and his posterity's liability to punishment, without defining the exact nature of the connection. The third view considered all sin as the fruit of man's own action. Paul utilized the first two for his soteriology. Rabbinic Judaism, while not wholly discarding the first two, generally upheld the third. The Rabbis were keenly aware of the difficulties in reconciling the goodness of God with the universality of moral evil, but they did not invest the subject with the importance which it held in Christianity. Paulinian Christianity, as we noted, placed the doctrine of original sin in the center of its thinking; Judaism left it on the periphery.

Rabbinic views on the subject have the character of random, informal, and private opinions without any dogmatic import whatever. The mystic Haggadah grapples with it most seriously, continuing the mythological notions of the Pseudepigrapha, and showing marked kinship to Parsi, Gnostic, and Christian views. The Rabbis often voice a polemical note, aiming to controvert heterodox teaching within the Synagogue and of other faiths. Their comments generally bear the mark of fanciful interpretations of Biblical texts, and reflect diverse and discordant viewpoints extending over many centuries. While they yield no precise doctrine of original sin, they exhibit certain general trends regarding what they deny and what they affirm.

The Rabbinic ideas on original sin become evident from their treatment of the main characters in the drama of the fall, of death, and the Yezer, the imputation of guilt and merit, and the ways of escaping the effects of sin.

A. Dramatis Personae

While Eve plays an important role in the drama, the leading character is Adam. The statement of Genesis that he was formed in the image of God, is amplified in the Apocrypha and presents a favorite theme of Rabbinic preaching. What did they understand by the "divine image?" Sirach 17.1 identifies it with rationality and supremacy over the beasts. The Wisdom of Solomon 2.23 associates it with immortality. The Targum Pseudo-Jonathan to Gen. 1.27, endeavoring to avoid anthropomorphism, makes the expression refer to the image of the ministering angels. Akiba speaks of man as "created after an image," i.e., a special likeness prepared for him.[30] The Midrash Aggada interprets "in our image," to mean that he shall have the spirit of life; and "in our likeness," that he shall have wisdom and understanding of divinelike character.[31] Ibn Ezra takes it to refer to the soul, which being immortal, is likest God.[32]

The glorification of Adam in the Haggadah exhibits Parsi and Gnostic elements. As with Gayomard,[33] so the dust used for the creation of Adam was

[30] Abot 3.14 and Rashi to Gen. 1.27. L. Ginsberg writes: "Akiba, who steadfastly denies any resemblance between God and other beings — even the highest type of angels — teaches that man was created after an image — that is, an archetype — or, in philosophical phrase, after an ideal, and thus interprets Gen. 9.6, 'after an image God created man,' an interpretation quite impossible in Gen. 1.27. Compare the benediction in Ketubot 8a, תומד סלצב ומלצב ותינבת, wherein God is blessed because 'He made man in His image (ומלצב), in the image of a form created by Him.'" Art. "Adam Kadmon," *Jew. Encycl.* I, 183.

[31] Ed. Buber, Bereshit, ch. 1.26, p. 4; see Nahmanides *ad loc.* See also Bereshit Rabbati, ed. Albeck, p. 19.

[32] Combining Gen. 2.7 with the Platonic theory of ideas (Allegorical Interpretation, I:12; On the Creation, 46), Philo distinguishes between the celestial Adam, made after the image of God, a perfect likeness of the Logos, an incorporeal object of intelligence, and the earthly Adam, compacted out of earthly substance or matter and an object of sense perception. Ginsberg suggests that Philo's idea is based on Pharisaic teaching. Gen. R. and Midr. Ps. 139.5 cite an opinion of R. Elazar b. Pedat interpreting *ahor vakedem zartani* as "before the first and after the last day of creation." This is taken to agree with another opinion of R. Elazar that the words, "Let the earth bring forth the soul of living being" (Gen. 1.24) mean the soul of Adam. This opinion is further identified with that of Simeon b. Lakish, who takes the verse, "and the spirit of God moved upon the face of the deep," as referring to the spirit of Adam. In Gen. R. 2.4 the same Amora is quoted as saying that the verse refers to the spirit of the Messiah. Prof. Ginsberg observes: "This contains the kernel of Philo's philosophical doctrine of the creation of the original man. He calls him the idea of the earthly Adam, while with the Rabbis the *Ruah* (spirit of Adam) not only existed before the creation of the earthly Adam, but was preexistent to the whole of creation. From the preexistent Adam, or Messiah, to the Logos is merely a step." *Jew Enc.*, I, 181. Cf. Paul's Christology in I Cor. 15.45-49.

[33] See Bundahis 3 in W. West's *Pahlavi Texts, Sacred Books of the East.* Vol. V.

gathered from all parts of the earth. The earth for his body came from Babylon; for his head, from Palestine; and for his limbs, from the rest of the
lands.[34] Another opinion is that he was fashioned from the navel of the earth
(cf. Ezek. 38.12), i. e., the Temple, and endowed with God's spirit.[35] His
stature extended from one end of the earth to the other (cf. Ps. 139.5). His
height reached to the very skies. As he stood up in his divine likeness, the
other creatures took him for their Creator, and began to prostrate themselves
before him. But he corrected them and said: 'Come with me, and together let
us clothe ourselves in majesty and strength, and crown Him as our God.' First
Adam and then the other creatures proclaimed God's kingship (cf. Ps. 93).

"Adam was the light of the world."[36] He was distinguished by surpassing
physical beauty and wisdom, brilliance which eclipsed the sun, and a heavenly
light, which enabled him to see the whole earth. And he was immortal. As
long as he was devoted to God, he enjoyed wisdom and power, counsel and
insight.[37]

The word *mimmennu* in Gen. 3.22 was taken by R. Pappias as a first
person plural. That is, the ministering angels declared: "Behold, Adam has
become like one of us." Akiba silenced him, explaining the word as a third
person singular, signifying: "Man is become like one who of himself may
choose the way of life or the way of death."[38] R. Judah bar Simon interpreted
it as a first person plural of majesty. That is, God says: "Man is become like
unto Ourselves," endowed with Godlike powers. Another opinion took it to
mean that Adam became like Gabriel. The verse was further understood to
mean that Adam was destined to be immortal like Elijah.[39]

The mystic Pirke de R. Eliezer comments on Gen. 2.18, "It is not good for

---

[34] Sanh. 98b; Pirke de Rabbi Eliezer, 11.

[35] R. Berechiah and R. Helbo said in the name of R. Samuel the Elder that God created
man out of the dust of the place where the Temple was to rise for the atonement of his sins.
Gen. R. 14.8 and note by Theodor. K. Kohler remarks: "Sin shall never be a permanent or
inherent part of man's nature." Art. "Adam," *Jew. Enc.*, I, 177.

[36] Cf. Prov. 20.27; Jeru. Sab. 2.6.

[37] Pes. 54a; Hag. 12a; Baba Batra 75a; Sanh. 38b; Pirke de Rabbi Eliezer, II.

[38] Mechilta, Beshalah, 7.

[39] Gen. R. 21.5.

Adam to be alone," etc. God showed special love for Adam by creating him out of a pure and holy place, out of the dust of the place where the Temple was to rise, i.e., that he might be free from sin, and brought him to his own preserve, the Garden of Eden. There he promenaded like one of the ministering angels. And God reflected: "I am unique in My world and man is unique in his. I do not procreate and he does not procreate. This may mislead the creatures to think that he created them. Hence, 'it is not good for Adam to be alone; I shall make for him a mate to help him.' "[40] As long as he was alone, he was called Adam, but as soon as woman, *ishah*, was created, he was named *ish*. God placed His name into their names (the *Yod* into the first and the *He* into the second), indicating that if they followed His teaching, they would be saved from all distress, but if they did not, God would withdraw His name from them and they would be consumed.[41] Adam's nuptials were celebrated with great pomp in Heaven. God prepared ten canopies for him in the Garden of Eden, all of them made of precious stones and pearls and gold (cf. Ezek. 28.13). The angels beat the drums and danced like maidens. The ministering angels served as the groom's companions, and God Himself officiated as *Hazzan*, blessing the couple (Gen. 1.28).[42]

The haggadic portrayal of the serpent is illuminated by the report of Bundahis 1.8 about Angra-Mainyu that "whatever he schemes he infuses with malice and greed till the end." As soon as he arose from the abyss, and came into the light, the evil spirit "desirous of destroying, and because of his malicious nature," rushed in to annihilate the light of Auharmazd (Ahura Mazda). Seeing that its bravery and glory were greater than his own, he rushed back to the gloomy darkness, and formed many demons and fiends, and together they rose to do violence (1.9–10). "His business is unmercifulness and destruction of this welfare (i.e., of the creatures of Auharmazd), so that the creatures which Auharmazd shall increase he will destroy; and his eyesight (referring to the "evil eye") does not refrain from doing the creature

---

[40] Cf. Gen. R. 8.10.

[41] By removing the Yod from one and the He from the other, the letters Aleph and Shin remain in both, spelling Esh — fire.

[42] We may have here a reaction to the Pauline idea of marriage as a mere concession to the flesh and to the Manichaean notion of the evil character of married life.

harm." "His body is that of a lizard whose place is filth" (28.1–2). Again we are told that "the evil spirit was a loglike lizard's body, and he appeared a young man of fifteen years to Geh" (3.9).

Of the wicked Geh, the Bundahis 3.3–9 tells that she comes "to cause that conflict in the world, wherefrom the distress and injury of Auharmazd and the archangels will arise." She announced: "in that conflict I will shed thus much vexation on the righteous man (Gayomard, the representative of mankind) and the laboring ox, that through my deeds, life will not be wanted, and I will destroy their living souls. I will vex the water, I wil vex the plants, I will vex the fire of Auharmazd, I will make the whole of creation of Auharmzd vexed." The evil spirit "kissed Geh upon the head, and the pollution which they call menstruation became apparent in Geh."[43]

Some of these traits of the evil one reappear in the Rabbinic portrayals of the serpent. R. Hoshaiah described him as double-horned, upright like a pole, and walking on two feet.[44] He is pictured also as camel. As in the Wisdom of Solomon 2.24 and in the Secrets of Enoch 31.3, so in the Haggadah he is identified with the devil, Satan or Sammael.[45] His characteristic attitude is that of jealousy and envy. He envied Adam's position in Eden. He envied Adam's lordship over creation, and above all Adam's possession of Eve. He therefore conspired to kill Adam and to marry Eve and to set himself up as king over the whole earth.[46] According to Gen. R. 18.6, the serpent was filled with lust for Eve when he beheld her conjugal relations with Adam.

Pirke de Rabbi Eliezer 13 treats a serpent as the instrument of Sammael,[47] who was a great prince in heaven. Whereas the *Hayot* had four wings and the *Seraphim* six, Sammael had twelve. He seems to have acted on behalf of the other ministering angels, who resented Adam's superiority over them, and resorted to stratagem to lead Adam to sin and thereby discredit him before

---

[43] See note 33. While the Bundahis dates from the 8th or 9th cent., it contains ancient Parsi teaching.

[44] Gen. R. 19.1 and notes by Theodor.

[45] Targum Jonathan to Gen. 3.6; Lev. R. 21.4; Deut. R. 11.9; P. R. E., 13; Zohar, I, 35b; cf. 2 Cor. 11.3; Rev. 12.9; 20.2.

[46] Sanh. 59b; Sota 9b; Abot R. Nathan, I, 1.

[47] In his commentary to Gen. 3.1 Ibn Ezra cites Saadia's opinion to the same effect.

God. Sammael descended on earth with his band of evil spirits. Surveying all of God's creatures, he found no one more skilled to do evil than the serpent (cf. Gen. 3.1). He at once mounted the serpent and prompted it to do his will.[48] Craftily the vile serpent proceeded to ensnare Eve, since woman is more readily enticed than man, suggesting to her that God prohibited the eating of the fruit of the tree because of His jealousy, for by partaking of the fruit one becomes like God. The trick worked. As Eve touched the fruit, she beheld the Angel of Death coming toward her. Fearing that she would die and that God would create another woman for Adam, she made him partake of the fruit so that, if they should die, they would both die, and if they should live, they would both live.

B. *Nature of the Sin*

The opinion is expressed that the serpent enticed Eve and cohabited with her.[49] The words "the fruit of the midst of the garden" (Gen. 3.3.) are taken as a euphemism for Eve (cf. Song of Songs 4.12). Out of that union Cain was born. Subsequently Adam begot Abel.[50] Hence Adam did not find consolation after Abel's death until Seth was born in his likeness. R. Ishmael is quoted as saying that the righteous generations descended from Seth and all the wicked ones from Cain. R. Meir held that the offspring of Cain behaved like animals, walking around stark naked, and indulging in all kinds of sexual excesses, including incest. It is of them that the fallen angels took wives. From their unions, according to R. Zadok, came the giants, who engaged in robbery, violence, and blood-shed. Thus their evil ways are hereditary.[51]

[48] Books of Adam and Eve, 9 ff.

[49] Cf. Gen. 3.13, taking the word *hisiani* in the sense of *nisuin*, marriage. Rashi to Sota 9b; and ntoes by Theodor to Gen. R. 18.25 and 19.13.

[50] Cf. 2 Cor. 11.3–5; Thackeray, *Relation of St. Paul to Contemporary Jewish Thought*, p. 55: A. Plummer, *Intern. Crit. Comment to 2 Corinth.*, p. 295. See also Tim. 2.13–15 and cf. IV Macc. 18.7–8 and notes *ad loc.* in Charles, *Apoc. and Pseud.* II.

[51] Cf. Targ. Jeru. to Gen. 4.1: Pirke de Rabbi Eliezer 21; Kasher, *Torah Shelemah*, I, p. 304, note 7. This curious notion regarding the parentage of Cain appears to have been current among the Gnostics. See Epiphanius. Haeresis 40.5; Tennant, *The Full and Original Sin*, p.

A crude theory of original sin states that by his union with Eve, the serpent, Sammael, polluted her posterity. R. Johanan teaches that "when the serpent had intercourse with Eve, he injected pollution into her. Israel, by receiving the Torah at Sinai, freed itself of the pollution; the gentiles who did not stand at Sinai have not rid themselves of it." R. Ashi holds that proselytes are included with Israel, for though they were not at Sinai, their *mazzal* (guardian angel) was.[52] R. Abba bar Kahana thinks that not even the Patriarchs were wholly free from that infection, for Abraham begot Ishmael, and Isaac begot Esau. Only Jacob begot twelve sons wholly free from blemish.[53]

The context in which R. Johanan's statement occurs in Aboda Zarah 22b suggests that the contamination was of the nature of lustful passion. The original sin thus consisted in awakening sexual desire in Eve.[54] Concupiscence as the cause of the fall is suggetsed by the saying of R. Aha that Eve's name signifies "serpent" (*Hivya,* a play on the name *Havvah*) because she was the serpent, i. e., the seducer of Adam as the serpent was her seducer.[55] In words that have an Augustinian sound, he comments on Ps. 51.7 ("Behold, I was shapen in iniquity, and in sin did my mother conceive me"), "Though one be the saintliest of saints, he cannot escape a trace of sin. Thus David said before the Holy One, blessed be He: 'Did my father Jesse aim only to beget me? Did he not rather aim to satisfy his own desire?'" R. Huna and R. Jacob report an opinion of R. Abba that Adam taught cohabitation to all creatures (cf. Gen.

159; R. Meir's idea may be related to the thought of the Bundahis 23.1 deriving the "tailed ape and bear and other species of degeneracy" out of the union of Yim with a demoness (cf. Lilit) and of his sister Yimak with a demon. See also Zohar, I, 36b; 145b. J. Rosenberg, in his comments on his edition of the Zohar, p. 40, "corrects" the Darwinian theory of the origin of species in the light of this idea.

[52] Cf. Bundahis 1.8 and note 2 by West.

[53] Yebamot 103b; Ab. Zara 22b; Sab. 145b–146a; cf. Jubil. 22.16 ff.; Zohar I, 36b, 52a: A. Kohut, *Aruch Hashalem,* sub *Zeham,* II, 273–4; *Die juedische Angelologie,* p. 66.

[54] L. Ginsberg, *Legends,* V, p. 133.

[55] Gen. R. 20.20. For a contrasting view see legend of union of Adam and Eve before the Fall. Gen. R. 18.25.

4.1). R. Huna bar Ido teaches that as soon as Eve was created, Satan was created with her,[56] i. e., the evil concupiscence.

As the incarnation of evil, Sammael is identified also with the evil impulse of man. R. Simeon b. Lakish teaches that Satan, the Yezer Hara, and the Angel of death are one and the same. He has a threefold function: he descends and misleads, he ascends and accuses, and he secures God's permission to take the soul.[57] Rashi comments on Gen. 2.25 that in their state of innocence, Adam and Eve had no sense of distinction between good and evil, but in consequence of their transgression, the Yezer Hara entered into them and they grew conscious of good and evil. In his commentary on Isa. 5.2, Rashi voices the same thought. He treats the chapter as an allegory of Adam. The words "And he removed the stones thereof" refer to the Yezer Hara, i. e., before Adam sinned, but as soon as he sinned the Yezer Hara entered into him. "And there will arise in it briars and thistles" (v. 6) signifies that "the Yezer Hara will rule over him and the generations following him, to do evil deeds." Rashi's Haggadic explanation implies that the Yezer Hara was in Adam from the first, but that it was removed from him during his state of innocence and was restored to him after the fall.[58] Rashi's opinion accords with the view of Aboth de R. Nathan, II, 42 that the Yezer Hara represents a punishment meted out to Adam for his sin. The Kabbalah follows the line of thought maintaining that in consequence of Adam's transgression, all men are born under the influence of the Yezer Hara.[59]

The Rabbis generally hold that God endowed man from the very beginning with two Yezers, one good and one evil. This they derive homiletically

[56] Lev. R. 14.5; Gen. R. 17.5; 22.2; Pirke de Rabbi Eliezer, 22.

[57] B. B. 16a; art. "Angel of Death," *Universal Jew. Encycl.*, I, 302–3.

[58] Nahmanides rejects the opinion that the fruit of the tree aroused sexual desire. He thinks that originally Adam and Eve were free from concupiscence, and cohabited only for procreation. Hence their sex organs were like other parts of the body of which they were not ashamed. By eating of the fruit man acquired the choice and the desire to do good or evil for himself and others, which is a godlike power, but also an evil in that man now possessed a Yezer. Commentary on Gen. 2.10.

[59] Zohar, I, 61a.

from the two *yods* in the word *vayyizer* in Gen. 2.7.[60] Furthermore, even the Yezer Hara is not absolutely evil. While, by rousing the passions, the Yezer "leads a man out of the world," he serves also a useful purpose. He is "the leaven of the dough." Without him there would be no family life and no enterprise whatever. "He is as necessary to the world as rain."[61] The Yezer is in reality neutral. Man can use his passional nature for good as well as for evil.

"The tempter appealed to the desire and ambition inherent in human nature (Gen. 3.5 ff.), and in yielding to this impulse man transgressed the commandment of God. This is the uniform doctrine of Judaism, as it is indeed the meaning of the story in Genesis."[62] In addition to concupiscence, drunkenness figures as the original sin. Thus I Enoch 32.4 considers the forbidden tree to have been a vine. We encounter the same idea in III Baruch 4.8, 16–17. Baruch is informed that the tree which led Adam astray is the vine, which the angel Sammael planted. In His anger, God cursed him and his plant, and forbade Adam to touch it. The devil, in his envy of Adam, managed to deceive him. As Adam was condemned through the vine and was divested of the glory of God, so his descendants "who now drink insatiably the wine which is begotten of it, transgress worse than Adam, and are now surrendering themselves to the eternal fire. For no good comes through it. For those who drink it to surfeit do these things: neither does a brother pity his brother, nor a father his son, nor children their parents, but from the drinking of wine come all the evils, such as murders, adulteries, fornications, perjuries, thefts, and such like."[63]

The idea recurs in Rabbinic Haggadah. This is the opinion of Rabbi Meir, of R. Judah b. Ilai and of R. Ibo.[64] As Noah was about to plant the vine, Shamdon (Asmodeus) came to help him, saying: "I desire to join you in your work, but be on your guard lest you come into my power and I injure you."[65]

[60] Targ. Jonathan *ad loc.*; Berachot 61a; Gen. R. 14.4.

[61] Abot 2.16; 4.28; Sefer Yezira 6; Midr. Temura I; Ber. 17a; Yoma 69b; Zohar I, 138a. On the whole subject see Frank C. Porter, "The Yezer Hara, A Study in Jewish Doctrine of Sin," in *Biblical and Semitic Studies*, Yale University, 1902, pp. 93–156.

[62] Moore, *Judaism*, I, 479.

[63] Compare the Christina interpolation ch. 4.9–15.

[64] Ber. 40a; Sanh. 70a; Gen. R. 15.6; 19.5.

[65] Gen. R. 36.3 and notes by Theodor; Tanhuma, Noah, 3; Num. R., Naso, 12.2, 8.

As through the serpent, who enticed Eve to drink wine, a curse came upon the earth (cf. Gen. 3.17), so through wine a third of the world, i.e., Canaan, the third son of Ham, was cursed (ibid. 9.24–25). As the viper divides between life and death, so wine separates man from the ways of life and sets him apart for the ways of death, for wine leads man to idolatry (cf. Prov. 23.33; Ps. 81.10). It was through wine that the Yezer Hara led Israel to worship the Golden Calf.[66]

C. The Effect of the Fall

The immediate effect of the fall was the expulsion of Adam and Eve from Eden. According to Pirke de R. Eliezer 14, as soon as Adam sinned, God came down to judge him. Adam had been clothed in a horny skin,[67] and covered with a cloud of glory. In consequence of the fall he was stripped of both. He cast the blame upon Eve.[68] She in turn blamed the serpent. Thereupon God meted out punishment to every one of the three, punishment consisting of nine curses and of death. He cast down Sammael and his troop from their holy place in heaven, cut off the feet of the serpent, and decreed that it should cast its skin in great pain, etc. The woman was afflicted with pains arising from menstruation, the rupture of the virginal membrane, of childbirth and of bringing up children. Her head was covered like that of a mourner,[69] and it is not to be shaved except in punishment of adultery (cf. Num. 5.18). Her ear is pierced like that of a perpetual slave. Like a handmaid, she waits upon her husband; and she is not believed in testimony. These curses are followed by death. Woman's entire status, physical, spiritual, and social, was determined by the fall. Adam's curses included the following: His strength was diminished and his stature shortened; he was to sow wheat and reap thistles; his food was to be the grass of the earth like that of beasts; and he was to earn his bread in

[66] Num. R. 10.8; Midr. R. Song 2.4.

[67] Accoridng to Targ. Jeru. Gen. 3.7 in an "onyx-colored" garment, and according to R. Isaac Ravia in a dress as smooth as the finger nail and as beautiful as a pearl. Gen. R. 20.12.

[68] The Midrash Aggadah, Bereshit, p. 8 refers the complaint against God Himself.

[69] Cf. 1 Cor. 11.5; Apostolic Constitutions 1.8.

anxiety and by the sweat of his brow. After all these comes death. Other opinions add that he was endowed with the Yezer Hara.[70]

The general view is that as soon as Adam sinned all things became perverted, and will not be restored until the advent of the Messiah.[71] The earth and the heavenly bodies lost their brightness. The course of the planets changed. Death came upon all creatures, because Eve gave the animals of the forbidden fruit. Only the phoenix refused to break the divine command. Hence he lives forever.[72] Adam's sin was followed by the loss of six excellences: his radiance, his eternal life, his stature, the fruitfulness of the earth and of the tree of Eden, and the lustre of the luminaries.[73] The Midrash applies Prov. 24.30 to Adam. "I went by the field of the slothful" refers to Adam who was too indolent to repent of his sin; "and by the vineyard of one devoid of understanding" refers to Eve who was enticed by the serpent; "and lo, it was all grown over with thistles" for the whole world was filled with woe; "the face thereof was covered with nettles" as it is said: "and thorns and thistles shall it bring forth to thee" (Gen. 3.18); "and the stone wall thereof was broken down," for Adam demolished the fence of the world.[74]

The chief penalty of Adam's transgression, according to both Apocryphal and Rabbinic literature is mortality. We meet with this view among the Palestinian as well as the Babylonian teachers.[75] This view was held by R. Meir. R. Jose teaches that because Adam violated one commandment given to him by

[70] Cf. Bundahis 3.15 ff. For a different view see Bereshit Rabbati pp. 50–52 and notes by Albeck; Ginsberg, *Legends,* V, pp. 101–102, notes 83–90. Secrets of Enoch 31.7–8 limits the penalties to the serpent Satan. Adam's ignorance and sin were likewise punished, but not Adam himself nor the earth nor the other creatures. Under Platonic influence, ignorance is here conceived as an evil in itself and forms the origin of moral evil. See note by Forbes and Charles in *Apoc. and Pseud.* II 450. n. 16. A. R. N. II, 42, knows of 40 curses, ten each for Adam, Eve, the serpent, and the earth. The number differs in A. R. N., I, 1. Num. R. 5.4 similarly speaks of 40 curses. The Zohar Hadash to Ruth, p. 158 refers to 39, corresponding to the number of stripes applied by a court to a human offender. See J. D. Eisenstein, *Ozar Midrashim,* "Perek Adam Harishon," I, 9–10.

[71] Gen. R. 12.5.

[72] *Ibid.,* 19.5.

[73] *Ibid.,* 12.6; Tanhuma, Buber, Bereshit, 18.

[74] Tanhuma, Buber, Bereshit, 22; Gen. R. 21.2.

[75] Geiger's claim that these ideas were acquired from the Christians in Babylonia lacks foundation. See *Juedische Zeitschrift,* X, 166–171.

God, death came upon him and all generations. R. Judah applies Deut. 32.32
to the sons of Adam, who brought the penalty of death upon all his descendants. R. Nehemiah limits the penalties to the gentiles, who are "the disciples
of the primeval serpent who misled Adam and Eve."[76] This is related to the
idea of R. Johanan, cited above, that the gentiles, by not accepting the Torah,
have not yet freed themselves from the pollution of the serpent. R. Judah
recognizes the universality of death. "No one hath power over the Angel of
death to keep him away from oneself."[77] In other words, "If Adam had not
sinned, men would not have been mortal."[78] He supports his opinion that if
Adam had not sinned he would not have died, with the case of Elijah, who
escaped death by his sinlessness.[79] Another view is that while mortality came
with Adam, every person deserves it for himself. This is substantially the
position of Paul.[80] Thus R. Ammi, basing himself on Ezek. 18.3 and Ps.
89.33, teaches: "There is no death without sin and no suffering without
iniquity." His view was controverted by the Tannaitic tradition that when the
angels asked God why He imposed death upon Adam, he replied: "I commanded him but one light commandment, and he transgressed it." They
retorted: "Did not Moses and Aaron keep the entire Torah? Yet, they too,
died." God answered in the words of Eccl. 9.2, "all things occur alike to all;
yea, one happening unto the righteous and the wicked." R. Ammi, it is
explained, followed R. Simeon b. Elazar, who held that Moses and Aaron,
too, died on account of their sin (cf. Num. 20.12). According to another
Tannaitic tradition, four men, Benjamin, Amram, Jesse and Chiliab, died not
because of personal guilt but on account of the serpent, i. e., the guilt of
Adam. Another tradition states that the Angel of death had no power over the
following six persons: Abraham, Isaac, Jacob, Moses, Aaron and Miriam.[81] In
keeping with R. Ammi's view, is the statement of R. Eliezer b. Hyrcanus that

---

[76] Erub. 18b; Sifra Vayikra 20.10; Sifre. Deut. 323.

[77] Deut. R. 9.3; Eccl. R. to Eccl. 8.8.

[78] Midr. Aggadah, p. 5.

[79] Eccl. R. 3.15.

[80] Rom. 5.12. See Moore, *Judaism*, I, 476.

[81] See Targum to Ruth 4.22; Eccl. 7.29; Sab. 55ab; B. B. 17a; cf. Prayer of Manasseh, 8;
on the immortals who entered Paradise during their life see Ginsberg, *Legends*, V, pp. 67–68, n.
67.

if God were to enter into judgment with the patriarchs, they would not be able to withstand the rebuke.[82]

A Midrash on Job 37.7 ("By the hand of every man will He seal") states that when God showed Adam all the generations that were to descend from him (cf. Gen. 5.1), Adam grieved over the fact that he had brought death upon the righteous, and implored God not to record that fact. God assented and promised him that in the hour of man's departure from this world, He will reveal Himself to him and order him: "Record thy deeds, for thou diest on account of thine own deeds." And in the future, when He will come to judge His creatures, He will produce all the books of the children of man and show them their deeds. Hence it is said: "By the hand of every man will He seal." When the righteous reprove Adam for causing them to die, he responds: "I committed only one transgression, but every one of you committed many sins." In order to sustain Adam's claim, they are punished with death even for light offenses.[83] Adam himself absolves God of the charge of having punished mankind with death, and takes the responsibility upon himself.[84]

R. Judah bar Simon, voices the thought that Adam was worthy of being immortal. Why, then, was he punished with death? "God hath so made it that men should fear before Him" (Eccl. R. to Eccl. 3.14). We have here the same motive which occurs in Gen. 3.22, viz., to draw a line between men and God. Gen. R. 9.5 makes the motive more explicit. R. Hama b. Hanina observes that Adam was punished with death on account of Nebuchadnezzar and Hiram who would set themselves up as gods. Because of them the entire human race was rendered mortal. Instead of posterity's suffering for the sin of Adam, it is Adam who suffered for the offense of some of his posterity.

That death is the natural lot of man was recognized in Rabbinic thought (cf. 1 Sam. 26.10; Eccl. 3.2). R. Joshua b. Korha argued that a subterfuge was employed in charging Adam with being the cause of human mortality (cf. Ps. 66.5), inasmuch as the Angel of death was made on the very first day of

---

[82] Arachin 17a.

[83] Yalkut Job 922; Tanh., Buber Bereshit, 29; *ibid.*, Hukkat, 39; cf. II Baruch 48.42–46; 54.15, 19. In the Book of Adam and Eve 10.2 it is Eve who is distressed by the fact that all sinners will curse her for not keeping God's commandment.

[84] Midr. Ps. 92.14.

creation and Adam was not created until the sixth.[85] Death is a part of the order of nature. It was with Death as a reality that God looked upon all that He had made and said: "It is very good" (Gen. 1.31).[86] R. Meir noted in the margin of his scroll the word *mavet*, death, by the side of *tob*, good. R. Samuel b. R. Isaac applied the words *Tob meod* to the Angel of Death.[87] The Midrash Lekah Tob (*ad loc.*) comments that "God looked upon the world and saw that death is good for the creatures, therefore it is said: 'and behold, it is very good.'"

How long will death reign? Gen. R. 24.4 connects Isa. 57.16 with Gen. 5.1, in this manner: "For I shall not contend forever" with Adam; "nor shall I always be wroth" with his descendants; "for the spirit fainteth before Me," i.e., He weakens the destructive spirit. R. Wolf Heidenheim interprets the statement that God will reveal (or release) the spirits which are "wrapped before Him." In keeping with the latter view is the saying of R. Tanhum bar Hiyya that the Messiah will not come before all the souls that appeared in God's plan of creation come to life. These are the souls referred to in the book of Adam (cf. Ps. 139.16). In Yebamot 63a the statement reads: the Messiah will not come until all the souls of the *Guf* (a supernatural chamber; according to Heidenheim's comment to Gen. R. 8.1, "the body of Adam contained all souls') will have gone through an earthly existence."[88] That will mark the end of death.

The subject is pursued further in connection with the interpretation of Gen. 2.17. The Midrash links it with Dan. 8.13 and applies the verse to Adam: How long will he and his descendants be trampled upon by the Angel of Death? The answer is found in the next verse: *ad erev boker* — until the morning of the gentiles will turn into evening and the evening of Israel into morning. In Messianic times "the sanctuary will be victorious." Adam will be absolved of the penalty to which he was subjected. The excellences that were taken from him when he sinned will be restored with the coming of the Messiah. The defects of nature will be remedied and the wound of the world

---

[85] Tanhuma, Vayeshev, 4.

[86] Tanhuma, Shemot, 17; cf. Gen. R. 30.8; Ex. R. 2.4.

[87] Gen. R. 9.5.9; Midr. Haggadol to Gen. 1.31; Midr. Aggadah, Bereshit, p. 5.

[88] Cf. II Baruch 23.4–5.

will be healed. Then, too, the Yezer Hara will be destroyed. With his elimination all suffering will disappear.[89]

D. *Imputation of Guilt and of Merit*

As in the Christian doctrine of Original Sin, so in the Rabbinic thought on the subject the idea of imputation plays an important part. The idea of transmission of both guilt and merit within families or of rewards and punishments to be visited upon one's descendants was shared by all the nations of antiquity, and forms the basis of the biblical doctrine of retribution. The second commandment declares that God visits the sins of the fathers upon their children unto the third and fourth generation of them that hate Him, and He shows mercy unto the thousandth generation of them that love Him and keep His commandments (Ex. 20.5–6; Deut. 5.9–10). In view of the descent of the human race from Adam, it was quite natural for the ancient thinkers to conceive of mankind as involved in the sins of its first parent. We encountered this belief in the Rabbinic teachings regarding the origin of death as an inheritance from Adam. The penalty imposed upon him must be borne by all his descendants. Midrash Lekah Tob explains the seemingly pleonastic expression *Mot temutun* in Gen. 2.17 as signifying death for Adam and death for his descendants.

The words "these are the generations of Adam" (Gen. 5.1) were interpreted by R. Judah bar Simon, in the light of Ps. 139.16; to mean that when God created Adam, He showed him all the generations, their interpreters and their sages, their scribes and their leaders.[90] In other words, humanity was

---

[89] Gen. R. 21.1; 12.6 and note by Theodor; Num. R. 13.12; Tanhuma, Buber, Bereshit 18, 40 cf. Yalkut, Gen. 42 on Gen. 5.29; A. R. N., I.2; Sukka 52a. Parallels appear in the Bundahis: "The creatures of Aharman (Angra-Mainyu) will perish at the time when the future existence occurs, and that also is eternity" (1.7). Ahura Mazda will overcome the adversary, and the guardian spirits of man will again become perfect, immortal, undecaying and undisturbed for ever and ever (2.10–11). Gayomard spoke thus: "Although the destroyer has come, mankind will be all of my race; and this one thing is good, when they perform duty and good works" (3.23).

[90] Gen. R. 24.1. Cf. Midr. Ps. 139.6; Ab. Zara 5a.

foreshadowed in idea in the mind of Adam. More explicitly the later Midrash Ex. R. 40.3, citing Eccl. 6.10 ("and it is foreknown what man is"), states: "While Adam still lay as an unformed mass, God showed him every righteous man that was to descend from him; one hung from his head, another from his hair, another from his eyes, another from his mouth, still another from his ear," etc. Mysticism enlarged upon this idea. R. Bahia b. Asher, for example, writes: Inasmuch as death was decreed upon Adam, who was the root of the world and of all the generations, no one may escape it. Had it not been for that sin, men would have been immortal. On the basis of Ps. 82.6–7, he maintains that the original plan of creation was to have men like angels in bodily forms, on the order of Enoch and Elijah, but because of Adam's sin that plan was upset. Nature shows that when the root of a tree decays, its branches, too, are affected. Death, which separates the soul from the body, corresponds to the sin which parted the fruit from the tree. As such it is the portion of the righteous and the wicked alike (cf. Eccl. 9.2; 3.19). However, this pertains only to their bodies. In the realm of souls, they are rewarded in accordance with their actions.[91] In the view of the Zohar, Adam's fall turned all things into disorder, and the heavenly channels through which divine influence streamed upon the world were broken. It destroyed the original harmony of creation and sent the Shechinah into exile.[92] In Luria's teachings, this idea takes on most fantastic forms. All souls were created together with the organs of Adam. Originally they were in pure and holy state, but following the fall they were mixed with evil. The confusion has continued ever since, so that there are no holy souls without some "sparks" of "uncleanness" and no unclean souls without some "sparks of holiness." This condition prevents the advent of the Messiah, for he cannot come until the sin of Adam is repaired and the good is separated from evil.[93]

The imputation of Adam's guilt to his posterity was acknowledged even by rationalists. Thus David Kimhi comments on Isaiah 43.27, ("thy first father sinned"): "how can you claim to be innocent in view of the fact that your first

[91] Kad Hakemah, Evel., ed. Warsaw, pp. 5ab.

[92] G. Scholem, *Major Trends of Jewish Mysticism*, pp. 220, 232, 272 and *passim*.

[93] S. A. Horodezki, *Torat Haari*, Kenesset, III, pp. 405–6; Vital, *Shaare Kedusha*, i.

father, Adam, sinned. Man is stamped with sin, "for the inclination of his heart is evil from his youth" (Gen. 6.5).[94]

Next to Adam's fall, the worship of the Golden Calf figures in Rabbinic literature as the most heinous sin which brought the direst consequences upon Israel. Death as the penalty of Adam's sin was cancelled at Sinai when Israel accepted the Torah, but by setting up the Golden Calf the Israelites came back under the sway of the Angel of Death. Another opinion is expressed that at Sinai God gave the Angel of Death dominion over all the idolatrous peoples, and reserved Israel for Himself that they might share in His immortality. But as soon as they acclaimed the Calf as their God, they reverted to their former mortality.[95]

The initiative for the Golden Calf came not from Israel but from the mixed multitude. That sin, which was trailed by the two other cardinal sins of incest and bloodshed was hereditary affecting twenty-four generations, till the final destruction of the Jewish state in the time of Zedekiah. R. Oshiah says: Down to the days of Jeroboam, Israel suffered for the sin of one calf and thereafter for three. R. Isaac expresses the thought that every chastisement which befalls the world is, in some part, a retribution for the sin of the Golden Calf. R. Jehudah said in the name of R. Jose: There is not a single generation that does not partake of the sin of the Calf.[96] According to R. Jehudah, Sammael entered the Golden Calf and began to bleat to mislead Israel (cf. Is. 1.3). However, not all the people were deceived by him. In the opinion of the Rabbi, the princes of the people were deemed worthy of beholding the Shechinah because they did not worship the Calf (Ex. 24.11). R. Jehudah similarly excludes the tribe of Levi from that offense (Ex. 32.26). When God first descended to give the Torah to Israel, sixty myriads of angels accompanied Him to crown every Israelite. Prior to that event the Israelites were better in the eyes of God than the angels, and the Angel of Death, as we noted

[94] On the other hand, Kimhi rejects Rashi's explanation of Hos. 6.7 as referring to Adam, and takes the word *adam* in the sense of person. The Targum renders the verse: "like the former generations they transgressed My covenant." Cf. S. Krauss, *Perush Madai, Isaiah*, p. 84 and A. B. Ehrlich, *Mikro Kipeshuto*, III, p. 99.

[95] Ab. Z. 5a; Ex. R. 32.1, 7; Lev. R. 11.1, 3; 18.2–4.

[96] Tanh., Ki Tisa, 20–21; Sanh. 102a; Mid. R. to Lam. 1.3, ed. Buber, 62.

before, had no power over them. But after that affair, God was wroth with them. On the night following the sin, the sixty myriad angels returned and stripped every Israelite of his adornments.[97]

Like these, so other sins are trailed by suffering. Rav Zutra calls out: "Woe unto the wicked! Not only do they incur guilt, but they involve their children and their children's children to the end of all the generations." In view of the solidarity of the Jewish people, each generation completely identifies itself with the preceding ones and assumes responsibility for their misdeeds. "Because of our sins have we been exiled from our land —" is the mournful confession of a penitent people.

Conversely, Rav Zutra exclaims: "Happy are the righteous. Not only do they acquire merit, but they bestow merit upon their children and their children's children to the end of all the generations."[98]

Not only guilt but righteousness as well may be transmitted and credited to subsequent generations (cf. Gen. 26.2–5; Ps. 103.18; etc.). In Judaism it is obviously not the righteousness of the Christ but the *Zachut,* the merit of the Fathers that is accounted to the Jewish people and affects their justification. This doctrine of merit is not, as S. Levy suggested, "a complete contrast of the Christian theory of Original Sin" and for which he proposed the name "Original Virtue,"[99] but a phase of the idea of imputation, which underlies the doctrine of Original Sin. The doctrine is clearly stated in Aggadat Bereshit 10.2, in connection with Prov. 20.7 ("He that walketh in his integrity as a just man, happy are his children after him"): "Happy are the children whose fathers possess merit, for that merit profits them. Happy are the people of Israel, for the merit of Abraham, Isaac and Jacob avails them. Because of their merit, God saved their descendants in Egypt (Ex. 2.24), when they departed thence (Ps. 105.42–43), in the episode of the Golden Calf (Ex. 32.13), in the days of Elijah (1 Kings 18.36), and in the reign of Hazael the King of Aram (2 Kings 13.22–23). God said to Israel: "Until now you had the merit of the Patriarchs; from now on, each person will depend upon his own

[97] Pirke de Rabbi Eliezer 47.
[98] Yoma 87a.
[99] See *Original Virtue and Other Short Studies,* p. 1.

acts." Another Midrash states: From that time on, the merits of one's own honest labor exceeds the merit of the Fathers.[100] The date of the cessation of the merit of the Patriarchs was variously given. Rab placed it in the days of Hosea (Hos. 2.12), Samuel in the days of Hazael (2 Kings 13.22–23). R. Joshua b. Levi in the time of Elijah (1 Kings 18.36), and R. Johanan in the reign of Hezekiah (Is. 9.6).[101] R. Aha is of the opinion that the merit of the Patriarchs endures forever. R. Judah bar Hanan says in the name of R. Berechiah, with reference to Is. 54.10: "When you see the merit of the Patriarchs declining and the merit of Matriarchs shaken, go and cleave to God's grace, for ("though the mountains [= Patriarchs] shall depart and the hills [= Matriarchs] be removed), My kindness shall not depart from thee."[102]

Rabbenu Tam remarks that while the merit of the Fathers has drawn to an end, the Covenant of the Fathers abides. Thus Lev. 26.42 states: "I will remember My covenant with Abraham, with Isaac and with Jacob," etc., i. e., even after the Exile. And (in the liturgy) we recall not the merit of the Fathers but the Covenant."[103] It is interesting that the original text of the Amidah, as represented by the Palestinian version, omits the words "who rememberest the goodness of the Fathers" in the first benediction. On the other hand, there is strong appeal to the covenant theme in the Zichronot in the Musaf for Rosh Hashanah. "It is in the later liturgy where the Zachut of the Fathers plays such an important part."[104]

The generations that suffer persecution cry out in despair: "Lord of the world! The former generations were protected by the merit of the Fathers, and 'we are become like orphans and fatherless' (Lam. 5.3), but Thou hast said, 'In Thee the fatherless find mercy'; 'Thou aidest the orphan' (Hos. 14.4; Ps. 10.14)."[105]

Particularly important is the merit accruing to the people in consequence of the Akeda, Sacrifice of Isaac. The Tahanun contains the prayer: "We

[100] Tanhuma, Vayeze, 13.
[101] Sab. 55a.
[102] Jeru. Sanh. 10.1; Lev. R. 36.4–6.
[103] Tosafot Sabbat 55a.
[104] S. Schechter, *Aspects of Rabbinic Theology*, p. 179; see S. Baer, *Abodat Yisrael*, p. 88.
[105] Aggadat Bereshit 84.3; cf. Midr. Ps. 121.1; Targum Jonathan, Deut. 28.15.

beseech Thee, O gracious and merciful King, remember and give heed to the Covenant between the Pieces (with Abraham), and let the binding (upon the altar) of his only son appear before Thee to the welfare of Israel." While the sacrifice of Isaac is passed over without further reference in the rest of the Bible, it figures prominently in Rabbinic literature. The Mishnah utilizes the incident in the special invocation for fast days: "He who answered Abraham at Mt. Moriah, may He answer us."[106] That incident is counted as the tenth test to which Abraham was subjected, and whereby he demonstrated his unswerving devotion to God. The Mechilta, on the other hand, refers to the blood of Isaac. Commenting on Ex. 12.23, "And when He seeth the blood," the Mechilta states, "He seeth the blood of the sacrifice of Isaac."[107] This agrees with the view that the Akedah took place in Nisan.[108] R. Jose the Galilean says that because of the merit of the Akedah God divided the Red Sea for Israel.[109] According to the Targum of Canticles 1.3, the merit of the Akeda atoned for the sin of the Golden Calf.

The Akeda looms large in the thought of the Amoraim. Two reasons are offered for covering the head with ashes on fast days. The first is that God may recall the merit of Abraham who spoke of himself as dust and ashes (Gen. 18.27). The second is that God may remember the ashes of Isaac as if they were heaped upon the altar.[110] R. Abahu says that the reason for blowing a ram's horn on Rosh Hashanah is that God may recall the binding of Isaac to the credit of his descendants and account it to them as if they had offered themselves up to Him.[111] The Babylonian Gemara assigns the reading of Gen. 22 for the second day of Rosh Hashanah, thus definitely linking the holiday with the Akedah.[112] The Jerushalmi presents the following homily of R. Johanan: Abraham said before God: "Lord of the Universe! It is known and

[106] Taanit 2.4.

[107] Tractate Pisha, II; cf. Ber. 62b.

[108] Ex. R. 15.11.

[109] Mechilta, Beshalah, 1.4.

[110] Jeru. Taan. 2.1. So too Babylonian Gemara, Rosh Hashanah 16a: "that God may remember in our favor the ashes of Isaac and have mercy upon us."

[111] Pesikta R., 40.

[112] Megil. 31a.

revealed before Thee that when Thou didst command me to offer up my son
Isaac, I could have pleaded: 'Didst Thou not promise me only yesterday that
"in Isaac shall seed be called unto thee?" And today Thou biddest me offer
him for a burnt offering, God forbid!' I did not speak thus, but I restrained
my inclination and did Thy will. Even so may it please thee, O Lord my God,
that when the children of Israel will be in distress, with no one to plead their
cause, mayest Thou intercede in their behalf." The words "the Lord seeth"
(Gen. 22.14) are explained: "He remembers in their favor the sacrifice of
Isaac, and is filled with mercy for them." R. Judah b. Simon says that when,
in the course of time, the descendants of Isaac will be entangled in distress of
oppressive kingdoms, they will be redeemed "through the horns of this ram,
'And the Lord will blow upon the horn,' etc." (Zech. 9.14).[113] These ideas
form the theme of the Zichronot in the Musaf for Rosh Hashanah: "Remember unto us, O Lord our God, the *covenant* and the *lovingkindness* and the
oath which Thou swearest unto Abraham our father on Mt. Moriah, and may
the *binding* with which Abraham our father bound his son Isaac on the altar
appear before Thee . . . and the binding of Isaac mayest Thou remember this
day to his seed."

The later Haggadah expatiates upon the Akedah, and invests some inci-
dents in that event with messianic significance, reminiscent of the Gospel
story. Isaac's birth formed the occasion of universal rejoicing, in which
heaven and earth, sun, moon, planets and stars participated, for had Isaac not
been created the world would not have endured.[114] The great event of the
Akeda was entered into by Isaac as well as by Abraham with unflinching

---

[113] Jeru. Taan. 2.4; cf. Gen. R. 56.14.

[114] Cf. Jer. 33.25; Tanh. Toledot, 2; cf. Luke 2.13. Philo represented Isaac as "the direct
child of God through Sarah to whom virginity has been miraculously restored." E. Goodenough observes: "How far this allegory of Isaac as the son of God by a virgin was carried out
in the *De Isaaco* it is impossible to know, and that impossibility makes it also impossible to
judge how literally Philo believed that Isaac as the ancestor of the race was the miraculous son
of God. There is at least a possibility that Philo developed the idea in a way so closely parallel to
the Christian doctrine about the birth of Jesus that Christian copyists suppressed the text." *By
Light, Light,* pp. 154-55.

faith, despite the devices of Sammael.[115] When Ishmael had vaunted his superiority over him for having suffered himself to be circumcised at the age ¦of thirteen, when he felt the pain more than Isaac who was circumcised on the eighth day of his birth, Isaac replied: "Thou pridest thyself in that thou didst offer up one part of thy body. If God were to ask me to sacrifice my whole being unto Him, I would gladly do so."[116] "He carried the wood for the offering as one who carries his gallows upon his shoulder."[117] The spot where Isaac was sacrificed was the place where subsequently the Temple was built.[118] The ass which figured in the drama was the offspring of the ass which was created during the twilight preceding the first Sabbath of the week of creation. Upon it Moses rode when he came to Egypt (Ex. 4.20). It will be ridden upon by the Messiah (Zech. 9.9; cf. Matt. 21.7). The altar was the same one upon which Adam, Abel, Cain, and Noah sacrificed.[119] When the knife touched Isaac's neck, his soul departed, but when the command resounded: "Lay not thy hand upon the lad" (Gen. 22.12), his soul returned to the body, which is symbolic of a future quickening of the dead. The ram, which was to serve as the substitute for Isaac, like the ass, was created on the eve of the first Sabbath. Sammael again tried to upset the offering of Abraham, but did not succeed. The ram was a perfect substitute for Isaac. R. Berechiah said: The sweet savour of the ram ascended before God as though it were the sweet savour of Isaac.[120] According to Hanina b. Dosa, not a part of the ram went to waste. The ashes of the parts burnt upon the altar formed the base of the inner altar of the sanctuary whereon the expiatory sacrifice was brought on the Day of Atonement. Its sinews were used for the strings of the harp upon which David played. Its skin served Elijah for his girdle, its left horn was blown by God at the revelation on Sinai, its right horn — the larger — will be used at the future ingathering of Israel's dispersed, when, "it shall

[115] Gen. R. 56.4.
[116] Sanh. 89b.
[117] Gen. R. 56.3; cf. John 19.17.
[118] Targum Jeru. Gen. 22.14; Gen. R. 56.10.
[119] Targ. Jeru. Gen. 22.9.
[120] See Zohar, I, 120b.

be blown upon the great horn," etc. (Is. 27.13).[121] (This passage links the
Akedah with Yom Kippur. The connection was favored by the Kabbalists.)[122]
These Haggadahs seem to indicate that the ideas of the sacrifice of Isaac in the
light of an atonement for the sins of Israel aimed to overcome the claims of
Christianity. The merit of the sacrifice of Isaac rendered the need of the
justification through the death of Jesus superfluous.[123]

The Targum of Canticles 1.3 claims that the merit of the Akedah expiated
the sin of the Golden Calf. R. Simlai taught that Moses expiated that sin; of
him the prophet said, "He bore the sins of many" who shared in the worship
of the Calf, and atoned for them by his self-sacrifice.[124] According to Pirke de
Rabbi Eliezer 45, when, in consequence of the sin of the Golden Calf, God
sent the five destructive angels, Wrath, Anger, Temper, Destruction, and
Glow of Anger, to destroy Israel, Moses appealed to the Patriarchs at the cave
of Machpelah for help. Because of their merit, three of these angels were
restrained, but two still remained as a menace. Moses implored God to keep
back Destruction for the sake of the oath which He swore to the people. God
assented, as it is said: "But He, being full of compassion, forgiveth iniquity,
and *destroyeth not*" (Ps. 78.83). Moses persisted, pleading that God hold back
also the last one, Glow of Anger, for the sake of His great Name (cf. Ex.
32.12). What did Moses do? He dug in the earth, in the possession of Gad, a
large dwelling place and imprisoned Glow of Anger therein.[125] Every time
Israel sinned, the angel arose and opened his mouth to blow his breath upon
Israel to destroy it. Hence his name is called *Peor*, the opener. But Moses
pronounced God's Name and brought him down beneath the earth. When

---

[121] Pirke de Rabbi Eliezer 31 and notes by Gerald Friedlander; cf. Kasher, *Torah
Shelemah*, p. 904, number 159 and note.

[122] See L. Ginsberg, *Legends*, V, pp. 252–53, n. 248, and *Hazofeh* III, 186–188; It is
instructive that Judah Samuel Abbas's piyyut, *Et Shaare Razon Lehipateah*, on the theme of
the Akedah which is recited in the Sefardi ritual before the blowing of the Shofar on Rosh
Hashanah, is used in the Italian rite during Neilah. See *Kimha D'abishuna* in Mahzor Roma,
ad loc.

[123] Cf. Geiger, *op. cit.*, pp. 170–71.

[124] Sota 114a.

[125] Cf. Jubil. 48.15.

Moses died, God buried him opposite Peor, so that whenever Israel sins and Glow of Anger opens his mouth threateningly, he is confronted by the grave of Moses and withdraws.[126] Thus in death as in life Moses continues to secure atonement for the sin of the Calf. Furthermore, the death of all the righteous was believed to effect atonement. To the question: why is the section dealing with the death of the sons of Aaron (Lev. 16), which was supposed to have occurred on the first of Nisan, read on Yom Kippur? the reply is given: to teach you that the death of the righteous atones (like Yom Kippur). Similarly, the proximity of the account of Miriam's death to the section of the Red Heifer (Num. 19 and 20.1–6) is explained as intended to teach that as the ashes of the red heifer cleanse Israel from impurity, so the death of the righteous atones for Israel's sins.[127]

E. Ways of Justification

The striking divergence of the Jewish and Christian conceptions of Original Sin comes to a climax in their difference of method in overcoming its effects. In Romans 6.2–12, Paul limits the way of salvation to mystic union with Christ. As by his death on the cross, Christ broke all contact with sin, which is a heritage of the first Adam, so the Christian, united with him in baptism, parts once and for all with sin, and lives henceforth a reformed life dedicated to God. Through baptism, the Christian incorporates himself into and identifies himself with Christ. Baptism also expresses a series of acts corresponding to the redeeming acts of Christ. "Through baptism we have been buried with him in death, so that just as he was raised from death to the Father's glory, so, too, we may live a new life. For if we have grown into union with him by undergoing a death like his, of course we shall do so by being raised to life like

---

[126] Cf. Deut. 34.6 and Rashi *ad loc.*, also Targ. Jerushalmi; Tosafot Sota 14a.

[127] Jeru. Yoma 1.1; Lev. R. 20.12; Zohar, III, 56b. At first the Shechinah dwelt on earth (cf. 3.8). When Adam sinned it moved up to the first heaven, and did not come down until the day of the dedication of the Tabernacle, (Ex. 25.7; Gen. R. 19.7; Num. 12.6). It was named *Mishkan Haedut* to "testify" that God pardoned the sin of the Calf and that the Shechinah returned to dwell in Israel. Tanh., Pekude, 2, 6.

him, for we know that our old self was crucified with him, to do away with our sinful body, so that we might not be enslaved to sin any longer; for when a man is dead he is free from the claim of sin. If we have died with Christ, we believe that we shall also live with him." The death of Christ, the second Adam, wins for the Christian immunity from the consequences of the sin of the first Adam. We have here a complete application to Christianity of the basic idea of the mystery religions. The believer identifies himself with his god, dies with him, and resurrects with him. Though the process must be undergone in a moral and spiritual sense, this system has no room for the Law, which, according to Paul's dialectics, only makes for sin, or for any observances whatever (Rom. 7.7–10). The Law is superseded by grace.[128]

In contrast to this method, Judaism — despite its doctrine of imputed merit —places full responsibility for salvation from sin, and from its effects, upon the individual person, upon his freedom of will, and his good deeds. Pivotal in this viewpoint is the doctrine of repentance. Adam and Eve are treated as types of penitent sinners in both the Apocrypha and in Rabbinic literature.[129] Pirke de Rabbi Eliezer 20 presents Adam praying that his sin be removed so that all generations may learn to know that there is repentance and that God receives the penitent. Indeed, repentance is regarded as one of the seven things that were created before the world was called into being.[130] R. Hanina bar Hama extols repentance for bringing healing to the world. In the view of R. Levi, repentance reaches to the throne of Glory. R. Jonathan teaches that repentance hastens the redemption.[131] That even the greatest sinner need not despair of being received by God is stressed by the example of Manasseh. "The Holy One rejects no creature, but welcomes every one. The gates are open and whoever wishes may enter."[132] Repentance directs man to a life of righteousness and is associated with prayer and charity as means of salvation.

---

[128] Sanday, *op. cit.*, pp. 153 ff.

[129] Book of Adam and Eve 1; 9; 27; 32; Erub. 18b; Ab. Z. 8a; Ab. R. N. I.

[130] Pes. 54a; Ned. 39ab; Midr. Ps. 90.12.

[131] Yoma 86ab.

[132] Ex. R. 19.4.

Another means of overcoming the effects of the fall is circumcision, the sign of the covenant of the Jewish people and God. Akiba explains the reference to the "covenant" in Ex. 19.5 as the covenant of circumcision and the covenant against idolatry.[133] The reference to the flaming sword "which turneth everyway" (Gen. 3.24) was taken to be Gehenna, and was set up immediately after the expulsion of Adam and Eve from Eden. It turns upon a man and sets him ablaze from head to foot. What instrument may save him from its flames? R. Huna says: the sword of circumcision (cf. Josh. 5.2). The Rabbis maintain: the sword of Torah (cf. Ps. 149.6).[134] R. Eleazar b. Azariah points to the contempt in which the Bible holds the lack of circumcision. R. Ishmael adds: Great is circumcision, with reference to which the word "covenant" is repeated thirteen times (Gen. 17.2-21). R. Judah Hanasi says: Great is circumcision, for despite all the commandments which Abraham our father fulfilled, he was not called "perfect" until he was circumcised, as it is said "Walk before Me and be perfect" (Gen. 17.1). Another opinion is expressed that were it not for the covenant of circumcision, God would not have created the world.[135] Still another idea is cited that circumcision outweighs all the commandments of the Torah, also that the covenant of circumcision outweighs the whole Torah.[136] This is understandable in the light of Paul's statement in Galatians 5.3 that any man who lets himself be circumcised is under obligation to obey the whole Law. In opposition to his claim that "if you belong to Christ, then you are true descendants of Abraham, and his heirs under the promise" (Gal. 3.29), Judaism emphasized the demand of circumcision of both Jews and Proselytes.

In place of the Christian emphasis on baptism, Rabbinic Judaism stressed circumcision as a means of escaping damnation. R. Levi teaches that in the future world, Abraham will be seated at the door of Gehenna and keep out of it every circumcised Jew. What does He do with Jews unduly steeped in sin? He removes the foreskin from children that died before they were circumcised

[133] Mechilta, Bahodesh, 2.
[134] Gen. R. 21.9.
[135] Ned. 3.11; Mechilta, Amalek, 3.
[136] Ned. 32a; Midr. Haggadol to Gen. 26.5.

and places them upon the sinners and causes them to go down to Gehenna.[137] Pirke de Rabbi Eliezer 29 states that Abraham was circumcised on Yom Kippur. Every year, God looks upon the blood of Abraham's circumcision and pardons the sins of his descendants. On the spot on which the blood of his circumcision fell the altar of the Temple was built whereon the blood of the sacrifices was poured out (cf. Lev. 4.2). By virtue of their circumcision, the prayers of the Jews reach God. R. Eleazar explains the repetition of the word *"bedamayich"* in Ezek. 16.6 as signifying that because of the merit of the blood of circumcision and of the blood of the paschal lamb, God redeemed Israel from Egypt and will redeem them again at the end of the fourth kingdom.

The idea of the saving power of circumcision is voiced by the prayer which the Mohel recites after the operation: "Praised be Thou . . . who didst sanctify the beloved one [Isaac] from the womb [i.e., who was sanctified for this command before birth; cf. Gen. 17.19], and didst set a statute in his flesh, and didst seal his offspring with the sign of the holy covenant [Jacob, who was believed to have been born circumcised]. Therefore, because of this, O living God, our Portion, ordain the deliverance from the pit, of our beloved one of our flesh, for the sake of the covenant which Thou hast set in our flesh."[138]

That the Torah saves from Gehenna is the universal belief of the Rabbis. According to the Midrash, when Adam recognized that his descendants would perish in Gehenna, he abstained from procreation, but on learning that after twenty-six generations Israel would receive the Torah, he lived with his wife and raised offspring.[139] The Torah is the instrument wherewith God created the world. Were it not for the Torah, the world could not abide.[140] It is one of the three pillars upon which the Jewish world rests.

The glorification of the Torah by the Rabbis appears to stem from their desire to overcome the antinomism of the Church (cf. Rom. 8.3–4; Gal. 5.2

---

[137] Gen. R. 48.8; cf. Erub. 19a; Tanh., Lech Lecha, 20.

[138] Tosefta Ber. 7.17; Sab. 137b and Rashi. The Tosafot *ad loc.* and in Menahot 53b cites Rabbenu Tam's view that this prayer contains references to all three Patriarchs. See S. Baer, *Abodat Yisrael*, p. 582; B. Lewin, *Ozar Hageonim*, Sabbat, pp. 135–36.

[139] Gen. R. 21.9.

[140] Gen. R. 1.1; Sab. 88a.

ff.; Heb. 8). The Torah is an everlasting possession. The words of Deut. 33.4, "Moses commanded unto us the Torah, an inheritance of the congregation of Jacob," are explained in the Sifre as "a heritage for ever." The word *morasha*, heritage, is read *meorasa*, betrothed, suggesting that the Torah is pledged to Israel for all time.[141] The scene at Sinai is pictured as a marriage ceremony. "God received Israel as a bridegroom come forth to meet the bride."[142] A late Midrash adds: "and the Torah formed the *ketubah*, the marriage deed."[143] The entire suggestion that heard God's voice at Sinai merited to be like ministering angels.[144]

We noted the saying of R. Johanan that the Torah removed from Israel the pollution of the serpent. The Midrash Haggadol to Gen. 3.24 (also Targ. Jeru. ad loc.) states that the Tree of Life which stood in the Garden of Eden was hidden by God, and was replaced for Israel by the Torah, which is a tree of life. By studying it, by perceiving the wisdom of God and His righteous ordinances and laws, by taking them to heart and by practising them, one acquires life both in this world and the next. With reference to Prov. 2.1, the Midrash observes: The Holy One said to Israel at Mt. Sinai: "If you will show yourselves worthy of receiving and treasuring My Torah and observing it, I shall save you from three visitations, from the wars of Gog and Magog, from the tribulations which will precede the advent of the Messiah, and from the judgment of Gehenna. (Mechilta, Vayasa, 5 names these as the reward of observing the Sabbath.) And if you will treasure the words of the Torah, I shall satisfy you of the good that I have stored up for the future." God further promised: "If you engage in the words of Torah, they will save you from the way of evil, for they are like a double-edged sword." R. Nehemiah takes the words "double-edged sword" to mean that it bestows life in this world and in the next.[145]

The Midrash inquires regarding the significance of the use of the words

---

[141] Sifre, Deut., 345; Ex. R. 33.7; cf. Rom. 7.2-4.

[142] Mechilta, Bahodesh, 3.

[143] Al-Nakawa, Menorat Hamaor, III, p. 347 and note by H. G. Enelow.

[144] Pirke de Rabbi Eliezer 41.

[145] Midr. Mishle 2.1; 12; Pesikta R. Kahana, Bahodesh Hashlishi, 37.

ishim and *bene adam* in Prov. 8.4. ("Unto you, O men, *ishim*, I call, and my voice is to the sons of men, *bene adam*.") R. Simeon b. Halafta offers the following explanation: If you keep yourselves meritorious and observe the Torah, you will be called *ishim* like Abraham, Isaac, and Jacob, who fulfilled the Torah; but if you do not, you will be called sons of Adam, who did not keep the Torah and was expelled from Eden. Another explanation is that through keeping the Torah Israel will be *ishim* or angels, but if not, they will be foolish men.[146] An older Midrash puts it this way: If they engage in Torah, they are like angels, but if not, they are like beasts and animals that do not know their owner.[147]

Deut. 5.26 evoked the comment that God said: If it were possible to do away with the Angel of Death, I would do so, but the decree was issued long ago. R. Jose remarked: It was upon this condition that the Israelites stood at Sinai, viz., that the Angel of Death should have no dominion over them; but they corrupted their ways and became mortal.[148] However, if the Torah cannot prevent physical death, it helps men overcome spiritual death. "The Torah is the antidote to the Yezer Hara. He who takes the words of the Torah to heart is freed from many evil thoughts, from the thoughts of hunger, of folly, of fornication, of the Yezer Hara, etc. When Israel engages in Torah and works of lovingkindness, their Yezer is within their power and they are not within the power of the Yezer."[149] Israel is told: "Your accepting the Torah is accounted to you as if you had never sinned."[150] The prayer "Let my heart be undivided in Thy statutes" (Ps. 119.80) is interpreted to mean that David asked God that, when he engages in the Torah, the evil Yezer may not be permitted to look into his heart and mislead him."[151]

A word must be added about the Day of Atonement. Not only were the circumcision of Abraham and the sacrifice of Isaac associated with it, but attempts were made to link the Torah with Yom Kippur, thus investing the

---

[146] Midr. Mishle 8.1.
[147] Sifre, Numbers, 119.
[148] Mechilta, Bahodesh, 9.
[149] Kid. 30b; A. R. N., I, 20; Seder Elijah Zutta, 1.
[150] Jeru. Rosh Hashanah 4.8.
[151] Ex. R., 19.2; Midr. Ps. *ad loc.*

day with the greatest possible efficacy. Pirke de Rabbi Eliezer 46 informs us that Moses ascended to heaven for the second time on Rosh Hodesh Elul. He spent forty days on the mount, and descended, carrying the second tables of the Law, on the tenth of Tishri. The people immediately learnt that it was Yom Kippur. The shofar was sounded, and the fast was proclaimed throughout the camp. "Were it not for the Day of Atonement, the world could not stand, for it effects reconciliation in this world and in the world to come, as it is said, 'It is a Sabbath of Sabbaths unto you' (Lev. 16.31) 'a Sabbath' refers to this world, 'Sabbaths' to the world to come. Moreover, when all other festivals shall pass away, the Day of Atonement will remain, for its effects reconciliations for weighty as well as for light offenses."[152]

Sammael pleaded with God to give him dominion over Israel as well as over all other nations. God yielded to his entreaty, and said: "Behold, thou hast power over them on the Day of Atonement if they have any sin, but if not thou shalt have no power over them." For this reason he is bribed on Yom Kippur (i. e., by the sacrifice to Azazel) in order that he may not interfere with Israel's atoning sacrifice to God.[153] Sammael was outwitted, and admitted that Israel is as pure from sin as the ministering angels in heaven. On Yom Kippur, God hears the petitions of Israel rather than the charges of the Accuser, and makes atonement for the altar, the sanctuary, the priests, and the people, both great and small.

On Yom Kippur, Moses sought to behold the Glory of God. The angels were jealous of him and sought to slay him, but God Himself protected him with the hollow of His hand (Ex. 33.22). As God passed by, Moses beheld the back of the Shechinah and exclaimed: "O Lord, O Lord, full of compassion!" (Ex. 34.6), and pleaded for the pardon of the iniquities of the people, incidental to the worship of the Golden Calf. Had he asked for the pardon of all the sins of Israel to the end of all generations, God would have granted his

---

[152] Jeru. Megil. 1.7, expressing the idea that all festivals will be abolished in Messianic times, except Purim.

[153] Midr. Abchir, cited in Yalkut Shimeoni, Gen. 44; Jellinek suggests that the practice of reading Lev. 18 in the Minhah service of Yom Kippur was intended to break the power of Azael or Azazel over the people, for he entices them to sexual immorality. See A. Kohut, *Aruch Hashalem*, art. "Aza," VI, p. 182.

plea, for it was a time of good favor (cf. Is. 49.8). God assented and said: "I have pardoned according to Thy word" (Num. 14.20).

In contradistinction to the doctrine of atonement in the early Church as the means of overcoming the effects of the fall and of original sin. R. Akiba taught: "Happy are ye, O Israel! Before whom do you purify yourselves and who purifies you? [No mediator, but] your Father in heaven, as the prophet states: 'And I will sprinkle clear water upon you, and ye shall be clean' (Ezek. 36.25). Similarly, [God is referred to as] *Mikveh* (literally, hope, but by a word play here construed as a ritual bath) of Israel (Jer. 14.8). As the ritual bath purifies the unclean, so the Holy One, blessed be He, cleanses Israel."[154] Though God's grace abounds, man must work out his own salvation. R. Isaac comments on the word *vaasitem* ("and ye shall make a burnt offering") in Numbers 29.2, that "God said to Israel: *Asu teshubah,* repent during these ten days of penitence between Rosh Hashanah and Yom Kippur, and I shall purify you on Yom Kippur and recreate you as a new creature."[155]

5. A Modern Appraisal

What significance may be attached by moderns to these searching efforts to penetrate the mystery of the persistence and diffusion of moral evil? The scientific study of the Bible excludes the acceptance of the Paradise story as "in some sense a veil of man's spiritual history," except in a homiletical way. Instead of being a divinely inspired answer to the eternal riddle, it forms an attempt on the part of an ancient thinker in Israel to deal with the troublesome facts of pain and death from the standpoint of the early religion of Yahvism, much on the order in which thinkers in Babylonia, Persia, Greece, and even among primitive peoples dealt with them in the light of their respective religions. It differs from them chiefly in the deeper moral consciousness with which it views life. Possibly not without justice it was taken to reflect a phase of man's moral and spiritual experience. By virtue of his endowment of

---

[154] Yoma 8.9.
[155] Pesikta R., ed. Friedmann, p. 160a and notes.

reason, which distinguished him from the animals around him, man was free to choose between good and evil. His freedom created a spiritual conflict within him. Temptation, which ever trails freedom, lured him on. Yielding to it, he involved himself in sin by disobeying God, thus bringing on himself the penalty of mortality. However, he did not forfeit his original gifts of reason and of freedom. Ever confronted by choices between obeying and disobeying the divine behest, he may range himself on the side of God or rebel against Him. Sin represents man's rebellion against his Creator, the disregard of His will, of right, and of holiness; it represents the pursuit of base pleasures. In consequence, conscience was awakened within him, and he began to hear the voice of God within his soul condemning his actions and filling him with shame and with guilt.

Does this story warrant the belief in the propagation of sin as an inheritance of the race, from Adam, or in the total corruption of man's physical and spiritual nature? Our investigation shows that the conclusions drawn from it by both Christianity and Judaism are without foundation. Tennant writes: "It is most doubtful whether the idea of original or inherited sin occurs in Holy Scriptures and that St. Paul made use of the conception of the imputation of Adam's sin, or of the solidarity of the race, in some undefined way, in the Fall of our first parent is ... no reason why the Church to-day should take the somewhat incidental utterances on the subject as the basis of its doctrine of human nature. The fictitious importance assigned by theology, in its most scholastic and artificial periods, to the doctrines of the Fall and Original Sin, is an accident of history, not the outcome of the necessary development of the Faith."[156]

Rabbinic Judaism, too, bound as it was to the text of Genesis, did not always recognize the naturalness of death and of physical suffering, and regarded them as penalties imposed upon mankind on account of Adam's transgression. However, its moral realism kept it from the quagmires into which Pauline Christianity fell. For all the artificiality of their methods of Biblical interpretation and for all the tenuousness of their ideas regarding imputed guilt and merit, the Rabbis bravely championed the dignity of human

---

[156] *The Origin and Propagation of Sin*, p. 150.

nature and consistently upheld the justice of God. While dwelling upon the striking changes that came upon Adam in consequence of his disobedience, they avoid the thought that he lost his divine image and his mental capacities or that he forfeited his freedom of choice between good and evil. Even the more mystic among them, who admit that "the pollution of the serpent" infected humanity, refuse to consider human nature as hopelessly corrupted. The "broken channels" of divine grace can be repaired by repentance, good works, and Torah. Spiritually every person enjoys complete autonomy. Against the despairing view of human nature as vitiated and depraved, Judaism consistently pointed to the divine capacities and endowments of man. Rejecting also the Greek idea of the corruption of matter, it taught that not only the soul but the body as well is God's handiwork. *Haneshama lach vehaguf paalach.* The capacity for goodness inheres in man as the bearer of the divine likeness.

The universality of moral evil, which fills the world with grief deserves from no mythical fall of a mythical father of the race in a mythical Paradise, but rather from man's slow advance in the scale of humanity. His appetites and impulses, which he carries within him as a member of the biological kingdom, have not yet been sufficiently mastered and subjected to religious and ethical purposes. However, it is gratuitous to call his heritage of instincts and passions a heritage of sin. It is a normal and necessary part of human nature, without which life could not go on. With the Rabbis we may speak of the Yezer as a neutral endowment, which we ourselves turn into good or into evil. Our instinctual responses and cravings become evil when they are permitted to run wild and to grow into lusts for pleasure, for glory or for power in disregard of reason and of social well-being. No inherited and ineradicable taint keeps the soul from virtue. Man never was vitiated to the point of losing his divine likeness or his ability to partake of God's grace. Sin springs from the mind and the will of man, from his weakness and ignorance. Salvation comes to him not through the mythical death of a divine savior on a cross or though magical rites and sacraments, whether they be baptism or circumcision, but through the resolute direction of the heart and mind away from darkness toward the light of God, through heeding the divine imperatives of personal and social duty, of goodness and of truth.

Palestine in Jewish Theology
Until the Year 70*

The felicitous combination of *God, the Torah, and Israel*[1] into the indissoluble unity that constitutes Judaism, appears also with the significant addition of *the Land of Israel*.[2] Indeed so close has been the kinship between Palestine and Israel, and of such far-reaching nature has this relationship been in the development of the Torah and of the idea of God, that it is impossible to trace the growth of any one of these foundations of Judaism without reference to the others. Palestine not only formed the background for the unfoldment of Israel's religious life, but has to a great extent determined both its lines of progress and its character. The physical atmosphere of Palestine formed the nursery of Israel's rich spiritual idealism. Nor has Palestine remained a mere museum of Jewish antiquities. Despite two thousand years of Jewish dispersion throughout the world, it has retained a powerful hold upon Jewish custom, law, and ritual. The land of ancient memories has been enshrined in Jewish hearts as the land of future promise. Linked with the Messiah idea and with the belief in the Resurrection, Palestine was transferred from the realm

* Published: HUC Jubilee Volume, Cincinnati 1925; in Spanish translation by Rebecca Trabb, *Davar* No. 18–20, December 1948, Argentina.

[1] Zohar, Leviticus 73a; ג׳ דרגין אינן מתקשרין דא בדא קב״ה אורייתא וישראל; and Israel Besht's Kether Shem Tob, pt. II. p. 2a: קב״ה ואורייתא וישראל כולא חד.

[2] Mostly in Modern Hebrew literature: קב״ה ואורייתא וישראל וארעא דישראל. This combination is not unknown in older Rabbinic literature. Thus Midrash Zutta, Shir Hashirim (ed. Buber) p. 8, reads: נקרא הקב״ה (בשבעים שמות) ובחר בישראל שנקראו בשבעים שמות ונתן להם את התורה שנקראת שבעים שמות והוא עתיד לנחם בירושלים שנקראת שבעים שמות.

of geography to that of faith. Not even the Reformation of Judaism has wholly separated the religion of the Jew from its native soil. The breath of the ancient Bible land inspirits many an institution and practice cherished by Reform Judaism. The Zionist movement has placed Palestine on the agenda of modern Jewish endeavor. The relation of Palestine to Judaism, therefore, assumes practical significance for Jews of every phase of religious belief.

The extent to which Palestine affected Judaism and its institutions, down to the Fall of the Jewish state and Temple, in 70 C.E. is the subject of the first part of the present study.

I

We must note at the outset that the union between Judaism and Palestine is historical rather than organic. It had not yet made its appearance in the days of Moses. Not alone tradition but also scientific investigation traces the origin of the Torah to No-man's land, to the desert. At Sinai (=Horeb), Israel entered into a covenant with Jahweh, and began to follow His ways and ordinances. Evidence tends to show that Jahweh was associated with that region. The Blessing of Moses speaks of His coming from Sinai.[3] The even more ancient ode of Deborah likewise describes His advent from Sinai, by way of Mt. Seir, to the aid of His people.[4] The Elijah stories also show that Horeb was considered "the Mountain of God."[5] This is unquestionably the belief of the narratives of the Exodus. At the Mount of God, at Horeb, Jahweh revealed Himself to Moses in the thorn-bush.[6] Thither too the newly freed slaves pilgrimed to receive the words of Jahweh.[7] The whole framework of Deuteronomy rests on this tradition. The same view faces us in the Psalms.[8]

While residing at Sinai, Jahweh moved before the Israelites not only on

---

[3] Deut. XXXIII: 1ff. cf. Habakkuk III: 3; Psalm LXVIII: 8 ff.

[4] Judges V:4–5.

[5] I. Kings XIX.

[6] Ex. III.

[7] Ex. XIX-XX; XXXIII: 17-XXXIV.

[8] Ps. LXVIII: 8–9. On the other hand Psalm XVIII and II. Samuel XXII regard the heavens rather than Sinai (=Horeb) as Jahweh's dwelling place.

their desert wanderings, but also into their new home. Whether in a pillar of cloud by day and a pillar of fire by night, or through His deputized angel, he led them on their perilous journey.[9] The Ark and the Tent of Meeting constituted His portable abode.[10] He received the ministrations of Israel's priests, and in turn protected the Israelites and gave them food and shelter. Their wars were also His wars — *milḥamoth Jahweh*.[11] He helped them to defeat the Amalekites.[12] He led them in their conquest of Palestine. In thunder and lightning He fought their battles and insured their victory.

It was in Palestine that the religion of Israel flowered forth in its variegated colors. There, too, a problem of foremost significance presented itself to the people: the problem of the relation of Jahweh to their newly acquired land. Children of their time, they shared the beliefs of their neighbors that even as nations, so their gods enjoy proprietory rights upon certain lands. Accordingly Palestine appeared to them not only as the land of the Canaanites but also of the Baalim. Whereas the Canaanites could be dispossessed, the Baalim belonged to the soil. As its *possessors*, they claimed the homage of its inhabitants. The situation was aggravated by the transfer of the Israelites from a nomadic to an agricultural economy. As part of their adjustment to the new conditions of settled life, they were compelled to learn from the old settlers the art of plowing, sowing, and harvesting, of tending orchards and vineyards. These were connected in the minds of the Canaanites, with the Baalim who, through union with the soil, produced all vegetation. They fertilized the land; they made the trees to grow and to yield fruit; they replenished the wells and the streams with water; they too sent down rain and dew from heaven. To secure their good will, proper rites had to be performed in their honor.[13] The very process of cultivation of the soil led the Israelites to worship the gods of the soil, to offer sacrifices to them, and to celebrate their harvest festivals.[14]

[9] Ex. XXIII: 21–33.
[10] Ex. XXIII: 7–11; Numbers X:33–36.
[11] Jud. V: 23; Num. XXI: 14.
[12] Ex. XVIII: 8–16.
[13] Cf. Hosea II.
[14] K. Budde, *Religion of Israel*, pp. 57–58.

Such worship did not involve a falling away from Jahweh. He was their covenant God who fought their battles and helped them gain a footing in the land. To Him they continued to turn for help in times of stress.[15] However in the land itself not He but the Baalim were the masters.[16] While the Baalim received homage, Jahweh was not wholly overlooked. Asyncretism followed. Both Jahweh and the Baalim were worshiped side by side. In the case of the city of Shechem where the population was mixed, a covenant god presided over the Canaanite and Israelite elements. It seems that while the former called him *Ba'al*-B'rith, the later knew him as *El*-B'rith.[17] The fusion of the two forms of religion is evidenced in the instance of Gideon. Though a strong champion of Jahweh, he is named *Jerubaal*. Saul, too, calls one of his sons *Ish-Baal*; and even David names one of his *Baaljada*.

As the God of the victorious people, Jahweh steadily extended His sway over the land. The desert deity was gradually transformed into the God of the land flowing with milk and honey. He banished the Baalim and established Himself in their place.[18] In fact He Himself became a sort of Baal. The use of the Canaanite dialect —שפת כנען[19] — by the Israelites facilitated their investing of Jahweh with the attributes of the Baalim.[20] The high places where they had formerly been worshiped, were consecrated to Him. Gibea, Rama, Mizpah, Penuel, Gilgal, Bethel, Beersheba, etc., became centres of Jahwism. Traditions arose connecting some of them with the Patriarchs.[21] Despite their transfer to another deity, these places retained their old cults. The agricultural character of their worship — as evidenced by the Code of the Covenant

[15] Judges VI.

[16] The people are so deeply attached to the Baalim that they clamor for the execution of Gideon for destroying the altar of Baal and cutting down the Ashera. Judges VI: 25-32.

[17] Judges IX: 4, 46.

[18] Budde, *Op. cit.* p. 106.

[19] Is. XIX: 18.

[20] Unsuccessful attempts were made to take over for Him, the name of Baal. Hosea II: 18.

[21] Gen. XII, XVIII, XXIII, XXVIII, XXXII: 25-33; XXXIII: 18-20; XXXV: 13 ff; XLVI: 1-3; etc. Cf. also Judges XVII-XVIII; Judg. I: 21; XIX: 11-12; II. Sam. V: 6-9; XXIV, etc. V. also Baudissen, *Studien zur Semitischen Religionsgeschichte,* on Heilige Gewässer, Bäume und Höhen, vol. II, pp. 145-269.

— remained unaltered. The Pesaḥ or the Spring festival which the Israelites celebrated in honor of Jahweh in their nomadic days, was now attached to the Ḥag ha-Mazzoth, the festival of the farmers. The festivals of First Fruits — Ḥag ha-Bikkurim — and of Ingathering or Autumn Harvest — Ḥag he-Osif — now formed part of Jahweh worship.[22] References are found also to festivals of sheep-shearing, vintage,[23] etc. These celebrations were marked by singing, dancing and merry-making at the sanctuaries. Though held in the honor of Jahweh, they retained much of the orgiastic nature of Baal worship.[24]

The adaptation of Jahweh and His cult to Baal levels was particularly marked in the North where agriculture stood on a higher plane than in Judah, and where Baalism was consequently more strongly entrenched; — hence the worship of Jahweh under the presentation of calves — symbols of Baal[25] — at Beth El and at Dan, following the disruption of the Monarchy.[26] Mazzebas, or pillars, representing abodes of the spirits, were reconsecrated to Jahweh.[27] Canaan's elaborate cult of divination was associated in the popular mind with Jahweh. Sacred trees appear to have been used for oracular purposes. Jahweh's voice was heard from the tree tops.[28]

By the time of the establishment of the Monarchy, Jahweh was so completely naturalized in Canaan, that David curses his slanderers because they had driven him out of "the inheritance of Jahweh" and compelled him, as a resident of foreign lands, to serve other gods.[29] As the Lord of the land, He could be rightly worshiped only within its precincts. Its soil became sacred property. A few centuries later, Na'aman the Syrian asks for a few mule-loads of Canaanitish earth which he desires to take to Damascus that he may be

[22] Ex. XXIII: 13 ff.; XXXIV; Dt. XVI; Lev. XXIII; Num. XXVIII.

[23] Judg. IX; 27 ff. (at Shechem); XXI: 19ff. (at Shilo, cf. also I. Sam. I-II: 13–17 and IX: 19–24); Judg. XI: 40ff. (at Gilead; cf. the weeping for Tammuz = Adonis).

[24] Cf. Isaiah XXVIII: 1, 7–8.

[25] Benzinger, *Die Bücher der Könige*, p. 90.

[26] I. Kings II: 27–33.

[27] Gen. XXVIII: 18, etc.

[28] Judg. IX: 37; II. Sam: V:24.

[29] I. Sam. XXVI: 19 cf. Gen. IV: 14, 16.

able to worship Jahweh there, and Elisha the champion of Jahwism of his day, grants the request.[30] As late as the fall of Samaria these beliefs held firm ground. The colonists that were transplanted by the Assyrians into Samaria "feared not Jahweh; therefore Jahweh sent lions among them, which killed some of them. Wherefore they spoke to the king of Assyria, saying: 'The nations which thou hast carried away, and placed in the cities of Samaria, know not the manner of the God of the land; therefore He hath sent lions among them, and behold they slay them because they know not *the manner of the God of the land.*' Then the king of Assyria commanded, saying: 'Carry thither one of the priests whom ye brought from thence; and let them [him] go and dwell there, and let him teach them *the manner of the God of the land.*' So one of the priests whom they had carried away from Samaria came and dwelt in Beth-el, and taught them how they should fear Jahweh."[31] As with the Israelites at the time of the conquest, so with the Assyrian colonists, the adoption of the local deity did not necessitate the abandonment of their own deities. "They feared Jahweh, and served their own gods, after the manner of the nations from among whom they had been carried away.[32]

As the Baalim, so Jahweh came to be identified with particular shrines. Beth-el, Shechem, Shiloh, Gibeon — each claimed that Jahweh placed His name within it.[33] It was Jahweh's connection with Jerusalem that was destined to exert the greatest influence on the religion of Israel. After conquering this Jebusite stronghold and turning it into the capital of the newly consolidated empire, David placed within it the Ark of the Covenant, which served as the Palladium of Jahweh.[34] Following the dire consequences of his census, David saw the destroying angel about to smite the city, when he was halted by Jahweh at the threshing floor of Arauna the Jebusite. On the spot where Jahweh revealed Himself so effectively as to stop the pestilence, David built an altar and offered a sacrifice. On it Solomon later erected the magnificent sanc-

---

[30] II. Kings V: 17.

[31] II. Kings XVII: 25ff.

[32] Ibid v. 33.

[33] Jer. VII: 12; C. O. Whitehouse, art. Hebrew Religion, in *Encycl. Brit.* 11th Ed. XIII; p. 180.

[34] II. Sam. VI; I. Chr. XIII; XV: 3, 12 ff, XVI: 1 ff, XVIII; XXI-XXII; cf. Ps. CXXXII.

tuary which permanently housed the Ark of Jahweh[35] and which served henceforth as the token of His presence.[36] "It was virgin soil. Only the plough and the threshingsled had reigned over it; no worship had been instituted there till Jahweh chose it for Himself as a place to reveal Himself and to dwell in. The legends of the Patriarchs could not compete with such attestation, and the course of events contributed its share to establish ever more firmly the preeminence of Jerusalem, until at last this single sanctuary remained the sole survivor, and became the centre of the religious world.

"With the dedication of the temple-site at Jerusalem Jahweh had taken final possession of Canaan and removed His residence thither. That was the close of this stage of development; but it was not fully recognized and preached until much later, in the time of Deuteronomy."[37]

As the seat of Jahweh's Ark and as the royal sanctuary, the new Temple gained preeminence over all other places of worship in Palestine. In a sense, it at once became the national sanctuary.[38] Thither people from all parts of the land pilgrimed to celebrate the autumn feast and possibly also the Passover. Nevertheless the new Temple could not check the progress of the local cults. Indeed, as the books of Kings and the sermons of the Prophets testify, Canaanitic rites invaded the Temple itself. Its entire worship, its festivals, and its sacrifices were Canaanitic. Not even Hezekiah's and Josiah's religious reformations totally eradicated its Canaanitic elements. In refined form they permanently entered into the higher religion of Israel.

II

It was only the original austerity of Jahweh that prevented His sinking into the swamps of Palestinian Baalism. To His champions He ever stood out distinct from all other gods, "glorious in holiness, fearful in praises, doing

---

[35] II. Sam. XXIV; I. Chr. XXI.

[36] II. Sam. XV: 25.

[37] Budde, op. cit. pp. 110–111.

[38] Cf. I. Kings XII: 27 ff. v. W. B. Smith: Prophets of Israel, pp. 437 ff. cf. Ps. XX.

wonders."[39] In the voluptuousness of the local cults (of the Kedeshim and Kedeshoth, etc.) as in the offering of human sacrifices, they beheld the degradation of Jahweh. The stories of Noah's cursing Canaan,[40] of the destruction of Sodom and Gomorrah,[41] and of the concubine of Gibeah,[42] as of the sacrifice of Isaac,[43] show the revolt of the leaders of Jahwism against "the excrescences of the overcivilization" of Canaan and its cults.[44]

This revolt found expression in Jonadab b. Rechab's cry: "Back to the desert."[45] Following the awakened enthusiasm for Baalism — due to Jezebel — he despaired of ever seeing Jahwism retain its true character in Canaan. He therefore established an order, and charged its men: "Ye shall drink no wine, neither ye nor your sons forever; neither shall ye build houses nor sow seed, nor plant vineyards, nor have any; but all your days ye shall dwell in tents, that ye may live many days in the land wherein ye sojourn."[46] The very atmosphere of agricultural life in Canaan appeared to the Rechabites as polluting. Jahweh the God of the desert could be worshiped aright only in the desert. As late as the time of the Babylonian Exile, they continued to lead a nomadic existence.[47] Their idealization of the desert period as the golden days of Israel's loyalty to Jahweh found its way into the words of Hosea[48] and of Jeremiah.[49] Their abstinence from wine may have survived in the Nazaritic order.[50]

---

[39] Ex. XV: 11.

[40] Gen. IX: 20–27.

[41] Gen. XVIII–XIX.

[42] Judg. XIX–XX.

[43] Gen. XXII.

[44] v. Budde, *op. cit.* p. 71.

[45] II. Kings X: 15.

[46] Jer. XXXV: 6–7.

[47] Ibid v. 11. According to Hegesippus, as quoted by Eusebius, the Rechabites existed in the first Christian century. Hist. Eccle. II. 23, 17. See *Encycl. Biblica* Col. 4020. Ta'an IV: 5 states that the appointed time for the service of the Rechabites in the Temple was the 7th of Ab. See *Jew. Encycl.* X: 341.

[48] Hosea II: 16; XII: 10.

[49] Jer. II: 1 ff.

[50] Amos II: 11–12; Num. VI.

More constructive was the attitude taken by the great prophetic reformer Elijah. The legends that cluster about him present the same idea of flight from the country of the Baalim. In despair, the prophet turns unto "the mountain of God, unto Horeb" for renewed courage.[51] But he does not remain there. The scene of his activities is Canaan. There he champions the nobler conception of religion. He not only refutes the belief that Baal controls either the fertility of the soil or the element of fire, but also denies the very reality of Baal.[52] His whole career is one long struggle to convince Israel that Jahweh alone is God, that He alone can send rain and fire, and that He demands absolute loyalty and justice, of His people.[53] It is significant that Elijah selects as his successor the prosperous farmer Elisha. The antithesis between agriculture and Jahwism, which drove the Rechabites back to the desert, completely disappeared in the teaching of Elijah and of his followers. While adjusting Jahwism to Canaan, prophetism succeeded in safeguarding the pure character of Jahwism.

This prophetic attitude to Palestine is reflected in the early Pentateuchal narratives, in the sermons of the prophets and in the Deuteronomic code. That Jahweh specially singled out Palestine for His people Israel stands out as their basic belief. In His covenants with Abraham,[54] with Isaac,[55] and with Jacob,[56] He swore to give the land to their children. As the Land of Promise, it formed the goal of Moses and of the Israelites whom he led out of bondage.[57]

"Thou in Thy love hast led the people that Thou hast redeemed;
Thou hast guided them in Thy strength to Thy holy habitation. . .
Thou bringest them in, and plantest them in the mountain of Thine inheritance,

---

[51] I. K. XIX.
[52] I. K. XVIII.
[53] I. K. XXI.
[54] Gen. XIII: 14–18; XV: 18–21; XVII: 8; XXVIII: 4.
[55] Gen. XXVI: 3.
[56] Gen. XXVIII: 13, 16–17; XXXV: 12–15; XLVIII: 4; L. 24; Ex. XXXII: 12; Ps. CV: 9 ff.
[57] Ex. III: 8, 17; VI: 8; XII: 25; XIII: 5; XXXIV: 11 ff.

> The place, O Jahweh, which Thou hast made for Thee to dwell in,
> The sanctuary, O Jahweh, which Thy hands have established."[58]

Though connecting Jahweh with Canaan, these narratives do not limit Him to Canaan. They speak of His call of Abraham at Haran[59] and of the help extended Abraham at the court of Pharaoh[60]; of His message to Jacob at Padan Aram[61] and of His protection of Joseph in Egypt.[62] There He manifested His power over the Egyptians and their gods, by delivering His people amid signs and wonders.[63]

Literary prophecy voices the same view. Amos, while rising to the religious height from which he beheld Jahweh as the cosmic God[64] who controls all nature, speaks of His revelation in Zion. Amos evidently thought of the Temple when he said: "Jahweh roareth out of Zion, and from Jerusalem He uttereth His voice."[65] Thither Jahweh led the Israelites and there He dispossessed the Amorites for their sake.[66] For them, any other land is *unclean*, possibly because it is not consecrated to Jahweh.[67] Hosea considers the union between Jahweh and Palestine so strong that the worship of any other deity within its borders constitutes rank harlotry and base ingratitude.[68] Not the Baalim but Jahweh is the master of the land. He alone produces her fertility. As for Amos, so for Hosea, the chief danger that threatens the Israelites through exile is their enforced estrangement from Jahweh:

> "They shall not dwell in Jahweh's land;
> But Ephraim shall return to Egypt,

---

[58] Ex. XV: 13, 17.

[59] Gen. XII: 1–4.

[60] Gen. XII: 17.

[61] Gen. XXXI: 1.

[62] Gen. XXXIX: 23.

[63] Ex. VI–XI.

[64] Am. IV: 6 ff, 13; V: 8; VII: 1–18; 15; VIII: 7–9; IX: 1 ff.

[65] Am. I: 2.

[66] Am. II: 9–10; IX: 7.

[67] Am. VII: 17; v. Marti's *Dodekapropheton*, p. 214.

[68] Hos. II: 7 ff.

And shall eat unclean food[69] in Assyria.

They shall not pour out wine offerings to Jahweh,

Neither shall they be pleasing unto Him;

Their sacrifices shall be unto them as the bread of mourners,

All that eat thereof shall be polluted;

For their bread shall be for their appetite,

It shall not come into the house of Jahweh.

What will ye do in the day of the appointed season,

And in the day of the feast of Jahweh?"[70]

Despite his universalism, Isaiah too, regarded Jahweh as linked with Palestine. His angel chorus singing the praise of the thrice Holy, indeed proclaims: "the whole earth is full of His glory" (more correctly: "the fullness of the whole earth is His glory").[71] But using his eyes of man, he beholds the majesty of Jahweh in the Temple of Jerusalem, and with his human tongue he speaks of the Temple as Jahweh's house, and of the rock on which it was built as the "Mount of the house of Jahweh."[72] Jerusalem was to him the religious centre not only of his own land,[73] but of the world. To it all nations will flow to be taught Jahweh's ways of righteousness and universal peace. "For out of Zion shall go forth instruction (Torah) and the word of Jahweh from Jerusalem."[74] Isaiah speaks of "Jahweh of Hosts who dwelleth on Mount Zion,"[75] of "the place of the name of Jahweh of Hosts, Mount Zion,"[76] and of "Jahweh who has a fire in Zion and a hearth in Jerusalem.[77] He looks to the day when

---

[69] Cf. Ezek. IV: 12. The later and more advanced idea is presented in Is. XIX: 19 ff.

[70] Hos. IX: 3-5; v. also III: 4, and Marti's *Dodekapropheton*, pp. 37-38, 70-71; G. A. Smith, *The Twelve Prophets* I. pp. 279-280; cf. M. Buttenwieser's *Prophets of Israel*, pp. 320-321.

[71] Isaiah VI: 3.

[72] Is. II: 2 (cf. Micah IV: 1) and XVIII: 7.

[73] Is. XXX: 29; XXXIII: 20 ff.

[74] Is. II: 3b, and Micah IV: 2b.

[75] Is. VIII: 18.

[76] Is. XVIII: 18.

[77] Is. XXXI: 9.

none "shall hurt nor destroy in all My holy mountain, for the earth shall be full of the knowledge of Jahweh as the waters cover the sea. And it shall come to pass in that day, that the root of Jesse, that standeth for an ensign of the peoples, unto him shall the nations seek; and his resting place shall be glorious."[78] In the ideal state of the future "he that is left in Zion, and he that remaineth in Jerusalem, shall be called holy, even every one that is written unto life in Jerusalem; when Judah shall have washed away the filth of the daughters of Zion, and shall have purged the blood of Jerusalem from the midst thereof, by the spirit of judgment, and by the spirit of destruction. And Jahweh will create over the whole habitation of Mt. Zion, and over her assemblies, a cloud and smoke by day, and the shining of a flaming fire by night; for over all the glory shall be a canopy. And there shall be a pavilion for a shadow in the day-time from the heat, and for a refuge and for a covert from storm and from rain."[79] The Psalm that is embodied in Isaiah XII interprets the spirit of the prophet in calling:

"Cry aloud and shout, thou inhabitant of Zion,
For great is the Holy One of Israel in the midst of thee."[80]

"To Isaiah the whole mountain land of Israel but especially the plateau of Zion is holy."[81]

Historical circumstances invested this belief with special significance. Sennacherib's invasion of Judah had cast the people into a state of panic. The fall of Jerusalem seemed imminent. Isaiah, who had frequently preached that evil threatened his people because of their disregard of the laws of Jahweh and of their being led astray by irresponsible leaders, now appeared with a message of hope: "Out of Jerusalem shall go forth a remnant, and out of Mount Zion they shall escape; the zeal of Jahweh of Hosts shall perform

[78] Is. XI: 9-10.

[79] Is. IV: 3-6.

[80] Is. XII: 6. Similar expressions appear in the Psalms, e. g. XX: 3; XLVI: 5-6, 8-12; XLVIII; LXXVI: 3; XCIX: 2; etc.

[81] W. R. Smith, *Prophets of Israel*, p. 438.

this."[82] Not for Israel's but for His own sake, will Jahweh deliver His city by crushing the Assyrians, who presumptuously vaunt their superiority over Jahweh.[83] The miraculous deliverance of Jerusalem was hailed as an undoubted confirmation of Isaiah's faith.[84] The city was rescued from the jaws of destruction, and not by human strength. What greater proof was required that "Jahweh of Hosts who dwelleth in Zion" protects His own house and city? Neither the righteousness of the people nor their wickedness affected the ultimate safety of Jerusalem, but the presence of Jahweh rendered it inviolable. "Isaiah, to be sure, left it to others to draw the dangerous inferences from his teaching. But *drawn*, they inevitably were."[85]

It is against these inferences that Micah of Moresheth raised his voice. He threatens the heads of the nation that abhor justice and "build up Zion with blood and Jerusalem with iniquity," also the priests and prophets that sell themselves to the highest bidder, and, in total ignorance of the moral character of Jahweh, confidently claim:

> " 'Is not Jahweh in the midst of us?
> No evil shall come upon us.'
> Therefore shall Zion for your sake be ploughed as a field,
> And Jerusalem shall become heaps,
> And the mountain of the House as the high places of a forest."[86]

Probably in response to Micah's stern message Hezekiah carried out his religious reforms, hoping thereby to render Zion worthy of Jahweh's pres-

---

[82] Is. XXXVII: 32.

[83] Budde writes: "It makes no difference if ever so many of the numerous prophecies in this strain are rejected as of later origin, the fact remains indisputable that Isaiah prophesied thus and no otherwise throughout the period of extreme necessity." *Op. cit.* p. 155. Cf. Is. X: 12, 28 ff; XIV: 24-27; 28-32; XVIII; XXIX: 1-6, 7 ff; XXX: 7 ff; XXXI: 4 ff; XXXVII: 27-29, 33-35. v. also W. R. Smith's *Prophets of Israel*, Lecture VIII. A different view is taken by M. Buttenwieser, *Op. cit.* pp. 283-285.

[84] Is. XXXIII.

[85] Budde: *Op. cit.* 159.

[86] Micah III: 12.

ence.[87] It may have been with the view of offsetting Michah's gloomy prediction, that the editor of his book appended to this prophecy of doom, the hopeful message which we meet in Isaiah.[88]

> "But in the end of days it shall come to pass,
> That the mountain of Jahweh's house shall be established as the top of the mountains,
> And it shall be exalted above the hills;
> And peoples shall flow unto it"[89] etc.

So firmly was this dogma of the inviolability of Zion established in the minds of the people that, a century later, Jeremiah ran the danger of being put to death for casting doubts upon it. He had warned the people that the Temple, which they regarded as Jahweh's personal residence, would not save them from Jahweh's offended wrath. "Will ye steal, murder, and commit adultery, and swear falsely, and offer unto Baal, and walk after other gods whom ye have not known; and come and stand before Me in this house whereupon My name is called, and say: 'We are delivered,' that ye may do all these abominations? Is this house whereupon My name is called, become a den of robbers in your eyes? Behold I, even I, have seen it, saith Jahweh. For ye go now unto My place which was in Shiloh, where I caused My name to dwell at the first, and see what I did to it for the wickedness of My people Israel."[90] Jeremiah's words sounded like the basest treason in the ears of the people. He escaped death at their hands only through the protection of Ahikam ben Shafan. Another prophet, Uriah ben Shemaiah, actually paid with his life for attacking the belief in the inviolability of Jerusalem.[91]

Nationalistic Judean philosophy accounted differently for the fall of Shiloh, and held out a brighter hope for the future of Jerusalem and the house

[87] Jer. XXVII: 18–19; II Kings XVIII: 4 ff.
[88] Is. II: 1–4.
[89] Micah IV: 1 ff.
[90] Jer. VII: 3 ff; cf. also Zephaniah I-III: 13.
[91] Jer. XXVI.

of David. Jahweh was provoked to anger by the disloyalty of His people, by their high places and graven images.

> "And He forsook the tabernacle of Shiloh,
> The tent which He made to dwell among men;
> And delivered His strength into captivity,
> And His glory into the adversary's hand. . .
> Then Jahweh awaked as one asleep,
> Like a mighty man recovering from wine.
> And He smote His adversaries backward;
> He put them a perpetual reproach.
> Moreover He abhorred the tent of Joseph,
> And chose not the tribe of Ephraim;
> But chose the tribe of Judah,
> The mount Zion which He loved.
> And He built His sanctuary like the heights,
> Like the earth which He founded for ever."[92]

To Micah, Uriah, and Jeremiah, the belief that Zion, as the residence of Jahweh, is indestructible irrespective of the low moral standards of its people, presented a serious stumbling block in the way of spiritual progress, for it removed all sense of moral responsibility. It was only the tragic fall of Jerusalem and the destruction of the sanctuary in 586 that effectively shook the people's complacency.

It must not be inferred that Jeremiah dissociated Jahweh from Jerusalem. He rather interpreted this relationship in the light of his loftier conception of Jahweh. In his teaching, all traces of monolatry vanish, and a complete ethical monotheism is proclaimed. For him Jahweh is "the true God, He is the living God, and the everlasting King. . . He hath made the earth by His power, He hath established the world by His wisdom, and hath stretched out the heavens by His understanding."[93] As the universal Creator, Jahweh transcends any

---

[92] Ps. LXXVIII: 60 ff.
[93] Jer. X: 10 ff. cf. Jer. V: 21 ff.

particular people or land. Thus, in his oracle against the nations, Jeremiah — unlike Amos I:2 — states:

> "Jahweh doth roar *from on high*,
> And uttereth His voice *from His holy habitation*."[94]

Nevertheless in a certain sense, Jahweh continues to be the portion of Jacob:

> "And Israel is the tribe of His inheritance."[95]

He is Israel's God and Israel is His people. He planted them in the land flowing with milk and honey, in fulfilment of his oath unto the Patriarchs.[96] Accordingly, Palestine was especially consecrated to Him. Its Temple is dedicated to His name.[97] Hence idolatry constitutes a defiling detestation.[98] To the exiled nation's cry: "Is not Jahweh in Zion? Is not her King in her?" Jahweh replies: "Why have they provoked Me with their graven images, and with strange vanities?"[99] He demands further: "What hath My beloved to do in My house, seeing she hath wrought lewdness with many?[100] Envisaging the impending doom of his people, the distressed prophet pleads:

> "Why shouldest Thou be as a man overcome,
> As a mighty man that cannot save?
> Yet thou, O Lord, art in the midst of us.
> And Thy name is called upon us;
> Leave us not."[101]

---

[94] Jer. XXV: 30.
[95] Jer. X: 16.
[96] Jer. XI: 4–5.
[97] Jer. VII: 10; XXIII: 11; XXXII: 34–35; XXXIV: 15.
[98] Jer. VII: 30; II: 7.
[99] Jer. VIII: 19 also II: 27, 28.
[100] Jer. XI: 15 ff.
[101] Jer. XIV: 9; cf. Zephan. III: 14 ff.

While counseling his brethren that were deported to Babylon to identify their welfare with that of their new home,[102] the prophet sounds the hope that "He that scattereth Israel will gather him. . . . And they shall come and sing in the height of Zion, and shall flow unto the goodness of Jahweh, to the corn, and to the wine, and to the oil, and to the young of the flock and of the herd."[103] The land of Judah, after her restoration, will again be called "the habitation of righteousness, the mountain of holiness"[104] and "Jahweh is our righteousness."[105] The whole city of Jerusalem "shall be built to Jahweh," and the entire valley shall be "holy unto Jahweh."[106] In the days of Israel's repentance, not the Ark of the Covenant but the whole city of Jerusalem will be known as "the Throne of Jahweh, and all the nations will be gathered unto it, to the name of Jahweh, to Jerusalem."[107]

The Deuteronomic Code, resting on the foundations of the prophets, shares their views on the relation of Jahweh to Palestine. While the framework of Deuteronomy stresses the importance of the Ark of the Covenant,[108] the Code itself makes no reference to it. The whole of Palestine is Jahweh's land. He lavishes special care upon it. "The eyes of Jahweh thy God are always upon it, from the beginning of the year even unto the end of the year."[109] He dispossessed the other nations and gave the land to His people of Israel, out of His special love for them and out of His desire to have them champion His cause of goodness and justice.[110] Within the land, Jahweh chose one place for His dwelling. Though not expressly named, Jerusalem is meant. There Jahweh caused His name to dwell, and there alone He is to be wor-

---

[102] Jer. XXIX.

[103] Jer. XXXI: 10–12.

[104] Jer. XXXI: 23.

[105] Jer. XXXIII: 16.

[106] Jer. XXXI: 39–40.

[107] Jer. III: 17–18. Duhm considers this passage of post-Exilic origin, but on wholly subjective grounds, v. his *Jeremia* pp. 40–41. A similar hope is expressed in Jer. I: 15.

[108] Deut. X: 1–8.

[109] Deut. XI: 12.

[110] Deut. IV: 37–38; VI: 18–25; VII-IX; etc.

shiped.[111] Thither the people were directed to pilgrim thrice annually, to celebrate before Jahweh.[112] The centralization of worship represented the final result of David's policy of making Jerusalem the center of the nation. As the central sanctuary, placed in the nation's capitol, the Temple on Zion came to be viewed by the people as the Palladium of Jahweh. Even the prophets, as we have seen, looked upon it as specially honored by Jahweh's presence. *"Under the conditions of the time,"* writes Driver, "the single sanctuary was a corollary of the monotheistic idea. Worship at different places would tend (as in the case of Ba'al and many other ancient deities) to generate different conceptions of the god worshiped, and might even lead to the syncretistic confusion of Jahweh with other deities. The concentration of worship in a single spot was thus a necessary providential stage in the purification of the popular ideas of God."[113]

The spirituality of God is impaired here and there in Deuteronomy. Thus we read: "Jahweh thy God walketh in the midst of thy camp, to deliver thee, and to give up thine enemies before thee; therefore shall thy camp be holy, that He may see no unseemly thing in thee, and turn away from thee."[114] In general however, the higher conception of Jahweh animates the entire book. "He is God in heaven above and upon the earth beneath; there is none else."[115] In His might, He produces fertility and brings drought, in order to reward or to chastise His people.[116] While he delights in the land of Israel, He is not dependent upon it. Hence should Israel stray from Him and break His covenant, He will forsake the people and hide His face from them, and "they shall be devoured, and many evils and troubles shall come upon them; so that

[111] Deut. XII: 11–14; XV: 19 ff; XXVI: 2. This is clearly a restriction of the earlier practice recognized in the Code of the Covenant, Ex. XX: 24, and illustrated in the historical books.

[112] Deut. XVI: 1–17.

[113] Driver, *Deuteronomy*, p. XXIX. His final conclusions are based, surprisingly for a scholar of his type, on doctrinal prejudice. Ibid.

[114] Deut. XXIII: 15; v. also IV: 19.

[115] Deut. IV: 39; X: 14 ff.

[116] Deut. XI: 13 ff; XXVIII–XXX; cf. Lev. XXVI.

they will say in that day: 'Are not these evils come upon us because our God is not among us?'"[117]

III

The prophetic conception of Jahweh as independent of Palestine, helped to save Judaism during the national calamity of 586. The priest-prophet Ezekiel, following Hosea and Jeremiah, denounced heathen worship as harlotry which defiles the soil of Palestine. In his vision, he beholds the chariot of the glory of Jahweh removing from the sin-laden city and from its contaminated sanctuary.[118] The idolatry, the immorality, and the injustice committed in them drive Him away.[119] "The iniquity of the house of Israel and Judah is exceedingly great, and the land is full of blood, and the city full of wresting of judgment; for they say: 'Jahweh hath forsaken the land, and Jahweh seeth not.'"[120] Having sinned against Jahweh, the land shall be delivered to destruction.[121] Through disloyalty, she forfeited the protection of her God. Indeed Jahweh shows His might by turning the land into a desolation. Consequently the Exile appears as the manifestation of His avenging justice. But Jahweh is a God of compassion. He is pained by the stern measures to which He is driven. He follows His people into captivity, where He is unto them "as a little sanctuary," and promises to bring them back to their own land where, purified in heart and renewed in spirit, they will be reunited with Him.[122] "For in My holy mountain, in the mountain of the height of Israel, saith the God Jahweh, there shall all the house of Israel, all of them serve Me in the land; there will I accept them, and there will I require

[117] Deut. XXXI: 17 ff, also Deut. XXVIII: 63–64; Cf. Josh. XXIII–XXIV, Jud. II; I. K. IX: 6–9; etc.

[118] Ez. I-II, X, XI: 22 ff.

[119] Ez. VIII: 6.

[120] Ez. IX: 9; also XXII: 29–31; XXIII: 38–39.

[121] Ez. XIV: 13 ff; XV: 8.

[122] Ez. XI: 16 ff. XXVIII: 25–26.

your heave-offerings and the first of your gifts, with all your holy things. With your sweet savor will I accept you, when I bring you out from the peoples, and gather you out of the countries wherein ye have been scattered; and I will be sanctified in you in the sight of the nations."[123] For His own name's sake will He restore Israel to His grace.[124] His dwelling place will again be in Israel. He will be Israel's God and Israel will be His people. "And the nations shall know that I am Jahweh that sanctify Israel, when My sanctuary shall be in the midst of them."[125]

The constitution which Ezekiel drafted for the restored nation is theocratic in character. It conceives of the people centered around the Temple, devotedly carrying out the sacred laws of Jahweh. It is indeed a kingdom of priests and a holy nation. Fittingly the rebuilt Jerusalem is renamed "Jahweh is there."[126]

A few of Ezekiel's fundamental ideas are paralleled in the Priestly Code and particularly in the Code of Holiness. They evince the same regard for the sanctuary[127] and "prescribe rules to guard it against profanation."[128] The people of Israel as Jahweh's people is linked with the holiness of the land: "Ye shall therefore keep all My statutes and all My ordinances, and do them, that the land wither I bring you to dwell therein, vomit you not out. And ye shall not walk in the customs of the nation which I am casting out before you; for they all did these things, and therefore I abhorred them. But I have said unto you: 'Ye shall inherit their land, and I will give it unto you to possess it, a land flowing with milk and honey.' I am Jahweh your God, who have set you apart from the peoples. And ye shall be holy unto Me."[129] Defilement of the land will be rigidly punished. The people will be scattered among their enemies and their land will be desolate, "and shall be paid her Sabbaths while she lieth

---

[123] Ez. XX: 40–41; v. XXXIV: 24–28.

[124] Ez. XXXVI: 8–38.

[125] Ez. XXXVII: 22–28. v. XXXIX: 25–29.

[126] Ez. XLVIII: 34.

[127] Lev. XIX: 30; XX: 3; XXI: 12; XXIII; XXVI: 2 and Ez. V: 11; VIII: 6; XXIII: 38 ff; XXV: 3; XLIII: 7 ff.

[128] Driver, *Literature of the O. T.*, p. 140 f.

[129] Lev. XX: 22–26; also XVIII: 24–30.

desolate without them; and they shall be paid the punishment of their iniquity." However, exile will not spell the rejection of the people by Jahweh. In keeping with His character He will remember the covenant with their fathers and restore them as His people.[130] To avoid such dangers, the elaborate body of law is prescribed, regulating every phase of the life of Israel.[131]

It is significant that Ezekiel, the most particularistic of the prophets, should have so effectively emphasized the universalistic doctrine that Jahweh is not limited to any particular land. Though declaring that the Israelites will be forced to eat their bread "unclean" in the lands of their exile,[132] he demonstrated the possibility of worshiping Jahweh in distant Babylonia. He thus taught the exiles that would hang their harps upon the willows, how to sing Jahweh's song in a strange land.

It was left to Deutero-Isaiah to blend the national hopes and the lofty universalistic aspirations into perfect harmony. He interprets the stirring events of his day, the crash of Babylon and the rise of Persia as a world-power, as parts of Jahweh's plan of universal salvation. Jahweh comforts Zion, makes her wilderness like Eden, and fills her with joy, with praise, and with song. The ransomed captives shall return jubilantly to Zion. They shall be protected by the shadow of Jahweh's hand, in order that heaven and earth shall be firmly established.[133] Israel's restoration in Palestine represents the practical manifestation of Jahweh's sovereignty. Rapturously the prophet hails Jahweh's return to Zion:

"Break into joy, sing together,
Ye waste places of Jerusalem;
For Jahweh hath comforted His people,
He hath redeemed Jerusalem. . . .
Depart ye, depart ye, go ye out from thence,
Touch no unclean thing;

[130] Lev. XXVI: 27-45. v. Ez. XXXVI: 16-36, XXXVII, XXXIX: 23-29.
[131] Lev. XXVI: 3-26; etc.
[132] Ez. IV: 12.
[133] Is. LI: 3ff; LV: 12-13.

> Go ye out of the midst of her; be ye clean,
> Ye that bear the vessels of Jahweh.
> For ye shall not go in haste,
> Neither shall ye go by flight;
> For Jahweh will go before you,
> And the God of Israel will be your rearward."[134]

The reunion of Jahweh and Zion holds out the promise of endless moral progress. It represents the kingdom of God on earth:

> "And all thy children shall be taught of Jahweh,
> And great shall be the peace of thy children.
> In righteousness shalt thou be established;
> Be thou far from oppression, for thou shalt not fear,
> And from ruin, for it shall not come near thee."[135]

An anonymous prophecy, strongly resembling Deutero-Isaiah, adds:

> "And a highway shall be there, and a way,
> And it shall be called the way of holiness;
> The unclean shall not pass over it."[136]

The universalistic and the national ideals likewise blend in the prophecies that are embodied in Trito-Isaiah. The righteous Jews and the God-loving aliens that keep the Sabbath and hold fast the divine covenant "will be brought to My holy mountain, and made joyful in My house of prayer;

> Their burnt-offerings and their sacrifices
> Shall be acceptable upon Mine altar;
> For My house shall be called
> A house of prayer for all peoples.[137]

---

[134] Is. LII: 7–11.
[135] Is. LIV: 11–14.
[136] Is. XXXV: 8. Cf. Pss. XCVI–XCIX.
[137] Is. LVI: 1–7.

The Temple stands out as the center to which all nations shall stream to worship God.

> "And they shall call thee The City of Jahweh,
> The Zion of the Holy One of Israel."[138]
> "Thou shalt also be a crown of beauty in the hand of Jahweh,
> And a royal diadem in the open hand of thy God.
> Thou shalt no more be termed Forsaken,
> Neither shall thy land any more be termed Desolate;
> But thou shalt be called My Delight is in Her,
> And thy land Espoused;
> For Jahweh delighteth in thee,
> And thy land shall be espoused.
> For as a young man espouseth a virgin,
> So shall they sons espouse thee;
> And as the bridegroom rejoiceth over the bride,
> So shall thy God rejoice over thee."[139]

Recognizing full well that the heaven is God's throne and the earth His footstool, and that no house can be properly built for Him, the prophet declares that nations from afar shall come to the holy mountain of Jerusalem.

> "And it shall come to pass,
> That from one new moon to another,
> And from one sabbath to another,
> Shall all flesh come to worship before Me,
> Saith Jahweh."[140]

Zechariah likewise predicts that "many peoples and mighty nations shall come to seek Jahweh of Hosts in Jerusalem, and entreat the favor of

---

[138] Is. LX: 14.

[139] Is. LXII: 3–5 and 11–12. v. also LXV: 18 ff. v. also Zeph. III: 14–20.

[140] Is. LXVI.

Jahweh."[141] For "thus saith Jahweh: I return unto Zion, and will dwell in the midst of Jerusalem; and Jerusalem shall be called The City of Truth; and the mountain of the Lord of Hosts, The Holy Mountain."[142] The whole country will again overflow with prosperity. Jerusalem will be so populous that her ancient walls will not be able to contain her. Jahweh Himself will be unto her a wall of fire round about, and will glory in the midst of her.[143]

In the additions to Zechariah, the same high hope is expressed. The Apocalypse that depicts the judgment of the nations that war against Jerusalem, states:

> "That living waters shall go out from Jerusalem:
> Half of them toward the eastern sea,
> And half of them toward the western sea;
> In summer and in winter shall it be.
> And Jahweh shall be King over all the earth;
> In that day shall Jahweh be One and His name one."[144]

Furthermore the nations that shall survive "shall go up from year to year to worship the King, Jahweh of hosts, and to keep the feast of tabernacles. And it shall be that whoso of the families of the earth goeth not up unto Jerusalem to worship the King, Jahweh of hosts, upon them shall be no rain."[145]

A dissenting voice was raised by Joel. Probably in response to the bitterness engendered by incessant warfare, he draws a different picture of the day of judgment. The nations shall be given over to destruction, while Israel will be saved:

> "So shall ye know that I am Jahweh your God,
> Dwelling in Zion My holy mountain;

---

[141] Zech. VIII: 22; II: 15.
[142] Zech. VIII: 3; I: 16–17.
[143] Zech. II: 9.
[144] Zech. XIV: 8–9, v. also Obadiah vs. 17, 21, and Is. XXIV: 23.
[145] Zech. XIV: 16–17, etc.

Then shall Jerusalem be holy,
And there shall be no strangers pass through her any more."[146]

IV

It was the glory of the Second Temple that it became the house of prayer
for many peoples.[147] In this regard it indeed exceeded the glory of the more
magnificent Temple of Solomon. The conviction grew general that God
cannot be domiciled in any structure whatever, for His majesty transcends all
earth and heaven,[148] also that His worship cannot be limited to any one land.
Malachi announces that "from the rising of the sun even unto the going down
of the same, My name is great among the nations; and in every place offerings
are presented unto My name, even pure oblations; for My name is great
among the nations, saith Jahweh of hosts."[149] The prophet may have thought
of the Jewish people living in distant lands and there continuing their religious life.

During the Second Temple the religious life of the Jewish people took on
new forms. On the one hand it grew more intimately connected with the soil.
The restored exiles felt that Jahweh had done wondrously for them. As from a
grave, the nations was restored to new life. The reorganized community took
the form of a theocracy. Ezekiel's ideal constitution, modified by the Priestly
Code and the Code of Holiness, took shape in the life of the people. Due to
political circumstances, the high priest became the head of the nation. Everything therefore centered around the priests and the sanctuary. Wherein the
Deuteronomic Reformation failed, the Reformation of Ezra-Nehemiah
succeeded. The Torah now became the foundation of Jewish life. What it
implied for the agricultural community in Palestine, is clearly seen in the
following pledge of the Great Assembly: "Also we made ordinances for us to

[146] Joel IV: 17. v. also II: 21–27.
[147] Cf. Ps. CII: 14–23.
[148] I. K. VIII: 16 ff. and II. Chr. VI; II: 2–5.
[149] Malachi I: 11, v. also Is. LXVI: 18–19.

charge ourselves yearly with the third part of a shekel for the service of the house of our God; for the showbread, and for the continual meal-offering, and for the continual burnt-offering, of the sabbaths, of the new moons, for the appointed seasons, and for the holy things, and for the sin-offerings to make atonement for Israel, and for all the work of the house of our God. And we cast lots, the priests, the Levites, and the people, for the wood-offering, to bring it into the house of our God, according to our fathers' houses, at times appointed, year by year, to burn upon the altar of the Lord our God, as it is written in the Law; and to bring the first-fruits of our land, and the first-fruits of all fruits of all manner of trees, year by year unto the house of the Lord; also the first-born of our sons, and of our cattle, as it is written in the Law, and the firstlings of our herds and of our flocks, to bring to the house of our God, unto the priests that minister in the house of our God; and that we should bring the first of our dough, and our heave-offerings and the fruit of all manner of trees, the wine and the oil, unto the priests, to the chambers of the house of our God; and the tithes of our land unto the Levites; for they, the Levites, take the tithes in all the cities of our tillage. And the priest the son of Aaron shall be with the Levites, when the Levites take tithes; and the Levites shall bring up the tithe of the tithes unto the house of our God, to the chambers, into the treasure-house. For the children of Israel and the children of Levi shall bring the heave-offering of the corn, of the wine, and of the oil, unto the chambers, where are the vessels of the sanctuary, and the priests that minister, and the porters, and the singers; and we will not forsake the house of our God.[150]

Here we have the germ of most of the distinctive elements of post-exilic Judaism. Under Pharisaic influence, there developed a vast body of law that was wholly contingent upon Palestine (מצות התלויות בארץ) and upon the Temple (בזמן הבית). It dealt with (1) sacrifices, first-fruits, tithes, pilgrimages, etc.; (2) civil and military government and administration of justice; (3) agricultural obligations (חובת קרקע); and (4) regulations concerning defilement and cleanliness (טומאה וטהרה). This legal material formed the basis of the Mishnah. Through it Jewish life in Palestine, and to a lesser degree in the

---

[150] Nehemiah X: 33-40.

Diaspora, found expression. A distinguished element of Jewry, that of the Kohanim and Leviim, was wholly dependent upon it.

On the other hand, the spread of the Jewish people over distant lands, during the Exile and the Second Temple, necessitated a readjustment of the relation of Judaism to Palestine. The Deuteronomic law provided for the centralization of worship in Jerusalem, and prohibited the establishment of Temples in other places. Before the new law could entrench itself in the life of the people, Jerusalem was destroyed. The Jewish refugees and exiles in foreign lands were faced with the alternative of falling away from Judaism altogether or of breaking with the Deuteronomic law. They chose the latter. Like Ezekiel in Babylon, so Jeremiah in Egypt urged the people to worship their God.[151] The Jewish colonists of Yeb in the Upper Nile region, even proceeded to erect a sanctuary, before the Persian conquest of Egypt, where they conducted sacrificial services for over a century.[152] There may have been similar places in other parts of the Diaspora.[153]

During the Maccabean struggle, Onias IV, the son of the murdered high-priest Onias III, fled to Egypt, where he obtained royal permission to build a temple and an altar to God, at Leontopolis, in the Heliopolite nome (some twenty miles north of Cairo). Josephus informs us that this temple was "like indeed to that in Jerusalem, but smaller and poorer."[154] On the basis of his excavations at Tell el Yehudieh, Flinders Petrie corroborates Josephus' report, and adds that the whole city of Oniah formed "as close a copy as could be arranged of the temple hill at Jerusalem," only on a smaller scale.[155] There "Onias found other Jews like to himself, together with priests and Levites, that there performed divine services."[156]

This Temple functioned uninterruptedly until the outbreak of the War of the Jews against Rome. To prevent its becoming the center of agitation among the strong and influential Jewish communities of Egypt, Vespasian ordered it

---

[151] Jer. XLIV.
[152] A. Cowley, *Jewish Documents of the Time of Ezra*, Intro. and Nos. 21, 30–33.
[153] Is. XIX: 18 ff. LXVI: 19 and Mal. I: 11.
[154] *Antiq.* XII: 3, 1–3.
[155] Flinders Petrie, *Israel and Egypt*, pp. 108–110.
[156] *Antiq.* XII, 3, 3.

demolished. But the Roman governors of Egypt were contented to strip it of its possessions and to close its gates.[157] It seems that it was subsequently reopened for worship. As late as the fourth century, R. Isaac, a contemporary of Rava, stated that he heard of the permissibility of offering sacrifices in the temple of Onias in his day.[158]

The Palestinian Jewish authorities shared different views about this temple. This division of opinion is reflected in the works of Josephus. In the *Jewish Wars,* where he regards Onias III, the son of Simon, as its builder, Josephus supposes that it was erected in order to spite the Jews of Jerusalem.[159] In his *Antiquities,* where he takes the more correct view that Onias IV built the temple, he speaks respectfully of it, setting forth the conversion of the Egyptians to the God of Israel as one of the motives that prompted its construction.[160] The Mishna naturally regarded this temple with displeasure, and considered the priests officiating in it disqualified for service in the Temple in Jerusalem.[161] Its sacrifices being offered outside of Jerusalem,[162] were not held proper. The Gemara presents one tradition that Onias erected an altar for idolatrous purposes and another that he built it for God's sake.[163]

Opposition to it may have existed among the Egyptian Jews, themselves. This may account for Philo's silence concerning it. On the other hand the Septuagint reading of עיר הצדק "the city of righteousness," for עיר ההרס "the city of destruction" in Isaiah XIX: 18, indicates the high regard in which the temple of Onias was held by some Jews in Egypt.[164] Its erection may have filled them with pride as betokening the fulfillment of Isaiah's prophecy

---

[157] *Jewish Wars* VII, 10, 2.

[158] שמעתי שמקריבין בבית חוניו בזמן הזה Megil 10a. References to the Temple of Onias are found in Jeru. Sanh. 1, 2, 5b-6a; and in Jeru. Ned. 6, 8, 23a. For its later history, see Maimonides, Mishnah Comment. Men. XIII.

[159] *Jewish Wars* VII, 10, 3.

[160] *Antiq.* XIII, 3, 1; XII, 5, 1; 9, 7.

[161] Men. XIII: 10.

[162] i.e. קרבנות חוץ.

[163] Men. 109b.-110a.

[164] Graetz, *Geschichte d. Juden* III, 34 ff. Jost, *Geschichte d. Judentums* I, 116 ff.

(XIX:19). However they did not permit it to replace the Temple of Jerusalem as the center of their religious interests.[165]

Jewish life in the ever widening Diaspora found its fullest expression in the Synagogue. As the only objects of its assemblies were the study of the Torah and the offering of prayer — and under no condition, any form of sacrificial worship — no possible objection could be raised against the Synagogue. In every Jewish settlement one or more Synagogues sprang into existence as rallying points for the Jewish people and as centers of culture and religion. As a "miniature sanctuary,"[166] the Synagogue linked the Jews of each community into a close bond of fellowship, and at the same time, united them with the rest of Jewry both of the Diaspora and of Palestine. It effectively fostered the sense of Jewish unity.

Thus Jerusalem, as King Agrippa proudly declared, had long before become "the metropolis,[167] not only of the one country of Judea, but also of many, by reason of the colonies which it has sent out from time to time into the bordering districts of Egypt, Phoenicia, Syria in general, and especially that part of it which is called Coelo-Syria, and also with those more distant regions of Pamphylia, Cilicia, the greater part of Asia Minor as far as Bithynia, and the furthermost corners of Pontus. And in the same manner into Europe, into Thessaly, and Boeotia, and Macedonia, and Aetolia, and Attica, and Argos, and Corinth, and all the most fertile and wealthiest districts of Peloponnesus."[168] Also in the islands of Euboea, Cyprus and Crete, in Babylon, and in all the countries beyond the Euphrates, Jews had settled.

While identifying themselves with the countries in which they lived, the Jews of the Diaspora piously looked upon "the holy city as their metropolis in which is erected the sacred temple of the Most High God."[169] Philo bears

---

[165] *Antiq.* XIII, 3, 4.

[166] Megil. 29a: ואהי להם למקדש מעט (יחזקאל י״א) א״ר יצחק אלו בתי כנסיות ובתי מדרשות שבבל. The great Synagogue in Alexandria is spoken of with pride by Philo (Younge's trans. IV, 129) and Sukka 51b.

[167] Cf. Ex. R. XXIII, 11 עתידה ירושלים להעזות מטרפולין לכל הארצות.

[168] Cited by Philo, on the Virtues and Office of Ambassadors, XXXVI. Younge's transl. IV. p. 161.

[169] Against Flaccus, VII, Younge, vol. IV. p. 70.

testimony to the respect in which "the most beautiful and renowned temple" is held "by all the east and by all the west, and regarded like the sun which shines everywhere."[170] The Jews of all lands considered it as a duty and privilege to assist the sanctuary of Jerusalem. Josephus writes that "all the Jews throughout the habitable earth, and those that worshiped God,[171] nay even those of Asia and Europe, sent their contribution to it [the Temple of Jerusalem]."[172] Philo too states that every year sacred messengers were sent from Jerusalem to Babylon and many other regions "to convey large amounts of gold and silver to the Temple, which has been collected from all the governments, traveling over rugged and difficult and almost impassable roads which they look upon as level and easy inasmuch as they serve to conduct them to piety."[173] In his treatise "On Monarchy," Philo glories in the hope that "as long as the race of mankind shall last, the revenues likewise of the Temple will always be preserved, being coeval in their duration with the universal world. For it is commanded that all men shall every year bring their first fruits to the Temple, from twenty years old and upwards; and this contribution is called their ransom. On which account they bring in the first fruits with exceeding cheerfulness, being joyful and delighted,[174] inasmuch as simultaneously with their making the offering they are sure to find a relaxation from slavery, or a relief from disease, and to receive in all respects a most sure freedom and safety for the future." Owing to the abundance of these contributions, "there is in almost every city a storehouse for the sacred things to which it is customary for the people to come and there to deposit their first fruits, and at certain seasons there are sacred ambassadors selected on account of their virtue, who convey the offerings to the Temple."[175] Philo makes special mention of the Jews of Rome "contributing sacred sums of money from their first fruits and sending them to Jerusalem by the hands of those who were to

---

[170] On the Virtues and Office of Ambassadors, XXIX. Ibid, p. 142. Also On Monarchy Bk. II, ch. II; Younge, vol. III. p. 192.

[171] i.e., converts to Judaism.

[172] *Antiq.* XIV, 7, 2; Shekalim III: 4.

[173] On the Virtues and Office of Ambassadors, XXXI, Ibid. p. 148.

[174] Cf. Bikkurim III: 3–4.

[175] On Monarchy Bk. II. ch. III: Younge's transl. vol. III. p. 193.

conduct the sacrifices."[176] The withdrawal of those funds from the Roman provinces was frequently objected to on the part of local officials. However, from the days of Caesar onward the sending of sacred tribute to Jerusalem was everywhere sanctioned, as a matter of state policy.[177]

Nor did the Jews of the Diaspora content themselves with sending tribute to the Temple. At great cost and much inconvenience, large bodies of Jews made regular pilgrimages to their mother country on festal occasions. "Innumerable companies of men from a countless variety of cities," writes Philo, "some by land and some by sea, from east and from west, from the north and from the south, come to the Temple at every festival, as if to some common refuge and safe asylum from the troubles of this most busy and painful life, seeking to find tranquility, and to procure a remission of and respite from those cares by which from their earliest infancy they had been hampered and weighed down."[178] From the pages of Josephus too we learn of the large numbers of pilgrims from all parts of the Diaspora to Jerusalem.[179] He estimates the number of Jews assembled at Jerusalem for the Passover celebration as 2,700,200, adding that "this multitude is indeed collected out of remote places."[180]

Josephus speaks of the altar at Jerusalem as "venerated by all Greeks and barbarians,"[181] and declares that the Temple mount "is adored by the whole world, and for its renown is honored among strangers at the ends of the earth."[182] Among the gentiles who honored the Temple with their gifts, he includes not only the numerous converts to Judaism for whom loyalty to it formed part of their adopted faith, but particularly those who remained heathens and would not care to confess their belief in the *superstitio Judaica.*

---

[176] On the Virtues and Office of Ambassadors, XXIII; Younge IV, 134.

[177] Ibid. XL. pp. 167-168; *Antiq.* XVI, 6, 2-7; XVIII, 9, 1, Schürer, *History of the Jewish People*, Divis. II. Pt. II. pp. 289-290.

[178] On Monarchy Bk. II. ch. I; Younge's transl. vol. II. p. 191. A good picture of the pious Jew of the Diaspora pilgriming to Jerusalem for the festivals, is presented in Tobit I: 4-8.

[179] *Antiq.* XVIII, 2, 2; XVIII, 9, 1. v. also Yoma VI: 4 and Ta'an. I: 3.

[180] *Jewish Wars*, VI, 9, 3-4.

[181] *Jewish Wars*, V, 1, 3.

[182] *Jewish Wars*, IV, 4, 3.

To be sure, their sacrifices were acts of courtesy toward the Jewish people and no real indication of genuine devotion to Judaism.[183] Nevertheless, as in older times so during the Graeco-Roman period, the offerings of the gentiles and their devotions[184] were viewed with special regard by the Jewish people. Non-Jews could not offer such sacrifices as were of an obligatory character, i. e. sin-offerings, trespass-offerings, and sacrifices presented by those who had issues, by women after child-birth, etc.;[185] nor could they because of their lack of the necessary Levitical purity, bring thank or peace-offerings. But they could bring votive and free-will offerings (נדרים ונדבות), burnt-offerings, meat-offerings and drink offerings. These sacrifices were sent from distant lands. And they occasionally came from people of great political prominence and from royal personages like Cyrus,[186] Alexander the Great,[187] Ptolemy III,[188] Antiochus Sidetes,[189] Marcus Agrippa,[190] Vitellius,[191] and Augustus.[192]

In addition to the sacrifices, it was common for gentiles to bestow gifts upon the Temple at Jerusalem. While some were prompted to do so by political considerations, others had no other motive than that of reverence for the famous house of worship. According to the Letter of Pseudo-Aristeas, Ptolemy Philadelphus on the occasion of his request that elders be sent to him to translate the Scriptures into Greek, donated "fifty talents weight of gold and seventy talents of silver and a large quantity of precious stones to make bowls and vials and a table and libation cups" and a hundred talents in money "to provide sacrifices for the Temple and for other needs."[193] While this story may belong to the realm of fiction, it faithfully depicts the Ptolemaic practice

[183] Schürer, *History*, Div. II. vol. I. pp. 299–300.

[184] Lev. XXII: 25; I. K. VIII: 41–43.

[185] Shekalim 1. 5; Tosephta Shekalim I: 7. Men. V: 3, 5, 6; VI: 1.

[186] Ezra VI: 10.

[187] *Antiq.* XI, VIII, 5.

[188] *Contra Apion* II, 5.

[189] *Antiq.* XIII, 8, 2.

[190] *Antiq.* XVI. 2, 1. and Philo, On Virtues and Office of Ambassadors, ch. XXXVII.

[191] *Antiq.* XVIII, 5, 3.

[192] Philo, Ibid, ch. XL.

[193] Vs. 33 ff. and *Antiq.* XII, 2, 5–9.

of presenting gifts to the Temple of Jerusalem.[194] The author of II Maccabees testifies that "even kings themselves did honor to the Place and glorify the Temple with the noblest presents; so much so that Seleuchus the king of Asia actually defrayed out of his own revenues, all the expenses connected with the ritual of the sacrifices."[195] The Romans too showed similar signs of respect to the Temple. After his conquest of Jerusalem, Socius offered a golden crown.[196] Marcus Agrippa, who on his visit to Jeusalem was so greatly impressed with the buildings and with the solemnity of the priestly service that he paid daily visits to the temple, as a token of respect presented gifts for its adornment.[197] Augustus too, despite his antipathy to Judaism, "commanded perfect sacrifices of whole burnt-offerings to be offered up to the most high God, every day, out of his own revenues," which — according to the claim of King Agrippa — were continued in his day.[198] Philo states further that Augustus "adorned our temple with many costly and magnificent offerings."[199] His consort, Julia Augusta, too, presented the temple "with some golden vials and censers, and with a great number of other offerings, of the most costly and magnificent description."[200] These together with other sacred utensils that were donated to the temple, were melted down by John of Giscala during the siege of Jerusalem. Josephus writes indignantly: "this man, who was a Jew, seized upon what were the donations of foreigners; and said to those that were with him, that it was proper for them to use divine things while they were fighting for the Divinity, without fear, and that such whose warfare is for the Temple, should live of the Temple.[201] Roman donations, it appears, were frequent at the Temple.[202] At the outbreak of the revolution in the year 66 C.E., Eleazar, the son of Ananias, the high priest, "who was at that time

---

[194] II. Macc. V: 16. *Antiq.* XIII. 3, 4.

[195] II. Macc. III: 2–3.

[196] *Antiq.* XIV, 16, 4.

[197] Philo, On the Virtues and Office of Ambassadors, ch. XXXVII.

[198] Ibid. ch. XL.

[199] Ibid. ch. XXIII.

[200] Ibid. ch. XL.

[201] *Jewish Wars,* V, 13, 6.

[202] *Ibid.* IV, 3, 3; II, 17, 3.

governor of the Temple, persuaded those that officiated in the divine service to receive no gift or sacrifice for any foreigner." Josephus considers this unprecedented step as "the true beginning of our war with the Romans; for they rejected the sacrifices of Caesar on this account." The leading priests and Pharisees, representing the peace party, were not slow to recognize that by rejecting the sacrifices of the Romans, the Jews ran the risk of not being able to offer their own.[203]

Sacrifices and prayers "for the life of the king and his sons"[204] became a standing feature of the worship of the Second Temple. These continued all through Persian and Graeco-Roman times. Even during the Maccabean wars, at a time when a large portion of the people warred against the King of Syria, sacrifices were offered for him.[205] When the gentile authorities did not defray the expense of the sacrifices, the Jewish people defrayed it.[206] During Roman times these offerings served the Jews as a partial substitute for the divine honors which the heathens paid the Caesars. Thus King Agrippa assures Caligula that the Jews are "inferior to none whatever in Asia or in Europe, whether it be in respect of prayers, or of the supply of sacred offerings, or in the abundance of its sacrifices, not merely of such as are offered on occasions of the public festivals, but in those which are continuously offered day after day; by which means they show their loyalty and fidelity more surely than by their mouth and tongue."[207]

Philo, The Pesikta, and the Talmud reflect the view of the Jewish masters, that the Temple was indeed a House of Prayer for all nations. (See essay on Proselytism, in this volume, page 319, 328-9.)

The union of the religious life of the Jewish people with Palestine had its bearings upon political conditions. To prevent trafficking with gentiles, during Maccabean times, Jose b. Joezer of Zereda and Jose b. Johanan of

[203] *Jewish Wars*, II, 17, 1-3.

[204] Ezra VI: 10. Cf. also I. Baruch I: 5-13.

[205] I. Macc. VII: 33.

[206] *Contra Apion*, II, 6. Possibly the sacrifices *for* the emperors were apart from those *by* them.

[207] Philo, On the Virtues and Office of Ambassadors XXXVI: pp. 161.

Jerusalem declared all countries other than Palestine *unclean*.[208] Demetrius I in his bid for Jonathan's friendship, declares: "let Jerusalem be holy and free, together with the outlying districts, (regarding) the tenths and the tolls,"[209] i.e. free from the tax on the Temple revenues that were exacted by the Syrian rulers. This was in part a confirmation of an older grant of Antiochus the Great that "It shall be lawful for no foreigner to come within the limits of the Temple round about; which thing is forbidden also to the Jews, unless to those who, according to their own custom, have purified themselves." A penalty of three thousand drachmae of silver was imposed for the violation of this law.[210]

The sanctity of the Temple was universally accepted and respected. Jewish tradition delighted in relating the horrible punishments that befell the impious strangers who entered its Holy of Holies.[211] In the Herodian Temple, between the outer and the inner courts, an inscription in Greek and in Latin, announced that foreigners were forbidden to enter the inner circuit under the penalty of death.[212] Philo pays glowing tribute to "the zeal of the Jewish people for their holy Temple." He speaks of it as "the most predominant and vehement and universal feeling throughout the whole nation; and the greatest proof of this is that death is inexorably pronounced against all those who enter into the inner circuit of the sacred precincts (for they admit all men from every country into the exterior circuit) unless he be one of their own nation by blood."[213]

In his treaty with the Romans, John Hyrcanus stipulated that Roman

---

[208] Sab. 14b. Herford sees in this measure opposition to the Zadokites who had withdrawn to Damascus. (*The Pharisees*, p. 26) This ingenious suggestion rests on the theory that the Zadokite Fragment is pre-Maccabean, a theory open to serious doubt. See A. Büchler, in the *J. Q. R.* (n. s.) vol. III, p. 429-485.

[209] I Macc. X: 31.

[210] *Antiq*. XII, 3, 4.

[211] *Antiq*. XV, 11, 5. Bousset, *Religion d. Judentums*, p. 193.

[212] Ptolemy Philopater, III Macc. I-II; Heliodorus, II Macc. III Apollonius IV. Macc. IV: 1-14; Antiochus Epiphanes II Macc. IX cf. XIII: 33; Nicanor II Macc. XV; Pompey Ps. Sol. II. Alcimus, for pulling down the wall of the inner court of the sanctuary — and thereby obliterating the difference between Israelites and gentiles — was stricken with palsy. I Macc. IX: 54-55.

[213] On the Virtues and Office of Ambassadors XXXI; Younge, IV, 147.

troops shall not pass through Jewish territory.[214] The Roman standards with their eagles were considered idolatrous. Accordingly the appearance of Pilate's cohorts in Jerusalem, with their standards bearing the effigies of the emperor threatened to rouse a public insurrection.[215] For this reason the Roman procurators took up their quarters in the half-heathen Caesaria rather than in the city of Jerusalem. The hope was strong in Jewish hearts that in the Messianic times all heathens will be removed from Palestine, that all the exiled Jews will be returned to it, and that Jerusalem will become the center of the world.[216]

The place that Palestine held in the religious life of the Jews is strikingly illustrated in the following regulations concerning prayer: "Those who stand up to pray in countries outside of the Land of Israel, direct their hearts toward the Land of Israel and pray,[217] for it is said: 'they shall pray unto the Lord toward the land which ... Thou hast chosen':[218] Those who rise to pray within the Land of Israel direct their hearts towards Jerusalem and pray, for it is said: 'they shall pray ... towards this city.'[219] Those rising for prayer in Jerusalem direct their hearts toward the Temple and pray, for it is said 'and they shall pray toward this place.'[218] Hence those standing north of Palestine face the South, south face the North, east face the West, and standing west face the East. Thus all Israel pray toward one place."[220]

The Mishnah distinguished between ten ascending grades of holiness within Palestine itself. (1) "The Land of Israel is holier than all other lands. Wherein does its holiness consist? In that from it alone, and from no other land, are brought the Omer, Bikkurim and the two loaves.[221] (2) The cities surrounded by a wall are of greater holiness inasmuch as lepers are sent out of them[222]; and dead bodies, though they may be carried from one place within

[214] *Antiq.* XIII, 9, 2.

[215] *Antiq.* XVIII, 3, 1.

[216] Ps. of Solomon XVII: 28–36. The place of Palestine in the Messianic hope will be presented in the second part of this paper.

[217] Dan. VI: 11.

[218] I. Kings VIII: 48.

[219] Ibid.

[220] Tosephta Berachot III: 15. Sifre, Deut. XXVIII.

[221] Lev. XXIII: 10, 17; Deut. XXVI: 2.

[222] Lev. XIII: 46.

these cities to another, may not be returned to the cities, once they were carried outside. (3) Of a higher degree of holiness is the city of Jerusalem, within the outer wall, where the lower grade sacrifices and the second tithes may be eaten.[223] (4) The Temple Mount is still holier, for men and women with issues, menstruating women and women soon after child-birth[224] may not enter into it. (5) The *Hel* is more sacred inasmuch as non-Jews and those defiled by contact with a dead body may not enter into it. (6) The Women's Hall is more sacred, for no unclean person may enter into it until he has had his bath of purification at sunset. However the infringement upon this rule does not incur a sin-offering. (7) The Israelites' Hall is holier, for no person may enter into it who had not made atonement, and if he did enter he must bring a sin-offering. (8) The Priests' Hall is holier, in that lay Israelites may enter into it only for the purpose of laying their hands upon the sacrificial animals, to slaughter them and to wave them before the altar. (9) The area from the Ulam (vestibule) to the altar is more sacred, inasmuch as priests with bodily defects or with uncovered heads may not enter into it. (10) The Hekal (Nave of the Temple) is more sacred, for no priest may enter into it before washing hands and feet. The Holy of Holies is more sacred than all the rest, for only the high priest may enter into it and only on the Day of Atonement."[225]

To these words, we would add the comment of the Sifre. On the basis of Numbers V: 2, it remarks that there are three camps within Jerusalem: "From the entrance of the city to the Temple Mount is the camp of Israel; from the entrance of the Temple Mount to the Temple Court is the Levitical camp; the area within the Temple Court is the camp of the Shechinah."[226]

The history of the Jewish people from the period of the Conquest to that of the fall of the State and the Temple, presents a steady tightening of the bonds of union between Palestine and Judaism. Simultaneously with its passing from Canaanite to Israelite control, Palestine — the land of the Baalim

---

[223] Deut. XII: 6, 11.
[224] Num. V: 2.
[225] Kelim I: 6–9.
[226] Sifre, Num. I. ed. Friedman, 1b.

— became "the possession of Jahweh." The whole country and particularly, after the erection of the Temple, Mount Zion became sacred to Jahweh. Despite the fears of the Rechabites, the agricultural economy of Palestine came to form the basis of the worship of Jahweh, as expressed in its sacrificial cult and in its festivals. Prophetic idealism, while aiming to lift Jahweh above any particular soil, yet linked His name with the home of His people, thereby seeking to transform Palestine into the center of the religious life of a re-generated humanity. The prophets of the Exile taught the people to find God also beyond the confines of their native land. Through them, the religious ideals of Judaism had progressed so far as to be able to maintain themselves beyond Palestine and its Temple. Yet they as well as the humbler exiles cherished Zion above their chiefest joy. Engraven upon their hearts, she was the object of their hopes and dreams. Ardently they prayed for her restoration to God's grace; and seized the first opportunity to reestablish her religious life by rebuilding the Temple at Jerusalem. Indeed large bodies of Jews remained outside of Palestine all through the Second Temple. However they too did not forget their ancient home and sanctuary. For the Jews of the ever widening Diaspora, Palestine became the symbol of spiritual unity. Though devoted in all things to the lands in which they lived, they turned in their prayers towards Jerusalem. Thither they directed their hearts in their daily worship and during the festivals. Thither too they sent their gifts and offerings. Whole-heartedly they prayed for the peace of Jerusalem,[227] and prospered spiritually in the love of her. For them Jerusalem ceased to be an earthly city and became the heavenly city of God. The Jews of the whole world profoundly shared the belief that Palestine was the Holy Land and Jerusalem the Holy City. The words of the Psalmist found universal response in the hearts of the faithful:

"The Lord bless thee out of Zion;
And mayest thou see the good of Jerusalem all the days of thy life."[228]

---

[227] Ps. CXXII: 6.
[228] Ps. CXXVIII: 5.

Proselytism

While Judaism was brought forth, preserved, and fostered by the Jewish people, its appeal has been worldwide. Monotheism spells universality. A prophet proclaimed to the Jewish people: "And nations shall walk in thy light, and kings at the brightness of thy rising."[1] And he called to the nations in God's name:

Look unto Me and be ye saved,
All the ends of the earth;
For I am God, and there is none else.
By Myself have I sworn,
The word is gone forth from My mouth in righteousness,
And shall not come back,
That unto Me every knee shall bow,
Every tongue shall swear.[2]

At the dedication of the Temple, Solomon prayed that the supplication of the strangers who might come to worship God in Jerusalem would be accepted. Instances are recorded of strangers who joined the Jewish community of faith. For example, Naaman, the Syrian general who was cured of his leprosy by bathing in the Jordan at the direction of Elisha, expressed his gratitude by avowing the God of Israel. The Book of Ruth tells the story of a

---

[1] Isa. 60:3.
[2] Isa. 45:22–23.

Moabitish woman who joined the Jewish fold, vowing to her mother-in-law: "Thy people shall be my people, and thy God my God."[3]

The Bible records also the conversion of whole tribes. During the conquest of the land, we are informed, the Gibeonites resorted to a ruse to ally themselves by covenant with the victorious Israelites.[4] Because of their ruse, they were assigned the menial place of hewers of wood and drawers of water within the people of Israel. More striking is the instance of the Samaritans. Transplanted by the Assyrian conquerors from distant provinces, these people mingled with the Israelite remnants of the country and adopted their faith. Because they retained certain ways from their heathen past, they were not recognized as pure Israelites. The short-sighted policy of some Jewish leaders at the time of the building of the Second Temple led to the repulsion of the Samaritans from the Jewish fellowship. But they have clung to the worship of the God of Israel, and to this day their remnants at Nablus, the ancient Shechem, adhere to the Torah and their inherited tradition with a zeal no less intense than that of the most devout Jews.

The relation of the Jewish people to the Samaritans illustrates their ambivalent attitude toward conversions of the gentiles. While some influential leaders were resolved to keep Judaism as the heritage of the Jewish people, there were others who cherished the hope of sharing their faith with all men. The prophets addressed themselves to other nations as well as to Israel.[5] Jeremiah and Deutero-Isaiah encompassed all mankind in the scope of their vision. A late prophecy expressed the hope that when God will show compassion on Jacob and again choose Israel and set them upon their soil, aliens will attach themselves to the house of Jacob.[6] Another prophecy states:

> And the foreigners who join themselves to the Lord,
>   to minister to Him, to love the name of the Lord,
>   and to be His servants,

[3] Ruth 1:16.
[4] Josh. 9.
[5] Jer. 3:17, 4:2, 12:14–17, 16:19. Cf. Isa. 19:19–25, Zeph. 3:8, Micah 4:1–5 = Isa. 2:2–4.
[6] Isa. 14:1.

Every one who keeps the Sabbath,
    and does not profane it,
    and holds fast my covenant —
These will I bring to My holy mountain,
    and make them joyful in My house of prayer;
Their burnt offerings and their sacrifices
    will be accepted on My altar;
For My house shall be called a house of prayer
    for all peoples.[7]

Zechariah looked to the day when many peoples and strong nations will come to seek the Lord of hosts. In those days ten foreigners will take hold of the robe of a Jew and say: "Let us go with you, for we have heard that God is with you." "And the Lord will become King over all the earth; on that day the Lord shall be one and His name one."[8]

Three terms came to express conversion to Judaism: *hanilvim el Adonai,* those who attach themselves to God; *mityahadim,* those who become Jews; and *Gerim,* proselytes. The early meaning of the word *ger* was civil and social rather than religious. Like the μέτοικος in the Attic state, so the *ger* in Israel was a *resident* alien.[9] He must not be confused with the *nochri,* the stranger who finds himself temporarily in Israelite territory, or with the descendants of the seven Canaanite nations who were dispossessed by Israel.

As among other Semitic peoples, so in Israel, the *ger*[10] was the protected stranger who lived by the side of the citizen אזרח,[11] his family, and slaves. Because of the *ger*'s distance from his own kin, Semitic morality offered him protection. The principle of inviolability of guests was universally recognized by Semites. "A man is safe in the midst of his enemies as soon as he enters a tent or even touches the tent rope. To harm a guest, or to refuse him hospitali-

---

[7] Isa. 56:6–7.

[8] Zech. 8:20–23, 14:9. Cf. Micah 4:1–5.

[9] Derived from גור. The hithpael in Mishnaic Hebrew connotes conversion to Judaism. Cf. התיהד in Esther 8:17.

[10] Arabic: *jār* (sing.), *jirān* (plural).

[11] Arabic: *sariḥ.*

ty, is an offence against honor, which covers the perpetrator with indelible shame."[12] The bond of hospitality was, of course, temporary, but while it lasted it accorded the stranger the full protection not only of the host but also of the entire tribe.

This obligation was confirmed among the old Arabs by oath at a sanctuary, and could not be renounced except by an act at the same place. The deity thus stood in the role of protector of the stranger's cause. In turn the stranger, without giving up his own gods, acknowledged the god of the land in which he lived.[13] If he lived there long enough — away from his own god — he even beame a permanent adherent of the god of his patrons, though not as their full equal.[14] Occasionally the deity was the direct patron of the stranger, "a thing easily understood," writes W. R. Smith, "when we consider that a common motive for seeking foreign protection was the fear of the avenger of blood, and that there was a right of asylum at sanctuaries."[15] In Phoenicia, "the Gerim formed a distinct class in the personnel of the santuary and received certain allowances."[16] The prevalence of such names as Germelkart and Gerastart in Phoenician inscriptions, and of Gairlos or Gerelos among the Arabs of Syria, and of Kosgeros in Idumea, corroborates this point. Numerous examples are found in the Bible of strangers who came to worship the God of Israel. Hence Solomon's request that the prayers of the strangers (nochri) be accepted by God, as those of the Israelites. A propagandistic note appears in his petition: "that all the peoples of the earth may know Thy name even as Thy people Israel." Deutero-Isaiah speaks of the bene hanechar, strangers attaching themselves to the worship of God.[17] Ezekiel reports that uncircumcised strangers ministered to God during the First Temple.[18] While he looked upon this phenomenon with disapproval, the postexilic prophets generally

---

[12] W. R. Smith, *Religion of the Semites*, p. 76. See also *Kinship and Marriage in Early Arabia*, pp. 48–49.

[13] I Sam. 26:19.

[14] Cf. דואג האדומי I Sam. 21:8.

[15] W. R. Smith, *Rel. of Sem.*, p. 77.

[16] Ibid.

[17] I Kings 8:41–43. See Isa. 56:3–8.

[18] Ezek. 44:6, 9.

looked forward to the conversion of the gentiles to the worship of the God of Israel.[19] Figuratively the notion of a temple-client, or *ger,* is used by the psalmist when he asks, מי יגור באהלך, "Who shall sojourn in Thy tent?"[20] The poet speaks of all men as *gerim* of God, that is, of living under His protection. The author of the Book of Ruth speaks of the *ger* as taking refuge under God's wing.[21] Whole tribes were spoken of as standing in the relation of *gerim,* or clients, to God. Israel itself was so considered — an idea which was conducive to high morality.[22] Whereas in the religion of his people, a person regarded himself as united with his god, as a client of another god, he was accepted only as long as his behavior was worthy.

In taking possession of a new land, the conquerors sometimes adopted its gods too.[23] Hence the Assyrians who were transplanted to Samaria maintained their old gods but also adopted the God of Israel. They also took over the local priesthood to teach them the ways of the local deity.[24]

Status of the Ger

Being without political rights and dependent entirely upon the sufferance of the people, the *ger* was occasionally the victim of injustice and oppression. Hence the injunction in the J and E documents not to oppress him is spoken twice.[25] Similarly Deuteronomy demands that he be treated kindly and justly,[26] and he is commended, by the side of the orphan and the widow, to the

---

[19] Zech. 8:20–23, Isa. 66:18–24.

[20] Ps. 15:1.

[21] Ruth 2:12.

[22] Lev. 25:23; Ps. 39:13; 119:19; 1 Chron. 29:15; etc.

[23] Cf. Israel in Canaan.

[24] 2 Kings 17:24–40. Wellhausen noted that the hereditary priesthoods of Arabian sanctuaries were often in the hands of families unrelated to the tribes of worshipers, but apparently descended from older inhabitants. In such cases the worshipers were really only clients of a foreign god. W. R. Smith, op. cit., p. 79.

[25] Exod. 22:20 and Exod. 23:9.

[26] Deut. 1:16, 10:19, 24:14, 17, 27:19.

Israelite's charity.[27] He is enjoined in J and E to rest on the Sabbath[28] and to observe it.[29] In Deuteronomy,[30] the *ger* is "included with the Israelites generally among those who enter into Jehovah's covenant, and are under the obligation of observing the Deuteronomic law; he may share in the joy of a sacred meal[31] at a festival. If Israel is disobedient, he will increase in importance,[32] and acquire supremacy over it."[33]

The conscious appeal of Judaism to the other nations made itself felt during the Second Commonwealth. The Book of Jonah may serve as an example of the breaking through the barriers of nationality by the prophetic message of Judaism, and of its reaching even to hostile nations to save them from doom. The conversion of Ruth shows that there was a conscious effort to

---

[27] Deut. 14:29, 16:11, 14, 24:19, 21, 26:11, 12, 13.

[28] Exod. 23:12.

[29] Exod. 20:10.

[30] Deut. 29:10 (11). Cf. Josh. 8:33, 35 (D2), and Deut. 31:12.

[31] Deut. 16:11, 14 and 26:11.

[32] Deut. 28:43.

[33] Driver, *Deuteronomy*, p. 126. "In Deut. the Ger does not stand formally on an equality with Jehovah's people: he is dependent upon the Israelites' forbearance and charity (cf. in H, Lev. 19.10, 33 f.); and though some conformity with Israel's religion is expected of him (29.10(11)), the only command laid expressly upon him is the observance of the Sabbath (5.14). In P the Ger is placed practically on the same footing as the native Israelite: he enjoys the same rights (Num. 35.15. cf. Ezek. 47.22), and is bound by the same laws, whether civil (Lev. 24.22), moral and religious (18.26; 20.2; 24.16. cf. Ezek. 14.7), or ceremonial (Ex. 12.19; Lev. 16.29; 17.8, 10, 12, 13, 15; 22.18; Num. 15.14, 26, 30; 19.10): the principle, 'One law shall there be for the home-born and for the stranger' is repeatedly affirmed (Ex. 12.49; Lev. 24.22; Num. 9.14; 15.15, 16, 29), — the only specified distinctions being that the Ger, if he would keep the Passover, must be circumcised (Ex. 12.48), and that an Israelite in servitude with him may be redeemed before the jubilee (Lev. 25.48 f.), a privilege not granted in the case of the master's being an Israelite (v. 40 f.). Indeed, in P, the term is already on the way to assume the later technical sense of προσήλυτος, the foreigner who, being circumcised and observing the law generally, is in full religious communion with Israel. (Schürer, *Neutestamentliche Zeitgeschichte* 2, ii, par. 31, p. 566). [English trans., div. II. vol. II, § 31]." Driver, *Deuteronomy*, p. 165. See also Moore, *Judaism* I, pp. 329 ff. Isa. 56; Zech. 8:20-23; Ps. 115:11, 13; *Sibyl. Oracles*; *Didache* — *Shab.* 31a.

welcome even Moabites into the community of God, despite the Deuteronomic law forbidding it.[34] Malachi pleaded with his people: "Have we not all one Father, Hath not one God created us?" and declared that

> From the rising of the sun unto its going down,
> My name is great among the nations,
> And in every place incense and sacrifice
> are offered unto My name.[35]

That is, all worship is in reality intended for the one living God. In this spirit, the opening chapters of the Bible proclaim the kinship of the entire race of man under God the universal Creator.

These universalistic expressions served as the leaven of the extensive Jewish propaganda for the spread of Judaism in the centuries before the rise of Christianity. In the Hellenistic world, many had fallen away from the polytheistic beliefs in which they were raised, and inclined toward Judaism. Some of them formed a fringe of adherents of the synagogue — though they formally remained outside of its pale — and were known as *yir'e Adonai* or φοβούμενοι τον Θεόν, σεβδμενοι τον Θεόν, or shortened, σεβόμενοι.[36]

Through the translation of the Bible into Greek, the gentile world became aware of Jewish teaching. In Alexandria, where Judaism and Hellenism met as friendly forces, the philosophy of Plato and the Torah of Moses were regarded as closely related. On the basis of their common elements Philo constructed his philosophy. Others labored in the same spirit to win the heathens for the worship of God. The rich Hellenistic literature of Judaism shows how serious was the effort on the part of the Jewish people in that direction.

---

[34] Deut. 23:4.

[35] Mal. 2:10, 1:11.

[36] Ps. 115:11, 118:4. See Moore, *Judaism* I, 325 ff. Cf. *Sifre*, Num. 111 and Deut. 54. כל התורה כולה מודה בכל בע"ז הכופר. Also *Horayot* III, 8; *Sanh.* 56b; *Gen. R.* XVI, 6; Ḥulin 5a. *Meg.* 13a: יהודי נקרא בע"ז הכופר.

Effect of Jewish Propaganda

The Jewish propaganda met with considerable success. Despite the lampoons of the satirists and the crude gibes of the Jew-haters in Alexandria and in Rome, Judaism gained the respect of many thoughtful non-Jews. Josephus speaks of the altar of Jerusalem as "venerated by all Greeks and barbarians,"[37] and declares that the Temple mount "is adored by the whole world, and for its renown is honored among strangers at the ends of the earth."[38] Among the gentiles who honored the Temple with their gifts, he includes not only the numerous converts to Judaism, for whom loyalty to it formed part of their adopted faith, but particularly those who remained heathens and would not care to profess their belief in the *superstitio Judaica*. Their sacrifices may have been mere acts of courtesy toward the Jewish people and no real indication of genuine devotion to Judaism.

Philo views the sacrificial service as intended not alone for Israel but "in behalf of all mankind."[39] He believes that Israel was consecrated to the priesthood "that it might forever offer up prayers for the whole universal race of mankind, for the sake of averting evil from them and procuring them a participation in blessing."[40] The *Pesikta*, too, regards the sacrifices offered on the feast of Tabernacles as intended for all the nations.[41] And the Talmud presents this homily of R. Eliezer:

> These seventy oxen[42] [offered up on the first seven days of the feast of Tabernacles], for whom are they meant? For the seventy nations. And for whom is the single ox [sacrificed on the eighth day] intended? For the single nation. It is like unto a human king who ordered his servants to prepare a large repast for him. On the last day he said to his friend:

---

[37] *Jewish Wars*, V.i.3.

[38] *Antiquities* XV.11.

[39] *On Animals Fit for Sacrifice* III; Yonge, vol. III, p. 213.

[40] *Life of Moses*, I, XXVII; Yonge, vol. II, 34. Jonathan's embassy to the Spartans assured them that they were remembered in the sacrifices of the Temple. I Macc. 12:11.

[41] Edition Friedman 202b. ‏כל ימי החג הייתם עסוקים; בקרבנות: של אומות העולם‎.

[42] Referring to Num. 29:13–36.

"Arrange a small meal for me, in order that I may have pleasure through you." Said R. Johanan: Woe unto the heathens who destroyed without realizing what they destroyed. As long as the Temple was in existence, the altar atoned for them; but now what atones for them?[43]

For the masters of Judaism, the Temple was indeed a house of prayer for all nations.

Furthermore the Jewish propaganda literature did not fail to find an echo in the hearts of non-Jewish thinkers. Accordingly, Strabo, writing of Moses with considerable sympathy, pictures him as a Stoic philosopher. Moses, he says, taught

> that the Egyptians had erred in making the divinity to resemble animals that such a thing was not done by the Libyans, nor even by the Greeks, who represented Him under a human form. For that alone is God which embraces us all as well as the earth and the sea, which we name heaven, and world, and the nature of things. But what man in his senses would venture to make an image of that, an image only resembling something around us? Rather must the making of images be given up altogether, and a worthy temple being consecrated to Him, let Him be worshiped without any image whatever.[44]

While Strabo and others like him, despite their sympathetic consideration of Judaism, did not become converts to it, there were those who boldly took the step. Josephus writes: "Many of the Greeks have been converted to the observance of our laws; some have remained true, while others, who were incapable of steadfastness, have fallen away again."[45] He testifies further that "among the masses of the people there has for a long time now been a great amount of zeal for our worship; nor is there a single town among the Greeks or barbarians or anywhere else, not a single nation to which the observance of

---

[43] *Sukka* 55b. See Tosephta *Maaser Sheni* V.27.
[44] Strabo XVI, 2.35 (p. 760sq.), cited by Schürer, div. II, vol. II, pp. 298–99.
[45] *Apion* II.10.

the Sabbath as it exists among ourselves has not penetrated; while fasting and the burning of lights,[46] and many of our laws with regard to meats, are also observed."[47] This can only mean, as Schürer argues, that Josephus refers to "the observance of practice of a specifically Jewish character by those who were not native Jews."[48] Proselytes are named in the Book of Acts, along with the Jews.[49] According to Josephus, the Jews of Antioch always got a large number of Greeks to come to their religious services, where they "treated them as, in a certain sense, a part of themselves."[50] In Athens, too, many Greeks joined the Jewish faith. In Damascus almost the entire female population was devoted to Judaism. Among them were women of rank.[51] The most interesting conversion was that of the royal family of Adiabene, the little kingdom situated on the confines of the Roman and Parthian empires. This story, as recorded in *Antiquities*,[52] reports that when the Jewish state was tottering under the attacks of the Romans, it received aid and encouragement from Helena the queen of Adiabene, a small kingdom to the northeast of Palestine. This queen, with her two sons, Izates and Monobazes, embraced the Jewish faith. In a time of famine she sent food to the starving people in Jerusalem, and she contributed costly gifts to the Temple. Izates had his five sons educated in Jerusalem. Helena made a pilgrimage to the holy city and built a palace there. Both Helena and Izates were buried in Jerusalem. Monobazes, as well as his mother, owned a palace in the holy city, and became the hero of many legends. During the Roman War, his relatives fought on the side of the Jews. It may be taken for granted that many subjects of the royal house of Adiabene also embraced Judaism. Azizus, king of Emesa,

---

[46] נר שבת.

[47] *Apion* II.40.

[48] Op. cit., p. 307, n. 271.

[49] Acts 2:9–11, 13:16, 26, 43, 50, 17:4, 17.

[50] *Jewish Wars*, VII.3.3.

[51] Acts 13:50, 17:4; Josephus, *Antiq.* XVIII.3.5.

[52] *Antiq.* XX.2–4. Rabbinic sources are: *Nazir.* III.6; *Yoma* III.9; *Gen. R.* 46:10; *B. Bathra* 11a; Jeru. *Peah* 1.1, 15b, and Tosephta *Peah* III (end); Jeru. *Suk.* 1.1, 51d; Bab. *Suk.* 2b; *Sifre* 70a (Num.).

and Polemo, king of Cilicia, the two brothers-in-laws of Agrippa II, were converts to Judaism.[53]

Among the famed Greek converts to Judaism was Aquila of Pontus, who, under the influence of R. Akiba, prepared a revised version of the Bible for the Greek-speaking Jews, and thus placed a weapon of defense in their hands against the newly born Christian movement, which had appropriated the Septuagint to its purposes. R. Eliezer and R. Joshua praised him for his zeal and applied to him the words of the psalmist: "Thou art fairest among the children of men."[54] Several rabbis were said to have been descended from proselytes, among them, Shemaiah and Abtalion, and R. Meir.[55]

The triumph of the Maccabees marked a general heightening of the Jewish spirit, and led to an aggressive policy of proselytism. John Hyrcanus forcibly converted the Idumeans. His son Aristobulus I converted the Itureans. And Alexander Janneus destroyed Pella because its inhabitants refused to be circumcised (i.e., converted).[56] Among the Idumean converts was Antipater, whose cruel son Herod became king of Judea.

In Rome, too, Judaism did not fail to make large numbers of converts. In the reign of Nero, Empress Poppea Sabina, his second wife, was inclined to Judaism. She was designated as Θεοδεβής and was ready to advocate Jewish

---

[53] *Antiq.* XX.7.1 and 3. Likewise the treasurer of Queen Candace of Ethiopia is named as a convert to Judaism. Acts 8:27–38.

[54] Ps. 45:3. Jeru. *Megilla* 1.11, 71c. Schürer, *History* II, III, p. 171. Perhaps a play on יפת = יפיפית.

[55] Mention must also be made of Miriam of Palmyra, who twice went to Jerusalem to offer Naziritical vows (*Nazir* VI.11). (It is not certain, however, that she was a proselyte. See Derenbourg, משא ארץ ישראל, p. 117 [59a].) Derenbourg argues that not only the women of Damascus but also those of Bethany (בטניה) and Haran were converted to Judaism. He cites as proof the names of three scholars of the first century: יוסי בן דורמסקית, אבא שאול בן בטנית, and יוחנן בן החורנית. These scholars were known by the names of their mothers because the women may have been converted without their husbands sent their sons to Jerusalem to study. (Derenbourg, op. cit., note; and art. in Ben Chananja, *Talmudische Forschungen* [1867].

[56] Possibly the disastrous results of some of these conversions, especially through the Herodians, led the masters of Judaism to look askance upon both גרי אריות and גרי שלחן מלכים. Jeru. *Kid.* 4. 1, 65b. וכן גרי אריות וכן גרי שלחן מלכים אין מקבלין אותן. See also *Yeb.* 24b.

petitions to the emperor.[57] Tactius remarks that after her death, she was not burnt according to Roman custom, but embalmed "after the fashion of foreign kings."[58] The success of Jewish proselytism in Rome may be judged from the fact that Horace speaks of the person who observes the Jewish Sabbath as *unus multorum*.[59]

Though most of the Roman aristocracy looked with contempt upon the Jews whom they had conquered, and ridiculed their imageless worship of God, their observance of the Sabbath — a practice which seemed to them rank idleness — and their abstention from swine-flesh, nonetheless some Romans were attracted by the belief in divine unity and spirituality and by the moral character of Judaism, which freed men from evil and from sorrow.[60] The conversion of Romans to Judaism appeared as a menace to the Roman empire and was checked by state law. Domitian punished converts with confiscation of property, exile, and even with death. His successor, Nerva, removed the prohibition on proselytism, but his reign was of short duraton (96–98); and with the accession of Hadrian to the throne, the restrictions were reinstated. Antoninus Pius, while permitting the rite of circumcision for Jews, prohibited proselytism. Septimus Severus, in 204, renewed the penalties for conversion to either Judaism or Christianity.

Jewish propaganda among the gentiles was further checked by the growth and expansion of Judaism's daughter religion. Christianity grew out of the messianic yearnings of the Jewish people and for a time continued as a Jewish sect. Through the energetic efforts of Paul, it was carried to distant parts of the world. Its proselytizers took over the seven Noachian laws as the sum of religious requirements (i.e., of a גר תושב).[61] Free from racial and national bonds, and containing a strong admixture of Greco-Roman elements in its beliefs and practices, it more readily recommended itself to the gentiles than did Judaism. When, after centuries of struggle, it emerged triumphant as the

---

[57] *Antiq.* XX.8.11; *Vita* 3.

[58] *Annals* XVI.6. Schürer, *Jewish People in the Time of Jesus Christ*, div. II, vol. II, p. 239, n. 74.

[59] *Sat.* 1.9, 68–72.

[60] Schürer, op. cit., II. 11, §31.

[61] Acts 15:20–29.

state religion of Rome, Christianity raised its head against its mother faith. The Jews were branded as a shameful, bestial sect," and "contemptible and perverse." Emperor Constantine imposed penalties both on the converts to Judaism and upon the Jews who converted them. Those who persecuted apostates from Judaism were punished with burning. The penalty of death and confiscation of property was imposed upon Jews who circumcised slaves and Christians. Furthermore, circumcised slaves gained their freedom. The intermarriage between Jews and Christians was forbidden under penalty of death.[62]

However, neither pagan nor Christianized Rome could stop the proselytical zeal of the Jewish people nor the appeal of Judaism to the non-Jews. Dio Cassius writes:

> The country has been named Judea and the people themselves Jews. I do not know how this title came to them, but it applies also to all the rest of mankind, although of alien people, who affect their customs. This class exists even among the Romans, and though often repressed, has increased to a very great extent and has won its way to the right of freedom in its observances. They are distinguished from the rest of mankind in practically every detail of life, and especially by the fact that they do not honor any of the usual gods, but show extreme reverence for one particular divinity. They never had any statues of Him even in Jerusalem itself, but believing Him to be unnameable and invisible, they worship Him in the most extravagant fashion on earth.[63]

Chrysostom is the authority for the fact that during the fourth Christian century, Christians in Palestine and Syria (i.e., after Christianity had been set up as the state religion) were attracted by Jewish modes of worship. At Antioch, Christian men and especially women attended synagogues on the Sabbaths and holy days, listened to the sounds of the shofar, participated in

---

[62] A. S. Hirshenberg, "Tenu'at ha-Hityahadut," in *Hatekufah* XIII, p. 192, n. 1.
[63] Dio Cassius, XXXVII, cited by Solomon Zeitlin, *JQR*, XXXIV, pp. 221–22.

Jewish devotions on Yom Kippur and Sukkot, and turned to Jewish courts for the settlement of their disputes.[64]

Pharisaic Attitude Toward Proselytism

That the Pharisees appeared as strong competitors of Paul in proselytical propaganda is evidenced in the Book of Acts.[65] Their zeal is the subject of the evangelist's denunciation: "Woe to you, you impious scribes and Pharisees! You traverse sea and land to make a single proselyte, and when you succeed you make him a son of Gehenna twice as bad as yourselves."[66] Graetz argued that this verse refers to the conversion of the consul Flavius Clemens, the nephew of Emperor Domitian, and his wife Flavia Domitilla, who together with other Romans were executed by the emperor because of their conversion. Graetz further thinks that the Pharisees referred to are probably the *tanaim* Rabban Gamaliel II, R. Joshua, R. Eliezer b. Azaria, and R. Akiba, who were in Rome at the time of Flavius Clemens's conversion.[67]

In the view of A. S. Hirshenberg, these elders made haste for Rome immediately after the death of Domitian, in order to engage anew in proselytical activity. The various debates on religious matters in which they participated show clearly their zeal in gaining followers for their faith.[68]

Akiba's extensive travels served the double purpose of strengthening the spirit of the Jewish people in the far-flung diaspora, and of doing missionary

[64] Graetz, II, 613–14.

[65] Acts 13:4–52.

[66] Matt. 23:15. In reality, the apostles followed the Pharisees in this respect. See Acts 13:17–22.

[67] *Monatschrift*, 1869, pp. 169–70. Possibly the talmudic reference to "the nephew of Titus" אונקלוס בר קלוניקוס בר אחתיה דטיטוס may intend Flavius Clemens. Hirshenberg, op. cit., p. 201, n. 6.

[68] R. Joḥanan b. Zakkai and the Roman officer. Jeru. *Sanh.* I, 19b; Bab. *Bech.* 5a; *Ḥulin* 27b; *Sifre Zut.* Num. 3:36; *Pes. R. Kah.* 40a; R. Gamaliel in Rome, *A.Z.* 4.7 and 54b; *Bech.* 8b.

R. Hash. 17b; *B.B.* 10a; *Sanh.* 39a, 91a; *A.Z.* 54b–55a; *Gen. R.* I. 9, X. 3; XI, 5; XIII, 6; XX, 4; *Exod. R.* XXX, 9; *Num. R.* IV, 9; XII, 4; XIX, 8;19; *Ruth R.* III.2; *Esther R.* IX, 11, etc.

work among the non-Jews.[69] With similar motives in mind, other leaders like
R. Judah b. Bathyra, R. Matitia b. Ḥeresh, R. Ḥanina the nephew of R.
Joshua, and R. Jonathan established schools in important centers in the
diaspora. R. Matitia b. Ḥeresh founded a school at Rome, which seems to
have functioned as a center of Jewish propaganda.

An interesting story is recorded by the glossator to *Megillat Ta'anit*. On
the twenty-eighth of Adar good news came to the Jews who had not strayed
from the paths of the Torah, that they need not mourn, though the kings of
Yavan[70] had decreed conversion on Israel, had proscribed study of Torah,
circumcision of their sons, and observance of the Sabbath, and had enjoined
the worship of idols. But a covenant had been made with Israel, that the book
of the Torah would not depart from among them, as it is said: "For it shall
not be forgotten out of the mouth of their seed" (Deut. 31:21). And it is said:
"If these ordinances depart from before Me, saith the Lord, then the seed of
Israel also shall cease from being a nation before Me forever" (Jer. 31:36).
And it is said: "As for Me, this is My covenant with them, saith the Lord. My
spirit is upon thee, and My words which I put in thy mouth, shall not depart
out of thy mouth, nor out of the mouth of thy seed, nor out of the mouth of
thy seed's seed, saith the Lord, from henceforth and forever" (Isa. 59:21).

What did Yehudah ben Shamua[71] and his friends do? They arose and went
to a certain matron in whose home all the Roman dignitaries assembled, and
solicited her advice. She said to them: "Come tonight and make a demonstration." They gathered at night, and raised a great outcry: "Oh, heavens! Are
we not your brothers? Are we not the sons of the same father? Are we not the
sons of the same mother? Wherein do we differ from other peoples and
tongues, that you should issue such harsh decrees against us?" And they
would not budge from the place, until they were granted three *mitzvot*: to
circumcise their sons, to study Torah, and to observe the Sabbath; also they

---

[69] E.g., *Yeb.* 98a: אמר בן יסאסין כשהלכתי לכרכי הים מצאתי גר אחד שנשא אשת אחיו מאמו.
אמרתי לו: בני מי הרשך? אמר לי: הרי אשה ושבעה בניה (גרים). על ספסל זה ישב רבי עקיבא ואמר שני
דברים...

[70] The name Yavan was applied also to Italy. Cf. the use of the term Magna Graecia for
Southern Italy.

[71] מתלמידיו של ר' מאיר.

would not be required to worship idols. That day on which they secured these three *mitzvot* they consecrated as a holiday.[72]

The three stories about heathens who turned to Shammai and then to Hillel with the request to be converted aim to reflect the erratic and uncompromising character of the one teacher and the mildness, patience, and humility of the other, rather than a fundamental difference on the question of proselytism. They are in line with other anecdotes in which Jewish people test the respective characters of the two sages.[73] It is hardly correct to maintain that the בית הלל favored the conversion of gentiles and the בית שמאי opposed it. Gamaliel II, a descendant of the house of Hillel, is reported to have been opposed to the admission of Ammonite *gerim*. On the other hand, R. Eliezer b. Hyrcanus, a Shammaite, is recorded as liberal with regard to converts.[74] All that we can say is that they held different viewpoints with references to the requirements for admission (i.e., טבילה or מילה alone, or both; etc.). But as heirs of the prophetic hopes all leaders of Pharisaic Judaism looked forward to the conversion of the world to the Torah.[75]

In the *Amidah,* the thirteenth benediction invokes God's blessing not only upon the righteous and the saintly of Israel but also upon the *gere zedek*: על הצדיקים ועל החסידים וכו' ועל גרי הצדק. The heroes of ancient Israel were pictured as missionaries. In romantic imagination, Abraham converted the men, and Sarah the women.[76] R. Jehudah bar Ilai maintains that the *ger* who brings *Bikkurim* may recite the confession of the twenty-sixth chapter of Deuteronomy[77] and may consider himself of the seed of Israel, for God said to Abraham: "For I have made thee the father of a multitude of nations. Before, thou wast father to Aram; and now, from here on, thou art father to all the nations."[78] The *ger* is thus placed on terms of equality with Israel. Further-

---

[72] *Megillat Ta'anit,* chap. 12, to Adar 28.

[73] *Shab.* 31a.

[74] *Gen. R.* LXX, 5; *Koh. R.* to Eccles. 8:8; *Num. R.* VIII, 9, and *Mechilta* on Exod. 18:5 (ed. Friedmann, 58a, b).

[75] Cf. עלינו and לעשות רצונך אגדה אחת כלם ויעשו הבראים, כל לפניך וישתחוו . . . פחדך תן ובכן בלבב שלם.

[76] *Gen. R.* XXXIX, 14. הנשים את מגיירת ושרה האנשים את מגייר אברהם.

[77] Deut. 26:5-10.

[78] *Jeru. Bikkur.* I, 4, 64a. Tos. *Bik.* 1.2 ascribes this statement to another *tana*.

more Jehudah, while demanding that *gerim* be received by a בית דין, accepted a *ger* who was converted without witnesses because he had children.[79] He was of the opinion that *milah* (circumcision) or *tebilah* (immersion) alone is sufficient.[80] His opponent, R. Neḥemiah, shares his view on proselytism.[81] Most striking is the accusation against Abraham that he did not accept all that wished to be converted. R. Joḥanan explains the subjection of Israel in Egypt as a punishment for the exclusivism of his conversions.[82] Moses too is credited with converting Bithiah, the daughter of Pharaoh.[83] The luxuriousness of Solomon is explained on the ground that he married many women in order to convert them to Judaism.[84] Hezekiah, without figuring as a missionary, relies upon the merit of his fathers.[85] Jethro and Rahab figure as model converts.[86] These haggadahs show that the effort to convert heathens to Judaism was intense.

Missionary Propaganda

From the church fathers we learn that the Jews held firmly to the prophetic hope of the conversion of the gentiles to their faith. Justin Martyr complains

---

[79] *Yeb.* 47a.

[80] *Yeb.* 46b.

[81] עמך נדבות ביום חילך שכנסתי לי כל אותן החיילות (Ps. 110:3) א"ל הקב"ה לאברהם: עמך הייתי (Gen. R. XXXIX, 8). See also *Sifre* (Friedmann) 73a on: ואהבת את ה' ומכניסן תחת והאוכלוסים Gen. R. XXXIX, 8; 48. *Cant. R.* to Song of Songs מלמד שהיה אברהם אבינו מגיירם. כנפי השכינה 1:3. (ללמדך שכל מי שהוא מקרב את העכו"ם ומגיירו כאילו בראו.) Rabba interprets the verse: נדיבי אלהי אברהם ולא אלהי יצחק ויעקב? אלא אלהי אברהם (Ps. 47:10) thus: עמים נאספו עם אלהי אברהם שהיה תחלה לגרים.

[82] (Ned. שהפריש בני אדם מלהכנס תחת כנפי השכינה, שנא' תן לי הנפש והרכוש קח לך (Gen. 14:21) 32a). *Sanh.* 99b contains the following: תמנע בת מלכים הואי . . . בעיא לאיגיורי באתה אצל אברהם יצחק ויעקב ולא קבלוה הלכה והיתה פלגש לאליפז בן עשו . . . נפק מינה עמלק דצערי נהו לישראל. מאי טעמא דלא איבעי להו לרחקה.

[83] *Pesikta* 17. According to the *Mechilta*, he is ordered: אני הוא שאמרתי והיה העולם אני המקרב ולא המרחק . . . אני שקרבתי את יתרו ולא רחקתיו אף אתה כשבא אדם אצלך להתגייר אינו בא אלא לשם שמים אף אתה קרבהו ולא תרחיקהו (loc. cit.).

[84] *Cant. R.* to Song of Songs 1:1.

[85] אבותי שקרבו לך כל הגרים הללו על אחת כמה וכמה שתתן לי את נפשי (Jeru. *Sanh.* X, 28c). See also *Meg.* 14b; *Cant. R.* to Song of Songs 1:3.

[86] See *Mechilta* יתרו and *Cant. R.* to Song of Songs 6:2; also *Cant. R.* to Song of Songs 1:3.

against them for sending emissaries in all directions to calumniate Christianity and to proselytize to their own faith.[87] Clement of Alexandria similarly
states that Judaism, though rent in factions, strives to win converts.[88] Origen
testifies to the great attraction which Judaism possessed for the heathens, and
attacks the Judaizers with indignation.[89] These Judaizers were active also
among the Christians. Thus many women kept the Sabbath and the Passover.
Origen accounts for this sympathy with Judaism as the work of Jewish
missionaries, who cajoled Christians to observe its rites.[90] Ephraem Syrus
informs us likewise that Judaism received many accessions from heathendom,
in consequence of Jewish propagandists.[91] Jerome is apprehensive that the
charity extended by Jews to Christians may corrupt the recipients and win
them over to the faith of the benefactors.[92] He testifies further that Christians
were so much attracted by the delights awaiting the righteous Jews that they
embraced Judaism.[93]

In the face of the general eagerness of the masters of the synagogue in
welcoming converts,[94] R. Ḥelbo, a fourth-century *amora*, stands rather
solitary in his derogation, "Converts are as troublesome for Israel as a sore on
the skin (ספחת), for it is written: 'And the stranger shall join himself with
them, and they shall cleave to (ונספחו) the house of Jacob' [Isa. 14:1]," a
remark which appears four times in the Babylonian Talmud.[95] Israel Levi

---

[87] *Dialogue*, c. 122. See Krauss, *JQR*, V (1893), 127.

[88] *Stromata* VII, 15. Cited ibid., 135.

[89] In *Matt. Comm.* ser. p. 16.

[90] *Hom. in Jerem.* XII, 13; in *Matt. Comm.* ser., p. 16, cited ibid., pp. 145–47.

[91] In 2 Reg. XIX, 1. Cited vol. VI (1894), p. 91.

[92] *Ep. LII ad Nepantinum*. Cited ibid., VI, 228.

[93] In Isa. 59:5; cited ibid., VI, 242.

[94] ואמר ר' אליעזר לא הגלה הקב"ה את ישראל לבין האומות אלא כדי שיתוספו עליהם גרים, שנאמר
כלום אדם זורע סאה אלא להכניס כמה כורין, ור' יוחנן אמר מכהא ורחמתי (Hos. 2:25) וזרעתיה לי בארץ
אותם שלא היו מעמי — דבקו בהם ותהיו לי לעם. (ibid.) את לא רוחמה: ואמרתי ללא עמי, עמי אתה
רש"י: כלומר בשביל שנפגשו עם ישראל עמי נתגיירו והיו לעמי. (כשדאי, המתיהדים, רעב/פ פסחים פז, ב.
א"ר אושעיה מאי דכתיב צדקת פזרונו בישראל? צדקה עשה הקב"ה בישראל שפזרן לבין האומות (רש"י:
שאינם יכולין לכלותם יחד) שם, שם.

[95] (a) *Yeb.* 47a, b. (מאי טעמא דאי פריש נפרוש . . . דאר' חלבו וכו').

(b) *Nid.* 13b. (הגרים והמשחקין בתנוקות מעכבין את המשיח וכו'). The *ger* is a danger to Israel,

calls attention to the interesting fact that though R. Ḥelbo taught in Palestine, his words are not quoted a single time in the Palestinian Talmud nor in
the Midrashim. Furthermore the very phrase (ונספחו)[96] upon which R. Ḥelbo
based his statement, served for a text for an opposite opinion,[97] preached by
R. Berechia, a disciple of R. Ḥelbo.[98] R. Ḥelbo's view seems to have been
shared by Rabba bar Rav Huna and perhaps also by R. Yitzḥak.[99] At first it
may appear that this is also the attitude of the *baraitha*[100] that proselytes are
not accepted in messianic times. In reality this view grows out of the aversion
to forced conversions and to conversions induced by political advantage. It
protests the type of proselytism carried on by John Hyrcanus, Aristobulus I,
and others. R. Ḥelbo's opinion may be understood in the light of historical
experience, notably the relations of converted Romans and the Jewish people,
in the reaction which set in after the Bar Kochba rebellion.[101] The general

for his unfaithfulness delays the Messiah. The idea is that the *gerim*, through their neglect of
the *mitzvot*, involve the Jewish people in punishment. On the other hand, *gerim* are credited
with being more observant than the Jews. *Pes.* 91b. אמר ר' יוחנן אין עושין חבורה שכולה גרים שמא
ידקדקו בו ויביאוה לידי פסל.

(c) *Yeb.* 109b. R. Yitzḥak's statement that one evil eye after another will befall those who
receive proselytes is followed by the opinion of R. Ḥelbo. Based possibly on Prov. 11:15: רע ירוע
כי ערב זר. Cf. *Kid.* 70b. On the other hand, in *Kohelet R.* to Eccles. 8.10 on proselytism: גם זה
הבל, אמר ר' יצחק איננו הבל, וזה הבל שאינן באים מאליהן.

(d) *Kid.* 70b. Rabba bar Rav Huna, the colleague of R. Ḥelbo, states: זו מעלה יתירה יש בין
ישראל לגרים דאילו בישראל כתיב בהו והייתם להם לאלהים והמה יהיו לי לעם (Ezek. 37:26) ואילו בגרים
כתיב. מי הוא זה ערב את לבו לגשת אלי נאם ה' והייתם לי לעם ואנכי אהיה לכם לאלהים (Jer. 30:21-22)

[96] Isa. 14:1.

[97] *Exod. R.* XIX. 4 contains the following: כנגד מי אמר בחוץ לא ילין גר (Job 31:32) אלא עתידין
ואין נספחו אלא (Isa. 14:1) גרים להיות כהנים משרתים בבהמ"ק שני' ונלוה הגר עליהם ונספחו על בית יעקב
ספחני נא אל אחת הכהונות שעתידין להיות אוכלין מלחם הפנים לפי שבנותיהן (1 Sam. 2:36) כהונה שנא'
נישאות לכהונה.

[98] *Hagoren* IX, p. 7. See Bacher, *Agad. d. Paläst. Amor.* III, 348.

[99] Cf. *Koh. R.* to Eccles. 8:10, above.

[100] *Aboda Zara* 3b, *Yeb.* 24b.

[101] Thus, reflecting this reaction, comes the statement of R. Ḥiyya: אל תאמן בגר עד כ"ד דורות
שהוא תופס שאורו. However, he proceeds to correct his statement: אבל בשעה שהגר מקבל עליו עולו
של הקב"ה באהבה ובוראה ומתגייר לשם שמים אין הקב"ה מחזירו שני' ואוהב גר לתת לו לחם ושמלה. This
quotation has been preserved only in the *Yalkut to Ruth* 601. R. Ḥiyya's opinion corresponds to

attitude of the synagogue to *gerim* may best be judged by the sermonic comments on the subject contained in the Midrashim.[102]

It is therefore not surprising to hear of important conversions to Judaism in Christian times. A few of these should be mentioned, in illustration of historical developments. The first is the case of Harit ibn Amr of Yemen (260–330). More dramatic is the story of Abu-Kariba, the powerful ruler of the Himyarite kingdom in South Arabia. This warlike ruler laid siege to the city of Yathrib in northern Arabia, the modern Medina. The Jews and the Arabs of Yathrib valiantly repulsed his attacks and succeeded in tiring his soldiers. During the siege, the king became ill; and, for want of fresh water, was tormented with thirst. Two Jewish teachers gained admittance to the exhuasted Abu Kariba, and prevailed upon him to lift the siege. They also succeeded in winning him over to Judaism (ca. 500). At his request, they accompanied him to Yemen to convert his people. Though the teachers were not able to convince all, they did bring great numbers into the Jewish fold. Not long thereafter, Abu Kariba was slain, reportedly by his own battle-weary soldiers. He was succeeded by his youngest son, Zorah (520–530), who proved to be an enthusiastic Jew and a zealous defender of Jews and Judaism. When he learned that the Byzantine king oppressed Jews, he seized and slew Byzantine merchants traveling on business through Himyar; and he levied heavy tribute upon the Christians of his land. These reprisals involved him in wars with neighboring kings, many forces being roused against him by a Syrian bishop. Apprised that his capital had been captured and that his queen and treasures were in the hands of the enemy, he, with his mount, plunged from a cliff into the sea. With him ended the short-lived Jewish kingdom in Arabia, which, in the words of Graetz, "arose in a night and disappeared in a night."

More enduring was the Jewish kingdom of the Chazars. These people of Finnish stock, related to the Bulgars and the Hungarians, at an early time established a powerful realm on the lower Volga, with their capital in the

---

the older opinion of R. Eliezer b. Hyrcanus: מפני מה גרים בזמן הזה (תחת ממשלת הרומאים) מעונין וסורין באין עליהן . . . לפי שאין עושין מאהבה אלא מיראה. *Yeb.* 48b.

[102] See *Num. R.* VIII.

vicinity of the later Russian city of Astrakhan. They were feared by the
Christian kings of Byzantium and by their heathen neighbors. The Slavs of
Kiev paid them an annual tax of a sword and a skin for each household.
About the year 735, their king Bulan and his grandees embraced the Jewish
faith and established Jewish schools for the instruction of the youth in Bible,
Mishnah, and Talmud. For some three centuries, Chazaria stood an oasis in a
fearsome wilderness of superstition, the only civilized center in vast reaches of
barbarism. Its tolerance to men of different faiths is shown by its unique court
consisting of two Jews, two Christians, and one heathen, to dispense justice to
men of all creeds. This kingdom was conquered by the Russians, and its
Jewish subjects fled for refuge to Spain, Babylonia, and Palestine, or scattered
in the Crimea and other parts of Russia.

The Ethiopian church preserved many distinctly Jewish elements, as is
evidenced by the practice of circumcision (professedly not for religious
reasons), the observance of the seventh-day Sabbath and the law of the
Levirate, and the prohibition of swine flesh and of things strangled.[103]

More significant is the Judaizing heresy in the Russian church.[104] It
firmly upheld the belief in the One God and denied the Trinity and the divinity of Jesus. Rejecting the New Testament, it insisted on strict adherence to the
Law of Moses. About the time of the expulsion of the Jews from Spain, it
made its appearance among high Russian state and church officials. In 1471,
a Jew, Zechariah of Kiev, had come to Novgorod and converted the priest
Dionis, also the archpriest Aleksei and, through him, many of the clergy of
Novgorod and Pskov. These priests were placed at the head of two important
Greek Catholic churches in Moscow by Grand Duke Ivan Vassilyevitch
(1480), where they had the opportunity of winning several members of the
grand duke's family to Judaism. It was not until a new ruler came to the
throne that Archbishop Genandi succeeded in breaking the power of this
heretical movement by burning its leaders (1504). Nevertheless the doctrine of
the group continued to spread secretly. In the year 1818, about fifteen
hundred members in the governments of Orel, Tula, and Saratov, openly

---

[103] F. J. Foakes Jackson, *The History of the Christian Church*, p. 557.
[104] H. Rosenthal, art. "Judaizing Heresy," *Jew. Encycl.* VII, 369–70.

adhered to the Judaizing sect.[105] Yet another such group, the Subbotniki, appeared near the end of the eighteenth century, met with similar governmental repressions and dispersions, and persisted — for the most part, clandestinely.[106]

In Christian lands, conversion to Judaism was a capital offense. Bishop Bodo, upon his renunciation of Christianity (838), took refuge with the Moors in Saragossa.[107] The Dominican friar Robert de Reddinge, after acceptance of Judaism (1275), escaped from England.[108] The Jews of Spain were expelled on the charge that as long as they remained in the land, their brethren who had been converted to Christianity would not be faithful to the church. The romantic soul Solomon Molko was burnt to death (1532) on the accusation of proselytizing. In the seventeenth century, an act of Parliament made the acceptance of proselytes to Judaism a criminal offense in England. Count Valentine Potocki, the famous *ger zedek,* was burnt in Wilna on the second day of Shabuoth, May 24, 1749, because of his conversion to Judaism. His aged teacher, Menachem Man bar Aryeh Löb of Visun, was tortured and executed a few weeks later (July 3, 1749).[109]

With all these obstacles in its way, Judaism naturally could not engage in a campaign of active proselytizing. In fact, the Talmud tractate *Gerim* advises that when a non-Jew applies for conversion, he should be dissuaded, and only if he persists should he be accepted into the Jewish fold.

However, Judaism has attracted many minds and hearts in an indirect way. It stood sponsor at the Protestant Reformation, at the birth of Unitarianism, and of the modernist movements which promise to transform the doctrines of the church. The early Judaizing Christians regarded their movement as a means of extending Judaism and of winning the gentiles for the Law of Moses. To them, Christianity appeared as a development of Judaism.[110] The energetic efforts of the Apostle unto the Gentiles were likewise, in great

---

[105] Ibid.
[106] Art. "Subbotniki," *Jew. Encyc.* XI, 577-78.
[107] *Jew. Encyc.* III, 283.
[108] *Jew. Encyc.* X, 345.
[109] *Jew. Encyc.* X, 147.
[110] See Acts 15:19-29.

measure, based on Jewish foundations. Saul of Tarsus carried the Gospel to many lands, frequently utilizing the synagogues of the spreading diaspora as centers of his activity. While absorbing the rites and customs of Greco-Roman heathenism, Christianity at the same time preserved the distinctly moral elements that it derived from Judaism. The cross in one hand and the Decalogue in the other, it made its triumphant march through the ages. With the aid of the Hebrew Bible and in the name of the God of Israel — despite the strange interpretation that it sometimes placed upon Him — it won its victories over licentiousness, degeneracy, and inhumanity in the pagan nations. "Through the Church," observed Woodrow Wilson, "there entered into Europe a potent leaven of Judaic thought." It is traceable in every phase of European civilization: its morality, legislation, thought, creeds and rituals, art, drama, and poetry.

Also directly, through its inherent truths and through the labors of its consecrated followers, Judaism continued to play a significant part in shaping the religious life of mankind. It roused Mohammed to undertake his great mission of religious reform among the Arabs, and to carry his campaign of conversion to distant lands. Deepened and enlarged in content through the Halachah (i.e., the legal portions of the Talmud) and the Haggadah (i.e., the narrative portions of the Talmud), it acted as a correcting check on the doctrines of both the church and the mosque. Through the refinement of religious values in consequence of the Karaitic schism in the eighth century,[111] Judaism developed a formidable body of philosophy of worldwide significance. Reconciling religion with Aristotelianism, the dominant science of the Middle Ages, Maimonides became the teacher of Thomas Aquinas, as was Gabirol of Duns Scotus, thereby affecting profoundly the foundations of scholasticism. The Jewish grammarians and commentators of the Bible — Ḥayyuj, Ibn Ezra, Rashi, Kimḥi — unequivocally held out before the world the thoughts of Judaism on the Bible and its message. Their labors yielded fruit in the Protestant Reformation. Christian Hebraists like Reuchlin, Pico della Mirandola, Melanchton, the Buxtorfs, Wagenseil, and many others,

---

[111] See S. Poznanski, art. "Karaites," Hastings, *Encycl. Rel. and Ethics,* vol. VII, pp. 662–72.

drank deeply from their fountain, and, exploring the Hebrew Bible, rabbinic and kabbalistic literatures, found many a new weapon in their struggles for a purer Christianity. Judaizing, to be sure, ever constituted a heresy, from which neither Catholicism in its Greek and Roman divisions nor Protestantism ever wholly freed itself. The Hebraic spirit manifested itself forcefully in the Puritan movement and in much that resulted from it in the life and literature of England and America. Through Spinoza and, to lesser degree, through Moses Mendelssohn, Judaism gained the respect of Lessing, Herder, Kant, Goethe, Matthew Arnold, Huxley, and hosts of other advanced intellects. Nor have the researches of the pioneers of the scientific study of Judaism —Zunz, Z. Frankel, Luzzatto, Geiger, Graetz — been without effect on Christian scholars. The modern restatements of Judaism by M. Lazarus, Steinthal, Hermann Cohen, Kaufmann Kohler, Claude G. Montefiore, and their renewed emphasis on the prophetic ideals of religion as based on justice and love, and their restressing of righteousness as the foundation of social progress, have heartened the general cause of religious liberalism.

Though long not an actively militant proselytizing faith, Judaism continues to leaven the thoughts and emotions of humankind. Recognizing other religions as beneficent forces, Judaism seeks not to supplant them but to labor with them in honorable fellowship, for the eradication of the impure spots of modern civilization, of hatred and prejudice, of ignorance and superstition, and for the enthronement of the One and Holy God in the lives of all men.

Studies and Notes
on Tefillin, Mezuzah,
Tzitzit, Tallit

Tefillin

The three external signs of Judaism, *tefillin, mezuzah,* and *tzitzit,* may be regarded as creations of Pharisaism. The rabbis speak of *tefillin* as based on the Torah and expanded by the *soferim.*[1] They are generally traced to Exodus 13:9, 16 and Deuteronomy 6:8 and 11:18. Attempts have been made to interpret these passages figuratively. It is argued, for example, that the sacrifice of the firstborn can hardly be carried as a sign upon one's hand and as frontlets between one's eyes. The words הדברים האלה and דברי אלה in Deuteronomy are not limited to the immediate texts, but apply to the entire code. It is obviously impossible to carry a whole book on the head or forehead. Passages like Song of Songs 8:6, "Set me as a seal upon thy heart, as a seal upon thine arm," show that these words must be understood to mean that the divine commands shall be constantly in one's consciousness, as if they were bound upon the arm or upon the forehead. However, the references to "writing" and "binding" and "writing upon doorposts," cannot very well be reduced to mere

---

[1] חומר כדברי סופרים מבדברי תורה. האומר אין תפלין כדי לעבור על דברי תורה פטור. חמש טוטפות להוסיף על דברי סופרים חייב. גמ׳. א״ר אלעזר אמר רבי אושעיא אינו חייב אלא על דבר שעיקרו מדברי תורה ופירושו מדברי סופרים ויש בו להוסיף ואם הוסיף גורע. ואין לנו אלא תפלין (פירש״י: שעיקרן בתורה ופירושן מדברי סופרים סופרים שהם ד׳ בתים וכו׳). והאיכא צצית דעיקרו מדברי תורה ופירושו מדברי סופרים וכו׳ (*Sanh.* X, 3, 88b).

metaphors, in the light of the common custom among the Jewish people and their neighbors, of marking their bodies and their homes with sacred signs, and of wearing charms and amulets to ward off evil influences and to ensure good luck.

The law of Exodus 13:16, combining the sacrifice of the firstborn of animals and the redemption of the firstborn sons with the "sign" upon the hand and "frontlets" between the eyes recalls the use of the blood of a sacrificial animal, among Semitic peoples, for marking a newborn child or an adult. Samuel Ives Curtiss gathered numerous examples of this character among the Semitic tribesmen in Iraq and in Syria. He was informed by a minister of the shrine at Zebedani that "the mother of a boy, when she slaughters a sacrifice in his behalf, takes some of the blood and puts it on his skin." This practice is known as *fedou*, "redemption."[2] Similarly, "a man who promised the *weli* (saint) a *fedou* in case a child should be born to him, puts the blood of the sacrifice offered in payment of his vow, on the child's forehead. The Mawali Arabs are accustomed to take the newborn infant to the shrine of the tribe to which their sheik belongs. The minister of the shrine sacrifices near the threshold. The child is anointed on the forehead or on the nose, with a mark of the blood of the victim." The Ismailiye slaughter the sacrifice for the child "in the courtyard in which he lives, and put a few drops of blood on his forehead and on his nose, to indicate that the sacrifice is in his behalf. The breaking forth of the blood is *fedou*. It redeems the child." At the shrine of Khudr (St. George) near the base of Mount Carmel, which is attended by Moslems, Christians, Druses, Babites, and Jews, if the animal sacrificed is for

---

[2] *Primitive Religion of the Semites*, pp. 200 ff. See also H. C. Trumbull, *The Threshold Sacrifice*, passim. Frazer, *Golden Bough*, index. Some light on this ceremony may be cast by the following report from Calcutta, India: "Until the English interfered, it was customary at the annual festival of this goddess [Kali] to bring a human sacrifice, but since this practice has been stopped by the enforcement of an English statute forbidding it, it has been customary for the one offering the sacrifice to hold a little boy in his arms, while another brought a kid in his arms, as the substitute for the son whom his ancestors would have offered." Curtiss, op. cit., pp. 216–17. The substitution of a ram for Isaac forms an exact parallel (Gen. 22).

a child or man, "they dip a finger in the blood and put it on the forehead of the boy or man for whom the sacrifice is made."[3]

This practice has been preserved by the Samaritans, in connection with their celebration of their Passover. H. Clay Trumbull reports from personal observation, that "the spurting life-blood of the consecrated lambs is caught in basins, as it flows from their cut throats; and not only are all the tents promptly marked with the blood as a covenant token, but every child of the covenant receives also a blood-mark, on his forehead, between his eyes, in evidence of his relation to God in the covenant of blood friendship."[4] This observance illustrates the biblical ordinance concerning the Passover prior to the exodus. The blood of the sacrificial lambs was to be "put on the two side-posts and on the lintel of the houses wherein they shall be eaten" (Exod. 12:7). And when Yahveh "shall go through the land of Egypt in that night, and will smite all the firstborn in the land of Egypt, both man and beast, . . . the blood shall be to you for a token upon the houses where ye are; and when I see the blood, I will pass over you, and there shall no plague be upon you to destroy you, when I smite the land of Egypt" (vss. 12–13). To ensure their full protection, the Israelites were ordered not to leave their homes that night until the morning (vss. 21 ff.).[5] This ordinance of the Passover was to be observed as a memorial forever (vss. 14, 24 ff.). In Exodus 13, it is linked with the institutions of the Passover and of the redemption of the firstborn sons (cf. *fedou*) and the sacrifice of the firstborn of the cattle. "And it shall be for a sign unto thee upon thy hand, and for a memorial between thine eyes, that the law of the Lord may be in thy mouth; for with a strong hand hath the Lord brought thee out of Egypt. Thou shalt therefore keep this ordinance in its season from year to year" (vss. 9–10). Verse 15 definitely connects the sign

---

[3] See Prov. 1:9, 3:3, 6:21, 7:3; Jer. 17:1, 31:32 and the comments of R. Samuel b. Meir and Abraham Ibn Ezra on Exod. 13:9; Hadasi, *Eshkol Hakopher*, p. 92; E. G. Hirsch, "Phylacteries, Critical View," *Jew. Encyc.* X, 26; Neubauer, *Aus der Petersburger Bibliothek: Beitraege und Documente zur Geschichte des Karaerthums*, Hebrew part, pp. 51–53.

[4] H. C. Trumbull, *The Blood Covenant*, pp. 232 f.

[5] In vs. 23, the "destroyer" is distinct from Yahveh and is kept by Yahveh from entering the houses of the Israelites.

with the sacrifice of the firstlings. In vs. 16, טוטפת, "frontlets," appears instead of "memorial" in vs. 9.

Such markings for the purpose of securing protection from destructive spirits are familiar to us from other sources as well. There is, for example, the sign of Cain placed upon him by Yahveh to prevent his being slain unavenged (Gen. 4:15).[6] Ezekiel 9:4, 6 refers to the letter *tav* that was written on the foreheads of the faithful in Jerusalem, to distinguish them from the idolators who were to be destroyed. We learn from Psalms of Solomon 15:10 and from Revelations 7:2 ff., 9:4, 13:16 f., 14:1, 9, 20:4, that these marks were made on the forehead or on the right hand.

In these practices, we may have the origin of tattooing, a practice indicating the person's belonging to a particular deity. Herodotus reports that at the temple of Heracles at the Canobic mouth of the Nile, a fugitive slave who had been marked with sacred stigmata could not be reclaimed by his master.[7] Marking in this manner was equivalent to branding cattle, slaves, or prisoners of war. Deuteronomy 14:1 and Leviticus 19:28 associate tattooing with cutting the flesh in mourning or in honor of the dead. Jeremiah 16:8, 41:5, and 48:37 (cf. Micah 4:14) indicate that ceremonial cutting of the flesh formed an ordinary custom of mourners. This widespread practice may have stemmed from the notion that the departed drank in new life with the blood that their bond of union with the living.[8] The ultimate origin of the stigmata may have been merely "the permanent scars of puncture made to draw blood for a ceremony of self-dedication to the deity."[9] The tattooing may have had

---

[6] Stade, "Das Kainzeichen," *Zeitschrift für die alttest. Wissenschaft*, 14 (1894), pp. 250 ff. Stade is of the opinion that this sign refers to the religious symbol of the Kenites. Cf. the mark on the prophet, 1 Kings 20:35–41.

[7] Herodotus, *History*, II, 113.

[8] Jer. 48:37 גדדת כי כל ראש קרחה וכל זקן גרעה על כל ידים גדדת ועל מתנים שק. refers to "ceremonial incisions" or more exactly, "all hands are cut into" (cf. Deut. 14:1: לא תתגדדו), Jer. 16:6: ולא יספדו להם ולא יתגדד ולא יקרח להם (cf. 41:5), 1 Kings 18:28: ויתגדדו כמשפטם, Hosea 7:14: על דגן ותירוש יתגודדו (in place of יתגוררו) "because of corn and new wine, they cut themselves," i.e., to propitiate the deity.

[9] Ball, art. "Cutting the Flesh," *Encyc. Bibl.* I, col. 972. 3 Macc. 2:29 states that Philopater

the force of a charm. This practice of marking a person with the sign of his deity is preserved in Isaiah 44:5. Speaking of dedicated people, he states: "One shall say: I am the Lord's; and another shall call himself by the name of Jacob; and another shall inscribe his hand: 'Unto the Lord,' and surname himself by the name of Israel."[10]

The word טוטפות is of uncertain etymology and meaning. Delitzsch suggested an Assyrian parallel, *tatapu*, "surround, encircle"; Gesenius and Dillmann offer an Aramaic root *tuf*, related to the Arabic *tafa*, of similar meaning. The word may thus be taken to denote "bands going around the head, a circle, or head tire." Accordingly, the word פאר in Ezekiel 24:17 and 23, is rendered *totefta* in the Targum. On the other hand, Knobel and Klein assume a root *tofaf*, "tap, strike," i.e., an actual sign or mark in the flesh.[11] As the primitive form of tattooing fell into disfavor on account of its connection with heathenism,[12] the *totafot* came into use in the higher religion of Israel. While in Exodus 13:16 it was applied to the blood mark on the head, in Deuteronomy 6:8 and 11:18 it distinctly refers to some sacred texts. The talismanic character of the *totafot* continued. Thus, in the report of 2 Samuel 1:10 that Saul wore, in battle, a crown on his head and a bracelet on his arm as protective charms, the Targum renders אצעדה, "bracelet," with *totefta*. That the "crown" had a similiar connotation is evidenced by its rendering עטרת in Esther 8:15, with *totfon* (cf. 2 Kings 11:12, where העדות was emended הצעדות). This is further evidenced by the Greek name *phylacteries*,[13] with which *totafot* are designated in the New Testament (Matt. 23:5), and by the

---

ordered the Jews to "be branded on their bodies with an ivy-leaf, the emblem of Dionysus." Cf. Philo, *De Mon.* 1.8. See also C. H. Toy, *The Book of Ezekiel*, p. 113.

[10] Paul writes in his Epistle to the Galatians 6:17: "Let nobody interfere with me after this, for I bear on my body the scars that mark me as a slave of Jesus."

[11] Art. טטפת in *BDB Lexicon*, p. 377; Driver, *Deuteronomy*, pp. 92–93. The derivation from נטף (cf. נטיפות, Judg. 8:26, Isa. 3:19), a round jewel worn as a charm is etymologically untenable.

[12] Hosea 7:14, Jer. 5:7, 1 Kings 18:28, Deut. 14:1, Lev. 19:28, 21:5; see also W. R. Smith, *Religion of the Semites*, p. 334, n. 1; Stade, op. cit., pp. 302 ff.

[13] From Φυλάσσειν, "to guard against evil, to protect," i.e., amulet.

rabbinic reference to them as *kameot* and by their linking *tefillin* with *kameot*,[14] assigning to them the power to ward off evil spirits and to prolong life.[15]

A possible connection of *tefillin* and tattooing is retained in the rabbinic derivation of binding the phylacteries upon the upper part of the head by analogy from Deut. 14:1: "Ye are children of the Lord your God: ye shall not cut yourselves nor make any baldness between your eyes." "Just as the expression 'between your eyes,' as used there, signifies the upper part of the head, so the expression 'between your eyes' used here, denotes the upper parts of the head."[16]

A higher meaning was read into the *tefillin* by both Hellenistic and Rabbinic Judaism. The *Letter of Aristeas* (158–59) states that the Lawgiver ordered the symbol to be fastened upon our hands,[17] "clearly to show that we ought to perform every act in righteousness, remembering (our own creation), and above all the fear of God." Josephus speaks of the record of the Law to be

---

[14] *Sab.* 6.2; *Shek.* 3.2; *Mikvaot* 10.2; *Kelim* 23.1; *Erubin* 96b; *Massek. Tefillin*; *Sab.* 57b. לא תצא אשה [בשבת] בטוטפת ולא בסרביטין בזמן שאינן תפורים ... מאי טוטפת. א"ר יוסף חומרתא דקטיפתא (רש"י: קשר שעושין לרפואות קיטוף עין רע שלא תשלוט) א"ל אביי ותהוי כקמיע מומחה ותשתרי. אלא אמר רב יהודה משמיה דאביי אפוזיינו (פירש הערוך: עיגול לשער הראש כו') .See *Aruch Completum*, under קמיע, טטפת.

[15] *Targ. Song of Songs* 8:3; *Midr. Tehil.* 91.4; *Men.* 35b; *Ber.* 23a–b; *Midr. Mishle* 31.28.

H. C. Trumbull writes: "In the primitive rite of blood-friendship, a blood-stained record of the covenant is preserved in a small leathern case, to be worn as an amulet upon the arm or about the neck, by him who has won a friend forever in this sacred rite. It would seem that this was the custom in ancient Egypt, where the red amulet, which represented the blood of Isis, was worn by those who claimed a blood relationship with the gods" (*The Blood Covenant*, pp. 232–33). He inclines to regard *totafot* as an Egyptian loan word, without suggesting the derivation. (M. Rodkinson's derivation of the word from the names of the Egyptian gods Thoth and Phath [Ptah] is fantastic. See Rodkinson, *Hist. of Amulets, Charms, and Talismans*, ch. 3, pp. 7–10.) Among the charms put upon the mummy, Ed. Naville names the buckle or the emblem of Isis, which is generally red in color. The text pertaining to it in the Book of the Dead (ch. clvi) reads: "The blood of Isis, the virtue of Isis, the magic power of Isis are protecting the Great One; they prevent any wrong being done to him," etc. Art. "Charms and Amulets, Egyptian," Hastings, *Encycl. Rel. and Ethics*, III, 432.

[16] *Mechilta, Pisha*, 17 (ed. Lauterbach, I, 150).

[17] Note the omission of the frontlets upon the forehead.

"written on the head and on the arm, so that men may see on every side the loving care with which God surrounds them."[18] The rabbis similarly conceived of the *tefillin* as a symbol of God's saving power, aiming to direct man's heart and mind to God and to His commandments.[19]

The word *tefillin* first appears in tannaitic literature and in *Targum Onkelos*.[20] The *Aruch* derives it from *tafal*, "attach." Elijah Levita rejected this derivation in favor of the root *polal*, i.e., a symbol employed in prayer.[21] Levy, while accepting Levita's etymology, relates the word to *palah*, "be separated, distinct." *Tefillin* would thus denote the symbols which distinguish the Jew from other people.[22] Levita's explanation ignores the fact that the *tefillin* were not originally confined to times of prayer, but were worn all day long. Like their biblical equivalent, *totafot*, *tefillin* signify sacred symbols attached to the arms and forehead.

The new name is indicative of a new emphasis on the phylacteries. Matthew 23:5 recognizes them as Pharisaic insignia. The rabbis speak of

---

[18] *Antiq.* IV.8.13.

[19] Cf. the meditation before putting on the tefillin in the prayer book. Its kabbalistic ideas are apparent.

[20] Onkelos uses tefillin not only for טטפת in Exod. 13:16 and in Deut. 6:8 but also for מצנפת in Exod. 28:37. Jonathan renders שם יהוה נקרא עליך in Deut. 28:10: שמא דיי חקיק בזמן דתפלין עלך כו׳. Cf. the saying of R. Eliezer in *Ber.* 6a.

[21] This produced the mistaken translation of tefillin as *Gebetriemen*.

[22] See *Aruch Completum*, art. תפילין, also arts. תפל and טפל. (Tos. Zukermandel *Pes.* 5, end: אין תופלין אותה בחרסית. (Cf. Levy, *Wörterbuch*, art. תפלה [In his *Chaldäisches Wörterbuch* II, 550, he follows the *Aruch*].) Cf. Ps. 119:69: טפלו עלי שקר כו׳. The word tefillin would thus correspond to the LXX ἀσάλευτον for *totafot*, i.e., something unmovable, or an amulet that is fixed upon the arm or forehead. Cf. Ezek. 23:15: סרוחי טבולים בראשיהם, with pendant and turbans upon their heads. See Rodkinson, *History of Amulets, Charms and Talismans*, p. 16.: "The names of tebhulim or tephillin are undoubtedly identical and even pronounced alike, differing only in orthography" (n. 21). "The name tebhulim is derived from a root tabhal, meaning to 'enwrap' or dress the head with ornaments, and is very appropriate to this amulet on account of its encircling the head while the fillets fall over the shoulders and breast" (pp. 16–17). Rodkinson's claim that tefillin were borrowed from the Babylonians is unsubstantiated. His rejection of Fuerst's explanation of tebulim as "turbans," in view of its derivation from the Assyrian *tublu*, "turban," is arbitrary. See *BDB Lexicon*, under טבל.

them as a sopheric institution.[23] More specifically they consider *tefillin* as characteristic of Pharisaic piety.[24] Among the criteria of an *am haaretz* (i.e., a non-Pharisee), R. Eliezer names anyone who does not read the *Shema* in the evening and in the morning. R. Jehuda states: Anyone who does not wear *tefillin*. Ben Azzai includes anyone who has no *tzitzit* in his garment, and R. Nathan, anyone who has no *mezuzah* on his door.[25] The use of *tefillin, tzitzit,* and *mezuzah* have figured as distinctive marks of a *ḥaber* or Pharisee.[26] We hear of a woman who, when married to a Pharisee, used to tie the *tefillin* on his arm; but when she subsequently married an *am haaretz,* she bound publican straps upon his hand.[27]

---

[23] *Sanh.* 88b. Cf. ר' נחמיה . . . עיקרו מדברי תורה ופירושו מדברי סופרים אומר ויתרון ארץ בכל אפילו דברים שאתה רואה אותן יתרון למתן תורה כגון הלכות ציצית תפילין ומזוזה אף הן בכלל (Eccl. 5.8) מתן תורה (*Eccl. R.* 5) מתן תורה (*Lev. R.* XXII). The Samaritans did not use tefillin, not necessarily because they interpreted the texts figuratively, but rather because they followed the older form of marking the heads and foreheads with the blood of the paschal lamb. Cf. *Men.* 42b: ס"ת תפילין ומזוזות שכתבן צדוקי (צ"ל מין) כותי עובד כוכבים עבד קטן ואשה מומר פסולין שנ' וקשרתם וכתבתם. כל שישנו בקשירה ישנו בכתיבה כל שאינו בקשירה אינו בכתיבה.

[24] Schorr ascribes the origin of tefillin to the Essenes, whom he regards as an offshoot of the Pharisees and as identical with the Hasidim Harishonim. Their emphasis upon external signs of holiness was taken over by the Pharisees, who extended them to all Jews (*Hehaluz,* V, 1860, 11–26). However, the reports concerning the Essenes in Philo, Josephus, and Hippolytus present no evidence that they wore tefillin. The talmudic reference to Elisha baal Kenafayyim (*Sab.* 49a) is too tenuous to establish his Essenic character. Neither is the identification of the Essenes with the early Hasidim justified. See Buechler, *Types of Palestinian Jewish Piety.*

[25] *Ber.* 47b. *Targum to Song of Songs* 2:6 שמאלו תחת לראשי: אנא קטרא תפילין ביד שמאלי ובריֹשי וקביעא מזוותא בסטריאינא דֹשי.

[26] *Menahot* 43b; cf. *Sab.* 13a–b, where the story is told about the wife of a *ḥaber* who died in his middle years, that she took his tefillin and went to the synagogue, demanding to know why her husband died so early, contrary to the promise that those who wear tefillin and engage in study of the Written and the Oral Law shall enjoy long life.

[27] *Bechorot* 30b. Rodkinson suggests that *kishre muchasin* means amulets of the *amme haaretz. Tefillah L'Moshe,* p. 105. ר"ש בן אלעזר אומר משום ר' מאיר מעשה באשה אחת שנישאת (*Bech.* 30b). לחבר והיתה קומעת לו תפלין על ידו, נשאת לעם הארץ והיתה קושרת לו קשרי מוכס על ידו ת"ר קטן היודע לנענע חייב בלולב, להתעטף חייב בציצית, לשמור תפילין אביו לוקח לו תפילין, יודע לדבר ת"ר איזהו עם הארץ כל שאינו קורא ק"ש ערבית ושחרית דברי (*Suk.* 42a) אביו לומדו תורה וקריאת שמע ר"א. ר' יהושע אומר כל שאינו מניח תפילין. בן עזאי אומר כל שאין לו ציצית בבגדו. ר' נתן אומר כל שאין

The earliest references to *tefillin* are to those of the grandfather of Shammai (and in a parallel passage, of Hillel).[28] R. Jehuda b. Betera claimed that his *tefillin* came from his grandfather, who descended from the dead bodies revived by the prophet Ezekiel.[29] The reference to *tefillin* in a legend connected with Simeon b. Shetaḥ, in Jeru. *Ḥagiga* 2.2, bears marks of lateness. R. Joḥanan b. Zakkai was said to have moved four ells without Torah or *tefillin*.[30] R. Eliezer b. Hyrcanus considered *tefillin* of the head as a special mark of the Jew's consecration to God.[31] He may have aimed to overcome the view which seems to underlie the *Letter of Aristeas*, limiting *tefillin* to the arm.

In their endeavor to extend their practices to all Jewry, the Pharisees made the wearing of *tefillin* obligatory upon all who were eligible to membership in their *ḥaburot*. This excluded slaves, women, and minors. The exceptional cases of Michal,[32] the daughter of Kushi (Saul), and of Tobi, the slave of Gamaliel II, who wore *tefillin*, are reported.[33] With regard to minors, the

---

ר' נחמיה: ויתרון ארץ בכל היא אפילו דברים שאתה רואה אותן יתרון למתן (*Ber.* 47b). מזוזה על פתחו וכו' תורה כגון הלכות ציצית תפילין ומזוזה אף הן בכלל מתן תורה כו'. סוף תוספתא ברכות: אין לך אדם מישראל שאין שבע מצות מקיפות מקיפות אותו תפילין בראשו ותפילין בזרועו כו'. J. H. Schorr, in *Hehaluz* V (1860), pp. 11–26.

[28] *Mechilta, Pisha*, 17 (ed. Lauterbach, I, 157); Jeru. *Erubin* 10.1, 26a–b.

[29] *Sanh.* 92a.

[30] *Succah* 28a.

[31] *Ber.* 6a, *Men.* 35b. See *Targ. Jonathan*, Deut. 28:10.

[32] Louis Ginzberg writes: "The legend about Michal's using phylacteries is of midrashic origin. The last section of Proverbs is said, by the Haggadah, to refer to the twenty-two pious women mentioned in the Bible (comp. Midash Haggadol I, 344, seq.; Mishle 31), each of the twenty-two verses of this section containing the praise of each of these pious women. It was therefore quite natural for the Haggadah to find in verse 25, an allusion to Michal, of whom one might have rightly said: 'And she rejoiced at the last day' (This is the literal translation of the Hebrew.), as it was in her very last day that she had the joy of motherhood [Sanh. 21a] (comp. *Legends*, IV, p. 117). The first half of this verse reads: 'Strength and dignity are her clothing.' Now, since in the Haggadah, 'strength' עוז is equivalent to 'phylacteries' (comp. Ber. 6a), it follows that the woman whose praise is sung in this verse (i.e. Michal) is lauded for having clothed herself with phylacteries." (*Legends*, VI, p. 274. See also *Comment, Palestinian Talmud*, I, p. 289.)

[33] *Mechilta, Pisha*, 17 (ed. Lauterbach, I, 154).

halachah states that "any minor who knows how to take care of *tefillin* may have them made for himself."[34] The Pharisaic ideal is expressed in the *baraita*: "Beloved are the people of Israel, for the Holy One has surrounded them with *mitzvot*, with the *mitzvah* of *tefillin* upon their heads and upon their arms, with *tzitzit* upon their garments, and with *mezuzot* upon their doors."[35] Wearing *tefillin* was regarded as equivalent to fulfilling the commandment of studying Torah. R. Eliezer teaches that Israel pleaded with God that they would like to engage in Torah day and night, but that they were too preoccupied. Whereupon God said to them: "Fulfill the commandment of *tefillin*, and I shall account it unto you as if you labored in the Torah night and day."[36] The obligation to wear *tefillin* was made universally binding upon *kohanim*, levites, and *yisr'elim*.[37] Rab includes among those who sin with their bodies, "the head that does not wear *tefillin*."[38]

Possibly to distinguish them from amulets intended to protect the wearer from demons, it was ruled that *tefillin* should not be worn at night, but only in the daytime. As "signs," they must be visible. *Targum Jonathan* renders Exodus 13:10: "And you shall keep this statute of *tefillin* at the time when it is visible, on days, on work days and not on Sabbaths and festivals, and in daytime and not at night." They were not to be worn on Sabbaths and festivals, because these days are themselves protective "signs." Originally, no such limitations existed.[39] The *tefillin*, having replaced the ancient amulets,

---

[34] *Ibid.*; *Succah* 42a.

[35] *Men.* 43b.

[36] *Mechilta*, loc. cit.; כל המניח תפילין כאלו קורא בתורה וכל הקורא בתורה פטור מן התפילין הכל קיימו מצות תפילין ומעלה אני עליכם. *Midrash Tehillim* 1.17; חייבין בתפילין כהנים לוים וישראלים כאלו אתם יגיעים לילה ויום.

[37] *Arachin* 3b; cf. *Shebuot* 3.8, *Ned.* 2.2. Cf. *Zebahim* 19a: כהנים בעבדתן ולוים בדוכנן וישראל במעמדן פטורין מן התפלה ומן התפילין. נשבע לבטל את המצוה שלא לעשות סוכה ושלא ליטול לולב, ושלא מי Cf. *Ned.* 2.2: להניח תפילין זו היא שבועת שוא שחייבין על זדונה כרות ועל שגגתה פטור. שבועות פ"ג,י. נשים ועבדים וקטנים פטורין מק"ש (*Ber.* 3. 1) שמתו מוטל לפניו פטור מק"ש ומן (התפלה) ומן התפילין כו' ומן התפילין וחייבין בתפלה ובמזוזה ובברכת המזון שם,שם ג'.

[38] *R.H.* 17a.

[39] *Men.* 36a, *Erubin* 95b–96a, *Mechilta*, loc. cit. (ed. Lauterbach, I, 157); Jeru. *Ber.* 2.3.4 bc. The probable reason for not using tefillin on the Sabbath was the need to carry them on that day. *Sab.* 6.1: לא יצא האיש בתפילין ולא בקמע בזמן שאינו 6:2: לא תצא אשה . . . ולא בסרביטין.

were tied in the same positions in which the amulets had been worn. We noted the attempt of the *Mechilta* to establish the rule that the phylactery of the head be bound in the place where the tattooing was done. With regard to the phylactery of the hand, it was not clear whether the right or the left hand was meant. On the basis of Gen. 48:13, Judg. 5:26, and Isa. 48:13, where "hand" is balanced by "right hand," it was concluded that the words "and it shall be a sign upon thy hand" refer to the left hand.[40] This may represent a conscious deviation from the Semitic practice of having the amulets on the right hand.

Tannaitic literature, while frequently referring to *tefillin*, prescribes no details regarding their preparation. Strangely, no controversies are recorded between the schools of Hillel and Shammai regarding the details of *tefillin*, their preparation and content, as in the case of other rituals of lesser importance. This circumstance would point to the lateness of the institution. Only a few minor points are mentioned, e.g., as to whether *tefillin* require periodic

---

מן המומחה עד מתי מניחן עד שתשקע החמה, רבי יעקב אומר עד שתכלה רגל מן השוק. וחכמים אמרים עד זמן שינה ומודים חכמים לר' יעקב שאם חלצן לבית הכסא או ליכנס לבית המרחץ ושקעה חמה שוב אינו חוזר ומניחן (*Men.* 36a). The Gemara cites contrary views regarding wearing tefillin on the Sabbath. The Mishnah, in *Erub.* 10.1: המוצא תפילין מכניסן זוג זוג. רבן גמליאל אומר, שנים שנים) וכו'). . . . גמרא: . . . והכא בשבת זמן תפילין קמיפלגי דת"ק סבר שבת זמן תפילין הוא ורבן גמליאל סבר שבת לאו זמן תפילין הוא ואיביעית אימא דכולי עלמא שבת זמן תפילין הוא והכא במצות צריכות כוונה קמיפלגי . . . ומאן שמעת ליה זמן תפילין ר' עקיבא דתניא ושמרת את החקה הזאת למועדה מימים ימימה. ימים ולא לילות. מימים ולא כל ימים פרט לשבתות וימים טובים דברי ר' יוסי הגלילי. ר' עקיבא אומר לא נאמר חוקה זו אלא לענין פסח בלבד . . . . וסבר ר' עקיבא שבת זמן תפילין הוא והתניא ר"ע אומר יכול יניח אדם תפילין בשבתות וימים טובים ת"ל והיה לך לאות על ידך. מי שצריכין אות, יצאו אלו שהן גופן אות. אלא האי תנא היא דתניא וכו' (*Erub.* 95b–96a). In the *Mechilta*, R. Isaac explains that "since the Sabbath is called a 'sign' and the tefillin are called a 'sign,' one should not add one sign to another" (ibid.).

The time for the wearing of tefillin was limited to the day, exclusive of Sabbaths and festivals. That the practice of also wearing them at night was current appears from the report concerning R. Abahu: ר' אבהו, יתיב מתני ברמשא ותפילוי עילוי. This practice was contradicted by his rule that he who puts them on at night transgresses a positive command: הנותן תפילין בלילה עובר ושמרת את החקה הזאת למועדה מימים ימימה. ימים ולא לילות (Exod. 13:10) ימימה פרט) בעשה ומה טעם לשבתות וימים טובים והא ר' אבהו יתיב מתני ברמשא ותפילוי עילוי . . . אית דבעי מימר לא אמרן אלא הנותן אבל אם היו עליו מבעוד יום מותר (שם) והיה לך לאות. את שהוא לך לאות אית דבעי מימר נשמעיניה מן הדא פרט לי"ט ושבתות שכולן אות (*Jeru. Ber.* 2.3).

[40] *Mechilta*, loc. cit. (ed. Lauterbach, I, 153).

inspection. The Hillelites prescribe examination every twelve months, whereas the Shammaites maintain that they need never be examined.[41]

From the comments of the *Sifre*, Deuteronomy 34 and 35, it appears that originally the Decalogue (i.e., as the epitome of the Torah) was inserted into the *tefillin*. From its connection with the *Shema* in the early liturgy of the Temple, we may infer that the four sections of the text enclosed in the *tefillin* at first consisted of the Decalogue and the three sections of the *Shema*.[42] Following the elimination of the Decalogue, Exodus 13:1–10 and 11–16 took its place, because of their references to a sign upon the hand and frontlets between the eyes. But the new arrangement consisted of five sections. In consequence, the third section of the *Shema* (Num. 15:37–41), which deals with *tzitzit* and does not refer to *totafot*, was removed, thus retaining the original number of sections.[43]

The final arrangement, as formulated in the *Mechilta*, consists of the four texts referring to "signs" and "frontlets," i.e., (1) Exod. 13:1–10; (2) Exod. 13:11–26; (3) Deut. 6:4–9; (4) Deut. 11:13–20. In the phylactery of the hand, the four sections are inscribed on one parchment, and in the head phylactery, on four separate parchments, but bound together in one container. They must be written in their scriptural order (otherwise they are unfit for use and must be hidden away).[44]

The external form of the *tefillin*, it seems, at first resembled amulets, and could be of any color save red, which was considerably unseemly,[45] and could

---

[41] loc. cit. (ed. Lauterbach, I, 157).

[42] *Ber.* 12a, Jeru. *Ber.* 1.8, 3d. On the basis of Exodus 28:36 and Isaiah 44:5 (cf. Zech. 14:20 ff.), the original amulets may have contained the simple inscription "Holy unto God" or "Unto God." Cf. שדי on the outside of the head phylactery and on the mezuzah.

[43] This would explain the Mishnah *Sanh.* 11.3 regarding the heretical idea in claiming five sections in the tefillin.

[44] *Mechilta*, ibid. (ed. Lauterbach, I, 150). The number four probably goes back to ancient custom, which R. Ishmael connects with the use of *totafot* twice in the singular in Exod. 13:16 and Deut. 6:8, and once in the plural in Deut. 11:18. R. Akiba derives the number from the word *totafot*, which he assumes to be a composit of two foreign words: *tot*-"two," and *phat*-"two": טט בכתפי *שתים פת באפריקי שתים Ibid.; *Men.* 34b, *Sanh.* 4b, *Zeb.* 37b.

* Jeru. *B.M.* IV.9c סלקו גבי ר' יוסי לגדפה. See Levy, *Wörterbuch,* גדפה.

[45] The Egyptian amulet of blood-friendship was red, representing the blood of the gods. H. C. Trumbull, *The Blood-Covenant,* p. 236. Cf. *Men.* 35a: אדומות לא יעשה מפני גנאי ודבר אחר.

be fastened with straps of blue, purple, or other colors. They were shaped not only square, but also circular or oval.[46] Toward the end of the talmudic age, they were standardized as square black boxes with black leather straps. Effort was directed against sectarians who either denied the obligation of *tefillin* altogether, on the ground that the Pentateuchal passages must be interpreted figuratively,[47] or prepared the *tefillin* in a nontraditional manner. Mishnah *Megillah* 4.8 states: "If a man makes his phylacteries round (instead of cube-shaped), he incurs a danger, for with such, one cannot fulfill his duty. If he ties them low on his forehead or on the palm of his hand (instead of on his forearm), his is the way of heresy. If he overlays them with gold or fastens them over his sleeve, his is the way of the sectaries (*hizonim*)." The Mishnah seems to refer to Gnosticism and early Christianity.[48] Every effort was made

---

Shibbole Haleket, p. 384, explains this statement: מפני גנאי שדומה לתכשיטי נשים ומפני דבר אחר מפני שנראה בראש כצרעת.

[46] *Men.* 35a.

[47] The Samaritans and possibly the Sadduccees. Cf. Ibn Ezra on Exod. 13:9. We have here the Pharisaic opposition to the sectarian views: העושה תפלתו עגולה סכנה ואין בה מצוה. נתנה על *Meg.4.8.* מצחו או על פס ידו הרי זו דרך מהינות. ציפן זהב ונתנה על בית אונקלי שלו הרי זו דרך החיצונים

[48] Von Dobschuetz writes: "From the East was derived the form of the medallion or small plaque (τέταλλον), often in gold with jewels or enamel. In Rome, the little head tube (bulla) had its home; and in later times, a small casket or locket (capsa, capsella). Under Christian influence these amulets took the form of the cross, but the medallion also survived. . . . It was soon sought in Christian circles to set these phylacteric objects on a level with the tefillin which were ordained in the O.T. . . . The Fathers contested this coordination (e.g. Epiphanius, *Haer.* 15) and the earlier Synods laid the penalties of the Church upon the manufacture of phylacteries by the clergy. . . . Chrysostom (in Matt. hom. 72) and Isidore Pelus (Ep. ii. 150) inform us that Christian women used to wear little gospels round their necks after the maner of Jewish tefillin; but these were very likely only single texts from the Gospels." Art. "Charms, Christian," Hastings, *Encyc. of Rel. and Ethics,* III, pp. 416–17, 425. "The present *encolpia,* generally regarded as decorative insignia of the Orthodox Church, and strictly regulated according to the rank of the wearer, according to Nicephorus, were originally called *phylacteria,* and served for the protection and assurance of life, for health of soul and body, for healing in sickness, and for the averting of attacks by unclean spirits. The Emperor and high imperial officials also wore phylacteries." Ibid., 416–17. "In the catacombs of Rome there have been found 'small caskets of gold or other metal, for containing a portion of the Gospel, generally part of the first chapter of John [with its covenant promises to all who believe on the true Paschal Lamb], which were worn on the neck,' as an imitation of the Jewish phylacteries. These covenant tokens were condemned by Irenaeus, Augustine, Chrysostom, and the Council

to overcome sectarian views and practices. In Isaiah 62:8, R. Isaac found support for his notion that God Himself wears *tefillin* (cf. 49:16). Simeon the Hasid interpreted Exodus 33:23 to indicate that God showed Moses the knot of His own head phylactery, to serve as a model for the people.[49] Every detail connected with *tefillin* was conceived as a *halachah* revealed to Moses at Sinai. These rules included that the *tefillin* must be prepared of the skins of clean animals, that their boxes be cubes, that both boxes and straps be black, that the hairs with which the rolls are tied and the veins used for stitching the boxes be from clean animals, that a square piece of leather be placed at the underside of the boxes (*titura*), that a loop be formed at the end of the boxes to permit the straps to pass through, that the straps ending at the back of the head be knotted in the form of the letter *dalet* (symbol of *Adonai*), and the strap passing through the hand phylactery, forming a noose near the box, be fastened into a knot in the shape of a *yod* (symbol of YHVH); also that the box of the head phylactery have, on its right side, the letter *shin* (made with three strokes, symbol of *Shaddai*) and on its left, a *shin* (made with four strokes, indicating that four sections are contained within). The *shin* of the head phylactery and the *dalet* and *yod* of the two straps spell *Shaddai*. The measurements of the boxes are not fixed. However, it is suggested that they be not smaller than the width of two fingers.[50] Though claimed to be of Mosaic origin, all of these regulations are stated by the *amoraim*, and must be regarded as late formulations.

While the time for wearing the *tefillin* was the entire day, they came to be connected particularly with prayer and with the *Shema*. According to one report, Rab held that "one should recite the *Shema* and then put on the

---

of Laodicea, as a relic of heathenism." (Jones, *Credulities Past and Present*, p. 188. Cited by H. C. Trumbull, *The Blood Covenant*, p. 328) (Tertullan states that Mithra marked his soldiers on the forehead in imitation of the Christian sacrament [*advers. haeret.* c. 40.] Stade, op. cit., p. 305).

[49] *Ber.* 6a, *Men.* 35b.

[50] Eighteen halachas derived by Moses from Sinai, dealing with the preparation of *tefillin*, are enumerated by the *amoraim. Sab.* 28b, 79b; *Jeru. Meg.* 1.9; *Men.* 35a; Tos., ibid., s.v. *shin*; *Erub.* 95b, Tos., s.v. *makom*; 97a, Rashi and Tos., s.v. *kesher shel tefillin.* Rodkinson, *Tefillah L'moshe*, pp. 20 ff.; *Jew. Encyc.* X, 22.

tefillin and pray." Another report has it that he followed the tannaitic tradition of putting on the *tefillin* before reciting the *Shema*. In Ulla's opinion, anyone who recited the *Shema* without wearing *tefillin* contradicts his own testimony. R. Joḥanan regards him as if he offered a burnt-offering without the necessary flour, or a sacrifice without libation. He who would accept the Kingdom of Heaven properly must cleanse his body, wash his hands, put on *tefillin,* and then recite the *Shema* and pray. If he acts thus, it is accounted to him as if he erected an altar and offered a sacrifice upon it.[51]

These comments indicate that the wearing of *tefillin* was neglected and that special exhortations were needed to strengthen the practice. The statement which we cited from the *Mechilta,* that wearing *tefillin* was equivalent to studying Torah, and that he who reads Torah is exempt from *tefillin,*[52] serves as a partial explanation of this neglect. There were also other reasons. The Mishnah teaches that the wearing of *tefillin* is not required in time of danger.[53] Rabbi Simeon b. Elazar comments that "any command which the Jews observed at the peril of their lives, in times of religious persecution [he refers to the Hadrianic persecutions], e.g., the laws regarding idolatry and circumcision, are still firmly held by them, but commands for which they did not sacrifice themselves are still held feebly by them."[54] The reference is not to a direct prohibition of *tefillin,* but rather to the Jewish people's fear of being recognized by their *tefillin.* This is probably the meaning of Jerome's statement that Jews feared to appear in the cities because they attracted attention.

[51] Jeru. *Ber.* 2.2.4 bc; *Ber.* 14b–15a. R. Joḥanan is further quoted: הרוצה שיקבל עליו עול מלכות שמים שלימה יפנה ויטול ידיו ויניח תפילין ויקרא קריאת שמע ויתפלל וזו היא מלכות שמים שלימה (*Ber.* 15a). R. Jannai states that *tefillin* require a clean body: א"ר ינאי תפילין צריכין גוף נקי מפני מה לא החזיקו בהן מפני הרמאים. עובדא הוה בחד בר נש דאפקיד גבי חבריה וכפר ביה א"ל לא לך הימנית אלא לאילן דבריישך הימנית. ר' ינאי היה לובשן אחר חוליו ג' ימים לומר שהחולי ממרק, מה טעם הסולח לכל עונייכי הרופא לכל תחלואייכי (תהילים ק"ג) רבי יוחנן בן זכאי לא הוון תפילוי זעין מיניה לא בקייטא ולא בסיתוא וכך נהג ר' אליעזר [הוא ר' אליעזר בן הרקינס] תלמידו אחריו. ר' יוחנן בסיתוא דהוה חזיק רישיה הוה לביש תרויהון. ברם בקייטא דלא הוה חזיק רישיה לא הוה לביש אלא אלא דאדרעיה. (ירוש' ברכות פ"ב,ה"ג) Ginzberg, *Legends,* I, 268.

[52] *Mechilta, Pisḥa,* 17 (ed. Lauterbach, I, 154).

[53] *Erub.* 10.1.

[54] *Sab.* 130a.

L. Blau suggests that he means to say: by their *tefillin*.[55] This circumstance tended to limit the wearing of *tefillin* to morning worship. Rab Sherira Gaon testified that in consequence of the persecutions to which they were subjected, the Jews of Palestine got out of the habit of wearing *tefillin*. On the other hand, the Jews of Babylonia observed the custom, particularly the scholars.[56]

The emphasis on cleanliness of body as a condition of wearing *tefillin*, and the attitude that only a *ḥaber* or a scholar may wear them, further weakened their hold on the people. Thus an inquiry was addressed to R. Joseph Gaon, asking whether a merchant who engages in a little study should wear *tefillin* during the recitation of the *Shema* and prayer, inasmuch as *tefillin* are worn only by distinguished scholars, and anyone else who puts them on appears presumptuous.[57] Since this practice was a sign of special piety, swindlers imposed upon the people by wearing *tefillin*.[58]

The rise of Karaism, with its denial of the obligation of *tefillin* helped to undermine the practice. R. Jehudai Gaon therefore stressed its importance. Repeating the talmudic glorification of *tefillin*, he adds that on account of them, the Jews were promised entrance into the Holy Land, and because of them, they will enjoy the hereafter. Anyone who does not wear *tefillin* will suffer punishment in Gehenna for twelve months. Furthermore, in the day of judgment, the *tefillin* will counterbalance a man's sins, "for there is no greater positive command in the Torah than that of *tefillin*, which is equivalent to both the Written and the Oral Law."[59]

A contributing factor to the neglect of *tefillin* was the difference of interpretation on the part of Rashi and R. Jacob Tam regarding the arrangement of the four texts in the phylacteries.[60] Rashi, in accordance with the

---

[55] Jerome, *On the Galatians*, IV.22; *Jew. Encycl.* X,27.

[56] L. Ginzberg, *Commentary on the Palestinian Talmud*, I, p. 262; *Shibbole Haleket*, p. 382.

[57] Cited by Rodkinson's *Tefillah L'moshe*, p. 73.

[58] *Bech.* 30b. See Ginzberg, *Legends*, VI, pp. 327–28, n. 58.

[59] Cited in *Shibbole Haleket, Inyan Tephillin*, p. 382. A responsum of Sherira similarly stresses the universal obligation of *tefillin*. Ibid. On the neglect of *tefillin*, see Tosafot כאליע, *Sab.* 49a, and קרקפתא, *R.H.* 17a.

[60] Hence the names of Rashi and Rabbenu Tam attached to *tefillin*. Their controversy dates back to the passage in *Men.* 34b–35a: "What is the proper order of the four sections in the

suggestion of the *Mechilta*, prescribes that they follow the order of their appearance in the Torah, from right to left of the reader, facing the wearer (i.e., Exod. 13:1–10; 13:11–16; Deut. 6:4–10; 11:13–20). R. Jacob Tam reverses the order of the third and fourth. The arrangement of the one is disqualified by the other. Rather than pronounce a benediction in circumstances of such uncertainty, some preferred not to wear *tefillin* at all.[61]

To encourage the wearing of *tefillin*, Maimonides wrote in his code: "Great is the sanctity of *tefillin*, for as long as the *tefillin* are upon man's head and arm, he is humble and God-fearing and is not drawn to laughter and to idle conversation, and he does not think evil thoughts, but devotes his heart completely to true and righteous words. Therefore man should try to have them on all day, for this is the law concerning them. . . . However, while it is the duty of man to wear them all day, it is particularly obligatory to wear them during prayer."[62]

In view of the general neglect of *tefillin*, R. Moses of Coucy, the author of the ritual work *Sefer Mitzvot Hagadol (SeMaG)*, set himself to correcting the situation. He was particularly challenged by the assimilationary trend among the Jews in Spain and France, and by the anti-Jewish measures of Pope Gregory. He traveled in those countries (1235), campaigning for a revived interest in Judaism and particularly for the observance of *tefillin, mezuzah,* and *tzitzit,* as well as of circumcision and the Sabbath. The line of argument that he pursued in his preaching ran thus:

phylacteries? *Kadesh* and *V'haya ki yebiacha* to the right, and *Shema* and *V'haya im shamoa* to the left. Is there not a *baraita* reversing the order? Abaye resolves the difficulty thus: the first follows the order of the reader (who faces the person wearing the *tefillin*) and the second, the order of the wearer, and the reader reads them in their order." Rabbenu Tam interprets the statement to mean that *Kadesh* and *V'haya ki yebiacha* are to be on the right of the reader, and to his left, the *Shema* on the outside and *V'haya im shamoa* inside, i.e., the two *V'hayas* are in the middle and the *Kadesh* to the outside on the right, and the *Shema* on the left. Rashi's arrangement is followed by Maimonides. The Shimmusha Rabba follows their order, but takes it to be the right of the wearer. The Rabad accepts Rabbenu Tam's order for the right of the wearer. Rodkinson, op. cit., VI. *Mahzor Vitry*, 640.

[61] The extrapious, to assure themselves that they follow the right order, wear sets of *tefillin* according to both arrangements. This is the practice of the Hasidim.

[62] *Hilchot Tefillin* 4, 25–26.

Out of 613 commandments, only Sabbath, circumcision, and *tefillin* are termed "signs." According to the Law, "by two witnesses shall a matter be established." No Israelite is a complete Jew without two witnesses to his Jewishness. Therefore, on Sabbath and the festivals, which are themselves signs, one is exempt from *tefillin,* for he has two witnesses, viz. Sabbath and circumcision. But on weekdays he must wear *tefillin* in order to have two witnesses, viz. *tefillin* and circumcision. Going without *tefillin* amounts to being left with only one witness, and to being an excommunicant in the sight of Heaven.

The requirement of bodily cleanliness as a condition for wearing *tefillin* can serve as a deterrent only for those who wear them all day; but during the hour of worship, even the most wicked may be fit to wear them. Indeed the Holy One is more desirous that the wicked lay *tefillin* than that the righteous do, for the *tefillin* are intended to serve as a reminder for the wicked, and to direct them to God.

The campaign of R. Moses bore fruit. According to his testimony, tens of thousands of Jews in Spain took upon themselves to wear *tefillin* during prayer.[63] This compromise arrangement is set down in the *Shulhan Aruch* as the law.[64]

---

[63] *SeMaG*, Positive Commands 3. Rodkinson, *Tefillah L'moshe, 83–85:* כן דרשתי פרשה זו בגלות ישראל להוכיח שכל אחד ואחד חייב בתפילין ומזוזות וכו' כי מתרי"ג מצות שנצטוו אין לך שום מצוה שתהא אות ועדות כי אם שלשה מצות והם שבת מילה ותפילין שנכתב בשלשתן אות כו' וע"פ שנים עדים יקום דבר: כל אחד מישראל אינו יהודי שלם אלא אם כן יש לו שני עדים שהוא יהודי, הלכך בשבת ויו"ט שנקרא שבת ושבת נקרא אות, פטור אדם מלהניח תפילין כי די שיש לו שני עדים שהוא יהודי. עדות שבת ועדות מילה, אבל בחול חייב כל אחד להניח תפילין כדי שיהיו לו שני עדים אות תפילין עם אות המילה. וכל מי שאינו מניח תפילין אין לו כי אם עד אחד שהוא יהודי ולכן חשבו כמנודה לשמים, בפ' ערבי פסחים. ואם תאמר מדוע היתה רפויה ביד ישראל, כבר פרשו רבותינו דבר זה כל דבר שלא מסרו עצמן עליה למיתה בשעת השמד ... עדיין היא רפוי בידם כגון תפילין ...

עוד זאת דרשתי להם כי מה שאמרו רבותנו תפילין צריכין גוף נקי כאלישע בעל כנפים כו' זהו באדם שמניחן כל היום כולו כמצותן פן ישכם עליו ויעשה בהם דבר שאינו הגון אבל בשעת תפלה אין לך רשע שלא ירא ראוי לתפלין ...

עוד זאת דרשתי להם כי יותר חפץ הקב"ה באדם רשע שמניח תפלין מאדם צדיק, ועיקר תפלין נצטוו להיות זכרון לרשעים ולישרם דרך טובה. ויותר הם צריכים זכר וחיזוק מאותם שגדלו ביראת שמים כל ימיהם. ... עוד אמרו רבותנו במנחות, כל מי שיש לו מזוזה בפתחו ותפלין בראשו ובזרועו וציצית בבגדו בחזקה שלא יחטא, שנאמר והחוט המשולש לא במהרה ינתק כו'. ...

Some authorities continued to view with disfavor the use of *tefillin* by the ignorant and by minors. The teaching of the Shimmusha Rabba continued to be voiced, declaring that only a person able to read *Torah, Nebiim,* and *Ketubim,* and Talmud, is fit to lay *tefillin*. (Of the books of the Torah, he should have read Genesis; of the Prophets, Samuel; and of the Hagiographa, Psalms. Of the Talmud, it is sufficient that he have studied Mishnah.)[65] R. Shimshon bar Zadok and R. Jacob Levy of Moeln objected to having unmarried boys and even young married men put on *tefillin,* since they do not keep their minds free from thoughts of sex.[66] Nonetheless, the view expressed in the

ויהי אחר ארבע אלפים ותשע מאות מאות וחמש שנים לבריאת עולם, היתה סיבה מן השמים להוכיח. ובשנת תתקצ"ו הייתי בספרד להוכיחם ואמץ הקב"ה זרעותי בחלומות היהודים ובחלומות הגוים וחזיונות הכככבים ויט עלי חסדו ותרגז הארץ ותהי לחרדת אלקים ועשו תשובות גדולות וקבלו אלפים ורבבות מצות תפלין מזוזות וציצית. וכן בשאר ארצות הייתי אחר כך ונתקבלו בכל המקומות ובקשו ממני לכתוב פרוש המצות בקצר. והנני שואל עזר מאלקי גליות ישראל וחפצו בידי יצליח ה"....

זאת נראה מהיוחסין ומצ"ד "שבזמן ההוא החלו השמדות להתחזק. בזמן ההוא היה האפיפיור גריגאר, שצרר את היהודים, אאוֹתות השמים נפלאים, שטף הארץ במדינת ווריזא וגם רעידת הארץ (בכיה) היו לפ"ד איך שהיה, רואים אנו כי השתדלותו והתאמצותו של הסמ"ג עשתה פרי זמן תחלת — 4990. היוחסין בשנת האלף הששי החלה המצוה הזאת להתפשט, אם כי לא בכל המקומות אך בארצות רבות בכל מקום שנסע הסמ"ג להוכיחם.

[64]*Orah Hayyim* 37.2: מצותן להיות עליו כל היום, אבל מפני שצריכים גוף נקי וכו' ואין כל אדם יכול. ליזהר בהם נהגו שלא להניחם כל היום ומ"מ צריך כ"א ליזהר בהם להיותם עליו בעת ק"ש ותפלה.

[65] Reproduced in *Mahzor Vitry,* p. 645: כת' בשימושא רבה. לא אכשר לאחותי תפילין אלא מאן דקרי בתורה נביאים וכתובים ותלמוד. בתורה בספר בראשית, בנביאים בספר שמואל. בכתובים בספר תילים. ואי הוי במשנה שפיר דמי. מסייעא ליה מתניתא לדשמואל. בן חמש שנים למקרא בן עשר למשנה בן שלש עשרה למצות. אמר רבא והוא דידע לתרגומי בכולהו. דכתיב ולמדתם, ושמרתם, ועשיתם, וקשרתם. אם אין למידה אין שמירה, אם אין שמירה אין עשייה, אם אין עשייה אין קשירה. עד כאן לשונם. אמנם בתלמוד שלנו קטן היודע לשמור תפילין אביו לוקח לו (*Suk.* 42a) לא מצינו כל זה. אלא אדרבא פרק לולב הגדל גרסינן תפילין. אע"ג שלא למד במשנה רק שיהא נקי לשומרם בטהרה כאלישע בעל כנפים וכו'.

[66] *TaSHBaZ,* no. 273; *MaHaRIL, Hilchot Tzitzit Utefillin.* אמהרי"ל שהוקפדה לו על הבחורים שאין נשואין עדיין לנשים שהם מניחין תפילין. וגם הנשוי כבר ועדיין רך בשנים לא ניחא שינויחם מפני שיצרן תקפם עליהן והתפלין צריכין גוף נקי שלא להרהר בעדן עליו ותמיהני מאין הרגלים שמניחין כ"כ בינקותן. ואני המלקט בתר לקוטים שוב ראיתי כ"כ בספר תשב"ק. תשב"ץ ס"י רע"ג: ועל הבחורים המהרהרים קריאת שמע לא יניחו תפילין דאפילו חולי מעיים אסור להניחם וכל מי שאינו יכול לשמרן שלא יפיח בהם ושלא יישן בהם כל שכן שלא ינהג בהם קלות ראש בתאות נשים. ועיין שו"ע או"ח סי' לב.

"במה שנוגע להתרשלות בני א"י במצות תפלין לא השמד גרמה אלא שקדושת תפילין היתה כל כך גדולה בעיניהם שהמון העם לא נועזו לגשת אל הקדש ורק החכמים והיחידים הניחו תפילין, וכבר היה הדבר קשה בעיני בעלי התלמוד ירושלמי על שלא מיחו החכמים ברב העם שמזלזלין במצוה זו ואמרו תפילין מפני מה לא

Mechilta and in the Talmud prevailed, insisting that a minor who knows how to care for them should be supplied with *tefillin*, even if he has not studied Mishnah.[67] In the stages of life, as presented by the rabbis, a boy was to begin the study of Scripture at five, and of Mishnah at ten. At thirteen he should assume his full responsibility for the observance of the commandments of the Torah. The assumption of religious responsibility, that is, as Bar Mitzvah, is marked by his beginning to wear *tefillin*.[68]

To the modern mind, the importance ascribed to *tefillin* appears exaggerated. The attitude of Reform Judaism stemmed from the break-up of the ancient modes of Jewish life, when, in consequence of the fall of the ghetto walls, customs and usages which had remained unaltered for countless generations, and were enshrined in the *Shulhan Aruch*, suddenly melted away like snow in a hot sun. Anything that seemed outlandish and irrational was spurned, in the age of the Enlightenment. Whatever ceremony appeared superstitious or excessively formalistic, or that had no particular claim upon the mind of the worshiper, had to be abandoned. The connection of *tefillin* with amulets discredited them in the eyes of the Reformers. Furthermore, inasmuch as Reform worship was limited to the Sabbath and holy days, the virtual discontinuance of daily worship automatically removed the use of the *tefillin*.

Mezuzah

The *Shema* follows up the command regarding *tefillin* with the order: "and

---

החזיקו בהן — לא הכריחו את העם — מפני הרמאים, ירוש׳ ברכות ב,א. Cf. Ginzberg *ad. loc.* See *Tefillah L'moshe*, pp. 73 ff.

[67] *Mahzor Vitry*, loc. cit.

[68] *Abot* 5.24; *Shibbole Haleket*, p. 382; Isserles, *Shulhan Aruch, Orah Hayyim* 37.3. חייב אביו לקנות לו (לקטן היידע לשמור תפילין בטהרה שלא יישן בהם ולא יפיח בהם) תפילין לחנכו. הגה וי״א דהאי קטן דוקא שהוא בן י״ג שנים ויום אחד [בעל העיטור] וכן נהגו ואין לשנות. המגן אברהם מוסיף: ועכשיו נהגו להניח ב׳ או ג׳ חדשים קודם הזמן. For details regarding the binding of the *tefillin*, see J. H. Greenstone, *Jew. Encyc.*, art. "Phylacteries, Legal View," X, 21–25; J. D. Eisenstein. *Otzar Dinim Uminhagim*, art. "Tefillin," pp. 443–46.

thou shalt write them upon the doorposts of thy house and upon thy gates?'
We note that Exodus 12:7 directed that the blood of the paschal lamb, offered
on the eve of the exodus from Egypt, was to be sprinkled upon the sideposts
and lintels of the house in which the lamb was eaten. While in the biblical
text, this command appears as an ordinance for a single event, the Samaritans
preserved the practice of marking with the blood of the paschal lambs the
tents as well as the foreheads of the children of the covenant, as a regular
annual ceremony.

This rite grows out of ancient practice, and is preserved among various
groups of Semitic peoples in Palestine, Syria, and Egypt. We cite a few
examples gathered by Curtiss, in addition to those already presented in
connection with the origin of *tefillin*. He reports instances, in villages near
Jerusalem, of Moslems' killing sheep and sprinkling their blood on the intels
and doorposts, in connection with the great pilgrim festival, *id dahhiheh*.[69]
"At Smed is on the Welli of St. George, an old Greek church with three Greek
inscriptions on it. The people take the blood of the sacrifices and put it over
the lintel; on the door posts and on the door itself one can easily trace the
marks of bloody hands."[70]

In Busan there is a *makam* known as Nebi Eyyub. This little building has
a dome which is plentifully smeared with blood. There is blood also on the
threshold, the doorposts, and the lintel. "In front of it were three pillars about
three and a half feet high; on the top of one of them was a peculiar-shaped
stone," of which there were many examples in the country, probably connected with ancient phallic worship. The broken pillars, too, were smeared
with blood.[71]

At the shrine of Abu Abeida (one of the companions of Mohammed, and a
famous general), at some distance northwest of Hamath, there is a small
building with a court in front of it, and graves behind it. On the door of the
court, blood marks were visible, in the shape of a capital T, "or possibly
designed to represent a cross." "On the door of the shrine itself there was a

[69] S. T. Curtiss, *Primitive Religion of the Semites*, p. 179, n. 1.

[70] Ibid., p. 187.

[71] Ibid., p. 188.

large T, also on the corners of the lintel, as in the accompanying diagram:
T ⌣⌢⌣ T   , and underneath it. There were twelve blood marks of the
same character on the inside walls and two in the prayer niche."[72]

Members of the Protestant congregation in Hamath reported that during
the cholera epidemic in their city in 1875, "the Christians sent to the slaugh-
terhouse, procured blood, and placed it in the sign of the cross on the door of
every room in the house. They also use red paint for the same purpose
whenever any serious calamity is feared in the house."[73]

In Urfu, in the vicinity of Aleppo, there is a well which is believed to
possess healing properties. The well is inside a house. The people kill a lamb,
goat, or pigeons, put their hands in the blood, and mark the inside of the wall
of the building. Curtiss adds that "such marks of the bloody hand or a hand
traced in red paint, are very common in Syria and Palestine — they are
supposed to be efficacious in protecting a house from the jinn."[74] Similarly, in
Iraq, the blood of the sacrifice is put over each door inside the court, "so that
there is the sign of the bloody hand."[75] According to Trumbull, the red hand
is seen on Jewish as well as on Syrian doors in Palestine and vicinity, and
probably represents a remnant of the Canaanitic practice of having lascivious
forms of Petachi or Kabirim, זכרונך, on the doorposts. (Cf. Isaiah 57:8,
Ezekiel 16:17.) The hand with its outstretched five fingers serves as an amulet
to ward off evil influence.[76]

To understand the significance of these practices, we must bear in mind
that the threshold, as Trumbull has pointed out, was the original hearthstone.
The doorpost had the blood sign and the guardian spirits or penates. (Cf.
Exod. 21:6, John. 6:26, 1 Kings 16:34.) If stepping on the threshold was not
prohibited altogether as a violation of its sacredness, it had to be crossed with
the utmost reverence. In Arabia, they say *Bismillah*, "in the name of God,"
when passing the door sill.[77]

[72] Ibid., pp. 192–93.

[73] Ibid., pp. 197–98.

[74] Ibid., pp. 215–16.

[75] Ibid., p. 216.

[76] Ibid.

[77] *The Threshold Covenant*, pp. 70 ff.; K. Kohler, *American Journal of Theology*, vol. 1, p.
800.

"Among the Egyptians we note a modification of this practice. The ancient Egyptians sometimes wrote a lucky sentence over the entrance of a house, for a favorable omen, as 'the good abode,' the *munzed mobarak* of the modern Arabs, or something similar; and the lintels and imposts of the doors, in the royal mansions, were frequently covered with hieroglyphics, containing the ovals and titles of the monarch. . . . [We find] even the storerooms, vineyards, and gardens placed under the protection of a tutelary deity."[78]

The *mezuzah*, as prescribed in Deuteronomy 6:9 and 11:20, clearly replaced the primitive protective symbols. Pharisaic usage adjusted it to the creed of Judaism by prescribing that the two sections of Deuteronomy containing references to the *mezuzah*, viz., 6:4-9 and 11:13-21, be written upon a parchment, enclosed in a cylinder, usually of metal, and affixed to the upper-right-hand post (as one enters) of Jewish homes. Unlike the *tefillin*, the *mezuzah* is obligatory for women and slaves. Minors, too, are trained to provide *mezuzot* for their dwellings. Synagogues and schoolhouses, which contain no dwellings, do not require *mezuzot*, for they are themselves sacred.

The outside of the *mezuzah* is inscribed with the word *Shaddai*. Maimonides contemns the writing of any other names, whether of angels or saints, and the inscribing of verses and signets: "For these fools not only nullify the commandment, but turn the great command of attesting the unity of God, of loving and serving Him, into an amulet for their personal use in accordance with their foolish desires." The purpose of the *mezuzah*, as Maimonides teaches, is not to serve as a prophylactic against evil influences, but to attract attention "as man goes in and out of the house, that he may be reminded of the unity of God, be aroused to love Him, and be awakened from the vanities and follies of the times."[79]

Tzitzit

The third outward mark of the Jew, the *tzitzit*, followed the same line of development as the *tefillin* and the *mezuzah*. In its earliest form, we

---

[78] Wilkinson-Burch, *The Manners and Customs of the Ancient Egyptians²*, 1878, I, pp. 361 f.; cited by Driver, *Deuteronomy*, p. 93.

[79] *Ahbah. Hilchot Tefillin, Mezuzah*, 5.4. Chyrsostom, in 1 Cor., hom. 43 (PG lxi, 373) mentions a εὐαγγέλιον hanging on the couch. Hastings, *Encycl. Rel. and Ethics*, III, 417.

encounter the ordinance regarding *tzitzit* in Deuteronomy 22:12, where it is named *gedilim*:[80] "Thou shalt make thee *gedilim* [twisted cords] upon the four corners of thy covering, wherewith thou coverest thyself." The more elaborate statement regarding this practice in Numbers 15:37–41, where the name *tzitzit* is used, specifies that a thread of blue must be intertwined with the tzitzit or fringes.

The talismanic character of the fringes is evident from the parallels among other peoples and from its usage among the Jews. The Egyptians are said to have worn fringed garments with blue threads as amulets.[81] The knotted form of the *tzitzit* suggests a similar purpose. Knots figured among many peoples as magical means of inflicting disease and of curing disease. "The ancient Assyrians seem to have made use of knotted cords as a remedy for ailments and disease. The cord with its knots, which were sometimes twice seven in number, was tied around the head, neck, or limbs of the patient, and then, after a time, cut off and thrown away, carrying with it, as was apparently supposed, the aches and pains of the sufferer. Somtimes the magic cord which was used for beneficent purposes consisted of a double strand of black and white wool; sometimes it was woven of the hair of a virgin kid."[82] "A modern Arab cure for fever, reported from the ruins of Nineveh, is to tie a cotton thread with seven knots on it round the wrist of the patient, who must wear it for seven or eight days or till such time as the fever passes, after which he may throw it away."

From India, too, we hear of the use of knots as charms. The *Khadira Grihya-Sutra* prescribes the following recipe for a prosperous journey for a person and his companions:[83] "On a dangerous road, let him make knots in the skirts of his garments (of those who travel together)." In Russia, also, amulets are said to derive their protective virtue from knots. "Often a Russian amulet is merely a knotted thread. A skein of red wool wound about the arms

---

[80] Bab. *gidlu*, "cord, a string"; Aram. *gedila*, "cord, rope." *BDB Lexicon*, sub גדלים.

[81] Crawley, art. "Dress," Hastings, *Encyc. of Rel. and Ethics* V, pp. 40–72.

[82] Frazer, *Golden Bough*, III, 303 ff.; C. Fossey, *Le Magie Assyrienne* (Paris, 1902), pp. 83f.; R. Campbell Thompson, *Semitic Magic* (London, 1908), pp. 164 ff.

[83] *Sacred Books of the East*, tr. H. Oldenberg, pt. I, p. 432; Pt. II, p. 127.

and legs is thought to ward off agues and fevers; and nine skeins, fastened round a child's neck, are deemed a preservative against scarlatina."[84]

The *tzitzit* may thus have derived from the original use of wearing amulets for protective purposes. It has been suggested further that it represents a survival of totemistic usage. "when animals were thought to be divine, the wearing of their hides would be one means of securing participation in their superhuman qualities; and it may therefore be suggested that a tasseled garment really represented a skin once worn in barbarious religious rites, the tassels at the four corners answering to the animal's four legs."[85]

The emphasis on the cord of blue points in the same direction. Like purple and scarlet, blue was required for ritual dress, as, for example, in the garments of the high priest (Exod. 28:6 ff.).[86]

The Priestly Code adjusted this survival of primitive magic or totemistic usage to Jewish religious practice. The Israelites were commanded to make them "fringes in the corners of their garments, and that they put with the fringe of each corner a thread of blue," that they may remember" all the commandments of the Lord, and do them," and not stray after their own hearts and their own eyes, and be holy unto God (Num. 15:37-41).

Though the law regarding *tzitzit* is Pentateuchal, the details governing its usage are all products of Pharisaic teaching. The early Hasidim are reported to have been particularly scrupulous in observing the law of *tzitzit*. However, it was left to the schools of Hillel and of Shammai to standardize their preparation. We are told that, after a discussion in the upper chamber of Jonathan b. Betera, the elders of these schools resolved that *tzitzit* have no fixed measurement.[87] From the plural usage of the word *gedilim* in Deut.

---

[84] Frazer, op. cit., pp. 306ff.

[85] G. W. Wade, *Peake's Commentary, Numbers*, p. 220.

[86] In contrast to the biblical usage, the *Atharvaveda* regards the combination of blue and red as savoring of witchcraft (Crooke, *Things Indian*, 1906, p. 165). The Yezidis hate blue (Milligen, *Among the Koords*, 1870, p. 277). This may represent a reaction to the Jewish regard for blue (cf. Hastings, *E.R.E.*, XII, art. "Yezidi," p. 830). In Roman Catholicism, blue or violet is the color of death. Blue is also associated with Mary, possibly as mourning her son. Crawley, art. "Dress," Hastings, *Encyc. Rel. and Ethics*, p. 47.

[87] An example of the exaggerated length of *tzitzit* is reported in the case of a leading citizen

22:12, the conclusion was drawn that *tzitzit* should not consist of just a single thread. The Hillelites demanded that *tzitzit* must be of not less than three; and the Shammaites maintained that it must consist of three of (white) wool and the fourth one of blue. The latter opinion was recognized as the halachah.[88] (Four threads must be passed through each of the four crners of the outer garment, with both ends tied together by a double knot. One of the threads, longer than the rest, is wound about the others, seven, eight, eleven, and thirteen times, a double knot made after each set of windings. Accordingly, each fringe consists of four sections, five double knots, and eight half threads.[89] The various minutiae in connection with the preparation of the *tzitzit*, and the manner of fastening them to the garments, formed the subject of discussion not only of the *tannaim* but also of the *amoraim*. The view was at first held that "everyone is obligated to wear *tzitzit*: priests, Levites, proselytes, women, and slaves." Minors who can dress themselves are likewise obligated. R. Simeon exempted women, inasmuch as *tzitzit* represents a positive comamnd which must be performed at a set time (i.e., during the day), from which women, on account of their primary duties as homemakers, and of their physical condition, are released.[90]

The blue cord of the *tzitzit* was dyed with the blood of the mollusk, *halzun*, which, according to legend, appeared but once in seventy years — a legend depriving from its scarcity.[91] There were probably various types of *halzun*. The Talmud reports that it was found in the mountains. It also speaks of *halzun* fishing in the area of the Phoenician border. "It appears certain

---

of Jerusalem, whose *tzitzit* trailed after him on a cushion. *Gittin* 56a: שהיתה ציציתו נגררת על גבי כסתו. Cf. Matt. 23:6.

[88] *Men.* 43a; *Arak.* 2b; *Sifre, Shelaḥ*, 115. ת"ר הכל חייבין בציצית כהנים לויים וישראלים גרים (*Men.* 43a) *Arak.* 2b; *Sifre,* נשים ועבדים. ר"ש פוטר בנשים מפני שמצות עשה שהזמן גרמא הוא וכו' *Shelaḥ*, 115.

[89] See J. H. Greenstone, *The Jewish Religion*, pp. 173–74; *Men.* 39a: הפוחת לא יפחות משבע והמוסיף לא יוסיף על י"ג.

[90] ראיתם אותו וזכרתם את כל מצות ה' ועשיתם אותם. מגיד הכתוב שכל המקיים מצות ציצית מעלים עליו כאילו קיים כל המצות (*Sifre, Shelaḥ* 115). הכל חייבין בציצית לאיתויי מאי? לאיתויי קטן היודע להתעטף. דתניא קטן היודע להתעטף חייב בציצית (*Arak.* 2b).

[91] *Men.* 44a.

that the genuine *ḥalzun* was found only in the land apportioned to the tribe of Zebulun, whose descendants were mostly engaged in this traffic."[92] On account of its scarcity, the authorities agreed to dispense with the cord of blue.[93] No substitute dye was permitted. Hence, since talmudic times, *tzitzit* have been prepared of white wool. In the original color, the rabbis read the primary meaning of the rite. The *Sifre* states: "It is not written, 'and ye shall see them,' but 'ye shall see Him.' Thus Scripture teaches that whoever fulfills the command of *tzitzit* is accounted as if he received the *Shechinah*, for the blue (of the *tzitzit*) is like unto the sea, and the sea unto the firmament, and the firmament unto the throne of glory" (cf. Ezek. 1:26).[94] While referred to by R. Nathan as a light commandment, it is extolled as equivalent to all others. The numerical value of the Hebrew word *tzitzit* plus the eight threads and five knots adds up to six hundred and thirteen, the number of all the Pentateuchal commandments.[95] It adds holiness to Israel. The outward act of

---

[92] J. D. Eisenstein, art. "Fringes" *Jew. Encyc.* V, 522. See *Meg.* 6a; *Sab.* 26a, Rashi. *Sifre, Deut.* 354. *Sab.* 74b. צדי חלזון (פירש"י: לצבע התכלת בדמו והוא כמין דג קטן ועולה אחת לע' שנה).
תני רב יוסף . . . יגבים אלו צַיָּדֵי (Jer. 52:16) ומדלות הארץ השאיר נבוזראדן רב טבחים לכרמים וליגבים
(Sab. 26a). חלזון מסולמות של צור ועד חיפה. (רש"י: לשון יקבים שעוצרין ופוצעין את החלזון להוציא דמו)
וזבולון מתרעם על מדותיו הוה כו'. . . . אמר זבולון לפני הקב"ה רבש"ע לאחי נתת להם שדות וכרמים ולי
נתת הרים וגבעות, לאחי נתת להם ארצות ולי נתת ימים ונהרות. אמר לו כולן צריכין לך על ידי חלזון שנ'
[עמים הר יקראו] . . . ושפוני טמוני חול. תני רב יוסף שפוני זה חלזון טמוני זו טרית (רש"י: דג שקורין
טונינ"א) חול זו זכוכית מגיליזה *Sifre Deut.* 354.

[93] *Men.* 4.1; 42a; *Tanh. Shelaḥ* 29: ועכשיו אין לנו אלא לבן.

[94] *Sifre, Shelaḥ,* 115; *Ḥullin* 89, where it is cited as a saying of R. Meir. The seven windings of the thread are compared to the seven heavens, and the thirteen to the seven heavens and the six aerial spaces between them. *Men.* 39a. תניא רבי מאיר אומר מה נשתנה תכלת מכל הצבעונין, מפני
(Exod. שתכלת דומה לים וים דומה לרקיע ורקיע דומה לאבן ספיר ואבן ספיר דומה לכסא הכבוד, דכתיב
24:10): (Hul. כמראה אבן ספיר דמות כסא (Ezek. 1:26): ויראו את אלהי ישראל ותחת רגליו וגו' וכתיב
89a). ר"מ אומר: וראיתם אותם לא נאמר כאן אלא וראיתם אותו. מגיד הכתוב שכל המקיים מצות ציצית
מעלים עליו כאלו הקביל פני שכינה שהתכלת דומה לים וים דומה לרקיע והרקיע דומה לכסא הכבוד שנא'
וממעל לרקיע אשר על ראשם כמראה אבן ספיר דמות כסא (Ezek. 1:26) (*Sifre, Shelaḥ,* 113).

[95] *Men.* 44a; *Shita Mekubezet, Men.* 39a; *Mahzor Vitry,* p. 636. ת"ר חלזון זהו גופו דומה לים.
תניא אידך (Men. 44a). ובריותו דומה לדג ועולה אחד לשבעים שנה ובדמו צובעין תכלת לפיכך דמיו יקרים.
וראיתם אותו וזכרתם את כל מצות ה'. שקולה מצוה זו כנגד כל המצות כולן. ותניא אידך וראיתם אותו וזכרתם
ועשיתם. ראיה מביאה לידי זכירה זכירה מביאה לידי עשיה. ורשב"י אומר כל הזריז במצוה זו זוכה ומקבל פני
שכינה וכו'. ת"ר חביבן ישראל שסיבבן הקב"ה במצות תפילין בראשיהן ותפילין בזרועותיהן וציצית בבגדיהן

looking at the *tzitzit* leads to remembering the commandments and to observing them, i.e., to inward conformity to the will of God. It is also spoken of as a good-luck charm.[96] *Tefillin, mezuzah,* and *tzitzit,* Maimonides says, "are the angels that save man from sin."[97]

Tallit

The *tzitzit* were worn on the outer garment and added to the distinctiveness of the garb of the Jew. Costume, it has been observed, despite the universality of its underlying principles, more than any other feature distinguishes race from race, tribe from tribe, and religion from religion. It marks off the social group and invests it with internal solidarity.[98] The garb worn in religious ceremonies itself acquires sanctity. It often takes on the form of the unusual or even the grotesque. It aims to symbolize the divine or to assimilate the priest to the deity, and the ordinary worshiper to the priest or to the sacrificial victim. In the case of Baal worship, garments were kept in the shrine and were donned on entrance (2 Kings 10:22). In certain Greek rites, both Dionysus and his worshipers wore fawn-skins. The Bacchanals wore the skins of goats.[99]

א״ר נתן אין לך כל מצוה (Men. 43b). (Ps. 119:164) ומזוזה לפתחיהן ועליהן אמר דוד שבע ביום הללתיך.
קלה שכתובה בתורה שאין מתן שכרה בעו׳ה׳ז ולבעוה״ב איני יודע כמה צא ולמד ממצות ציצית וכו׳ (Men.
44a).

[96] Sifre, Shelah, 115; Men. 44a, 43a: ר׳ עסקייהו ואצלח דקמך קמאי עבוד הכי סבא ההוא ל״א
חנינא בן אנטיגנוס אמר כל המקיים מצות ציצית מהו אומר בימים ההמה אשר יחזיקו עשרה אנשים מכל
לשונות הגוים ובחזיקו בכנף איש יהודי (Zech. 8:23). וכל המבטל מצות ציצית מהו אומר לאחוז בכנפות
והייתם קדושים לאלהיכם — זו קדושת ציצית מגיד Sifre, loc. cit. (Job 38:13) הארץ וינערו רשעים ממנה.
שהציצית מוסיפת קדושה לישראל (Sifre, Shelah 113).

[97] H. Tefillin umezuza 6.13. Additional References: Men. 41a אבל ,קטינא לרב מלאכה ל״א
השתא שאין העולם רגילים במלבושיך כאלו אין צריך לקנות. אך טוב לקנות טלית ולברך עליו בכל יום כו׳.
See Tosafot to B.B. 74a. (Tosafot to Shab. 32b) תכילתא הא יהודה רב בר שמואל לרב אביי ל״א
היכי צבעיתו לה. אמר ליה מייתינן דם חלזון וסמנין ורמינן להו ביורה [ומרתחינן ליה] ושקלינא פורתא
הכל חייבין בציצית (Men. 42b). בביעתא וטעמינן להו באדרא ושדינן ליה לההוא ביעתא וקלינן ליה לאדרא
(Hulin 2b).

[98] Crawley, art. "Dress," Hastings, *Encycl. Rel. and Ethics,* V, p. 46.

[99] Ibid., p. 65; Frazer, *Golden Bough,* II, 166.

Also in nonritual uses, men wore the tokens of their social religion, which served them as charms and means of divine protection.[100] Thus Jews attached *tzitzit* to the corners of the outer garment, which, like the *abaye* of the modern Arabs, formed a blanketlike cloth of coarsely woven wool, thrown around the body in the manner of a Scotch plaid,[101] as a protection from rain and from sun. A *tallit* of fine linen, similar in quality to the Roman *pallium*, came to be used by distinguished men, rabbis, and scholars.[102] With the adoption of Greek and Roman dress, the *tallit* remained as a ceremonial garb. Particularly in the Middle Ages, when the distinct garb of the Jew marked him for persecution, and he was forced to adopt the costume of the gentile world, the wearing of the fringed *tallit* was reserved to the hours of morning worship.[103] It was replaced by the *tallit katon* or *arba kanfot*, an oblong cloth with *tzitzit* at its corners and an opening in the center large enough to slip over the head. It was worn as an undergarment. The *tallit* itself then acquired the religious character of a prayer-shawl. In talmudic times, it was worn in Babylonia only by married males, whereas in Egypt, as in Palestine, it was worn by all males. In Morocco, its use was limited to scholars. In some places, scholars used to cover their heads with the *tallit*, whereas the rest of the men merely threw it over their shoulders.[104] It became customary for a bride to present her groom with a *tallit*, in which he was wedded. In Western communities, the *tallit* is generally used by all males above the age of bar mitzvah, and in some places, even by younger boys. Fine cotton and silk are used, as well as wool.[105] The *hazan* attires himself in a *tallit* for *minhah* as well as for

---

[100] W. R. Smith, *Religion of the Semites*, p. 437.

[101] Driver, *Deuteronomy*, pp. 253–54; *Midr. Lekah Tob, (Pesikta Zutarta) Shelaḥ*: ועטיפתו כעטיפת ישמעאלים.

[102] *B.B.* 98a; *Gen.R.* XXXVI, 5; *Ex.R.* XXXVII, 9.

[103] Tosafot *Sab.* 32b; I. Abrahams, *Jewish Life in the Middle Ages*, pp. 209–10. R. Jacob Tam remarks: אין מנהגנו ללבוש תמיד ציצית; Tosafot *Ber.* 18a: למחר.

[104] J. D. Eisenstein, art. "Tallit," *Ozar Dinim Uminhagim*, pp. 151–52.

[105] The *tzitzit* are of wool. The prohibition of *shatnes* does not apply to the fringed *tallit*. *Men.* 39b; *Targ. Jonathan* to Deut. 22:12 and Ibn Ezra ad loc.

shaharit, and for *kabbalat shabbat* and *ereb yom tob.* The reader of the scroll, in Sabbath *minhah,* likewise wears a *tallit.* The *kohanim* cover their heads and faces with their *talletim* during *duchan,* the blessing by the *kohanim,* in order not to gaze upon the *Shechinah* above them. The *tallit* is used also for wrapping the bodies of dead males. In Ashkenazi communities, the custom arose of untying the *tzitzit* of the dead.[106]

By reason of its antiquity and its ceremonial character, the *tallit* gained special significance. A saying of R. Johanan states that God Himself appeared to Moses in a fringed *tallit.*[107] The kabbalists invested it with other worldly symbolism. In the prayerbook meditation on donning it, the worshiper is taught to say: "As I cover myself with the *tallit* in this world, so may my soul merit to clothe itself in a beauteous robe in the world-to-come, in the Garden of Eden."[108]

While Rabbinic Judaism regarded the fringed *tallit* as the sacred garb of the Jew,[109] the sectarians differed from the rabbis in the matter of *tzitzit.* This opposition made itself felt in talmudic times. The law of *tzitzit* is connected, in the Haggadah, with the rebellion of Korah, which follows it immediately in the biblical text. His opposition to Moses, the protesters asserted, stemmed from his resentment of the inconsistencies and absurdities of the requirements

---

[106] Tosafot *Baba Batra* 74a: אבל קשה על המנהג שנוהגים להסיר ציצית מטליתות של מתים. ואר"ת ששמע מזקני לוטי"ר לפי שציצית עדות הוא שקיים כל התורה דציצית עולה ת"ר וה' חוטין וה' קשרים הרי תרי"ג ועכשיו שאין חשובין כל כך הרי הוא כאילו מעיד עדות שקר. וה"נ דרשינן במדרש ועשו להם ציצית לדורותם לדור תם. ואור"י דבימיהם היו כולם מקיימין מצות ציצית לפי שהיו לכולן טליתות של ד' כנפות ולכך היו עושין להם אף במותן אבל עתה שאין לכולן בחייהן אין לעשות במותן אפי' מי שהיה לו בחייו שלא לבייש את מי שאין לו. . . . וכן נוהגין בארץ אשכנז להשים ציצית בטלית של מת שיהא ניכר שקיים מצות ציצית ומיד מסירין.

[107] *Pesikta R. Kahana, Hahodesh,* p. 49a; *Pes. R.,* pp. 78a–b.

[108] Morning service. See Singer-Abrahams *Daily Prayerbook,* p. 14.

[109] The belief is expressed that in messianic times, all nations will be converted to Judaism and will don *tefillin* on the head and arm, *tzitzit* in the garments, and mount *mezuzot* on the doorposts. However, when the wars of God and Magog break out, they will rise up against God and the Messiah, and will "break their bands asunder," i.e., their *tefillin* and *tzitzit,* "and cast away their cords," i.e., the other commandments which they had accepted. *Midr. Ps.* 2.3; *Ab. Zara* 3b; and Jeru. *ad loc.* 2.1.

regarding fringes, the *mezuzah*, etc. Laws so irrational as the insistence that a blue cord be attached even to a garment that is made wholly of blue, or that a *mezuzah* be fixed to a doorpost of a house filled with sacred books, could not have come from God, but are the pure invention of Moses.[110]

In the Jerusalem Talmud, Rab is quoted as calling Korah an Epicurean, i.e., a sectarian. The opposition to *tzitzit* reappeared in Karaism. Thus Aaron ben Elijahu of Nicomedia takes issue with some of his fellow Karaites for following the rabbinic ideas of *tzitzit*. He cites older authorities for the interpretation of the law in Numbers 15:37, staring that the children of Israel "shall make tassels at the ends of their garments, and shall put upon the tassels a cord of blue." *Tzitzit*, he says, denote threads at the end of the cloth, paralleling the meaning of the word as used in Ezekiel 8:3, where it signifies the hair of the head. The *tzitzit* might therefore form part of the garment itself, that is, the ends of the threads which the cloth was woven, or threads attached to the garment. The Torah requires that a cord of blue be placed upon the border tassel, but says nothing about the number of threads or that the blue be one of them. It uses the word *petil*, which means a cord of at least three threads. Neither does the Torah command that there be any knots or that the threads be wool. As in some rabbinic sources, the word *tzitzit* is taken to mean an object of sight (from the root *tzutz*, as in Song of Songs 2:9).[111] Instead of one law, says the interpreter, there are really two laws, namely, first that there be a tasseled border upon the garment, and second, that the *petil techelet*, the cord of blue, should serve as a visible sign, to remind the people of their duties to God. Unlike the Rabbanites, the Karaites do not require the blue of the *tzitzit* to be derived from the *halzun*, and therefore still retain the cord of blue.[112] Ibn Ezra cites the opinion of some Karaites that the

---

[110] Jeru. *Sanh.* 10.1, 27d–28a; *Targ. Jeru.* Num. 16:1 ff.; Rashi ad loc.; *Chronicles of Jerahmeel*, chap. 65; Ginzberg, *Legends*, III, 289; VI, 100.

[111] *Gan Eden, Inyan Tefillah*, pp. 80a–81a; David Alfasi, Pinsker's *Likkute Kadmoniyot*, p. 126.

[112] Mordecai b. Nissan, in Neubauer's *Beitraege u. Documente*, pp. 97–98, Hebrew part, p. 19.

requirement of *gedilim* is for night use, and of *tzitzit* for use by day.[113] The use of the *tallit*, they limited to the time of prayer.[114]

[113] Commentary on Numbers 15:38-39. יתכן על שני פרושים האחד שיעשו ציצית כמו בציצית והם החוטים היוצאים שאינם ארוגים. על כנפי בגדיהם: על כל בגד חלוק או מכנסים כי אם (Ezek. 8:3) ראשי תחלקה הנה הוא כדמות כנף. פתיל תכלת: על מציצית . . . והיה לכם לציצית: והנה ישוב הפתיל להיותו בקצה כמו מציצית. R. Samuel b. Meir accepts some of these views. He והפירוש השני כאשר העתיקו חז"ל. ציצית, כמו בציצית ראשי. קבוצת פתילים תלוין בשער הראש. והיה לכם לציצית. הציצית הזה יהיה :writes לכם לראייה שתראו אותו כמו מציץ מן הכרכים. וכן מצות (Sifre, *Shelah* 115). See S. Schechter, *Documents of Jewish Sectarians*, II, 25. אמרו מהבחשים שהוא מצוה בלילה כמו הציצית ביום.

A note of comparison: The sacred girdle, *kosti*, which is worn by every Parsi, man and woman, from the fifteenth year, forms the "badge of the faithful," by which he is united with both Ormusd and his fellow believers. "He who does not wear it must be refused water and bread by the members of the community; he who wears it becomes a participant in the merit of all the good deeds performed all over the Zarathustrian world. The Kosti consists of seventy-two interwoven filaments, and should three times circumvent the waist. . . . Each of the threads is equal to one of the 72 *Hahs* of the *Izashne*; each of the twelve threads in the six lesser cords is equal in value to the *dawazdih hamaist*. . . .; each of the lesser cords is equal in value to one of the six *Gahanbars*; each of the three circumventions of the loins is equal in value to the *humat*, good thought, *hukat*, good speech, *huaresta*, good work; the binding of each of the four knots upon it confers pleasure on each of the four elements, fire, air, water, and earth," (Edal Daree, *apud* Wilson, *The Parsi Religion Unfolded*, p. 163). In the Brahmanical system also, the faithful are bound to their God by means of a sacred girdle, the *mekhala*.

"Another piece of clothing which every Parsi is enjoined to wear is the *Sadarah* or sacred shirt, a muslin shirt with short sleeves, that does not reach lower than the hips, with a small pocket at theopening front of the shirt" (James Darmsteter, *Zend Avesta*, pt. I. *The Vendidad*, p. 191). The *Vendidad* states that "the man who continues for three years (?) without wearing the sacred girdle makes the unseen powers of death increase" (nos. 8-9; cf. no. 54).

[114] Ibn Ezra, loc. cit.